conversations
on the written
WORD

conversations
on the written
W O R D

■ ■ ■ essays on ■ ■ ■
language and literacy

JAY L. ROBINSON
The University of Michigan

with essays by

Cathy Fleischer
Carol Lea Winkelmann
Patricia Lambert Stock

and a foreword by
Maxine Greene

Boynton/Cook Publishers
Heinemann
Portsmouth, NH

Boynton/Cook Publishers
A Division of
Heinemann Educational Books, Inc.
361 Hanover Street   Portsmouth, NH 03801
Offices and agents throughout the world

The following have generously given permission to use material in this book:

Excerpts from the Preface to *Discourse Analysis* by Gillian Brown and George Yule. Copyright 1984 by Cambridge Textbooks in Linguistics. Reprinted with the permission of Cambridge University Press.

Excerpts from "Blurred Genres: The Refiguration of Social Thought" by Clifford Geertz. Reprinted from *The American Scholar*, Volume 49, Number 2, Spring, 1980. Copyright © 1980 by the author. By permission of the publisher.

Excerpt from *Of Wolves and Men* by Barry Lopez. Reprinted with permission of Charles Scribner's Sons, an imprint of Macmillan Publishing Company, from *Of Wolves and Men* by Barry Lopez. Copyright © 1978 Barry Holstun Lopez.

Excerpts from *The Medusa and the Snail: More Notes of a Biology Watcher* by Lewis Thomas. Copyright © 1979 by Lewis Thomas. Reprinted by permission of Viking Penguin USA.

"Ceremony" by Leslie Marmon Silko. From *Ceremony* by Leslie Marmon Silko. Copyright © 1977 by Leslie Marmon Silko. Reprinted by permission of Signet Books.

Versions of some of the essays have been published previously:

"What Is Literacy?" *Federation Review* 8:4 (July/August 1985), 1–5. Reprinted by permission of *Federation Review* and the Federation of State Humanities Councils.

"The Social Context of Literacy," in *fforum*, ed. Patricia L. Stock. Reproduced with permission from Patricia L. Stock: *fforum* (Boynton/Cook Publishers, Portsmouth, NH 1983).

"Literacy in Society: Readers and Writers in the Worlds of Discourse," in *Literacy and Schooling*, ed. David Bloome (Norwood, NJ: Ablex). Copyright 1987 by Ablex Publishing Co. Reprinted by permission of the publisher.

"Literacy as Conversation: Classroom Talk as Text Building," in *Literacy in the Classroom*, ed. David Bloome (Norwood, NJ: Ablex). Copyright 1989 by Ablex Publishing Co. Reprinted by permission of the publisher.

"Literacy in the Department of English," *College English* 47:5 (1985), 482–98. Copyright 1985 by the National Council of Teachers of English. Reprinted with permission.

"Constitutive Literacy," in *Profession 86* (Modern Language Association), 36–40. Copyright 1986 by the Modern Language Association. Reprinted by permission of the publisher.

Library of Congress Cataloging in Publication Data
Robinson, Jay L., 1932–
   Conversations on the written word : essays on language and
literacy / Jay L. Robinson with essays by Cathy Fleischer, Carol
Lea Winkelmann, Patricia Lambert Stock.
      p. cm.
   Includes bibliographical references.
   ISBN 0–86709–252–1
   1. Literacy.   2. Sociolinguistics.   I. Fleischer, Cathy.
II. Winkelmann, Carol.   III. Stock, Patricia L.   IV. Title.
LC149.R63   1990
302.2'244—dc20   89–35894
                                                                      CIP
Designed by Maria Szmauz
Printed in the United States of America
90 91 92 93 94 9 8 7 6 5 4 3 2 1

This book is dedicated to all who try to teach. It is dedicated especially to those teachers who are reflective enough to know that try is all teachers can do and yet courageous enough to keep on trying.

The book is dedicated, too, to students in Saginaw, Michigan, who have taught me in their attempts to learn that what I know about literacy isn't quite enough and probably never will be.

Contents

Part Three
Literacy and Learning

Part Four
Literacy and Our Institutions

Foreword

The authors of this book invite us to join a particularly significant conversation. It is one that touches upon some of the crucial themes in our culture today. They center around what is presented as the problem of literacy, ordinarily conceived in purely functional terms and assessed in the light of what the new technologies demand. Jay Robinson and Patricia Stock, along with their diverse collaborators, open novel perspectives in these pages, perspectives expanded and enriched by the tapping of multiple voices and multiple points of view.

Familiar dichotomies, such as those setting the academic up against the "educational," are overcome. The primary authors here are acknowledged scholars of literature and rhetoric; they have taught composition and writing to liberal arts students; they have been close to the interpretive and critical communities that shape the course of our intellectual life today. Not only is it unusual for such scholars to inquire into the work of public schools, but it is rare and wonderful to see them involving themselves in the lives of students. They have taught English classes in Saginaw high schools; as importantly, they have done collaborative work with teachers in those schools. This has meant stimulating research and writing among those teachers and their students, becoming participant in an ongoing search for meaning that transmutes learning and renders it vibrant and new.

Dealing as they do with the "politics of literacy," the authors confront directly the tension between the authoritative discourses of "school literacy" and what they speak of as an "in-forming" literacy within the discourse of the students themselves. They make particularly clear the socially constructed nature of literacy and trace the implications of what this means when it comes to the silencing of many young people whose voices or whose dialects resist articulation in the dominant of "standard" language. The swelling contemporary interest in journal-writing and group evaluation is captured here and given fresh exemplification. Indeed, the examples taken from journals and student-written texts infuse this book with an immediacy and even a kind of drama. When one of the authors, now a full participant in the conversation in a high-school classroom, writes a story of her own life in a letter to the students in the class, she creates a space into which one of the students can move. The account of the interchanges that follow, the growth of young Sanchez into a kind of "artistry," and the consciousness of collaborative co-learning may well provoke readers to devising pedagogies of their own. Robinson and Stock keep reminding us that none of what is accomplished guarantees against imposed marginality; but the enriched view of literacy they develop makes the pedagogical effort look like an effort to confirm human rights— at the very least, the right to be heard.

Offering instances of the damage done by habitual treatments of what Mina Shaughnessy called "errors and expectations" (including the poignant formality of some of the writing traditionally considered simply "incorrect"), Jay Robinson involves his readers in an evaluation of traditional "handbook" corrections, which ordinarily led nowhere. We are reacquainted with the discussions of the relation between speech and writing, and we are made to feel included in the effort to replace punishing (and futile) assessment with diagnosis, or with formative evaluation, or with voluntary group examination of what is done in class. A panoply of linguistics, critics, and practitioners—Shaughnessy, Labov, Heath, Scholes, Culler, Bakhtin, Freire—are consulted for the light each one can throw on the nurture of an "in-forming" literacy. By the end, they have begun to play new roles in the context created by the book: the context of a critical literacy.

Through subtle readings of the literature of educational critique and through explorations of the types of hegemony that coerce consciousness even as they impose illiteracy, the several authors here—Fleischer, Winkelmann, as well as Robinson and Stock— allow us to experience the necessity for "learning as conversation" because they engage in it themselves. Moreover, they make us feel intensely the existential importance—as well as the political importance—of liberating persons to find and use their own voices. If they do not, they remain effectually mute. It is not simply a question of rights or equity. It is a question of the culture's articulate life, as it is of the health of our public space. John Dewey, in

The Public and Its Problems, wrote of the significance of a "subtle, delicate, vivid and responsive art of communication" in such a space. Then: "Democracy will come into its own, for democracy is a name for a life of free and enriching communion. It had its seer in Walt Whitman. It will have its consummation when free social inquiry is indissolubly wedded to the art of full and moving communication." This book on literacy proposes a practice for such consummation. Doing so, it invites multiple readers into the conversation. There is much to be discovered just ahead.

Maxine Greene
Teachers College
Columbia University

Introduction

. . . any speaker is himself a respondent to a greater or lesser degree. He is
not, after all, the first speaker, the one who disturbs the eternal silence of
the universe. And he presupposes not only the existence of the language
system he is using, but also the existence of preceding utterances—his own
and others'—with which his given utterance enters into one kind of relation or another (builds on them, polemicizes with them, or simply presumes that they are already known to the listener). Any utterance is a link
in a very complexly organized chain of utterances.

MIKHAIL BAKHTIN

It is the human condition, and complicatedly that of humans who
live in literate societies, to always enter conversations in the middle. And the more important conversations that engage societies—
those in which the meanings of self and other are negotiated, those
in which values are contested, those in which mysteries and puzzlements about the human condition raise always newly formulated questions—have been in process for very long times. In oral
societies, and in those communal groups in literate societies whose
members retain the capacity to talk and tell stories to one another,
memory serves as a capacious enough repository to store the traces
of past conversations. But in literate societies, libraries always
stand as a reminder that present conversations could be infinitely
expanded, through the reach of their citations, allusions, and references, through the depths of the echoes and resonances of inscribed
voices, into pasts that have somehow shaped us, even if we do not

1

remember the words those voices spoke. In oral societies, the past is ever present and ever renewed, for memory is reshaped in stories told to present others. In literate societies, old stories seem less changeable, since they are inscribed; yet it is only in the re-telling of old stories, if only to oneself when reading them, that they take on meaning—present meanings for human beings engaged in conversation with present or absent others. We read our pasts to shape them into our futures whether we are literate or not.

These essays, which are a part of my past, are offered as traces of conversations I have had—conversations always entered in the middle. But they are less a record of that past and of those conver-sations than they are invitations to future conversations: conversa-tions about our preoccupations and activities as professionals—as teachers and writers; conversations about our profession (or our professions); conversations about the fit of our roles as profession-als to our obligations as human, hence social beings; conversations about the fit and functions of our professions in the various social communities, including possible ones, we seem to inhabit.

In my professional life, I have been invited into the middle of many kinds of conversations, and have intruded into others un-invited. To those writers—scholars, researchers, committed and informed amateurs, whose works impel responses and who leave space in what they say for other voices to respond—the gratitude of a reader and writer who finds profit in talk with others. To those teachers whose words have been always conversational because they are always tentative, the gratitude of a lifelong student-teacher who has always preferred the seminar room to the lecture hall.

As background to the particular conversations that follow in this collection, some reminiscences of contexts for past conver-sations:

I did my graduate work at the University of California, Berke-ley, preparing to be a medievalist; in my dissertation, which was a sources and analogues kind of thing, I entered—or tried to enter—scholars' and critics' conversations about Chaucer's *Prioresses Tale*. I was naive enough then to title my dissertation "The Context of *The Prioresses Tale*"; in remembering the composing of it (I haven't read it in decades), I think I really thought then that the past was so open to my view that I could say something rather uncompli-cated—even something sensible—about what the tale must have meant to Chaucer's audience: a close reading of the tale as it would have been done by the Black Prince.

After graduate school, I plied my trade as a medievalist for some years (never publishing anything in that field), while prepar-ing myself—largely on my own time—for a transformation from medievalist to linguist. One of the reasons for that change was that I was teaching the history of the English language (one of the things that all medievalists were presumed able to do) and I got interested in linguistics in preparing to teach it in an informed way. But another reason had to do with conversations—contentious ones—I heard outside my graduate classrooms at the University of California, Berkeley. During my schooldays there, in days when politics had to be contested off campus (no Free Speech Movement yet), there were some interesting on-campus fights in progress. Both the New Critics (who were then second-generation not-so-young Turks) and the New Linguists (who were then mostly first-generation structuralists—also Turkish in temper) were battling it out with the philologists, who were retiring or dying off, but who still ruled over requirements, finding allies among a similarly dwindling number of older-generation literary historians. When the New Critics and the New Linguists took time out for a breather, they battled among themselves. The second, to a newcomer like me, seemed the livelier fight.

So when I got to Northwestern for my first real teaching job, I read linguistics and some literary criticism to find out what the fight really meant. I don't think I did find out, but I decided to take sides anyway, perhaps because I liked the way linguists talked (some of them hadn't bothered to change their regional dialects into English Department Received Standard). By the time I moved on to the University of Michigan, four years later, I had co-edited a collection of essays titled *An Introduction to English Linguistics*, and was hired to teach, besides Old English and Chaucer, a course in English language for teachers and a course in contemporary grammatical theories. Armed with my new knowledge of phonemes, morphemes, and substitution classes, I arrived in Ann Arbor to encounter Noam Chomsky, though not in person. *Syntactic Structures* was the first on a list of books that introduced me to hard, undreamed-of conversations: my new dreams were decorated with algebraic proofs and tree diagrams. But there was also something familiar in certain of the claims that Chomsky and his colleagues were making: echoes of more humane conversations in which humans were conceived as shapers of the meanings they make with language. These echoes led me to act as eavesdropper on disputes psychologists as well as linguists were having: Are humans conditioned by stimuli to make predictable responses in the language they are learning or do they bring their own native genetic equipment to the challenge of making a language and, with it, their worlds? Behaviorism giving way to nativism and native creativity: new voices entered the conversation.

At Michigan, while teaching a course or two of literature each term (which helped me, as much as Michigan's strong tradition of language study, to avoid the lot of marginalization that falls upon so many English department linguists), I was given a chance to extend my reading and thinking in English language and English linguistics. Some work in historical lexicography, looking with others into the feasibility of reviving the long-dead Early Modern

English Dictionary project, let me explore and write about how dictionaries are and should be made and how computers might be used in their making. It also led me to suspect that the lexicons modeled in generative syntax and generative semantics, while interesting, weren't going to teach me as much as I needed to know if my task was to recover and record the meanings of words that human beings had employed in their attempts to make sense. Some work on English dialects, mainly social ones, led both to the co-editing of another book in language studies—*Varieties of Present-Day English*—and to the realization that generative grammars didn't come close to answering the questions that could be asked about what happens when individuals in social groups use language in the settings in which they happen to talk or to write. Abstract models and formalisms often had quite powerful heuristic value, and they were a good deal of intellectual fun: but when I asked questions about present uses of language, when I asked questions about how language use is itself shaped in response to the situations of use, abstract models and formalisms didn't prove to be all that helpful. The shift in linguistics (persuasively argued for by William Labov among others) from a focus upon a presumed competence of a hypothetic ideal speaker-hearer, who is presumed to be free of psychic and social constraints, to a focus upon real speakers and the languages they use as these are shaped by social and sociopsychological constraints gave me other conversations to get in the middle of. From linguist, I metamorphosed into sociolinguist, a member of the growing number of hybrid, hyphenated academic species that were making their appearance in academies that encouraged interdisciplinary work.

And then there were voices from outside the academy. My thoughts in my own study, at Northwestern and Michigan, and my words in my own classrooms, were shaped and continue to be shaped by conversations with teachers and students who work in other classrooms—conversationalists who rarely enjoy the luxury of thinking in a study. At Northwestern, because I was learning about English language and linguistics, and because the metaphor of the tripod still guided English curricula in precollegiate schooling, I was invited to join a staff of faculty teaching teachers in NDEA summer institutes—something I continued to do at Michigan. And because I taught in these institutes, and taught regular university courses judged useful for school teachers—courses they were sometimes even required to take—I was invited into school classrooms. My first glimpse of the inside of an inner-city classroom came in 1963, on Chicago's near-north side, when I visited a racially, linguistically, and socioeconomically mixed high school as a supervisor and counselor of an MAT candidate who had graduated from Smith College. Trying to listen and to talk with her, and with teachers who had spent and would spend more time there, I got into the middle of conversations very different from my academic ones, conversations I am still trying to understand even as I try to continue them in classrooms and hallways in other cities.

Conversations with teachers (to interrupt the temporal flow of my autobiography with a bit of reflection—something I'm told by theorists that the genre allows) have been very important to me as a conversationalist myself, and in two ways I would inscribe. In conversations with teachers, especially public-school teachers, I hear echoes (if I listen carefully enough) of the conversations they have had with students who will never enroll in my university, never sit in my classrooms, never write a paper in their study or talk about one in my seminar room. I want my study to resound with voices I will never hear, for in those voices are framed the questions that really matter, the questions teachers—hearing those voices—help to frame: What is the usefulness of our thoughts and our theories? What is their reach toward students in classrooms, toward students whose differences from one another and from us test the comprehensiveness and humanity of any thoughts we think, any theories we manage to construct?

When I rehear conversations that have shaped my mind—a mind Clifford Geertz tells me I find myself having because I have played a role as an academic specialist (linguist, sociolinguist)—the questions school teachers have asked are the ones that re-echo when I am tempted, as the academy tempts, to narrow my mind. Good and experienced teachers—teachers from public schools, teachers from community colleges, teachers of remedial courses in universities, teachers of introductory courses in universities, teachers of more advanced courses in universities whose commitment endures to enable them to listen to voices not yet shaped into patterns of academic discourse—always enliven ongoing conversations with intrusive questions that test the limits of academic understandings, understandings earned in the privacy of one's study. Questions that open to voices not yet heard in our academic conversations test far more than our capacity to hear: they test more crucially how we live in the world with others.

But back to the obligations of autobiography and to the perfectly legitimate constraints of "Introduction" as a genre, brevity among them: Questions I could not answer as a sociolinguist, especially teacherly questions about how students compose texts and comprehend them, using such language as they have, led me from sociolinguistics, within whose disciplinary constraints I could answer too few of the questions that are increasingly important to me, to rhetoric, because such questions are being asked and answered in that domain: questions particularly about how human beings use language to define themselves in relation to others. And more recently, working in classrooms and reading in rhetoric, trying to puzzle out relations of composing to comprehending, I have been led to readings and rereadings of literary critics (who read texts) and literary theorists (who reflect on what it is and means to read texts). Conversations in these two domains, at present, are increasingly open ones. In them may be heard the voices of language philosophers, students of epistemology, cognitive and developmental psychologists, philosophical and cultural anthropologists, sociologists studying power and the social distribution of knowledge. These conversations invite something even beyond interdisciplinary inquiry; in them, blurred genres are the customary forms of speaking.

Working in the intellectual world I seem to inhabit at the moment, reading and writing blurred genres, trying to find a place for myself while living in a collage (as Clifford Geertz characterizes the present human condition of acting and thinking), I find it far less easy to name myself with a convenient academic label for a disciplinary role: linguist, sociolinguist, rhetorician, literary theorist do not seem at the moment accurately descriptive labels for the mind I find myself to have. I am interested in literacy—what it is, how it is acquired, how it functions (or does not) in classrooms, how it functions (or does not) in worlds outside classrooms. Like many others nowadays, I characterize my present work in literacy as the study of discourse; and like many others nowadays, I recognize that the study of discourse necessarily entails a study of discursive practices—real actions in a social world comprised of roles and relationships that determine the uses and limits of reading and writing as situated actions, as sociocultural practices. Thinking in that way makes it hard to stay within the comfortable confines of a discipline or even an interdiscipline, let alone a department; thinking in that way prompts a readiness—perhaps an obligation—to get into the middle of as many conversations as possible. Perpetual neophytes, persistent amateurs, which is what interdisciplinarians turn out to be when they ask tough questions, need all the help they can get if their constant questions are to result in useful answers.

I have had the benefit always in conversations I have had to talk and work with others who ask good questions, and there are traces of them in the essays gathered in this volume. Present work with students, teachers, and university colleagues in inner-city classrooms has led to questions and toward answers that capture for me the kind of complexity that is required for thinking well while living in a collage. In our work (which is described in the last essay in this collection), we are trying to understand how literacy develops, when it does, in the adolescent years of schooling. We are trying to understand how members of a school class come to constitute themselves (if they do) into a social community of a particular kind: something Stanley Fish might call an interpretive community. And we are trying to understand how social and sociointellectual interactions among members of the forming community both effect and affect individual development of those competencies and the enactment of them that we comprehend with the term "literacy." We are trying to understand and describe not so much the peculiar culture of *the* classroom as the particular cultures of particular classrooms as these are shaped by personal and institutional histories and as they take shape in anticipation of future, perhaps possible worlds.

To advance our conversations with one another, we are conceiving the terms "writer" and "reader" as social roles in communities made through uses of the written word. We are trying to discover how, through social interactions, writers and readers inscribe themselves in a way that gives them a place in the communities they are constituting, a place that allows for and enables a reading writer to become a speaking person who may expect responsive understanding from others who speak from their own places in the social community.

That is in outline the way we are trying to capture the development of literacy: as, in essence, sociocultural development, not merely cognitive development, a notion that seems to imply an isolated learner and not one who lives and learns as a social being in conversations with others. Learning, we are trying to say—and especially language learning—is a particular kind of sociohistorical process. Becoming literate, we think, crucially involves a glimpse of some future—a sight, however blurred, of what Jerome Bruner or Nelson Goodman might call a possible world; but it also involves, as crucially, some sense that one may find habitable space in that future as a self who can speak and act meaningfully. Becoming literate also involves, we certainly know, recapturing the past: both a personal past of understandings and stories scripted in memory, but also more alien pasts inscribed in texts others have made—pasts that must also be made one's own in order to be made meaningful.

To describe a meaningful interaction in a literacy classroom, we are finding out—in a composition or a literature classroom— requires one both to live in a collage and to explore the limits and possibilities of that community's collective self-consciousness in the process of its collective formation. Reading and writing are always present engagements, but like good conversations they are much more than that. Present in good conversations are always the pasts that they presuppose and the futures that they inevitably prefigure. Reading and writing, as human activities, are shaped by what is past; but they have the potential, as means to make the past communally known in engagements necessarily shaped by some vision of the future, to refigure a past into a future worth the telling. And that's why questions about students' developing literacy are very important ones; that's why the study of students' developing literacy is a centrally important humanistic concern.

But an "Introduction" probably should not be a statement of a book's conclusion, or a record of the most recent in a history made of conversations. Yet in assembling this collection, I have thought about its possible purposes and have chosen in most cases to ignore chronology in favor of something like a loose thematic arrangement for the conversations inscribed here in essay form. Late pieces sometimes come early in the collection, early pieces later. Brief headnotes name the themes in essays gathered into a section and describe the occasions that brought them forth and the audiences for whom they were originally composed. Discourse is always, of course, situated action.

Part One

Literacy
and
Its Uses

The public's present concern with literacy—with something they have been encouraged to think of as a literacy crisis—has now lasted long enough for us to try to become reflective about the situation. What are the roots and causes of the public's concern? What are the capacities that are named by the terms literate and literacy? What are the deficiencies that are named by the terms illiterate and illiteracy? Why do such deficiencies place our nation at risk—if they do? These are questions that pop up in many of the essays in this collection; the following three essays begin reflections on issues that the questions raise—reflections about what the term literacy both means and should mean, reflections about what its presence or absence means for schooling and for society, about what the implications are when we use its related forms—literate and illiterate—to label people, reflections about how literate activities relate to other social activities when people use written language to get something done—or undone.

The first essay, "What Is Literacy?", was written upon request for the reader-audience of *Federation Review: The Journal of the State Humanities Councils,* an audience comprised of "members and staff of state humanities councils and their colleagues in public life, civic and cultural organizations, schools, and colleges." The second, "The Social Context of Literacy," took first shape in a talk to a symposium of teachers and students of English education sponsored by members of Michigan's Joint Ph.D. Program in English and Education (May 1982); then most of its present shape came about in a revision for Patricia L. Stock's collection *fforum: Essays on Theory and Practice in the Teaching of Writing,* a collection intended for writing teachers and one of the first to address teachers of writing as members of a wider community of teachers and scholars interested in literacy. The third essay, Cathy Fleischer's "Re-forming Literacy: A Collaborative Teacher-Student Research Project," also entered the world as talk: hers for the varied audience that attended the MLA conference titled "The Right to Literacy" in Columbus, Ohio, September 1988. Her essay, especially, began in conversation, and closes this section as an invitation to other ones about how literacy takes shape, and has the potential to take on new shapes in American classrooms.

"What Is Literacy?", the first of these essays, is less an attempt at definition than an exploration of the implications—social, ethical, and political—of definitions of literacy that interested parties in our society construct. Fleischer also touches on institutionally constructed definitions of literacy to test them against others that are constructed outside school. She seeks to understand what can happen when students are encouraged to act as co-researchers who reflect upon their own uses of language outside of school in order to come to understand both the limits upon and the potential of in-school literacy.

"The Social Context of Literacy," the second essay in the collection, also asks questions about literacy and its institutional settings. When I first wrote the published version of the essay, I began it this way:

> This essay, like most in the genre, has its roots in experiences—past, past continuous, and even future since anticipation works on one's mind. Past are seven years as an English Department Chairman; past and continuing is my work with the English Composition Board at the University of Michigan helping to develop a writing program for undergraduates; and in my future is a chairmanship of a Ph.D. program in English and Education. All of these lumped together with reading that a sabbatical has allowed me to do have provoked me to think about the topics addressed in these pages: how literacy functions (and does not function) in our society; how society influences what we do as learners and teachers of literacy.

The sabbatical is now long past, though other opportunities to read have presented themselves, and I hope I have made use of them. Other experiences have accumulated too: a review of the University of Michigan's English Composition Board while I was its chair; participation with seriously committed others both in the Ph.D. Program in English and Education and in an invented Center that involves university faculty with faculty and administrators from public schools in collaborative work on learning and teaching, work of the sort reported in the third essay in the section.

All of my reading and the accumulation of new experiences would cause me to write now quite another essay, one I would now title "The Social Contexts of Literacy." But I leave this one more or less as it was then because I still believe in the importance of the subject and because neither my reading, nor my experience either, has changed my misgivings about how well our profession is constituted and motivated to meet challenges that seem so apparent in the public's concern for literacy and in the unequal distribution of its potential benefits among the public that we are.

1

What Is Literacy?

We use the word *literacy* so often, and the related words *literate* and *illiterate* so easily, that it is hard for us to think of them as problematic terms—and yet they are. For most people, the words denote either absolute or at least easily identifiable states: one can read or one cannot; one can write or one is left with speech only. But in fact, for those who must use the terms *literate* and *illiterate* carefully and with consequence, as labels for people, the terms must be qualified carefully.

Take for example these two perfectly common usages of the term *illiterate*:

> With modern electronic communication as widespread as it is, there are now few peoples of the world so completely isolated as to be accurately labeled illiterate.

> Randolph, your reading of that poem is quite illiterate!

In the first example, the term means something like "untouched by 'letters,' " that is, by the effects of literate culture; in this usage it is customarily applied to humans who cannot in fact read. In the second, where the term is clearly applied to someone who can read, it means something like "untouched by certain socially approved ways of reading, ignorant of certain bodies of socially valued knowledge." In our culture, cut up as it is into various professional and academic specializations, and with education differentially distributed along various socioeconomic hierarchies, it is perfectly possible for a person who can read and write to be labeled "illiterate."

13

There is snobbery involved, of course, in some such usages of the terms *literate* and *illiterate,* but more serious forms of social sanction accrue to the terms as well. To be illiterate, or thought to be so, is to be considered unqualified generally for employment at any but the most demeaning and unrewarding jobs. To be illiterate, or thought to be so, is often—very often—to be denied access to education or even training that might prepare one for more rewarding employment. Almost all tests now in use to screen students for any form of voluntary education presume the prior achievement of a relatively advanced state of literacy. Even in community colleges, write Cohen and Brawer, where in principle doors should be open:

> Literacy is certainly related to success . . . : transfer courses demand proficiency in reading, writing, and mathematics, and licensure examinations admitting students to practice after completing technological programs typically demand the same. Many community college programs are closed to students who cannot pass an entrance examination that is based on literacy (1983, 210).

To base entrance and licensure examinations on literacy is both inevitable and legitimate, for ours is a society that requires facility with the written word in almost all of its workaday activities. But there can be problems with such tests—they can be radically unfair and discriminatory—if those who construct and administer them do not specify, in concrete terms, both what competencies literacy should encompass and the functional necessity of these competencies in school or in the workplace. We say so easily: "Students should read but don't; students should write well but can't." We are not so good at saying: "This is what reading and writing are, as functional competencies"; "These are the competencies that are requisite for productive achievement."

An Issue for the Nation

Our uncertainties about what literacy is and what its real uses in society are lead not only to public handwringing about perceived literacy crises but also to disputes—with serious implications for public policy—over how severe the crises might or might not be. Estimates of the number of "illiterate" Americans, for example, range from a low of 23 million to a high of some 60 million, a figure provided by Jonathan Kozol in his angry book, *Illiterate America.* His figure is compounded of "25 million American adults [who] cannot read the poison warnings on a can of pesticide . . . " and "an additional 35 million [who] read only at a level which is less than equal to the full survival needs of our society" (1985, 46). The figure includes, of course, a disproportionate number of blacks and Hispanics, because in the United States as elsewhere in the world, illiteracy correlates—in more ways than statistically—with poverty and powerlessness. His figure also includes a large number of ill-prepared students from urban schools, most of whom are members of minority groups and most of whom lack all chance, upon early exit or graduation, for future education.

If the lower figure is correct, a mere 23 million, the scope of human suffering it implies is a national scandal, for that many men, women, and children lack means for economic if not physical survival; if the higher figure is correct, Kozol may be right in looking toward a national catastrophe. How does a democratic nation govern itself if one third of its citizens have no access to printed matter? How does an information society operate if so high a percentage of its workforce is disabled, if so high a percentage cannot act even as consumers, save of images and sounds? What are the financial and spiritual costs to a nation that disenfranchises and thrusts into inevitable poverty almost a third of its citizens?

The numbers vary in the grim business of toting up the number of illiterates not only because some definitions of literacy vary but also because those more adequate ones that are similar—those that add the qualifier "functional" to the term "literacy"—point to something that is relative, not absolute. A widely accepted definition of functional literacy is that framed in 1962 by UNESCO:

> A person is literate when he has acquired the essential knowledge and skills which enable him to engage in all those activities in which literacy is required for effective functioning in his group and community and whose attainments in reading, writing, and arithmetic make it possible for him to continue to use these skills toward his own and the community's development (Hunter and Harman, 1979, 14).

The implications of this definition are clear: a person may possess the capacity to function in one group, in one community, perhaps in more than one, but not necessarily in others; a functional literate may be rendered dysfunctional as community or societal demands for attainment in reading and writing change—as of course they will. To be schooled once, as most of us know, is not to be functionally educated forever, not in times of rapid social and technological change. We mandarins of print culture who have earned our high literacy through serious engagements with books and struggles with the pen could possibly be rendered illiterate by the electronification of the word, unless we keep up or hold on to power.

Literacy changes in nature more or less in pace with technological changes (though conservative elites, if they remain powerful, can remain relatively immune to change, as can the educational structures that sustain them). Industrializing societies demand more readers able to comprehend and make use of information, and more writers able to provide it. Information societies will demand many more readers, though what *reading* means may change;

they may, perhaps, demand more, or perhaps fewer, writers, depending on whether the means for producing information are
decentralized or centralized. The nature of literacy is as subject to
political change—to alterations of power—as it is to technological
change.

In school and society, at least in Western cultures, criteria for
what counts as literacy have changed in response to new demands.
In the seventeenth century, one could be called a reader if he or she
were able to read aloud a familiar Biblical or catechismal text and
answer some few simple questions about it; one could be called a
writer if he or she were able to sign a name to a contract or to a will.
Even in the early years of the twentieth century, in the United
States, readers were those who could read a text aloud correctly;
for one to be considered productively literate and be honored for
it, it was almost enough to win a spelling bee. Now, of course, a
minimum standard for functional literacy includes these criteria:
(1) the ability to read unfamiliar material (silently), (2) the ability
to gain information from a text, (3) the ability to extrapolate from
a text, (4) the ability to apply information in new contexts when it
is demanded, and (5) (at least for a possibly growing number) the
ability to create texts—to write, and write coherently and cogently
for various audiences.[1] The functional literate, according to
UNESCO's standard, is "one whose attainments in reading, writing, and arithmetic make it possible for him to continue to use these
skills toward his own and the community's development." The
functional literate will be the reader/writer who is able to change.

To speak merely of functional literacy is both to ignore what
literate societies have been able to achieve beyond economic well-
being and to invite charges of philistinism. To speak of literacy and
illiteracy, of millions of functional or full illiterates, of large per-
centages of school-leavers and school graduates who read below
grade level and have no chance to pass entrance or licensure examinations, is to invite the questions: Have our schools failed? Have
they failed those who would survive only? Have they failed those
who would not live by bread alone?

Deeper Than the Schools

The answer to these questions is tied, interestingly, to two other
questions: What is literacy? How does literacy develop?

"[R]eal literacy," writes Michael Clark, "is always a specific response to a concrete situation and never a generalized touchstone
for personal development, social respectability, or pedagogical
success" (1983, 60). Those of us who have achieved a "higher literacy," one that enables beyond the capacity to fill in the short form
provided by the IRS or spell all words correctly on an application

form, have done so because we have found ourselves in "concrete situations" that both demand and permit a certain kind of "specific response": an essay for readers of a journal, a brief for a corporate legal action, a budget request to a board of regents, a poem, a position statement on terrorism in the Middle East, a journal for one's daughter that is both published and reviewed, a seminar paper that receives an A, a letter to a United States senator that is read, acknowledged, and acted upon. All such specific responses presume a particular place in the world: a privileged place well above the poverty line.

"A person is literate," goes the UNESCO standard, "when he has acquired the *essential knowledge* [emphasis mine] and skills which enable him to engage in *all those activities in which literacy is required for effective functioning . . .*" James Boyd White, lawyer, legal scholar, and professor of English and Classics at the University of Michigan, offers this definition of literacy:

> I start with the idea that literacy is not merely the capacity to understand the conceptual content of writings and utterances, but the ability to participate fully in a set of intellectual and social practices (1983, 56).

To "engage in all . . . activities" and "to participate fully in a set of intellectual and social practices" presumes opportunities to do so. Such opportunities are not extended to all citizens in the United States; certain easily identified groups are always denied them. If we one day find ourselves citizens in a fully developed information society, how many opportunities will there be for all of us to develop and make use of the full range of competencies imaginable as essential for active, not merely passive, participation in such a society? In our culture, producers benefit and consumers merely consume—if they have money enough to do so.

Historians of literacy such as Harvey J. Graff have come to speak of a "literacy myth," a notion that literacy inevitably results in social progress, in the liberation of the individual:

> The rise of literacy and its dissemination to the popular classes is associated with the triumph of light over darkness, of liberalism, democracy, and of universal unbridled progress (1979, xv).

Robert Disch speaks of two tendencies in the mystique about literacy endowed to us by our predecessors:

> One, essentially utilitarian, was committed to the functional uses of literacy as a medium for the spread of practical information that could lead to individual and social progress: the other, essentially aesthetic and spiritual, was committed to the uses of literacy for salvaging the drooping spirit of Western man from the death of religion and the ravages of progress (1973, 3).

The utilitarian benefits of literacy, so goes the myth, are economic, social, and intellectual. Economic benefits include enhanced access to employment and to information leading to a better life. Social benefits include the broadening of personal perspective beyond the tribal or local—perhaps beyond group or community. Claims for the intellectual benefits of literacy have gone beyond the obvious ones of access to stored knowledge to stronger ones asserting a causal relation between literacy and general learning as well as between literacy and full cognitive development.

Whatever the validity of these claims, all presume access not merely to the means for acquiring literacy but to opportunities for practicing its competencies in specific responses to concrete situations. Language does not develop save in contexts of use. There is no point in reading if there is no purpose for doing so; there is no point in writing if no one reads and acts upon what has been written.

Have schools failed? How many opportunities has our society provided for all graduates "to participate fully in a set of social and intellectual practices"? It is that kind of participation that motivates and promotes literacy.

Historians have called our attention to the double-edged character of literacy as it is embodied in educational and other social institutions. This from Harvey Graff's study of some nineteenth-century Canadian cities:

> ... literacy ... a phenomenon suggestive of equality—contributed regularly as an element of the structure of inequality, reinforcing the steep ridges of stratification, and also as a force for order and integration. It also served as a symbolic focus of other forces of inequality: ethnicity, class, sex, and age (1979, 19).

Some things never seem to change. Consider these statistics from Jonathan Kozol's book:

> Sixteen percent of white adults, 44 percent of blacks, and 56 percent of Hispanic citizens are functional or marginal illiterates. Figures for the younger generation of black adults are increasing. Forty-seven percent of all black seventeen-year-olds are functionally illiterate. That figure is expected to climb to 50 percent by 1990 (1985, 4).

Are the schools failing? Consider this finding from John Goodlad's study of schooling in the United States:

> Reading instruction in the junior and senior highs appeared to be a matter of remediation involving the mechanics of word recognition, phonics, and vocabulary development. In English there was still a substantial emphasis on the basics of grammar and composition—punctuation, capitalization, sentence structure, paragraph organization, word analysis, parts of speech. *In line with the findings* [all emphasis mine] *of our analysis of tracking reported in Chapter 5, lower track classes tended to emphasize the mechanics of English usage,*

whereas high-track classes were likely to stress the intellectual skills of analysis, evaluation and judgment. . . . The low track classes were unlikely to encounter the high status knowledge dealt with in the upper tracks normally considered essential for college admission (1984, 205).

Functional literacy, we are told, is a matter both of knowledge and skills; "literacy . . . is the ability to participate fully in a set of intellectual and social practices." But some students only do drills and apparently pay the price.

Are the schools to blame for such myopia? Who teaches the teachers who drill the students in low-track classes? Who provides them with materials? How much are such teachers paid, and how many students do they have to teach, and in what surroundings? Who tells them what to teach and how? Do they like being told, and do they think they are being told the right thing? What kinds of tests do their students have to take? How much control do they have over the motivations of their students? What opportunities do they and their students perceive for the exercise of an expansive literacy, one that might result in the use of competencies toward their own and their communities' development?

Such literate communities as exist are comprised of writers and readers bound together by a common language, which in turn is reflective of common knowledge and values. Drawing upon what is common, writers and readers constitute community (i.e., construct common meanings) by participating in a set of intellectual and social practices that are sanctioned, supported, and rewarded by the broader society. Readers of essays like this one, like those who write them, are members of such a community, and it is, like most literate communities, a privileged one. With privilege should come an obligation to ask questions: Is our community a closed or an open one? Is the common language that constitutes it for members only, or may others come to use it, even if they change it in the process of doing so? In forming our community, whom and how many have we systematically excluded, and at what cost to the possibility of common understanding and social cohesion?

Literacy is precious when it is put to uses that are worth valuing; literacy can be pernicious when our concept of it is used to deny any possibility of its use by others whose lives and values the privileged literate do not value. To be reflectively literate in a humanely literate society is to understand that the term *illiterate* does not name an absence or a disability, but a place in the world in which one's actions have been both limited and limiting.

Note

[1]The discussion here borrows from essays by Resnick and Resnick (1977) and by Clifford (1984).

2

The Social Context of Literacy

It is important to discuss the social context of literacy for several reasons, some of them perfectly obvious. It is obvious, for example, that teaching—any teaching—takes place only in some one or another social context: We teach something to somebody some place at some particular time in some particular setting. What we do is influenced not only by the *what* but also by the *when, to whom,* and *where*. It is also obvious, when we think about it, that the teaching of literacy is especially sensitive to the pressures of social context. Language in all of its uses is an intimate part of human experience: Language is expressive of identity and personality, but it is also socially binding and expressive of collective values. Written language is peculiarly public, more so than speech, and as a consequence its forms are carefully scrutinized; reading and writing are highly valued activities so that society monitors their acquisition—as we know from myriad articles in the public media about Johnnies and Janes who can't read or write. We teachers of literacy meet students in a charged atmosphere. We need to be sensitive to the prevailing currents, if for no other purpose than to avoid electrocution.

A compelling reason for talking about the social context for literacy is that our profession has usually avoided the subject in spite of its importance, leaving it to sociologists, sociolinguists, and social historians. Let me cite just one example, borrowed from an essay by Frank D'Angelo (1983, 97–114). Richard Ohmann, when he was Editor of *College English*, requested manuscripts for a special issue on the publicly proclaimed literacy crisis. This was his challenge to his colleagues:

> Is there a decline in literacy? in writing ability?
>
> If so, what are its causes? To what extent is it accountable to changes in schooling? To changes in American society? What can—or should—college English teachers be doing about it? Are there college programs that successfully make up deficits in verbal skills? Is "bonehead English" an idea whose time has come again? Do competency requirements for graduation help? Should this be a problem of the English department, or the whole college or university? Can we distinguish between the traditional basics—spelling, usage, etc.—and some others that have more to do with intellectual competence? Can English teachers usefully shape the national concern with verbal competence, rather than simply respond to needs expressed by pundits, legislators, regents, and businessmen?
>
> If, on the other hand, there has been no significant decline in reading or writing ability among college students, what explains the outcry? What can English teachers do to correct public misconceptions? Is our responsibility confined to the classroom, or does it include social and political action? (1976, 819).

Ohmann asked us to look not merely at alleged symptoms but also at the social dimensions of the literacy crisis and at the social meaning of the public's concern; to decide whether or not a crisis existed and if so to discover its causes; and only then to reach decisions about how to deal with it. But when the special issue of *College English* appeared, Ohmann published his disappointment at the contributions:

> A large proportion merely reiterated the public concerns and in terms very similar to those employed by the media. Others devoted most of their energy to suggesting better ways to teach writing. We might infer from these facts that the profession accepts not only the public assessment of the literacy "crisis" but also the blame for it. Our original call queried whether in fact there has been a significant decline in reading and writing ability among students. Yet not one contribution reviewed and analyzed in any detail the assumptions, methods, and statistics of the testing on which so much of the public outcry seems to be based. Are these assumptions, methods, and statistics as invulnerable to criticism as our professional silence suggests? (Ohmann and Coley, 1977, 441).

Nastier questions than Ohmann's last can be put: Does our profession's silence on such topics suggest that we are willing to let others tell us what to do and then develop methods for getting it done better or more efficiently? Does our silence imply contentment with the status quo?

The world may very well need a better rat trap, but does it really need a better sentence combiner?

A fact of life in our world is that the possession of literacy correlates almost perfectly with the possession of power and wealth. And in general, the more literacy one has or can control, the more power one can exercise—real power, not something metaphorical like the power of self-expression. Now I intend no causative implication in the statement; to achieve literacy does not necessarily earn one power, as we well know. But the powerful are usually themselves literate, or if not, they can purchase the services of those who are.

Another fact of life in our world is that the *profession* of literacy, as contrasted with its possession, correlates not with power and wealth but with relative powerlessness and relative poverty. English teachers do not exert much influence in the world of raw power, even though they live and work in it. The humanities, when compared with the sciences, the social sciences, or professional schools, are underfunded both within their own institutions and nationally, and humanists are underrepresented both in academic governance and in government.

These facts of our own social existence are more than unpleasant, they are dangerous. The danger is not to our persons, yours and mine, or even to our sense of personal worth. The danger is rather to our profession—to our collective sense of endeavor and to the ethics we apply in the teaching of literacy. We have or can claim to have two things useful to those who possess power—namely, the ability to make students literate and squatting rights in classrooms where literacy is assumed to be taught. But as poor cousins, we are particularly vulnerable both to the temptations of utility (we call it service) and to the temptations of the money that pays for our services. Methods can be endlessly adjusted to ends and aims, to the aims and ends of others as easily as to our own.

And what if our academic discipline does not enjoy intellectual prestige? We can always try to achieve status by borrowing prestigious theory and adapting it to the demand for new methods. But when we do, does the right brain always know what the left brain is doing?

I am oversimplifying and being facetious, and with issues that are neither simple nor funny. We do have a responsibility to the society that sustains us, and at least equal responsibility to students whose pragmatic needs must be met. But we can meet these responsibilities only if we understand at least something of the social context in which literacy presently functions.

What kinds of things constitute the social context of literacy in our time? More than I can mention, of course, but I will touch on these four: First, on inherited conceptions of literacy and the values we attach to them; second, on real and socially perceived needs for literacy; third, on ideal and ethically conceived needs for literacy; and fourth, on some few of our institutions for the fostering of literacy.

Inherited Concepts and Values

Practice is always rooted in concepts even when the concepts are unstated or even unstatable; but what we practice most energetically is not always that which we value most highly. The *concept* of literacy is highly valued in our own as in other Western and Westernized industrial societies. Historians, recognizing this special phenomenon and testing values against social practices, are now writing about a "literacy myth"—a configuration of generally held and privileged notions about literacy and its functions in modern society. Harvey J. Graff, for example:

> The rise of literacy and its dissemination to the popular classes is associated with the triumph of light over darkness, of liberalism, democracy, and of universal unbridled progress. In social thought, therefore, these elements relate to ideas of linear evolution and progression; literacy here takes its place among the other successes of modernity and rationality. In theory and in empirical investigation, literacy is conceptualized—often in stark and simple fashion—as an important part of the larger parcel of factors that account for the evolution of modern societies and states (1979, xv).

With its wide acceptance, the literacy myth benefits us poor cousins, of course. Foundations fund our programs, deans find money for English departments, enlightened school boards reduce loads for writing teachers (though rarely), and in general our public and professional stock rises. In the short run, we prosper; but we might be better off in the longer run if we try to find out how much truth the myth contains and then act on that. What we inherit is not always to our good.

Robert Disch, in his introduction to *The Future of Literacy*, writes that

> the twentieth century inherited a mystique of literacy born out of . . . two tendencies. One, essentially utilitarian, was committed to the functional uses of literacy as a medium for the spread of practical information that could lead to individual and social progress; the other, essentially aesthetic and spiritual, was committed to the uses of literacy for salvaging the drooping spirit of Western man from the death of religion and the ravages of progress (1973, 3).

The utilitarian benefits of literacy, so goes the myth, are economic, social, and intellectual. Economic benefits include enhanced access to employment and to information leading to a better life (for example, information about birth control or about sanitation). Social benefits include a broadening of personal perspective beyond the tribal or local; acquisition of societal norms and values leading to public spiritedness; participation in democratic means of governance. Claims for the intellectual benefits of literacy have gone beyond the obvious ones of access to stored knowledge to stronger ones asserting a causal relation between literacy and general learning as well as between literacy and full cognitive development.[1] How many of these claims correspond to established fact?

In fact, we do not know, but in some few cases we are beginning to find out. And what we are discovering, when the myth is tested, is that it proves to be mythical. For only one example, consider the following results of historical research into the correlations of literacy with liberalized social attitudes and with expanded economic opportunity. In a study of literacy in Colonial New England, Kenneth A. Lockridge (1974) found that Protestantism was a stronger impetus to literacy than secular school laws; that schools were dominated by conservative, not progressive, educational impulses; and that when literacy became nearly universal in New England near the end of the eighteenth century, attitudes toward society and the larger world were not discernibly modified. In another study, treating some nineteenth-century Canadian cities, Harvey Graff found that:

> ... literacy—a phenomenon suggestive of equality—contributed regularly as an element of the structure of inequality, reinforcing the steep ridges of stratification, and also as a force for order and integration. It also served as a symbolic focus of other forces of inequality: ethnicity, class, sex, and age. Literacy, then, did not universally serve to benefit all who had attained it, but neither did it disadvantage all those who had not (1979, 19).

Graff does not claim that literacy holds no potential for liberalization; rather he demonstrates that powerful, deeply embedded social forces can override its potential. Literacy can be an effective means of social control when educational institutions use it for this purpose; or it can be a means of social liberation when individuals are encouraged to think, read, and write for themselves. Ohmann presses the pertinent question: Where do we stand as teachers when we emphasize means over ends or methods over purposes? In answering the question, we do well to be mindful that ours is a society that has sanctioned a back-to-basics movement, that is enamored with competency testing, and that presently values vocational over liberal education. Few vocations in our society encourage an exercise of literacy that is liberalizing and liberating.

Even if all of our students were to achieve literacy, not all would benefit unless allowed and encouraged by society to put their competencies to use. Our aims and especially our methods have to accommodate to this brute fact of social reality. We need to know much more than we now do about the forces and institutions in our society that constrain literacy, both those that inhibit its exercise and those that make it serve as an instrument of unconscious socialization to mores and values we would not endorse. Without such knowledge, we could well help create a reality more malignant than that figured in the literacy myth.

Real and Socially Perceived Needs for Literacy

So far I have been talking about literacy as a "buzz word"—as a concept or a symbol incorporating notions of aspiration and value. Now I want to define the term, or at least to limit its reference. Let *literacy* mean *functional literacy;* and let *functional literacy*, for the moment, mean only this: the ability to read and write well enough to compete for economic sufficiency. Such literacy is essential for all students and for all citizens, and insofar as we are able and insofar as social circumstances will allow, we must help provide it. I quote some expert views on the demographics and consequences of functional literacy and its absence:

> Ralph W. Tyler: . . . in 1800, the unskilled in all categories constituted more than eighty percent of the labor force; in 1900 they made up sixty percent; and in 1980, about six percent. It was only after World War II that rapid changes in the occupational and social structure created sharp new demands for education and many more opportunities for employment in such fields as education, health, recreation, social services, administration, accounting, and engineering. Now jobs requiring no schooling are few in number, while tasks requiring at least a high school education make up nearly two thirds of employment opportunities. Consequently, schools are now expected to educate all (or nearly all) children rather than to sort out high performers and proficient test takers and to encourage members of that group alone to go on with their education (1983, 198).

> Paul A. Strassman: Since the 1950s our country has become predominantly occupied with the creation, distribution, and administration of information. By 1990, only about fifty percent of the work force will be manufacturing objects and producing food. The rest will occupy most of the time just communicating. From an economic standpoint it is important to be concerned about the effectiveness with which all these people carry out their tasks. Literacy is therefore a special concern since it is one of the underlying capabilities that enable our economy to function effectively (1983, 116).

> Arthur M. Cohen and Florence B. Brawer: Literacy is certainly related to success in nearly all community-college programs: transfer courses demand proficiency in reading, writing, and mathematics, and licensure examinations admitting students to practice after completing technological programs typically demand the same. Many community-college programs are closed to students who cannot pass an entrance examination that is based on literacy (1983, 210–11).

> Robben W. Fleming: Meanwhile, it is estimated that there may be as many as 57 million adult illiterates in the United States (1983, 64).

> John Oxenham: In 1971, some 780 million people over the age of fifteen all over the world were classed as illiterate . . . by 1980 they will total perhaps 820 million (1980, 2).

Since functional illiteracy does correlate with poverty and power-lessness, the problem of illiteracy is as urgent as any in our society.

But ironically, the needs of the poor could well be forgotten because recently we have discovered other needs among the better-off and the more influential. We have discovered that middle-class students don't write very well, not even those who enroll in prestigious schools; that businessmen don't write very well, or at least don't think they do; that bureaucrats and lawyers write even worse; that the new information-society requires a new kind of literacy—in software rather than in ordinary printed language. The *influential* public is now more often asking "Why can't Johnny write?" than it is "Why can't Johnny read?" Yet as Edward Corbett so accurately points out, reading is far more important for economic sufficiency (even for survival) than is writing:

> ... writing will never be as crucial a skill for surviving or thriving in our society as reading is. Functional illiterates who cannot even write their names may suffer embarrassment because of their deficiency, but they somehow manage to subsist in our technological society. But those functional illiterates who cannot even read street signs and simple directions are so severely handicapped that it is questionable whether they can survive, much less thrive, in our society. Thirdly, only a minuscule portion of the total population will regularly have to compose important, influential documents. The majority of literate people have to do some writing occasionally—letters, notes, fill-in-the-blanks forms—but only a minority have to write regularly and seriously in connection with their jobs (1981, 47).

The present emphasis upon writing over reading doubtless reflects a bias in favor of the upper of our social classes, where needs take precedence.[2] If not restrained or balanced against the need for reading, the bias could well contribute to a widening of the gulf between rich and poor that now seems so permanent a feature of our national topography. As Richard Hendrix writes:

> The emphasis on writing clarifies the gap between a commitment in principle to universal opportunity and the fact of unequal opportunity. Writing ability is unevenly distributed in our society along class lines. Indeed, writing and access to writing improvement is as good an indicator of the difference between, say, white collar and blue collar career tracks as we are likely to find (1981, 53).

Our problems are made more difficult to solve because just when we begin to recognize the number and complexity of them, the public develops an aversion to taxation and politicians develop a preference for bombs over books.[3] How, then, are we to react to the perfectly legitimate demands placed upon us in our social role as teachers of literacy when we know that resources will be limited—perhaps severely?

We could, of course, take battlefield medicine as our model and practice triage on some principle of social utility, fitting our teaching to present social realities and comforting ourselves with some resigned or basically optimistic notion of social inevitability. Maybe only a minority do need to learn to write; maybe the masses need only to learn to read, and then only marginally; and maybe, because of technology, the masses don't even need to read. And maybe the socially disintegrating effects of such specialization can be avoided if some such vision of social interdependence as John Oxenham's turns out to be an accurate one:

> [F]or the masses to enjoy literature without literacy, a minority would need to be highly literate. The paradox evokes two reflections on technological change. One is that, as science and technology introduce new changes in production and services, a growing majority with decreasing skills seems to become increasingly dependent on a highly skilled but shrinking minority. The trend appears to lead to a dictatorship of technocrats. On the other hand, while a necessary consequence of the extension of specialization may well be the dependence of majorities upon minorities, oppressive technology is not the necessary end. The reason is simply that the proliferation of specializations generates a net of interdependence and a homeostatic distribution of power (1980, 131).

Perhaps a stable and healthy interdependence can result from a planned distribution of the assets of literacy. Perhaps we can focus our attention and concentrate our resources on training a fully literate elite without oppressing the masses. Perhaps that is what we are doing anyway, without much thought about it.

There is nothing of the conditional in these two assertions: Resources will be limited as we seek to meet needs for literacy; priorities will be set—either by us or by others, either by intention or through thoughtless inertia. Policy should be at least as well planned as good writing. Right now we need good policy more than better lesson plans.

Ideals and Ethics

In June 1981 the English Composition Board of the University of Michigan sponsored a conference on "Literacy in the 1980's."[4] Experts from various occupations and professions were invited to the conference and asked to respond to this question: "What will be the needs for literacy in your field as we look from now toward the end of the century?" As I review the conference, two presentations stand out: one by a lawyer and professor of law; another by a scientist who is also Manager of the Central Research Division of the Mobil Research and Development Corporation. These two impressed me because they called not for more emphasis on utilitarian writing (and reading), but for a more expansive and humane literacy.

James Boyd White, Professor of Law at the University of Chicago[5] and the author of a distinguished book on lawyers' use of language (1973), described what he calls "the invisible discourse of the law":

> unstated conventions by which the language [of] law] operates . . . expectations about the ways in which [words] will be used, expectations that do not find explicit expression anywhere but are part of the legal culture that the surface language simply assumes (1983, 48–49).

But White did more than describe. First, he enriched existing definitions of (functional) literacy:

> I start with the idea that literacy is not merely the capacity to understand the conceptual content of writings and utterances but the ability to participate fully in a set of social and intellectual practices. It is not passive but active, not imitative but creative, for participation in the speaking and writing of language includes participation in the activities it makes possible (1983, 56).

Then he described a course in writing and reading that might be taught to invite such participation. White would help his students to perceive how rule and procedure constitute social organization and govern social cooperation; how language is the means of such constitution; and how law is related to everyday social behavior. In so doing he would demystify the law, making it more subject both to lay understanding and to personal control. According to White:

> All this could be done with materials from the student's own life, without the use of legal terms or technicalities. It need not even be done in Standard English: the student's writing . . . should indeed reflect the way people actually speak in their own world. One important lesson for us all might be the discovery that it is not only in the law, or only in the language of the white middle class, that community is constituted, or that argument about justice proceeds (1983, 58).

Paul Weisz, a scientist and businessman, called for clarity and broad comprehensibility in scientific language: for the development and use in science of a common language enabling more citizens "to benefit from the knowledge which abounds around us," a language that would also serve to combat the socially and intellectually fragmenting effects of specialization. He sees the need as essential:

> The relationship in our society between division of knowledge and presence of social tension is clear. As knowledge and activity become more sophisticated, the bridges of understanding and interaction grow weaker and weaker. Now, more than ever before, such bridges are needed for both social and psychological survival (1983, 131).

Weisz's concern echoes that expressed in the report of the Rockefeller Commission on the Humanities:

> Our citizens need to become literate in a multiple sense. We all need to understand the characteristics of scientific inquiry and the repercussions of scientific research. We must all learn something about the use of the media and of new technologies for storing, transmitting, and expanding knowledge. Without this sort of literacy, our society as a whole will be less able to apply science and technology to humanistic needs, less able to measure the human effects of scientific achievements, less able to judge the information we produce and receive (*The Humanities*, 1980, 18–19).

Our profession has begun to recognize that its own notions about needs for literacy do not always match day-to-day needs outside the classroom. But most who have argued for adjustment to the real world have addressed only economic needs. White and Weisz, both practitioners in the world of work, suggest other ways: White by linking language use with social behavior and to intellectual activity rooted in social practices; Weisz by linking the aims of writing with a democracy's needs for information and knowledge essential for the solution of human problems. Both programs are *ethical* in conception.

Caesar exacts his due, but we need not pay the taxmaster so unthinkingly as to leave in his control all decisions about what social reality ought to be. Societies exist in the mind as well as in fact, in ethical standards for behavior as well as in behavior patterns. It is our particular obligation as teachers of literacy to recognize this, and with our students' help to frame ideals constructive of a world we would willingly inhabit. Ideals and ethics find their most permanent expression in public language.

Institutions: Who Teaches the What to Whom?

Existing institutions, like inherited concepts and values, are part of the social context for literacy. As things are now established, we English teachers are the ones customarily assumed to be responsible for teaching literacy (along with elementary-school teachers, who can do anything). But given existing and shifting needs for literacy, it is not at all clear that we will continue to be held responsible or considered responsible enough to be so held.

In an article in a volume containing the proceedings of a conference sponsored by the National Institute of Education, Richard Hendrix—who is associated with the Fund for the Improvement of Postsecondary Education—asks this question: "Who is responsible for improving writing?" He says this about English departments:

> Writing instruction was for years a stepchild of English departments, who have always dominated it. As recently as fifteen years ago many

colleges dropped composition altogether—partly on the basis that the high schools were handling the job, but mainly to give still greater emphasis to literary study. That development should make us hesitate about trusting that English departments, as they are presently constituted, will solve the problem.

Now there has been a resurgence of active involvement by English faculty along with others. Writing instruction could be a boon for underemployed humanists, a large and influential group. But teachers trained in literature may not necessarily be well situated to work with beginning students, or to prepare students for the kinds of writing tasks they will likely face after school. English professors are not even necessarily good writers themselves, and their commitment to specialization has been at least as strong as any other discipline's (1981, 56).

There are grounds for Hendrix's suspicion. They exist in the prevailing attitudes of most college and many high-school English teachers toward the teaching of writing; in the way composition teachers are treated in their own departments; and in the way composition programs are funded, staffed, and managed. And in the meantime societal needs are not being met, either by instructional programs that address vocational needs or by research programs that address the need for better understanding of the relations of literacy to society, to learning, and to the determination of value. Can and will English departments change enough to meet such needs? My own experiences as a teacher of writing, as a program planner, and as an English department chairman give me grounds for doubt at least as strong as that expressed by Hendrix.

The trouble with literacy is that it enters all aspects of human life in literate societies. The trouble with questions about literacy is that the important ones are general in their application to human discourse and its functions. The trouble with our answers, when we are English teachers, is that we are all specialists. And it is possible—at the least arguable—that a specialization in literature is less adaptable than many to a broad understanding of literacy.

Raymond Williams, in a challenging critique of dominant trends in literary study, reminds us that the term *literature* once applied more broadly than to imaginative works of a certain kind and quality. In one of its earlier usages, "it was often close to the sense of modern *literacy*"; its reference was to "a condition of reading: of being able to read and of having read" (1977, 45–54). Histories, biographies, works of philosophy, political and scientific treatises were once all works of literature. In his argument, Williams traces the specialization of the term to the domain of "creative" or "imaginative" works, and the development of literature departments in academies as units concerned exclusively with this narrowed domain and with the practice of criticism.

The problem arising from this development is that it invites us, as inheritors of the tradition, to equate "literacy" with knowledge of a special kind of literature, without recognizing that such an equation is a socially privileged and economically self-serving one: more a matter of status and value than of fact. The study of imaginative literature may well contribute to the complex of abilities, capacities, and attitudes that function in good reading and good writing; but to claim that it necessarily and sufficiently does is patently absurd.

If departments of English continue to define themselves as departments of literature and mean by that term imaginative works only, and if English teachers restrict themselves to reading only such works and commentaries on them, then there is need for new kinds of departments just as there is for differently prepared teachers. Harvey Graff gets to the heart of the problem:

> Discussions of literacy are confused and ambiguous—an ironic, and even startling, phenomenon, which contrasts sharply with the high value we assign to the skills of reading and writing. Vagueness pervades virtually all efforts to discern the meaning of literacy; moreover, there is surprisingly little agreement on or special evidence for the benefits of literacy, whether socially or individually, economically or culturally. Rather, assumptions preempt criticism and investigation, and agencies and specialists whose business it is to promote literacy shrink from asking fundamental questions in their campaigns to disseminate skills (1981, 3).

Certain questions cannot be avoided any longer. Serious research is needed into literacy and its place in our present social context, and such research should take precedence over concern with method. There is little profit in trying to do better what cannot or should not be done.

Notes

[1]These last claims are now much in the literature, especially the literature justifying writing programs. Before believing them completely, teachers and administrators should read the very important book by Sylvia Scribner and Michael Cole, *The Psychology of Literacy* (1981).

[2]Part of the problem, too, of course, is the present dichotomy in education, as institutionalized, and in schools as they are structured, between something called "reading" and something called "writing." "Reading" is in the domain of elementary education and "writing" is the domain of secondary education, even though many secondary students do not read well. Literature courses in high school, strangely, are rarely thought of as reading courses; history, science, math courses even more rarely. Perhaps recent developments in early literacy, in both research and teaching, will lead the way toward better integration of reading and writing into all subjects at all levels.

[3]The problem is now exacerbated in the later 1980s by the politicians' recognition that "education" is a hot issue: our nation is at risk.

[4]A volume of essays records the proceedings of some part of this conference. See Bailey and Fosheim (1983).

[5]Now a colleague at The University of Michigan, with appointments in Law, English, and Classics.

3

Re-forming Literacy: A Collaborative Teacher-Student Research Project

Cathy Fleischer

I start with the idea that literacy is not merely the capacity to understand the conceptual content of writings and utterances, but the ability to participate fully in a set of intellectual and social practices. It is not passive but active; not imitative but creative for participation in the speaking and writing of language is participation in the activities it makes possible. Indeed it involves a perpetual remaking both of language and of practice.

JAMES BOYD WHITE

Critically speaking, illiteracy is neither an "ulcer" nor a "poison herb" to be eradicated, nor a "disease." Illiteracy is one of the concrete expressions of an unjust social reality. Illiteracy is not a strictly linguistic or exclusively pedagogical or methodological problem. It is political, as is the very literacy through which we try to overcome illiteracy.

PAULO FREIRE

If we believe with Jay Robinson and James Boyd White that literacy is always socially constructed, we must inevitably turn to the question implicit in Paulo Freire's words: What are the politics of the literacy through which we might try to overcome illiteracy? A literacy situated in the realm of the social must respond to the world of the political as we delve into what defines the expectations and the limitations of that social world. For our students today, such expectations are firmly situated in the world of schools. Recently, as I co-taught in a high school English class, I began to look seriously at the implicit definition of the literacy valued and taught in schools, a normative definition of what I want to call a literacy of conformity. What counts as literate in the school world is often adherence to a set of norms, a set of values, and, most particularly, a set of forms. If a student can fill the muffin tin—as Ann Berthoff would say—he or she is considered to be at least minimally literate. Such a literacy reifies the five-paragraph essay, the structured research report, the rigidly designed and frigidly delivered book report—forms that are imitative of *nothing* in the real world and thus conspire to make school an unreal world. These forms are artifacts of what Knoblauch and Brannon call a ceremonial view of discourse, what Jenny Cook-Gumperz sees as a schooled literacy, what James Paul Gee calls an essay-text literacy: a kind of literacy constructed by and for the schools whose demands correspond to the specific set of discourse practices required of those who will survive in the social worlds of schooling.

In a school world where literacy is defined as conformity, forms and genres become the invisible content of students' language learning and the visible center of the energies they devote to writing. As students write and as teachers read their writing, form takes precedence over content, so much so that students often fail even to think about the subject matter they are writing about, so much so that students see writing as "a process of honoring the conventions that matter to English teachers," as Knoblauch and Brannon tell us, "rather than a process of discovering personal meanings, thinking well in language, or achieving serious intellectual purposes" (1984, 31). As it is practiced in schools, writing all too often becomes a game in which students strive to communicate with their teachers—but are able to communicate only in limited ways and only if they say what it is they have to say in sanctioned ways.

When literacy is viewed as conformity, structures and rules become the reality, a reality that is independent of meaning in the processes of composing. For students so caught up, in-school discourse exists as a phenomenon quite separate from the other kinds of discourse in which they constantly engage. Because the rules for classroom discourse seem to be invented only for use in the classroom, and because they are so unlike those that regulate discourse in students' worlds outside school, they assume a mysterious nature for student writers. Both the invented genres of classroom writing (the five-paragraph essay or the formulaic research paper) and the regulations that dictate language use ("never start a sentence with a conjunction" or "never use passive voice") leave the student at the mercy of the teacher: the genres are her genres, the rules are her rules for a language that is her language, if it is anyone's at all. Writing thus becomes for many students a game of choosing the right rules from a perplexing array of must-do's, never-do's, and sometimes-do's—a constantly shifting array as students move from class to class and from teacher to teacher. Caught up in the game of choosing, students have little time to think about writing as an activity of discovering personal meanings, thinking well in language, or achieving some serious intellectual purpose by communicating discoveries and thoughts to others.

The English class in which I recently co-taught, the class that produced the collaborative research described in this essay, taught me a great deal about a world of literacy conceived as conformity, and taught me to think hard about how what Freire calls the politics of literacy impinges upon various groups of students in schools. The students with whom I worked live in a classroom world labeled "discover level"; in other communities, that classroom might be labeled "basic," "at risk," "skills"—whatever euphemism is currently in vogue as the means to separate out and name groups of high school students whose literacy does not meet the standards set by the institution. These particular high school juniors, like others so labeled, are typically asked to do very little writing during their schoolday—maybe fill in a form; write a structured two-paragraph summary (including what the chapter said and what you think); define a list of words from the textbook—and they are generally assumed to resist or to be unable to manage any other kind of writing tasks. Not only can't they do it, the story goes, but because they don't know how to do it, they hate it so much that they'll *never* do it, and they probably won't need it to get a job anyway, so it's not worth it, right?

Sheila Smith, my co-teacher, and I decided to go against the expectations that attach themselves to labels: to ask questions that might form new expectations. We chose to base at least part of the classroom agenda for the term on the notion that these students probably were the best sources of knowledge about their own writing and that by calling upon their own understandings formulated in their own language, we could all learn something about these students' own literacy. When we asked our students to join us as co-researchers in this project, which honored their intuitions and their experiences, we discovered to our initial surprise that they knew a lot about writing and were willing to share that knowledge with us. They were aware of the demands various teachers of various subjects made upon them; they had intuitions about the differences between in-school and out-of-school discourse; they understood some important things about their own processes of writing. Even more to our surprise, we discovered that many of them enjoyed various kinds of writing, a notion that seemed antithetical to all expectations called up by the labels they brought with them to class.

Our process of learning just how much our students knew was a journey, a journey that began that first weekend of the semester as I sat at home, flipping through the pages of their first journal entries. We had halfheartedly asked them to write about how they

feel when they write, expecting to read equally halfhearted attempts to explain their notions of writing. Instead, I found myself
increasingly intrigued by what these students were telling me. I
read Scott's entry early on, an entry that got my interest rolling. He
wrote, "When I am writing I never think about what I am writing.
Then I read it over to see if I made any mistakes and if I should add
something to it. When I am writing I block out everything. And
I have to be comfortable." Pretty interesting, I thought; he shows
some self-analysis, some understanding of the process he uses to
compose. I was encouraged to continue reading, this time a bit
more carefully, when I came to Stephanie's:

> When I write I like to be at the kitchen table where it is usually quiet,
> at night. With one light on to make it relaxing. Our kitchen is fur-
> nished in earth-tone colors; it makes it very relaxing. Then I pull out
> paper that is colorful (red, green, yellow, blue) and write on and on
> without stopping. When I make a mistake I scribble it out just to make
> the letter more laid back. Not real neat because the way you write
> your words and letters brings out your personality to other people, I
> think. I like to make my letters funny, full of jokes and scribbled out
> words, because that's my personality. And I make it a point *not* to
> copy the letter over.

I began to wonder why this student had been placed in a basic
class. Sure, there were some problems with sentence structure and
punctuation, but I was impressed by her understanding of some
very complicated issues that surround the connection of authorial
voice and style. "The way you write your words and letters," she
said, "brings out your personality to other people," a fairly sophisticated notion of intentionality in one's writing, a notion I had
failed to think of as an informing one for "these students." I began
to sit up and take note now as I read on and on, surprised at how
many students articulated a similar understanding of their own
writing, bolting upright when I came to Andrea's:

> When I am writing a story, I usually find myself on a beach and fill my
> lungs with ocean air. In the background I hear no seagulls, not even
> the ocean. Just the sensation I get from that very first breath, I guess
> it's similar to the feeling you get when you're being hugged or when
> you yawn. It relaxes my imagination as the blank wall that sits in
> front of my typewriter fills with the images of the people, places, and
> situations my mind creates.

A short-story writer, I told myself. Look at the metaphors, the
rhythms. Not only does she understand a lot about her own writing,
but she writes artfully about her understanding. Again, I asked
myself why a student who writes like this would be labeled "at risk."

As I continued to read the other journals, more carefully now,
I recognized that while not all the students were this articulate
about their own writing, they all showed a greater understanding

of their own composing processes than I had expected. While these
students were resisting the writing they were assigned to do in
school classes (a resistance that manifested itself in a variety of
ways, from being absent on days when writing was due to simply
refusing to write in class to writing the bare minimum expected,
often on the way into class as the bell rang), they were writing up
a storm at home—fully one half of this class admitted their interest
in and practice of writing outside the bounds of school. While these
students were vehemently denying any interest in writing when we
had class discussions in school, they were penning journals, poems,
short stories, and plays at home. Melvin, for example, the self-
appointed class poet, maintained an initial silence about his composing when we tried to elicit talk from students in class about
their writing selves, but then wrote in his journal about why he
writes what he does:

> *I feel that journals help me*
>   *realize things,*
> *Stories make me think what*
>   *I lack,*
> *Poems help me chill, you know,*
>   *lay back and relax.*

His choices for writing, if not his reasons, seemed typical for
those who slowly began to admit to not only writing on their own
but also enjoying that writing. Marty, an almost nonwriter in
terms of school assignments, said, "Sometimes I sit down and write
short stories" just when there's nothing else to do; Jenny, a well-
mannered but fairly nonproductive school writer, writes poems
because "they give me a great feeling"; Traci, a good student who
always fulfills assignments, but generally doesn't go beyond her
teacher's expectations, likes journals because they "bring back a lot
of memories." How could these be the same kids who moaned,
complained, even refused to write when asked to do so in class? The
same kids who would say in unison during a class discussion on the
subject that they hated writing? The same kids who were labeled
at risk or illiterate or preliterate or semiliterate—labels of which
they were well aware. Clearly these students weren't illiterate,
but they did fail to measure up to the standards of a conforming
literacy, the only kind their school—and a host of other schools—
seemed to recognize and value. Maybe, Sheila and I began to think,
these students possessed a different kind of literacy—what we've
come to call an in-forming literacy, in which students formulate
literacy from within themselves, using their own forms that emerge
from their own backgrounds and experiences, forms that seem to
be disparate from the school forms.
    The interplay between this in-forming literacy of the individ-
ual within his or her own discourse and the conforming literacy of

the schools remains integrally linked to issues of authority. In Bakhtin's terms, the school forms of literacy are an "authoritative discourse . . . the word of a father, of adults, and of teachers." He continues, "The authoritative word demands that we acknowledge it, that we make it our own; it binds us, quite independent of any power it might have to persuade us internally; we encounter it with its authority already fused to it" (1981, 342). Bakhtin sees the authoritative word as a set entity, a kind of discourse unto itself in which no deviation is allowed, no heteroglossia is possible.[1] He believes "[Authoritative discourse] enters our verbal consciousness as a compact and indivisible mass; one must either totally affirm it or totally reject it" (343).

For Bakhtin, the struggle between an authoritative discourse and its dialogical opposite, what he calls an internally persuasive discourse, is an important struggle. Internally persuasive discourse, that which is "backed up by no authority at all and is frequently not even acknowledged in society" (342), enters our consciousness not in the rigid and unchanging manner of authoritative discourse, but rather as "intense interaction, a *struggle* with other internally persuasive discourses" (346). Whereas authoritative discourse denies heteroglossia, internally persuasive discourse celebrates it.

This struggle between authoritative and internally persuasive discourse is, for Bakhtin, a struggle that is central to one's formation of an individual ideology. He argues that as we begin the "process of assimilating the words of others," an assimilation that is based in a constant dialogue with these various internally persuasive and authoritative discourses, we begin to formulate our own ideologies (341). Only then can our own voice begin to emerge from this cacophony of voices to which we are exposed, and only then "can one's own discourse and one's own voice . . . begin to liberate themselves from the authority of the other's discourse" (348).

In many ways, Bakhtin's notions of individual ideology and its formation relate to the notions of literacy acquisition held by such diverse scholars as James Boyd White, Jay Robinson, and Paulo Freire, notions that informed the research Sheila and I undertook. Adolescents in particular continue the forming of their literacy in a kind of warfare similar to Bakhtin's struggle: the school notions of discourse—the conforming notions of literacy—stand as authoritative discourse; the other kinds of discourse—those that make up an in-forming literacy—stand as internally persuasive discourse. The consistent dialogic interplay between these two, in its most positive moments, helps constantly to re-form students' literacy. But more often, this interaction is played out in a less positive way in schools, and the interaction truly becomes a battle in which students all too often are the losers.

The real problem for schools, it seems, becomes what to do with these two very real types of literacy. An in-forming literacy alone, while it celebrates the personal and encourages exploration of ideas, often is too private a means of creating shared meaning, and such sharing is a necessary end in the public sphere of school. A conforming literacy, on the other hand, when it is conceived as narrowly as it seems to be in schools, relies on forms sanctioned in isolation by schools and is, thus, viable neither in real public nor in private worlds. The dilemma becomes how to create a space in school settings that allows for a positive enactment of the interplay between the two through which students might begin to formulate a new literacy based in dialogue, based in heteroglossia.

Calling upon our inclinations about these two literacies, Sheila and I decided to explore their implications for student writers and to search for a new space by asking the students in this class to search with us for answers to the dilemma, beginning with the questions their journals had raised for us and for them. We asked them: Why don't the schools recognize and value your words, your language, your forms? What are the differences between your kind of literacy and the literacy expected by the school? What's wrong with the school forms? Why can't you seem to meet the expectations for literacy demanded by schools when you can clearly use written language so effectively in other settings? When it comes to school writing, why do so many of you not only fail to meet the expectations but simply refuse to take the challenge—a resistance to school literacy that results in your designation as preliterate or illiterate or just plain at risk? Why is it that you who show us both pleasure and interest in out-of-school writing seem to have little or no interest in in-school writing? Our search for answers took the students in a number of directions: interviews with their peers in the classroom and out, analysis as a class of specific pieces of their writing, surveys and other information gathered to research specific projects about literacy that they designed.

As our students joined us in the search, we all began to understand some of the implications of our initial questions and of the notion of students and teachers researching together, both of which seem to be central to Freire's query: What are the politics of literacy through which we try to overcome illiteracy? For me, the answer might begin with Stephanie and her responses, responses that became fairly standard as the students started to explore these issues. She began to inform us all when she told us this after conducting an interview with one of her peers:

> Sally likes to write about herself but doesn't like English or poetry. She likes to write in her kitchen or out under a tree. When learning how to write she had to do introductory paragraphs and had to be neat. In elementary she never wrote anything very long. In junior high and high school, she said it was a different story. Rough drafts, outlines, brainstorming, essays, etc. She said it got harder for her to write. Rules teachers told her to remember were writing in blue or black ink or typed, very neat, no mistakes and put things in specific order.

This interview and others led researcher Stephanie to conclude, "Most students don't really do much free writing [in school]. They seem to write to communicate with others [i.e., teachers] and that is all. As for writing in school we have to and write enough to answer the question or get the job done."

This contrasts sharply with the image of writing many of these students remember from elementary school. Many remember enjoying writing, being praised for their writing, and writing lots of different kinds of pieces in lots of different ways. For these students writing in high school clearly has lost whatever appeal it once had; it's now seen in the businesslike context into which Stephanie placed it: they have to do it, and they have to do enough of it to get the assignment done. Writing in school to fulfill teachers' preordained notions of communication serves the function of a commodity, its trade value seen in terms of a grade. As such, school writing has come to lose most of the value or meaning that these students themselves at one time assigned to it, as a means to come to understand something, a way to discover something new, to help remember your past or come to grips with your present or even to give you pleasure. We all began to ask ourselves why this had happened.

As we teacher and student researchers looked carefully together at students' writing practices, our students' understanding of form informed our understanding of their failure to master the literacy of conformity. As teachers, we first began to see this as we listened to the student researchers try to describe certain pieces of writing that various class members had done—again and again the only descriptive words they could come up with would be the "name" of the particular form or genre the writing took. For example, on one occasion a group of students was looking at a list of definitions one student had written in a consumer economics class, taken from a unit on the stock market. The group decided the subject matter, the actual content of the writing, was "definition." When I suggested that "definition" might not describe the subject matter, but might instead be the form, an argument ensued. I asked the students, "If you read a story about animals, would the subject matter be 'story'?" Although these students acknowledged the distinction I was making in my example, they insisted that the content of their classmate's written list was, nevertheless, definition. "We don't have any idea what this is about," they told me. And the implication followed, if you don't know what it's about, how can you possibly see a content? We could begin to see that an emphasis on form had become so ingrained for these students that it completely overshadowed content for them. We began to see why the question "what are you writing?" inevitably would be answered, "a report," "a research paper," "a paragraph," "a summary"—not "I'm writing about one of the characters in this short story" or "the effects of AIDS testing on the workplace" or "a film we saw in class."

There seems to be a cart-before-the-horse mentality about this approach to writing in which students see form as the substance of their writing, with content, if it follows at all, coming in a distant second. I'm reminded of a comment that Sarah, a high school student in another setting, once made to me.

> For school, they say "Write a descriptive piece," and you can choose what you want to describe, but you still have to write descriptively. . . . You have to rack your brain to think of something to describe. . . . You start off thinking descriptive instead of being struck by something and saying, "I want to describe that, I want to capture that."

There seems to be, for all these students, a world of difference between writing primarily because they have something to say, then finding a form in which to say it, and writing in a form whether or not they have anything to say. In schools, where students are often placed in situations in which they have nothing much to say, they seem to revert to the sanctioned forms, the safe structures that allow them to get by without composing their own informed selves into the writing.

The students with whom we worked seem to have at least one clear belief about form: they know not only that such structures are safe, but that they need the structures if they are to survive in their school worlds. They acknowledge, at least implicitly, a split between form and content and accept the preeminence of form. Despite this knowledge, however, they often still choose to reject and resist such forms.

Fred comes to mind immediately as I think back to how and what we teachers learned with our students about resistance to the school forms. His "theme" about writing—the notion that kept coming up for him again and again throughout the term—was one of subject matter—or the lack of subject matter in most of the writing he knows about. Fred is a student who told us from the start that he hated writing. Why? we wondered, and as the term progressed we began to piece together a few clues to answer that question. Early on in the semester when he interviewed a peer about *his* writing, Fred came up with this conclusion: "He thinks his writing could be good if he could have a subject matter to write on, otherwise he doesn't like it." He went on, "People can write if they feel like it. When they do write they do a good job of it." Occasionally in class, Fred would mention this belief that he can write but that he doesn't because he has nothing to write about. By March he was able to articulate this a bit more, as an entry in my teaching journal reflects:

> It was an interesting class today—I handed out notebooks as some of the students came in and tried to comment specifically on what some of the kids wrote. I told Fred especially that I liked his imagery about

the car a lot. [Fred had written a nice response in his notebook to the question "What is observation?" He wrote, "I think when you observe you look at things around you, you are aware of what is happening in almost every direction. It's like when you drive a car you can't just look straight forward. You have to look around and see what is happening."] . . .

We brainstormed questions about personal background and about writing together and then they went at it alone. . . . Fred was particularly interesting. He talked about how little he cared about writing—how he hated it, wouldn't do it. Started by talking about how he'd get letters from girls and wouldn't write them back. Why not? He didn't know; he just didn't know what to say. Moved later into talking about history class—he wouldn't outline chapters, so he kept failing. Why not? "I don't know much about history," he said, "so how do I know what's important and what isn't?"

Fred, clearly a thoughtful student as you can see by his creative use of the car metaphor, explains here that he can't do outlines because he doesn't know or understand the subject matter—and if he doesn't know the subject matter, he can't know what's important and what isn't, and thus he can't possibly conform to the genre of the regimented outline with its Roman numerals and capital letters. While this does seem a serious concern to Fred, at first I wasn't sure how seriously to take his resistance to the task of outlining chapters in history. Is it true that Fred's lack of understanding of content kept him from filling the forms—or is it just Fred's way of avoiding the task? I later recalled a student in another high school in this same city talking to me about how she did outlines. This student, Akemi, who is an academically successful student, pointed to the lack of subject matter she needs in order to write outlines, a view almost opposite to Fred's. What an outline says—its content—isn't what's important, she believes. It only has to "*look* like it's outlined," she told me; "it's got to be in a little format."

For both students, the form's the thing. For Akemi, whose academic success means that she has learned how to conform to the school rules, an understanding of the subject matter isn't important; she knows how to take any subject matter and make it fit into a preordained format. For Fred, who doesn't conform, who either hasn't learned to or has chosen not to negotiate the rules that govern school discourse successfully, subject matter is closely tied to the form—so much so that finding the right form without knowing the content is either an impossibility or a meaningless task he refuses to undertake. His lack of understanding of the subject matter and thus his inability to fit into a form lead to his failure to conform—a failure that is costly in this setting: Fred eventually failed the history course for a second time.

For Andrea, another student in Fred's class, it isn't the lack of subject matter that causes resistance, but rather the limitations placed on what the subject matter can be. In her view when students are limited to certain kinds of contents, they are necessarily limited to certain kinds of forms. Students in school thus write both in prescribed ways and with prescribed opinions. She says, "[s]chool writers are sometimes phony. Instead of writing what they feel, they write what's expected of them without expressing what their opinions really and truly are." For her this leads to the following conclusion: "I don't like writing assignments but I love writing on my own." In other words, the limited contents and the limited forms that define school writing for her result in her resistance to school assignments; when she can write what she wants and how she wants, she does, and she does so copiously, outside of school. When she has to write in the school ways, ways she thinks force her to limit her own ideas, she opts out. Stephanie seems to agree with this characterization. Her perception about school writing is that "When it comes to school work we really don't have a lot of choices in writing. Because of our homework 'rules': most teachers have an answer key in their books and we have to have that answer in order to get it right." As with Andrea, this emphasis on "correct" structure and form leads Stephanie to a rejection of school writing, but she too stresses, "I love to free write and be different in every way possible." Again the distinction these academically unsuccessful students make about free writing, which rejects the school forms and which they value, and school writing, which is based in specific forms and which they don't value, brings to mind the academically successful Akemi. She values what she calls "freestyle writing" in out-of-school settings but when, for whatever reasons (lack of time, interest, and so on), she writes an in-school piece in that freestyle format, she ends up rejecting that writing. The great pleasure she finds in writing "off the top of my head" outside school becomes *just* writing off the top of her head when transferred to school-type tasks. Like her notions of outlines, her school writing has to look like an essay, a report, a summary in order for it to "count" in her world.

For Akemi and for Stephanie, Andrea, and many others in their class, the preference for writing on their own or free writing carries with it an element of resisting the school rules, the school forms. Students described for us writing outside the bounds of school assignments as less rule-bound, freer, with more of an element of themselves involved. For all these students, though, their resistance doesn't go so far as to allow them to write in school settings in the ways they know and in many cases value—that is, to reject the conforming literacy in favor of their in-forming one within the structured setting of the institution of school. Instead, Fred refuses to write at all; Andrea and Stephanie resist school writing strongly (although they do it at times), while they write furiously outside school; Akemi keeps the two kinds separate and writes copiously in both ways. The two kinds of writing, reflective of the two kinds of literacy, remain separated for many students, particularly for those called illiterate by the schools.

As our students began to raise questions with us teachers about the limited and form-based notions of literacy put forth by the schools, we teachers consciously strove to create a place in our classroom where both a literacy of conformity and a literacy of informity might be explored. We took Bakhtin's words to heart as we searched for a space within the confines of the classroom in which the two forms of discourse might struggle with each other, resulting, we believed, in a positive dialogue, a dialogue that might help students to think and to act more critically as they began to forge, in Bakhtin's words, "an individual ideology." Perhaps not surprisingly we found our students showing less resistance to writing and in fact writing more effectively. By the end of the term, many students who initially had refused to write and to talk about their writing began to join with us to research the issues and to write up the results they uncovered.

Such participation in their own critical literacy brings us back to the words of Paulo Freire that opened this essay and the implications his work has for all of us literacy workers. As Freire explores the politics of the literacy by which we might overcome illiteracy, he stresses the basis of such a literacy: people must learn to be critical, participating members of the literacy club they join; people must name these worlds for themselves as they first critically reflect on the world at present and then act to change it. In our classroom, our students' continually expanding literacy depended on just these elements: students learned first to reflect critically on the literate worlds they inhabit by naming the forms that surround their school and home discourses and then to act upon that new knowledge by trying to bridge the gap between the two. As students began to name these forms, we all began the long process of expanding our critical consciousness about why such forms exist and what limitations they have, while at the same time recognizing what benefits forms—when more openly defined—might offer readers and writers. Such critical questions challenge the elements of the literacy of conformity put forth by our schools as the end-all of what students need to know—a notion of literacy that results in labels for students who do not conform, labels that are inaccurate and harmful as characterizations of capacity and interest. As a result of their reflection on such issues, students and teachers in this classroom began to take action: to push toward establishing an environment in which we all could reformulate the definitions of what truly might be called literate, allowing the struggle between the two literacies to surface and to begin to be resolved. If we agree, as we came to do, that the literacy of conformity so common to the schools is a limiting and thus unsatisfactory means of teaching and learning writing and that a literacy of in-formity, while personally satisfying, needs to make meaning in more publicly shared ways, then a new space must be created where students and teachers can explore the implications—a space in which we can re-form what exactly literacy might mean.

One group of students in our class chose to define that re-formed notion of literacy in their final report, the culmination of a short research project in which they looked into a question about literacy they chose to explore: in this case, "do boys and girls write differently?" After surveying, interviewing, and analyzing their own and their peers' writing, these students chose to share their information with the class, in part, in an oral rap:

Wrote this rhyme last night
Trying to help our group pass
Trying to scrape up a grade
for a literature class

Explaining the female whole lifestyle
Story of lyrics
When they write a letter
It's long, neat, and serious.
This rhyme is far from over or done
Cause they express their feelings like a slow song.
This is not a person, place, or thing
Like a pronoun, fraction
This is strictly a verb
Cause they show nothing but action . . .

Boys are in the other direction
If they make mistakes they don't make corrections
If you don't assign to type it
You won't understand their handwriting
They destroy your brain, mess with your red blood cells
If it was a crime for writing
Boys would be under the jail.

This is a rhyme about the triple S
Sloppy, short, and serious.

Here is a piece that clearly does not conform to the genres of school writing but is instead situated in an in-formed literacy. But in using this form, the students were able to meet some of the desires we teachers have for all our students. The students who wrote this show me critical thinking and a sense of play with language. These are students who were writing to discover personal meaning, who were thinking well in language, and who were achieving serious intellectual purpose. Writing such as this piece can only be viewed as a beginning for our students, but for me it seems like great place to start. Could the rap be better? Of course. But for the students who wrote this, students who had refused to participate in the reading and writing of most of their classes, students who continue to be labeled illiterate, this rap, a start toward a mix of their own form of literacy with that of the schools, is a big step forward.

And for me, this kind of action, action based in critical reflection, is a big step forward as well. For me it's the way we who are teachers can join with those who are our students in order to make real and attainable for them and for ourselves the implications of Freire's notion. It seems to me that these are the politics of the literacy through which we can and and we will overcome illiteracy.

Note

[1] In *The Dialogic Imagination* Bakhtin defines heterogolossia in this way: as "another's speech in another's language, serving to express authorial intentions in a refracted way" (324). Michael Holquist, in his introduction to that book, sees heteroglossia as celebrating "the immense plurality of experience"(xx).

Part Two

Literacy
and
Its Users

In trying to answer the questions they raise, the essays in this section wander from the field of sociolinguistics to the field of rhetoric. But in them may be found common themes and common concerns: a concern for students and other citizens whose language or language use excludes them from communities that get things done in school or in the world of work; a concern, too, for those of us, especially those teachers among us, who participate through attitudes or actions in processes of exclusion. These essays are about people—mainly students—who find it hard to talk and write to certain others; but they are also about people—mainly teachers—who find it hard to listen to certain others because of what they hear in the languages those others use.

These essays, no matter what they draw upon, are embedded in teacherly concerns, mine as well as others. Some are arguments for ways to apprehend another's language; some are arguments for arguably better ways to teach language use. All are probably better read as reflections on the obligations that accrue from presuming to try to teach another how to use language, or which language to use.

As these essays wander from sociolinguistics to rhetoric, meanings of the term *language* change. In the first essay, *language* means something akin to what *code* means, and the essay is about the social attitudes and cultural values that attach themselves to codes in ethnically mixed and hierarchically ordered societies. In the second essay, *language* has shifted to mean something like what James Boyd White means when he uses the term: language not as a code but as a set of meanings and moves, as a cultural resource that members of communities have available to them when they attempt to say something circumstantial and substantive to one another. When, that is, they wish to seek membership in community with others and are allowed to enact their wish.

The first essay in the section, the oldest in the whole collection, took form as an intrusion into the often angry conversations that broke out in the 1960s and 1970s about the feasibility and ethics of teaching Standard English to speakers of Nonstandard English. In re-offering the essay I have left most of its original headnote to give something of the flavor of the social context in which the conversations were taking place. Reread now, the essay seems very dated, as much for its raising of the issues it does as in the linguistics used in its various arguments. And yet black students, and Hispanic students, and many of those other students who are perceived as "other," continue to predictably fail, as we do who are their teachers. Why are the marginally literate always marginal people, and who put them there? The absence of questions like these in mainstream conversations about education in America is a silence that speaks loudly, especially about the absences of certain students and citizens from academic and professional communities that enjoy privilege.

The second essay in this section, "Literacy and Conversation: Notes Toward a Constitutive Rhetoric," moves beyond sociolinguistic issues to rhetorical ones and shows the influence of James Boyd White as well as that of Mina Shaughnessy. The essay was not the first in which I used the term *community* as central in discussions of literacy, but it was one of the first in which I explored an explicit link between processes of social formation and literacy development, a topic developed more fully in later essays in this collection. The term *community* is now in so many mouths, and serves as the centerpiece of so many dinner and other social conversations, that it is time for us to test its too easy uses. That is what Carol Lea Winkelmann does in the last essay in this section, "Talk as Text: Students on the Margins." Hers is a teacher's self-challenge to understand potential dangers in classroom work designed to encourage the formation of community and to foster the social construction of meaning and knowledge. What happens when students resist? How may the concept *resistance* be used as a means to better understand the meanings and uses of community? What are the creative potentials in resistance, marginality, isolation, and what are their costs? Winkelmann's are questions we all need to ask one another in our conversations about self and community.

4

The Wall of Babel; Or, Up Against the Language Barrier

The profession of teaching English faces a crisis in that the easy verities of the Great Tradition have given way to a new uncertainty. The drive toward "behavioral objectives," "defined outcomes," "accountability," and "contract teaching" cuts in one direction; the paradox of good intentions and harsh realities in another. And meanwhile, a cost-conscious public is inquiring ever more closely into what actually happens in the classroom. Like other activities in the corporate state, teaching faces mechanization, and the schoolmaster with only a book and a piece of chalk may shortly find himself "technologically unemployed."

More than in any other way, the new pragmatism reflected in these trends focuses itself on the teaching of "communication skills," the second "r" of the traditional three. Computer programs have been available for almost a decade to identify "errors" of the sort usually called mechanical: spelling mistakes, the comma splice, the run-on sentence. Because failures of this kind are easier to measure than is excellence, they have become the prime object for those who would replace expensive teachers with cheap machines.

Beset by "linguistic engineers" and engineers of a more traditional sort, an English teacher is being asked again and again to justify himself, not by an apologia defending his dedication to the humanities, but by the tangible, measurable results he produces in "altering behaviors."

The effect of these trends comes, ironically, just at the point where teachers are repenting past failures and looking for new ways to focus on effective—rather than merely correct—writing. One anonymous writer, thinking of himself as a rat in a behaviorist's maze, puts his change of heart this way:

> My own research has convinced me that red-inking errors in students' papers does no good and causes a great many students to hate and fear writing more than anything else they do in school. I gave a long series of tests covering 580 of the most common and persistent errors in usage, diction, and punctuation and 1,000 spelling errors to students in grades 9–12 in many schools, and the average rate of improvement in ability to detect these errors turned out to be 2 percent per year. The dropout rate is more than enough to account for this much improvement if the teachers had not even been there. When I consider how many hours of my life I have wasted in trying to root out these errors by a method that clearly did not work, I want to kick myself. Any rat that persisted in pressing the wrong lever 10,000 times would be regarded as stupid. I must have gone on pressing it at least 20,000 times without any visible effect (Quoted in Farrell, 1971, 141).

What is to be done? As I show in the following essay, the Great Tradition has failed to confront the issue; surface "errors" are confounded with cognitive "disabilities," ignorance of written conventions with chaos and old night. Even the "enlightened" are guilty of smearing over the hard facts of failure with a kind of semantic goo: deprivation *for* different, *divergent dialect* for *language not like their own. The task to be faced does not involve "explaining away errors" or linguistic "permissiveness"; it is, rather, to help all students feel at home in their language and to make linguistic prejudice repugnant to good men.*

Ralph Ellison's invisible man is suddenly very conspicuous. Whether incarnated as a black militant or as one of the growing number of black professionals working for change within the system, the black man in America is no longer content to be ignored, pushed aside, patronized, or whitewashed into the background of white. Others from America's "different" cultures push just as vigorously for visibility and recognition—organizing in strongly ethnic unions, as in California, or building larger, more demanding, more politically active groups than the cultural clubs and the street gangs that have been characteristic of ethnic life in big cities. In California, American Indians seize an island formerly used as the site of a federal prison, hoping to found there an educational center for Indian youth and to renew contact with their largely vanished native culture (one group of white businessmen had offered alternative plans to convert the island to an amusement park—a disneyland of the Northwest). In Michigan, Indians sue the state university to honor early treaties promising free education for land and petition the state bureau of natural resources to honor traditional fishing rights. In their relations with governmental agencies, minority groups have substituted mau-mauing for deferential petitions, the up-thrust fist for the humbly extended palm in demands not just for money but for the right to control it and the power it brings. The movement for local control of poverty funds is based on the perception that such funds have too often been used for the hypothetical good of the state and the real benefit of the middle class rather than for the needs of the poor and the nonwhite, particularly their needs for dignity and self-determination. The movement for local control of education is based in the perception that the needs of real children are not being met when the expectation is that all are alike in needs and desires. The melting pot may have been a congenial metaphor for the European immigrants flocking to the United States between the Civil War and World War I, eager as they apparently were to put behind them their languages and their old ethnic identities; but it does not appear to describe the aspirations of all groups in the latter half of the twentieth century.[1]

With its experiments in democratic education and mass literacy, the American schoolroom is the microcosm of the larger society, quite naturally subject to the same turmoil and the same stresses that operate outside its doors. And we are beginning only now to recognize that for too long too many children have been invisible in our classrooms, given over as classrooms have been to the socialization and acculturation of every child, no matter what his background or interests, to a single and dominant mode of living—one congenial to a mass technological state. If there is a unifying theme in the current outpourings of books critical of American education—books by the Kohls, the Kozols, the Bruners, the Silbermans, the Faders—it is that our educational institutions have neglected the individual in favor of certain societal norms; and that the neglect has been most severe of those individuals who happen to come from America's "different" cultures.[2]

The facts of cultural and ethnic diversity cannot be ignored. Glazer and Moynihan reported in *Beyond the Melting Pot* (1963) that in New York City the pot had yet to boil: ethnic patterns still shaped life styles, values, aspirations, and political choices for the people crowded into America's biggest city. From his work with American Indians in the Southwest, Sol Tax concluded that the problem of American Indian education is alienation rather than lack of opportunity, and he found causes of the alienation in value conflicts between Indian and middle-class culture (1965; Tax and Thomas, 1969). William Labov found clear evidence of group fidelity among young urban blacks to social and linguistic norms running counter to the middle-class norms that dominate the American classroom, and he showed that reading failure is more severe among young blacks who have the social skills to join the countergroup than among youngsters who do not (Labov & Robins, 1970). We are beginning to realize that powerful and positive values link members of countercultures and subcultures. The recent work by sociologists, cultural anthropologists, and linguists has centered on those forces that cause minority cultures to exist and persist, and findings have suggested a new conception of American society: we are not a monolithic culture guided by common assumptions, beliefs, and goals so much as a loose conglomerate of cultures, sharing some attitudes, conflicting violently about others.

The facts confront teachers and teachers-to-be with new tasks. The most urgent one is learning how to operate comfortably and effectively in a multicultural world—learning how to mediate between the several worlds created by our students out of their own personal and social experiences and the world we have created for ourselves out of different experiences. A first and necessary step in the learning process is recognizing that as teachers of English our education has rarely prepared us for working effectively in cultural and linguistic diversity. Most of us have studied only one literature; most of us control only one language. With other teachers, our experiences are limiting: most of us come fresh from institutions of higher learning purged of the culturally divergent by entrance requirements and by standardized tests; many of us come from suburbs comfortably homogeneous in status and skin color.[3] Our ethnocentrism is accurately measured by our militant monolingualism; finer shades of measurement can be traced in the degree of surprise we feel when we read facts like these:

> Between 1930 and 1964, almost a million Germans immigrated to the United States. Between 1951 and 1960, over 125,000 immigrated from the Philippines and Asia. In the single year 1964, over 60,000 entered the U.S. from Mexico and South America; over 100,000 from Castro's Cuba.

> Students in the schools of New York City come from "fifty-eight different language communities" in which "more than forty different nationalities are represented." Probably "more than three-fourths of the non-English-speaking children are Spanish-speaking Puerto Ricans."

> In 1966, the Phoenix Indian School enrolled 1,041 students coming from fifteen different tribal groups. About 75 per cent came from homes where English was not spoken.[4]

> Conservative estimates derived from the mother-tongue data reported by the 1960 census indicate that nineteen million white Americans have a mother tongue other than English. Roughly half of these individuals are American-born (indeed, approximately a quarter are children of parents who are themselves American born). . . .

> [There are] fifty to sixty million white Americans who are the first generation of individuals with English as the mother tongue in their families.[5]

English is the universally required school subject. But what of common experience, of a common language, may English teachers assume among their charges in classrooms? Yet no university English department offers an adequate program for preparing bilingual and bicultural teachers; few prepare teachers adequately to face the dialectal complexity typical of the urban classroom.

A second step in the learning process of teachers is to recognize that our national language mythology is in fact mythological; based not on fact so much as on feeling, picked up in bits and pieces like the hagiography of national heroes and stored in the darker recesses of our memories with images of watermelons and shuffling feet on dusty roads. Ignorance of language facts, particularly facts about the nature and significance of language diversity, is as widespread as it is pernicious: as much a property of the otherwise educated as it is of people innocent of education. When subcultures exist and persist, it is inevitable that language differences exist too. Ours is a big country, and dialect differences follow inevitably from geographical separation. Because we are divided into social classes by money and status, our linguistic differences are class marked. Because ethnic groups are set off from one another by a complex of preference and prejudice, linguistic differences sometimes match ethnic lines as each group learns and clings to speech patterns peculiarly its own. Yet the English profession has been generally content to rest in the presumption of a single common and uniform language and to ignore the fact and implication of difference within it. The ethnocentrism that has governed the teaching of English generally is nowhere more noticeable than in the teaching of language and of language use.

The ruling conception in the mythology of language has been termed *Standard English*. We have assumed the existence of such a thing, connecting it vaguely with the language of writing. Because we associate Standard English in our minds with literacy, and particularly with the high literacy of literature, we assume as our duty the teaching of Standard English. And because a standard is something against which we can measure, we derive standards of writing and speaking from our conception of Standard English, conscientiously marking and correcting deviations with little thought for why we do it. The complementary term in the neat dichotomy is *Nonstandard*, or the less euphemistic *Substandard*, which matches better with practice. Nonstandard or Substandard English is that collection of deviations from the standards of Standard that are written or uttered by individuals who do not share our values or inhabit our neighborhoods. Entry to the literate world is available only to those who conform.

Because the mythology has been comfortable for those who sit with the catbird and croak his tones, we have assumed too much about the nature of Standard and the nature of Nonstandard. We have rarely made an attempt to define either term with precision or to listen to those who have tried; we have rarely checked existing or operational definitions (which are often contradictory) against reality, which is usually more complex than our definitions allow. The assumptions that Standard English must be taught to every student at every level of every classroom is almost universally held. But we rarely expose that assumption to hard questioning: What are prevailing conceptions of Standard English and how do they differ from one another? What is Nonstandard English and what relation does it bear to Standard English? Is there any correlation—more important, any causal connection—between possession of a nonstandard dialect and educational failure? Is there any necessary correlation between possession of the standard language and intellectual achievement? What are the personal, social, political, and ethical implications of decisions to teach or not to teach Standard English?

The purpose here is not to give definitive answers to such questions: no one can, and no one should pretend to be able to. I will attempt instead to examine and evaluate some prevailing conceptions of standard and nonstandard and discuss their implications for educational practice, trying to make such recommendations as are warranted by the evidence I have examined. The chapter is divided into three sections. The first, "The Great Tradition," examines the conception of nonstandard dialects as deficit systems—as inherently deficient or functionally limited. In the opinion of those who hold such a conception, possession of a nonstandard dialect necessarily results in some kind of educational or cultural deprivation that must be countered by the teaching of Standard English. The second section, "The Enlightenment," examines the conception of standard and nonstandard dialects as differing linguistic systems, neither inherently superior or inferior as systems, but differing in structural detail, use, and the sociology of their speakers. "The New Frontier" treats educational proposals that purport to issue from the difference position. The section is concluded with some counterproposals that permit the writer to slip from behind the facade of scholarly objectivity to defend the bias not very well hidden in the section titles and in the commentary each section contains.

The Great Tradition

Though the tradition, like all traditions, has a past, it is its present we are most concerned with.[6] The view that Standard English is inherently superior to other dialects sprouted in the sixteenth and seventeenth centuries, ripened in the intellectual climate of the eighteenth, and was harvested and preserved in nineteenth-century pedagogy. Bottles of it are still being opened.[7] "... Mr. Hogan believes with the linguist," writes an English professor who has written two highly successful composition texts and is now jousting with the Executive Secretary of the NCTE:

> Mr Hogan believes with the linguist that all languages are equally good: namely, that the dialect of the ghetto is as good as standard English. And of course it is—but only for daily communication. "We need to accept the fact," says Mr Hogan, "that if a child can survive for twelve, fourteen or sixteen years on the streets of Harlem, his linguistic resources have had to be pretty sophisticated." He further sees that with the rise of black capitalism: "Within the separate black economy the children can speak whatever dialect works there." Such thinking hardly touches the concept of literacy, of reading and writing, and it sees reading and writing as little more than functional instrumentation (Baker, 1970, 13).

But how does the concept of Standard English touch the concept of literacy? By equating Standard English, of course, with what is written down in English—with our rich and valuable legacy of literary documents and with access to what they contain through education. The literate man controls Standard English because he is literate; the man who does not control Standard English cannot be literate. The confusion of the two concepts—literacy and Standard English—is both blatant and misleading: "Literacy," says our English professor, "... is of the highest importance to thought, to maturity, to civilization." No one can disagree; but by the equation, Standard English is of equal importance, and certain usages receive divine sanction:

> Praise of nonliterate dialects as "highly sophisticated" is simply irresponsible—compassionate, no doubt—but damaging to society and to individuals as it damages our faith in literacy, makes education superfluous, and encourages us to think of language as only a communicative convenience and not as the highest intellectual and moral instrumentality we have (1970, 15).

In 1851, the New England Quaker schoolmaster Goold Brown put the case more directly and without the attendant sneer in the direction of soft-minded liberals:

> But *language* is an attribute of reason, and differs essentially not only from all brute voices, but even from all the chattering, jabbering, and babbling of our own species, in which there is not an intelligible meaning, with division of thought, and distinction of words (Brown, 1970, 42).

So much for the spoken word.

But the practices of linguistic aristocrats have seldom reached their high conceptions of the standard language. Goold Brown wrote that "grammar is to language a sort of self-examination"; and because language is a faculty of reason and bears a direct relation to thought, to correct the former is to instruct the latter. But in practice, Goold Brown was as content as are current prescriptive grammarians to offer lists of "improprieties for correction," bits and pieces of sentences for tinkering, lists of usages to be avoided. Our latter-day traditionalist in a chapter called "Grammar"[8] refers to parts of speech as "the sentence's vital organs," but changes the metaphor quickly when "Correcting Bad Sentences" is the topic: "Now let us contemplate evil," he begins "—or at least the innocently awful. . . ." Fallen man, pen in hand as he faces the world, must have rules to guide him, for "writing is devilish," and rules must correct our natural tendency to "waste our words, fog our thoughts, and wreck our delivery." The pilgrim is offered another list, appropriately hortatory: "Avoid the passive voice"; "Beware the of-and-which disease"; "Beware *the use of*"; "Break the noun habit." Edit thy words and reason wilt follow, for if grammar be flesh yet must it be scourged by the spirit. And generations of teachers have applied the red pencil, convinced that scrupulous attention to surface form affects processes of thinking.

Apparent support for the antique concept of nonstandard dialects as inherently inferior or severely restricted has come from the recent research of educational and cognitive psychologists working with "disadvantaged" children, usually very young disadvantaged children. The most extreme view is that disadvantaged children virtually have no language at all, certainly no language that can be of any use in the schools. Carl Bereiter and Siegfried Engelmann characterized the speech of preschool children from poverty backgrounds in this way:

> When the children first arrived, they had, as expected, a minute repertoire of labels to attach to the objects they used or saw every day. All buildings were called "houses," most people were called "you." Although Urbana is in the midst of a rural area, not one child could identify any farm animals. As obvious as their lack of vocabulary was their primitive notion of the structure of language. Their communications were by gesture (we later discovered that one boy could answer some questions by shaking his head, but that he did not realize that a positive shake of the head meant yes), by single words (Teacher: "What do you want?" Child: "Doll."), or a series of badly connected words or phrases ("They mine." "Me got juice.").
>
> The pronunciation of several of the children was so substandard that, when they did talk, the teachers had no notion of what they were saying. . . . Although most of the children could follow simple directions like "Give me the book," they could not give such directions themselves, not even repeat them. Without exaggerating, we may say that these four-year-olds could make no statements of any kind. They could not ask questions. Their ability to answer questions was hampered by the lack of such fundamental requirements as knowing enough to look at the book in order to answer the question, "Is the book on the table?" (1966, 113–14).

In sum, these psychologists conclude that the language of the culturally deprived "is a basically nonlogical mode of expressive behavior which lacks the formal properties necessary for the organization of thought." The fit between the view of the humanist and the view of the educational psychologist appears more than coincidental. The humanist asserts that "the dialect of the ghetto" is adequate "only for daily communication"; the psychologist offers support by finding the language of poor children lacking in the formal properties essential for thought. The humanist finds the requisite properties in Standard English; the psychologist argues that a proper goal of early language instruction is "not that of improving the child's language but rather that of teaching him a different language which would hopefully replace the first one, at least in school settings." That "different language," when one examines the program and practices instituted by Bereiter and Engelmann, bears a striking resemblance to Standard English.[9]

It is such a singular event when a humanist and a psychologist agree that one should perhaps not question the basis of agreement. But on the other hand, their mutual conception of the nature of nonstandard is so widely held, and its implications for pedagogy so far reaching, that one *must* question. For if nonstandard dialects as linguistic systems—as systems of concepts and formal properties—are inadequate to the organization of thought, some other linguistic system *must* be taught if children speaking nonstandard dialects are to succeed in school. But could it be that the whole basis of such an argument rests not on empirical proof leading to a necessary conclusion, but on a common assumption—unproved and unacknowledged—an *assumption* that Standard English is superior?

The Enlightenment

Linguists have attacked the Great Tradition for several generations and from several points of view. In maintaining that nonstandard dialects are merely different from standard and not inherently inferior they have agreed in suspecting that a very old myth underlies the concept of inferiority—the myth of the primitive language. A primitive language, the story goes, is one spoken by a people who have never developed a writing system or borrowed one, and it exhibits certain characteristics: it is limited in vocabulary (often so limited that gesture must supplement speech to make communication possible); it is lacking in the abstract terms necessary for thinking; it is restricted in semantic reference to the concrete world of discrete objects. That myth was exploded, for all who would read it, by the careful descriptive work of anthropologically oriented linguists who recorded and analyzed many of the aboriginal languages of the Americas and other regions of the world; the remains

of the myth should have been swept away by more recent findings
in theoretical linguistics and in language learning. But it is still
possible to find the myth printed and quoted. Of Eskimos, "There
are no abstract words and all verbs are verbs of action. The Eskimos, though extraordinarily quick and alert mentally, are not
thinkers in our sense. . . . [Theirs] is a language of people whose
lives are lived in their bodies and not in their minds."[10]

Leonard Bloomfield some time ago pointed to a tendency
among literate people to rationalize the structure of their own
language—to see in external features of linguistic form the perfect expression of a universal logic or a universal aesthetic. Such
"logic" has been the frequent appeal of prescriptive grammarians,
and linguists have found it operative as well in the assumptions
of intervention programs. Carl Bereiter says that his program's
major concern

> . . . is the acquisition of grammatical statement patterns and a grasp
> of the logical organization of these patterns. Precise pronunciation is
> seen as a critical requirement for mastery of grammatical structure,
> for even in our relatively uninflected language a good deal of gram-
> matical structure is mediated by little affixes, variations, and parti-
> cles which cannot be differentiated by the blurred pronunciation
> typical of culturally deprived children. The child who says "Ih bwah"
> for "This is a block" is in a poor position to understand, much less
> communicate, such contrasting statements as "This is not a block,"
> "These are blocks," and "These are not blocks" (1966, 112).

According to such a view, there can be no alternate grammatical
means for the expression of conceptual niceties: if pronunciation
"blurs" past tense markers, for example, the conceptual contrast
between present and past disappears. Bereiter claims that the
utterance *Ih bwah* (which suggests the nonstandard pattern with
copula deletion, loss of final consonant on *it*, and the childish substitution of /w/ for /l/—i.e., a complete nonstandard sentence with
subject and predicate) has no pattern. The child who says "Me got
juice" (another of Bereiter's examples) confuses subject and object
and may be presumed to have drowned.

Direct and empirically based counterevidence to findings of
verbal deprivation among poor children is appearing with increasing frequency. [11] But because such research proceeds from assumptions about language quite different from those held by deprivation
theorists, it is more relevant to contrast basic assumptions and their
support than merely to weigh the gross tonnage of accumulated
evidence.

As we have seen, deprivation theorists base their argument for
the inadequacy of nonstandard on observations of the language
behavior of "deprived" children. Because they reject, as untenable,
hypotheses of hereditary inferiority or universal mental retardation

on the part of poverty children, deprivation theorists find causes of linguistic deprivation in environment—in the absence of parents in slum homes, in the linguistic modes used for adult-child interaction, in noise and distraction levels in crowded slum dwellings. William Labov, the linguist whose work with nonstandard dialects has been as comprehensive as any yet done, vigorously questions both the accuracy of the observations and the adequacy of the findings made by deprivation hypothesists. Labov claims that the concept of verbal deprivation has "no basis in social reality"; and that the limited language behavior observed in tests and classrooms results from tensions in the test situation, not from the child's lack of language capacity (see 1970, 1972a, 1973). He charges further that the concept of deprivation results from assuming that any utterance divergent from standard norms is by that reason deficient: in other words, Standard English is better because we assume it to be better—hardly a convincing proof.

Linguists, says Labov, in spite of disagreements over theory and detail, all "agree that nonstandard dialects are highly structured systems." All linguists seem to agree, too, in what has been called the principle of linguistic relativity: an assumption that from the point of view of structural complexity, adequacy to serve the cognitive and communicative needs of the speech communities using them, all dialects are equal. The two assumptions have guided all twentieth-century linguistic work, and the resulting descriptive and comparative grammars based on them clearly prove their accuracy as descriptive statements about human language. *No human language, no form* of any human language, is a random collection of words put together haphazardly. All human languages have rules governing phonetic and syntactic processes, and organize such rules in a systematic way. But these two principles do not in themselves disprove the idea of functional discontinuities between dialects. One may grant that a nonstandard dialect is systematic and adequate to serve the needs of, say, the ghetto in which it is spoken, yet still maintain that it is inadequate for the requirements of the school.

However, Labov and others make a further claim: As linguistic systems, nonstandard dialects are not just equally systematic, but fundamentally similar to Standard English. The dialects differ in detail, to be sure, but not in kind; and because of their fundamental similarity nonstandard and standard are equal in their capacities to serve communicative, cognitive, and logical requirements. Summarizing his work with some nonstandard dialects spoken by urban black children, Labov says,

> They [the children] have the same basic vocabulary, possess the same capacity for conceptual learning, and use the same logic as anyone else who learns to speak and understand English (1972a, 201).

For a long time, linguists have insisted that the regional and social varieties of American English are relatively uniform. Even the dialectologists most concerned with differences among dialects—those engaged in mapping variants for the Linguistic Atlas of the United States and Canada—have reached the general conclusion that "dialect differences in American English are relatively small" (McDavid, 1958, 482). But conventional dialectology, focusing as it does on surface differences, has lacked adequate means for revealing underlying similarities. More recent studies, by employing and extending ideas and methods borrowed from generative-transformational theory, have had better bases for describing similarities among dialects. In addition, because the study of meaning has been central in generative theory, recent studies have been based on a clearer appreciation of the complexity involved in the relations of language to cognition and logic—a degree of complexity that shows as inadequate and inaccurate earlier assumptions of direct relations between language form and thought.[12]

Generative theory, to offer a brief and much oversimplified summary, is much concerned with what linguistic systems have in common. A language is conceived of as an unlimited set of sentences; a grammar as a system of rules describing principles of sentence construction and accounting for the relation between meaning and sound. Some rules in a generative grammar (base rules) describe deep structure—a system of semantic and syntactic categories and their relations that determine meaning most directly; other rules (transformations) relate deep structures to the surface structures of sentences as they are actually spoken; still other rules (phonological rules) account for how a sentence is pronounced. Two ideas are central to the theory: deep and surface structure may differ (e.g., sentences may differ in surface form but not in meaning, or differ in meaning but not in surface form); deep structure is more important for meaning than surface structure or phonological structure. Let us see how such a framework functions in showing basic similarities among some contrasting features of Standard English (SE) and of what has been termed Black Vernacular English (BVE).[13] Although the illustration is long it is necessarily so to demonstrate the basis of Labov's claim about logicality. If the length strains patience, rest assured that the writer has spared the kind of detail that would be necessary for a fully detailed grammatical account.

One feature consistently placed high on the list of proscribed usages by prescriptive grammarians is the double negative. Since the eighteenth century, the form has been called illogical on a quasimathematical analogy: two negatives make a positive. Dialectologists have reported the following patterns in BVE (no attempt is made to render pronunciation differences by "dialect" spellings):

BVE	SE
1. He don't know nothing.	⌈ He doesn't know anything. ⌊ He knows nothing.
2. Nobody know it.	
3. Nobody ⎰ doesn't ⎱ know it. ⎱ ⎱ don't ⎰	Nobody knows it.
4. Didn't nobody see it.	Nobody saw it.
5. It ain't no cat can't get in no coop.	There isn't any cat that can get into any coop.[14]

Clearly, nonstandard and standard dialects contain negative sentences. But are the nonstandard sentences as systematic as the SE sentences, or are negatives thrown at the speaker's whim? Are the nonstandard sentences as logical as the SE sentences? A third question relevant to classroom practice is, "Are the nonstandard sentences intelligible?"

Because SE and BVE both contain negative sentences, generative grammarians assign a feature NEG to the deep structures of both grammars. Thus a very gross rule for a negative sentence would be: *NEG + sentence.* The feature *NEG* appears in various surface realizations in a SE sentence, but normally, for clausal negation (that is, denying the assertion made by the clause), *NEG* is attached transformationally to the verb by means of the verbal auxiliary *do* (if no other auxiliary is present), which serves to carry tense and negative marking:

$$\text{NEG} + \text{He sings} \longrightarrow \begin{array}{l} \text{He doesn't sing} \\ \text{not *He singsn't} \end{array}$$

Standard English has another transformational rule, however, that permits what has been called negative attraction. The rule says, essentially, that in a sentence containing an indefinite noun, *NEG* may be attracted to the first indefinite noun. Attraction is obligatory when the *subject* is an indefinite noun, optional when the indefinite occurs after the verb. Thus we have negative sentences in SE like *Nobody sings* (but not *Anybody doesn't sing*) where the subject is indefinite; alternative forms *He doesn't know anything* or *He knows nothing* occur when the indefinite comes after the verb. In SE, there are constraints on the negative rule: the negative may be attracted to one indefinite only; when it is attracted, negative marking is removed from the verb. Thus only one negative appears in the deep and surface structures of SE sentences.

As we see in sentences 1 through 5, nonstandard sentences may contain more than one surface negative. But negatives are not thrown in at whim; rather, their occurrence is governed by rules that are essentially the same as the rules for SE negation. First, the deep structures are identical, because both SE and BVE have negative sentences. As in SE, *NEG* is regularly attached by transformation to the verb by means of the auxiliary *do:* "He *don't* know nothing." "Nobody *don't* know it." And so on. As in SE, *NEG* may be attracted *only* to indefinite nouns and not to other sentence elements: thus, "He don't know *nothing.*" "Didn't *nobody* see it." And so on.[15] The clausal negation rules of BVE differ from SE rules only in lacking the two constraints limiting *NEG* attraction to one indefinite only and erasing negative marking from the verb. It is illuminating that rule differences like these—showing elimination of special conditions or constraints from rules to permit them to apply more generally—have been widely found in studies of linguistic change. Rules similar to those for negation in BVE have been reported in studies of child language acquisition, with children from environments in which Standard English is spoken, showing the tendency for complex grammatical rules to be simplified in normal language learning.

Most of us do not need such sophisticated analysis to accept the fact that the standard and nonstandard versions of sentences 1, 2, and 3 are identical in meaning. No nonstandard speaker misunderstands another nonstandard speaker; no nonstandard speaker has the slightest difficulty understanding that "He doesn't know anything" denies knowledge on the part of *He*; no standard speaker takes "He don't know nothing" to mean *He* must know something, unless that speaker has swallowed the foolishness that $(- \times - = +)$ is a formula applying to language. But such formulas *are* the bases for charges that nonstandard dialects are lacking in formal properties essential to logical thinking. Their absurdity is demonstrable through analysis and through common sense operating on some knowledge of language. If $(- \times - = +)$ were a formula applying universally to language structure, we could offer the following formula for measuring the logic of Chaucer's Middle English[16]: count the negatives and divide by two; if the resulting number is even, the sentence is illogical, if odd, logical. Attitudes and spurious knowledge inhibit communication at least as effectively as differences in linguistic structure.

Sentences 4 and 5, however, do present a slightly more complicated problem, because they might conceivably be misunderstood by a standard speaker who had had limited social contacts. "Didn't nobody see it" (4) could be taken as a question, though intonation would make doing so unlikely; (5) "It ain't no cat can't get in no coop," a structure termed rare in BVE, might be understood as meaning "There isn't any cat who can't get into any coop," the opposite of the intended meaning. But Labov shows convincingly that the two structures can be related to their equivalents in SE and their differences explained by such minor rule differences as the removal in nonstandard of the constraints on negative attraction that we have just discussed.

Sentence 4 has auxiliary *do* with a negative particle preposed before the subject, making it superficially similar to SE questions

(Didn't John do it?). But Labov argues that the nonstandard sentence should be compared not to SE questions that do prepose auxiliaries, but to SE sentences with "negative foregrounding" (1973, 13), stylistic variants in which negative elements are brought to the front of sentences for emphasis: "*Never* did anyone see it." "*Seldom* did he come." "*At no time* did he enter the bank." In the SE sentences, indefinite adverbials may be foregrounded. Nonstandard sentences like 4 suggest that BVE permits the foregrounding of more kinds of negatives than SE; thus the difference again involves not a major rule change but the removal of a constraint on a rule—the constraint restricting foregrounding to indefinite adverbials.

Sentence 5 shows the further generalization of negative attraction. The sentence contains two clauses, each containing an indefinite noun:

CLAUSE 1   CLAUSE 2

There isn't *any cat*   that can get in *any coop.*

Only the first clause is negative, the second is positive. In the SE sentence, only one negative element occurs in the surface structure; should a second negative occur in the second clause in SE, the meaning would change:

6. There isn't any cat that *can't* get into any coop.

The deep structure for 6 would thus contain two *NEG*'s, one for each clause: *NEG + Clause 1 + NEG + Clause 2*. But nonstandard 5 differs in meaning from 6 and is synonymous with standard 5. It has the deep-structure *NEG + Clause 1 + Clause 2*. The multiple-surface negatives simply show negative attraction by those elements that regularly attract negatives: indefinites (any cat → no cat, any coop → no coop) and first position in a clause (can → can't, when the relative *that* is deleted). Thus the multiple negation in the nonstandard sentence, though perhaps troublesome for the standard speaker, is not random but systematic. The rules that govern negation are basically similar in SE and BVE and differ in relatively minor ways: essentially by the removal of rule constraints or conditions in the nonstandard dialect. The standard constructions are not more logical in any way than the nonstandard, unless we are willing to attribute some abstract logical quality to the surface appearance of one rather than more than one negative element. Negation is as available for use in nonstandard dialects as in standard when its use is needed. There is no justification for the traditional practice of equating logic with the superficial features of one's own speech.

Although the existing research on nonstandard dialects is limited (no one has produced even a reasonably full grammar of a nonstandard dialect), the systematic study of dialect features now being conducted seems to confirm the conclusion that differences between standard and nonstandard are relatively superficial and easily explained with reference to SE rules. Few linguists have postulated deep structure differences. One exception is the form *be*, which occurs in sentences like "I be making hats" and "If somebody hit him, Henry be mad" to signal a verbal aspect (generic, nontense marked) that is not a part of the aspect system of SE. Most have found differences only in phonological rules, in transformational rules, and in lexicon.

Such differences in rules can, of course, result in surface differences wide enough to occasionally hinder communication. The lexical replacement of *it* for anticipatory *there* could lead a standard speaker to misinterpret the sentence:

> Doesn't nobody really know that *it's* a God, y'know, 'cause I mean I have seen black gods, pink gods, white gods, all color gods, and don't nobody know *it's* really a God.[17]

by taking *it* as a personal pronoun. But once learning that *it* serves the same function in certain dialects as does *there* in SE, we are not likely to misunderstand. Similarly, phonological rules can operate to remove grammatical signals that seem essential to the standard speaker. Word final consonant clusters, for example, are consistently simplified in some nonstandard dialects, particularly /st/, /sp/, /sk/, /st/, /zd/, /ft/, /vd/, /md/, /nd/, /ld/, /pt/, /kt/. Some of these clusters result from the past-tense marking of verbs: pass + *Past* → passed [pæst], fish + *Past* → [fišt], join + *Past* → [joind], and so on. When the clusters are reduced in pronunciation, the overt past tense marker disappears: [pæst] → [pæs], [fišt] → [fiš], [joind] → [join]. But past *tense* does not disappear from the nonstandard dialects with the loss of overt marking. The sentence "Yesterday I fish off the pier" does not contain a present tense. Standard speakers similarly reduce consonant clusters in casual speech and under certain phonetic conditions (try, e.g., The house burn*ed* *d*own; Charlie walk*ed* *t*o town; the desk*s* *s*eemed out of place). Again, the nonstandard dialects merely extend tendencies, that is generalize rules, that operate as well in SE.

More examples could be offered, but perhaps the major point is clear. When linguists like Labov assert the equality of dialects, they assert that dialects are equally systematic, equally adequate to serve needs for communication felt by the people using them. When they further assert that nonstandard speakers "possess the same capacity for conceptual learning, and use the same logic as anyone else who learns to speak and understand English," they are basing such assertions on the theory that language relates to logic and cognition through its deepest structure—a theory well supported by present research and on findings of virtual identity in the deep structures of American dialects. Nonstandard dialects are as capable of supporting cognitive uses as SE because they are virtually identical in deep structure to SE, and because such differences as do exist are restricted to surface features and are easily related to features of SE.

We must see that such a concept is antithetical to many present practices, especially those guided by the Great Tradition. But we must also see how the concept applies to the teaching of language use—of composition and reading—before we rush, as so many have done, to ill-guided application.

First, the concept is abstract. Linguists study linguistic systems and linguistic communities. We must teach individuals. Linguists write dictionaries of American English, or of English, not of the words possessed by Jay Robinson. A grammar is a description of rules for sentences in English, not a catalog or analysis of the sentences used by Jay Robinson. But as a grammar or a dictionary probes deep beneath the surface to discover general rules for word and sentence formation shared by Jay Robinson, by other speakers of Standard English, and by speakers of so-called nonstandard dialects, it begins to reveal what we all have in common by virtue of our common language, by virtue of our common humanity, by virtue of the similar structuring of our knowledge through innate mental capacities. The concept of linguistic equality speaks to our expectations and preconceptions about the students who come into our classroom. It says, no one is disqualified by the accident of learning one system of English rather than another from entering and running well in the race for knowledge.

The concept is neither vaguely humanitarian nor disrespectful of education, as Great Traditionalists charge; nor is it irrelevant to everyday practice, in spite of its abstraction. The contrary assumption—of linguistic deprivation resulting from cultural deprivation—can have and has had damaging effects. To identify a particular group of children as disadvantaged, as needful of special *remediative* teaching, isolates those children from their schoolmates, makes their educational needs seem somehow peculiar and not quite normal, urges us to view such differences as may appear between their behavior and language and our behavior and language as corruptions of some sacrosanct norm. The deprivation hypothesis offers an all-too-convenient escape hatch for teachers of poor children and nonwhite children: its premise is that the *children* are lacking—that they do not bring to the classroom the competencies we have every right to expect. If such children fail, it is easy to convince ourselves that they do so because of what they are, not because of what we have failed to do. As the twig is bent, the saying is, and who ever heard of a tree growing in a gutter. The deprivation hypothesis translates easily into the self-fulfilling prophecy: if we expect little, that is what we usually get; if we expect failure, we will have little trouble allowing it to happen.[18] If we see every departure from Standard English as a lapse in logic, every nonstandard form as inappropriate to the classroom, we build failure into our very system of evaluation and guarantee it for the groups we seek to help.

The concept of dialect equality does not reduce the complexity in the task of teaching effective language use, nor does it remove from the teacher the responsibility for teaching his or her students to expand and develop their native linguistic resources. To say that nonstandard speakers have the same basic linguistic competence as standard speakers does not mean that all nonstandard speakers know all the vocabulary they must know, can manipulate complex sentences effectively, or control styles appropriate to a wide range of topics and audiences. We must teach them, just as we must teach the immature users who bring Standard English to the classroom with them. All students bring to the classroom systems we can work with; and rejecting the notion of verbal deprivation on the part of some students may force us to look hard at factors other than dialect that *can* cause failure in language use: inadequate intellectual preparation for addressing a topic, failure on the part of the teacher to indicate what is required, lack of trust between teacher and students, the students' lack of experience in the whole process of writing, and their failure to see how writing can possibly be of importance to them. All too often in English classrooms we have preferred the direct frontal attack on language use, wielding the red pencil against the barbarian assaults our students make on standards, defending our language from chaos and non-sense. If the concept of dialect equality is abstract, the abstractions on which it is based are not of the sort that govern Great Tradition practices. There the abstraction is not theory but the thing to be taught. One searches in vain the pages of prescriptive grammars for adequate, precise, and realistic definitions of Standard English, or for reasoned justification for preferring it to Nonstandard; one hunts just as fruitlessly for the cognitive system underlying the language drills imposed by Bereiter and Engelmann.

There is, of course, a major difference between Standard and Nonstandard English: the difference of social status, specifically, the social status of the speakers using them. That idea is very old, but few have accepted it in spite of overwhelming evidence, perhaps because accepting it imposes a very difficult burden on those who would teach Standard English. Once we accept the fact that the terms Standard/Nonstandard refer to the social status of speakers, we uncapitalize standard and make it multiform, not uniform. High-status speakers in Atlanta use different forms from those used by high-status speakers in Boston; such speakers in Atlanta have different language attitudes from those held by comparable speakers in Boston. To teach standard once we recognize its diversity requires a painstaking collection of current information on usage and opinion, the translation of such information into effective teaching materials, and inhuman patience to endure hours of mind-dulling drill. Most Great Traditionalists prefer simple lists of *do's* and *don'ts*, and find no need to relate them to reality since mythology serves. In the face of complexity, do something simple.

The New Frontier

It would appear from the preceding discussion that linguists and linguistically oriented applicators would assign low priority to the systematic teaching of standard English. The best linguistic evidence seems to prove that nonstandard is as fit for logical and cognitive uses as standard; that differences between nonstandard and standard "are largely confined to superficial, rather low level processes which have little effect upon meaning" (Labov, 1970, 40); that communication between standard and nonstandard speakers is rarely and then not seriously hindered by such superficial differences as do exist. Linguists working on problems of dialect have rightly pressed the attack against the cultural chauvinism implicit in Great Tradition and neo-Great Tradition conceptions; they have been right in insisting that standard English must be realistically and concretely defined with reference to the speech and beliefs about speech of the controlling class, generally taken to be the great white middle; but many, while believing everything said in this paragraph, have still seen the direct teaching of standard English as a vitally important task. In the face of complexity, do something simple.[19]

Complexity is amply provided by the chaos in urban schools, by the conflict in American society. Present circumstances in society and school—disastrous urban riots, soaring crime rates with an emphasis on crimes of violence, dropout and rates of failure in ghetto schools, racial trouble in integrated schools—have sent the current generation of social scientists on a frantic search for causes. In their dash, too many have been more impressed by the size of the problems than by the complexity of their causes. When cautious statements are offered, like the following by Labov, they are too often pruned of their qualifying modifiers and conditions by those who would rush pell-mell to oversimple "solutions":

> One of the most extraordinary failures in the history of American education is the failure of the public school system to teach black children in the urban ghettos to read. The fact of reading failure is so general, and so widespread, that no one school system, no one method, and no one teacher can be considered responsible. We are plainly dealing with social and cultural events of considerable magnitude, in which the linguistic factors are the focal points of trouble or centers of difficulty rather than the primary causes (1973, 238).

Such a position offers cold comfort to those who would change the world tomorrow: it says the causes aren't yet known and are likely to be plural rather than singular. It is easier to take *centers* or *focal points* to mean *cause;* it is easier still, given generations of like practice, to look at language for *the* cause:

> In regard to the supposed substandard language of lower-class Negroes, school investigators are just beginning to recognize that Negro speech is a language system unto itself which differs from "standard" English in everything but vocabulary (Abrahams, 1969, 11).

Because so little is known about "the language system unto itself," the opening is there for the dash to application. Many have hurried through.

DIALECT AND READING PROBLEMS   If more black children than white fail to learn to read, perhaps the cause is "the language system unto itself":

> . . . the one major fault of our urban educational system is its failure to understand why teaching an urban Negro child to read is so difficult. But the explanation is really quite simple. A cultural variable is at work which is basic to the difficulty that the Negro child experiences in attempting to learn to read. Evidence has been accumulating that the Negro ghetto child has a different language system (call it Negro nonstandard dialect) which is part of his culture and which interferes with his learning to read. Unless and until this variable is considered, and specific educational innovation based on it, the majority of the inner-city Negro children will continue to fail despite the introduction of all sorts of social improvements to the educational setting (Baratz & Baratz, 1969, 13).[20]

A simple cause calls forth a simple solution: if dialect difference is the cause of reading failure, teach the dialect that will remove it. Teach standard English (presumably the dialect of books) and reading problems disappear for nonstandard speakers.

The argument is given persuasiveness by the obvious need for literacy: we *must* teach our students to read and write. With that requirement, no one can quibble. However, the argument rests on two assumptions: (1) that the system of written English represents the system of standard spoken English better than it does nonstandard spoken English; (2) middle-class children (i.e., standard speakers by the linguists' own definition) learn to read more readily *because* of the match between the written and spoken systems. The assumptions seem valid until we again raise the questions of the *nature* rather than the details of differences between the two dialects and place the assumptions in the context of the use of English around the world.

As we have seen, a fundamental tenet of generative grammar is that deep and surface structure may differ. Thus, when we observe that nonstandard speakers sometimes say *tess, dess, wass, han, col* where standard speakers (sometimes) say *test, desk, wasp, hand, cold,* we speak of the actual phonetic realization of these words— their actual pronunciation—not the shape in which they are stored in the speaker's mind. For reasons too complicated to discuss here, linguists postulate more similarities than differences in underlying representations for lexical items used commonly by standard and nonstandard speakers. In a generative lexicon for nonstandard English, the words above would have final consonants in the under- lying representation, even though they are not always pronounced (they do appear in some environments). There is every reason to believe that these underlying forms are more crucial in learning to read than the surface forms.[21]

The point might be made clearer by another example, treated in a highly simplified way. Some nonstandard sentences of the patterns Subject + Copula + Adjective; Subj + Cop + Predicate Nominal; Subj + Cop + Locative lack the copula (the *be* form) nearly always present in SE. Thus we find sentences like "He wild," "She a pretty girl," "They in the closet." It would appear that these sentences show a major difference: that learning to read the stan- dard sentences, "He's wild," "She's a pretty girl," "They're in the closet," might pose a major problem. But the copula *is* present in the deep structure of BVE, although sometimes it is deleted in the surface structure. The copula appears regularly in certain con- structions: elliptical forms "He is too"; tag questions "He ain't here, *is* he?"; comparatives "She taller than he *is* "; clauses with relatives "That's what he *is.* " Labov proposes a general rule: "Wherever standard English can contract, BVE can delete *is* and *are,* and vice versa; wherever SE cannot contract, BVE cannot delete *is* and *are,* and vice versa" (1970c, 61). Again, deep-structure analysis reveals similarity and suggests that concentration on surface differences can overexaggerate the effect of structural conflict on learning to read.

Furthermore, the case for dialect interference in reading be- comes weaker when we ask what *real* dialect the writing system of English does represent. How different are the written productions of Southern Americans and Northern Americans, British novelists and Australian novelists? The same writing system serves for the *r*-less and *l*-less dialects of American English as well as the *l*-full and *r*-full; for spoken systems as different as British English in its variable manifestations, Australian English, Canadian English, Indian English, and Nigerian English. But the literature on dialect and reading still offers statements like the following:

> Further problems in teaching reading to some black children arise because of the fact that they come to school speaking the Negro dialect—Black English. The middle-class child brings to school essen- tially the same dialect he will be taught to read, i.e., standard English (Fasold, 1969, 76).

Dialect problems—instances where the structure of a native dialect interferes with the structure of that being learned—can emerge, of course, in the process of learning to read and write, particularly in the latter, because writing demands productive and not merely receptive control—a more difficult accomplishment in language learning as those of us know who can read a foreign language but not speak or write it with facility. But structural interference as a causative factor in reading failure must not be overexaggerated, as it has been in much recent work. Dialect-related problems that emerge in reading do so early, and are essentially mechanical—matters of sound-letter correspondences. But such problems can easily be solved by a teacher who knows nonstandard phonologies and can tell a correct nonstandard reading from a failure to decipher the written symbol. More serious types of reading failure—problems in analysis and comprehension of *matter*—are not so easily handled. Real reading takes place as a student moves from deciphering to interpretation, learning to draw inferences and conclusions from what he or she reads. Structural interference of one dialect with another does not hinder that kind of reading; teaching standard English by any method yet proposed will not facilitate it.

THE SOCIAL ARGUMENT: BIDIALECTALISM OR BILOQUIALISM

The argument that standard English must be taught to young children from the ghetto *before* they are taught to read is too obviously impractical and too patently ludicrous ever to have proceeded very far, though neither condition kept it from being made. Roger W. Shuy, the director of the sociolinguistics program of the Center for Applied Linguistics in Washington, D.C., grants in a recent article: "the simple truth is that speaking Standard English, however desirable it may be, is not as important as learning to read" (1969, 118), and that one can teach reading by modifying materials to suit the child rather than "changing the child to suit the materials," that is, systematically teaching him Standard English. In fact, he comments: "It is hard to imagine how we ever got so sidetracked on this issue." But Shuy is reluctant to question the "social value of learning Standard English" (118). *Social Value* has been the phrase and the concept motivating the many proposals offered over the past few years, usually funded, and sometimes implemented, for teaching Standard English as a second dialect—code word *Bidialectalism* or *Biloquialism*, to use the more recently coined and clearly euphemistic term. [22]

The basic idea behind either learned term is the same simple one: nonstandard speakers must be equipped by the school with a second dialect—standard English—if the school hopes to prepare them for life in the real world—technological, industrial, corporate, middle-class and white-dominated America.[23] The idea is not without precedent: Fries argued in 1940 that: "It is the assumed obligation of the schools to attempt to develop in each child the knowledge of and the ability to use the 'standard' English of the United States—that set of language habits in which the most important affairs of our country are carried on, the dialect of the socially acceptable in most of our communities" (15). In 1940, Fries' charge to the schools rang with enlightened liberalism; now a phrase like "the socially acceptable" starts less harmonious overtones. [24]

The discord is made more striking by the biloquialists' acceptance of the principle of linguistic relativity. All of them grant that there is little to choose between standard and nonstandard, middle- and lower-class English on grounds of grammaticality, logicality, fitness to serve communicative needs. Few claim that there are serious communicative difficulties when standard and nonstandard speakers converse. None claim that possession of standard English better equips a young student to understand the principles of engineering, the laws of finance, or the customs of politics. Social utility lies in none of these; social value does not incorporate such criteria. The social value of learning standard English is simply that those in power demand that those without power learn it; the value of acquiring standard English lies in overcoming pejorative judgments some speakers make about others, not by teaching the judges that their attitudes are irrational, but by urging the judged to change. "The linguistic relativity," says the humane bidialectalist:

> The linguistic relativity . . . does not take into account the social reality. Middle-class individuals still rate Standard American English as more desirable than Negro speech. Pejorative ratings are associated with Negro nonstandard speech despite its viability, complexity and communicativeness as a linguistic system. (Baratz, 1970a, 25).

So *there* is social value. In the class game choose sides, and do not play for the loser. The arbiter is the middle class, and we play by its rules, within boundaries drawn by attitudes of ugly Americans toward the speech of Americans they find ugly. What we are to teach are the forms considered prestigious by the dominating class, irrespective of any intrinsic value or lack of it, without consideration for our own preferences, tastes, and beliefs, or those of our students. If we reject the position and the criteria as too obviously based on prejudice, not reason or taste, we become dropouts and threaten our students with economic ruin:

> . . . not teaching the black inner-city child standard English not only further hinders his ability to ultimately compete in the mainstream of society in terms of oral skills [sic], but also makes the child's task of learning to read considerably more difficult (26).

As we have argued earlier—and as the quoted bidialectalist would likely admit in a less polemical moment—oral skills are not the exclusive property of middle-class speakers; as we have argued earlier, there is every reason to question the assertion that literacy—effective control of reading and writing—requires control of spoken forms of standard English. The argument for bidialectalism—for the painstaking and systematic teaching of standard English—finally reduces itself to the naked fact of prejudice against some forms of spoken English reflecting social and racial prejudice against the people who utter such forms.

Conclusions: Or, What Other Answers Are There?

Some who have found the morality of the biloquialist position repugnant, or at the least difficult to reconcile with humanist tenets, have nonetheless accepted the task of teaching standard English as a second dialect on the grounds that the position is realistic. After all, who *can* change the world?[25] But those who are tempted must ask themselves two questions: Is the position indeed so realistic? If it is, can we afford a brand of realism that wastes so much talent?

Critics of bidialectalism have questioned whether the goal of a two-dialect speaker is in fact attainable. James Sledd, an early and persistent critic of doublespeak finds "the complete bidialectal, with undiminished control of his vernacular and a good mastery of the standard language ... as mythical as the unicorn" (1972, 441). Reasons for the rareness of the beast are not difficult to imagine. The would-be biloquial must first desire to adapt his speech to middle-class norms and then be able to. Speakers are rarely successful in erasing all traces of their native dialect. In Great Britain, where large numbers learn the standard language in school, few avoid speaking it with the regional accent that separates the newcomer-to-status from the aristocrat born with a silver Eton and Oxford in his mouth. In our country, even carefully trained newscasters, if Southern-born, betray their origins with an occasional /ɪ/ rather than /ɛ/ before a nasal, no matter how carefully they monitor their network English. Biloquialists in fact set an unattainable goal when they speak of complete enough accommodation to middle-class English to overcome "pejorative ratings associated with Negro nonstandard speech"; i.e., passing for white. A simple list of features, such as is usually offered, will not suffice because even the most ardent biloquialist would agree that many features identify a speaker's race (including many such as "voice qualifiers"—intonation patterns, rhythms, voice placement—not yet described). Were all such features erasable, or neatly variable to suit occasion, what would finally prevent *The Man* from changing the features he identifies as the badge of status? To say that a man's speech disqualifies him for a job is more acceptable than saying his color does, and is not illegal. For those who need such excuses, any bit of language will serve.

The argument that the schools have a responsibility to teach standard English because the system demands it rests on the assumption that nothing can be done to change the system—that prejudices against nonstandard forms cannot be eradicated. It assumes, too, that the values of the system will remain fixed as human nature clutches to her bosom her most cherished stereotypes. But are these assumptions valid? It seems to me that many of my undergraduate students are less hung up on the trappings of status than are their middle- and upper-class parents.[26] And black awareness seems to be having some effect on cherished prejudices. Much has been made of the existence in the United States of linguistic self-hatred and of the fact that many blacks seem to share white prejudices against black dialect features. Judgments of that sort are changeable and changing. A social realist less committed to the status quo might find a more satisfactory role for himself or herself in helping to change such judgments, rather than seek to perpetuate them.

It is realistic for us as teachers to visualize clearly the relationship with our minority students forced on us if we accept the goal of biloquialism. If I urge nonstandard speaking students to learn Standard English—even if I magnanimously "allow" them to keep their nonstandard in its "appropriate" setting—I must say to those students: your dialect is as good as any other, as systematic, as grammatical, as logical, at least as expressive, as the new dialect I am going to teach you; but you must learn this new dialect because those in power demand it. Without it, you will not pass the right tests, you will not get the right jobs, not because you are ignorant and inarticulate, not because you won't be understood (though some may claim not to understand you), but because you don't make the right noises. If the students are alert, they will know that I have other alternatives. And they will know, too, if they have been listening to my talk about literature and the human spirit, that my social realism fits ill with the values I profess to hold as a humanist.

The alternatives to the biloquial position and the Great Tradition are not escapist and idealistic, nor need they devalue the great aims of education. Things can be done to change the system— things that are philosophically and educationally defensible. If we are convinced by the dialectologists who assert that standard and nonstandard are equivalent systems and that attitudes toward nonstandard reflect snobbery and prejudice, we can attack snobbery and prejudice in our classrooms by teaching what the best research teaches us about dialects. Classroom teaching has done much to keep alive the myth of the superior language form: it might do as much to expose it as myth. We can banish the deprivation model from our own classrooms by questioning the assumptions of remediation programs and by looking to ourselves or to the broader society instead of to our students for causes of failure. We can assign to oblivion ill-constructed and badly motivated teaching materials simply by refusing to teach them. And we can, as members of a profession, draw on the special knowledge that gives us our professional status to extend our activities outside the classroom: to scrutinize the standardized tests that govern admissions, placement in tracks, and hence career goals—tests that in the market place are often used to determine employability and promotability. If such tests, under the pretense of measuring intelligence or necessary linguistic competence, really only measure conformity to standard usage; if they perpetuate myths about usage preserved in the folklore of correctness and purism; if they measure only one's degree of adjustment to middle-class behavior and morality, we have every obligation to mistrust and attack them. In a society that can be split over the question of whether or not children should ride buses to school, quiet acceptance of corporate standards is more cynical than realistic.

Inside the classroom, we can effect change by making our everyday practices conform to what is known about language learning, language structure, and language variation, throwing out badly worn practices based on questionable assumptions and seldom justified by unquestionable results. A place to start might be the marking of papers—that mundane activity that vexes the waking hours of all English teachers. To make the discussion concrete, here is a paper written for a remedial English class by a young black community college student (the title is mine):

[AN EMBARRASSING EXPERIENCE]

When I were in High School we had a football Banquite and I   (1)
had not Ben to a fromer accesson Befor. and I also included a   (2)
young Lady along.   (3)
    I were like the young man in the story we read in class.   (4)
    I came to the Banquite Proper dressed But I did not have no   (5)
table Manner. Everyone Began to set down, I did not know I   (6)
sirpose to assit the young lady with chair until she told me. after   (7)
about 30 min the guss spoke Began to spake & I did not know   (8)
when to Began to eat & after I saw all the other People eating I   (9)
look around for my silverware, But I did not have any, than I   (10)
tryed to get the water attanson. They finily Brage me my silver-   (11)
ware. I though that were the lose embarrassment monet for   (12)
tonight, But they had just Began. The main dish were chicken &   (13)
it were fride cripe & when I Bit off it, it would make a loud nose   (14)
and the other people would look aroung at me & my date would   (15)
look the other way. From then on I promer myself I would learn   (16)
good table manner.   (17)

FIGURE 4–1

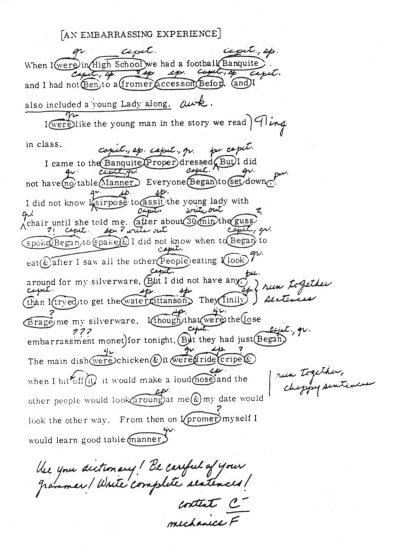

A paper like this frequently elicits a response from a teacher similar to the one in figure 4–1.

While the comments and "corrections" here are mine, I do not think that they caricature so much as epitomize the art of paper grading as practiced in American classrooms, an art dominated by the approach-direct to deviations from norms and expectations. It is a commonplace of English methods courses that similar excesses of red often warn insecure students away not from the errors circled but from the act of writing itself; the unsubmitted paper is less public than a gaily decorated one, and a less laborious way to fail. But I am less concerned with the psychological effects of such comments, assuming again that they are fairly representative, than with their general unhelpfulness to the student who wishes to improve his writing. So-called corrections that merely identify and vaguely name mistakes a student has made, or that we think he has made, do little to show him how to correct or why he should.

If we approach a paper like "An Embarrassing Experience" armed with a few facts about language and how it works, we may be less likely to make the paper or the student bleed. We know that every student has a language that he uses every day, one that generally serves him well. We know that whatever language system the student possesses, that system is rule governed, as is the student's use of the system. In ordinary conversation, the student rarely makes mistakes—certainly not any serious enough to hinder his ability to communicate. We know that his system, whether a variety of standard or some less prestigious dialect, equips him to think as well as his knowledge and intelligence allow. Why then all that red? Assuming that the student writer of "An Embarrassing Experience" does have a usable language system at his command forces us to search out other causes for his very real problems than some vague notion of linguistic deprivation, smacking as that notion does of original sin and incorrigible deficiency. Do his problems occur because the language of writing has special features not shared by oral language, features that this student does not yet know because of limited experience with reading and writing? Do they occur because we are asking the student to write in an unfamiliar dialect, an unfamiliar register, or an unfamiliar style? Do they occur because of pressures in the act of writing for a teacher-critic armed with a red pencil and the power to dispense grades? Problem solving can begin when we ask ourselves precise questions—questions that recognize writing as a very complex process requiring many skills and subject to many influences. Problem solving can begin when the teacher rejects the role of *grader* and accepts a role as *diagnostician*, equipped with detailed knowledge about language and its working.

Most English teachers have read enough professional and amateur writing to be able to trust intuition as a guide to where a writer is going astray. But intuition is not enough in the process of diagnosis, which requires more than vague feelings that "something is wrong with this sentence." Scattergun or random marking—the circling or underlining of any and every problem perceived—does not direct the student's attention to major problems or suggest bases or sequences for solving them. The use of a lean marking

FIGURE 4–2

___

After about 30 min the guss

spoke Began to spake & I did not know when to Began to

eat. After I saw all the other People eating, I look

around for my silverware, But I did not have any(.)

___

vocabulary—*gr.* for grammar, *punc.* for punctuation, *awk.* for almost anything we don't like but haven't the time or knowledge to name—neither identifies for the student what he has done wrong nor suggests how he might do better. Language structure is complex; the rules governing effective selection of language forms for topic, audience, and occasion are more complex still. Any marking vocabulary we use must be sophisticated enough and rich enough to handle such complexity. The greatest danger in the use of a vague or lean vocabulary is that general labels can be misapplied, leading teachers to attribute to students problems that do not really exist.

For example, in marking the sample paper in figure 4–1 as a "grader" might, I used the traditional notations "run-together sentence" and "gr." as I have seen them often used by school and college English teachers. These notations appear to name quite serious language problems—more serious, for example, than spelling. As a diagnostician, I would want to discover just how serious these problems really are—whether they reflect some deep troubles or, like the spelling mistakes, the less serious problems of "getting it down right on paper." I might begin by asking the student to read me his paper, noting the intonation patterns he uses to see if they identify "correct" sentence divisions; or I might simply repunctuate the paper myself, seeing whether a judicious sprinkling of commas, periods, and the deletions of a few conjunctions might leave well-formed sentences (see figure 4–2).

To make well-formed, if not elegant, sentences the student needs only one additional period (a semicolon would suffice in a pinch), one deletion of &, one comma, and the replacement of a comma with a period. If "But I did not have any" looks like a sentence fragment because of the capital letter on "But," we might note that the student consistently capitalizes, or appears to capitalize, *b*—a feature more easily explained from the handwritten version in which he does not distinguish *b* and *B*, a scribal problem. To teach such a student to make accurate punctuation is not easy, of course; but it is much easier than to teach him what he at first appears to need to know: how to make English sentences. He already knows how to make them, and we need teach only the rules for marking their limits in writing.

As diagnosticians, we might look at the forms marked "gr." What are the problems? What causes them? Two, "I sirpose" (line 7) and "with chair" (line 7), appear to involve the omission of necessary grammatical forms: "I *was* supposed" and "with *her* chair." *I sirpose* may show the weakening of the unaccented auxiliary *was* in speech with attendant loss of vowel and /w/ glide, a spoken form sometimes represented in literary nonstandard dialect with the spelling "*Ise* suppose"; loss of /s/ from *was* would reflect assimilation with the initial /s/ of *suppose*; *with chair* may similarly reflect weakening of /hə/, the r-less pronunciation of *her*. If the analyses are right (they should be checked against the student's casual speech to be entirely trustworthy), the "omitted" forms do not represent random errors, much less ignorance of grammatical signals, but faithful phonetic spellings of the student-writer's dialect. The apparent inconsistencies in verb forms may well represent similar phonetic spellings: *sirpose* the expected past participle with simplification of /zd/; *look* (line 10) the expected past tense with simplification of /kt/, not the misuse of present for past; *to Began* the infinitive *to begin* with nasalized vowel. Other "grammatical errors" show similar reflections of the student's vernacular dialect. *Proper* (line 5) instead of *properly*, and *set* (line 6) instead of *sit* show the selection of less prestigious but equally meaningful usage variants in instances where American English contains alternative but socially graded synonyms. Even the puzzlingly consistent use of *were* where *was* is expected ("When I were in High School . . . ", "I were like the young man . . . ," "The main dish were chicken . . . ", and so on) may well reflect dialect conflict—reverse interference on the vernacular from a formal register of the pattern, "If I were . . . ", picked up by the student as a hyperformalism. If teacher prefers "If I were" to "If I was," why not go him or her one better and use the high-class *were* at every opportunity?

The purpose of such diagnostic analysis is not to explain away the writing problems that do exist but to identify them and in so doing get a better sense of where the student really is in terms of his language skills. The writer of "An Embarrassing Experience" is not languageless; he does not lack knowledge of the rules of English grammar; he does not have to be taught English—a task that, if we really faced it, might well cause us to throw up our hands. He is inexperienced in writing, probably in reading; he has much to learn about the writing system—the accepted marks for recording English; he must learn when he can trust the spelling system to reflect his pronunciation and thus rely on analysis, but when he cannot, and must rely on memory of written forms and on the dictionary. Information like that in table 4–1 will enable us to help him by showing the greatest disparities between his phonology and the

TABLE 4-1 SOME PROBABLE DIALECT-RELATED SPELLING PROBLEMS

1. **r-lessness**
   1. 2: *fromer* for formal. Letter *r* intrusive in first syllable as student tries to use orthographic *r* where he lacks it phonetically; *-er* spelling extended to unstressed syllables realized as [ə] (that is, the second syllable shows loss of final /l/).
   1. 7: *sirpose* for suppose. *-ir* spells [ə] (compare *-er* on *former* for formal).
   1. 8: *spoke* for speaker. *e* spells [ə](?)
   1. 16: *promer* for promise. *-er* spelling again extended to unaccented syllable pronounced [ə] after loss of final consonant.

2. **Reduction of consonant clusters**
   1. 7: *sirpose* for supposed. Loss of final dental in cluster [zd].
   1. 10: *look* for looked. Loss of final dental in cluster [kt].
   1. 12: *lose* for last. Loss of final dental(?). Possible confusion with lose, vb.(?)
   1. 14: *cripe* for crisp. Metathesis [krips] and simplification(?).

3. **Loss of final dental after vowel**
   1. 12 *though* for thought. But the form is not phonetically spelled.

4. **Loss of consonants in unaccented syllables**
   1. 2: *fromer* for formal. [ə] for final syllable.
   1. 8: *min* for minute. Shortening influenced by loss of final [t](?) or the standard abbreviated spelling(?).
   1. 16: *promer* for promise [ə] for final syllable.

5. **Problems spelling final nasals**
   1. 11: *Brage* for brang.(?) The *-g* must go somewhere.
   1. 15: *aroung* for around. Final sound is probably [n]. Same source of interference as in *Brage*.

---

system of written standard. For certain audiences and for certain types of writing, he may well have to add some syntactic structures to those of his native vernacular, and learn to change certain selections from among status-marked usage variants. But it is important for us to realize that there is nothing peculiar about these learning tasks themselves, although there may be more of them for the nonstandard speaker. All students, standard-English speaking as well as nonstandard speaking, must learn to employ the writing system—a system that does not always match the pronunciation of spoken standard any better than it does nonstandard (*peace, piece, elite, concrete, feet, key, quay* serve as reminders); all students, if they are to become accomplished writers, must learn to extend their syntactic resources and their vocabularies, learn new registers and styles, and sharpen their feel for language variants.

As students learn to explore new uses of language, it is foolish and damaging to expect the error-free paper so often worshipped by the priests of correctness and institutionalized as a behavioral goal. If we ask our students to stretch their linguistic muscles, we must be ready for them to stumble; if we are getting "perfect" papers, we are likely not asking them to learn anything useful. The writer of "An Embarrassing Experience" is attempting to write in a formal register, seeing such a register as appropriate to what teacher is demanding but also to the topic of his essay—manners and the use of them on formal occasions, something he identifies as foreign to him as the linguistic register itself. As we have seen, his misuse of subjunctive *be* is the misuse of a formal usage. His choice of vocabulary is likewise formal (*banquet, occasion, young lady, young man; assist* rather than *help; speak* rather than *talk*), and in one case gets him again into minor syntactic difficulty when he uses the lofty *include* rather than *brought* (avoiding *brang*, perhaps? See line 11). He puts *include* into the syntactic frame for *to bring*, resulting in the "awk." "And I also included a young lady along," a subcategorization error of the sort often made by immature language users who are trying to extend their linguistic knowledge to new uses. Suppose this were the first attempt made by this student to use a formal register in his writing: suppose it were his first attempt at the formal *include*? Would marking the error in red likely motivate him to try again, or urge him to play it safe? For finally, the psychology of paper marking does matter, and matters very much. If students in attempting the language of writing incorporate forms from their natural speech, we have no right to mark those forms as wrong, offering no further explanation. We have no right to isolate speakers from backgrounds different from our own by drawing attention to their own language. To suggest or insist that nonstandard language forms are not good enough for the classroom or for polite society is the surest way we can take to alienate the human beings who use those forms.

If we are to become better at teaching *all* of our students to be literate, we must do a better job of reconciling our practices in teaching language use with what we profess to believe as humanists and as teachers of literary art. We must set realistic goals tailored to individual needs and abilities, but informed by larger ends than corporate and material good. We must establish priorities that include our highest educational aims, which may not be the state's, and the needs of our students, which may not be the middle class's. We must make use of our own best knowledge. As English teachers, for example, we are usually trained in sophisticated analytical skills for discovering how a piece of literature works for what it is, how its parts fit into a unified whole. But when we approach an essay written by a student, we throw our analytical skills out the window with our appreciation for imaginative and original language and go busily to work on sentences and parts of sentences, forcing conformity to very narrow linguistic norms and in the process choking off fluency and experimentation. Do we ourselves really care so much if a student writes *proper* instead of *properly*, *set* instead of *sit*? That he occasionally omits an orthographically precise *-d* or *-ed* at the end of a verb? Measuring by the values we perceive in literature, would "An Embarrassing Experience" be all that much better if it were impeccably spelled, punctuated, and expunged of low-status usages? What ultimate goals do we set for ourselves in our work with composition: producing an employable secretary for General Motors? a copywriter for Time-Life?

Humans learn language by using it. Few six-year-olds have seen a grammar book or been exposed to usage drills. And it is obvious from the persistence of stigmatized forms in the face of attacks by purists and English teachers, or tinkering by bidialectalists, that humans use those forms of a language that are important to them—*personally* important. Personal language is what we must seek to draw from our students, shaping it to be sure, but for their uses; not seeking to replace it with some chloroformed specimen from the pages of prescriptive grammars or the depersonalized and word-processed language of the business letter. If we are to cure the alienation of many young American men and women, the alienation of some groups of Americans from the larger culture, we must be ready to listen to individual voices no matter what their variety, to understand the forces that make them individual and various, to appreciate what they might tell us. In encouraging all voices to be heard, we may have to shelve our most cherished handbooks; in giving them time to be heard and to develop, we may have to neglect our spelling drills, our punctuation drills, and our usage drills—throw them out entirely if they contribute to the isolation and denigration of the nonstandard-speaking student. In neglecting drill, I do not think we need to feel guilty: writers need something to say before they need to shape an essay; they need words before they need to spell them correctly. When student writers feel that what they have to say is significant enough, they will seek larger audiences and in doing so find the need, perhaps even the means, for making language publicly acceptable. Proofreading is, after all, the task you do last.

As teachers whose primary job it is to encourage students to find a voice—to recognize and control the power of the word—we cannot afford to denigrate some voices. Too many chasms already separate America's rich and poor, her white and nonwhite. Many are trying to build bridges through the teaching of minority literatures—a hopeful sign that we seek to find out about each other and begin to recognize that ethnic experience is valuable to the outsider as well as the insider. When we teach literature, we often

praise its language for fidelity to character or to the unique experience the author invites us to share. Some of us have doubtless
urged our students to admire the cadences of urban Jewish speech
as we have taught Malamud's *The Assistant*, or those of the Southern black preacher in Baldwin's *Go Tell It on the Mountain*. We
admire language with the human in it and in our composition
classes we often tell our students to emulate such writing, to write
from their own experiences and hearts, to be forthright and honest
in the telling. But to some students we say: Don't write it in your
own language, use mine.

Could it be that standard English is sometimes *not* appropriate
to the composition class?

Notes

[1]The problems of diversity have only grown more acute in the years that
separate first publication of this essay from its present one. Most of us
know both present situations and demographic projections, but here are
a few salient claims from the latter:

> By 2030, the population will have increased by 18 percent through
> immigration alone, mostly Asian and Hispanic (16).

> One out of every three Americans, by the year 2000, will be nonwhite
> (16).

> Already, in California, the majority of elementary school students
> are now nonwhite; in Texas, 46 percent of students are Hispanic and
> black (16).

> Between 1985 and 1993, elementary-school enrollment is expected to
> increase by 4.5 million; yet the white fertility rate is now at an all-
> time low (20).

> Thus, by the year 2000, about 38 percent of the under-eighteen popu-
> lation will be black, Asian, Native American, and Hispanic, and as
> their portion of the child birth rate continues to grow, the population
> will become more racially and ethnically diverse than ever (38).

> See *Education Week*, May 14, 1986.

[2]More recent critiques carry much of the same message and both extend
and deepen our understanding of forces in schools and schooling that
enforce hegemonic values and sharpen class distinctions. See particularly: Everhart (1983); Giroux (1981, 1983); Aronowitz and Giroux (1985).
See also the important reports sponsored by the National Coalition of
Advocates for Students: *Barriers to Excellence: Our Children at Risk* (1985)
and *New Voices: Immigrant Students in U.S. Public Schools* (1988).

[3]It is painful to think how accurately descriptive these words still are, in
spite of various, now largely aborted, programs to open doors to higher
education. The absence of minority members from the ranks of practicing

and prospective language-arts teachers defines some large part of the present problems culturally divergent students have in schools.

4The statements are adapted from Allen (1966).

5The statements are from Fishman (1969, 41–42). Patterns of recent immigration have made the situation more complex. Here is how it is described in the report *New Voices* (1988).

> Many immigrants of previous decades brought new languages with them, but often shared a common heritage with Latin roots and a Roman alphabet. Spanish—a major language of the new migration—is familiar on that basis to many Americans.
>
> The Cambodian, Laotian, and Thai languages have little relation to the English sentence structure, and their system of writing doesn't use the Roman alphabet. Creole-speaking Haitians first began to put their language into written form only 50 years ago. Hmong arriving from the hills of Laos have survived for centuries with no written language until the last 30 years.
>
> People from the Caribbean are also linguistically diverse, with Cubans and Dominicans speaking Spanish, Jamaicans speaking English, and Haitians speaking both French and Creole.
>
> Many recent Asian immigrants are literate in English: 69% of Vietnamese; 44% of Lao; and 38% of Cambodians (Moffat and Walker, 1987). A study of employed Latin American immigrants who arrived between 1975 and 1980 showed that 60% of Mexicans and 75% of Central Americans have some use of English (Wallace, 1986).
>
> Some newcomers have yet to be literate in any language. Limited or disrupted schooling in their native land, a language only recently evolving into written form, or a purely oral tradition are among the factors involved.

6Its present has now, of course, been considerably extended, though along different lines, by those who argue with Hirsch (1987) that cultural literacy—defined as common knowledge and a common language—is essential both for enlightenment and national cohesion.

7As is obvious, if in no other form than the sporadic attacks of various individuals and groups on NCTE's relatively innocuous assertion of "the Student's Right to His Own Language." Ann Arbor's celebrated Black English Case (see "Martin Luther King Junior Elementary School Children *v.* Ann Arbor Schools District Board, Defendant") showed how shallowly below the surface of public discourse about language issues lie powerful biases against certain forms of language use.

8To the end of the paragraph, the quoted bits and pieces are from Sheridan Baker, *The Practical Stylist*, 2nd ed. (1969), Chaps. 5 and 6.

9Engelmann argues in "How to Construct Effective Language Programs for the Poverty Child," in *Language and Poverty*, Frederick Williams, ed. (1970), that the Bereiter–Engelmann program is based not on a particular dialect but on concepts and language structures determined to be essential to cognition and learning. But although Bereiter and Engelmann deny that the requisite structures exist in the language of poverty children, they find them easily enough in fully explicit structures from standard English. They do not demonstrate how these structures relate to cognitive processes and appear to operate from very primitive notions of relations between language structures and their uses. For example, in Bereiter, Engelmann, et al., the following distinction is made between expressive and cognitive uses of language and their supporting structures: "Language covers such an enormous territory, however, that setting up language development as an objective for preschool education narrows the field hardly at all. The field can be narrowed considerably by separating out those aspects of language which mainly serve purposes of social communication from those aspects which are more directly involved in logical thinking. The former include lexical items—nouns, verbs, and modifiers—and idiomatic expressions. The outstanding feature of the latter aspect of language is the manipulation of statement patterns according to grammatical and syntactic rules" (106). No linguist would propose such a dichotomy of language structure; no linguist would agree that the formal properties of language could be so neatly separated by the uses to which they are put. Bereiter and Engelmann simply deny the possibility of statement patterns in nonstandard dialects, and consequently do not recognize them when they occur in the speech of children from poverty backgrounds. It is interesting that the assumption that English was a grammarless language was made in the sixteenth century, and served as a push toward the writing of pedagogical grammars. Some notions die a slow death, for the assumption is a typical feature in Great Tradition concepts of nonstandard dialects.

[10]Katharine Scherman, *Spring on an Arctic Island* (56). Quoted first by J. C. Carothers, "Culture, Psychiatry, and the Written Word," *Psychiatry*, 22.4 (1959): 307–20; then by Baker in "The Literate Imagination."

[11]Representative studies are Joan Baratz and E. Povich, "Grammatical Constructions in the Language of the Negro Preschool Child," a paper presented at the national meeting of the American Speech and Hearing Association, 1967; Joan C. Baratz, "Teaching Reading in an Urban Negro School System," in Williams (11–24), which gives a partial report of research done by herself and Povich; Doris R. Entwisle, "Semantic Systems of Children: Some Assessments of Social Class and Ethnic Differences," in Williams (123–39). Entwisle's report concerns word association tests with young children from slums and from suburbia. Her aim was to gauge the development of semantic fields for selected lexical items, where development was measured by the child's ability to associate words by form class (nouns with nouns, verbs with verbs, and so on), or by some other discernible semantic framework such as generic class or synonymy. Her findings: "Word associations of black and of white elementary school children reveal, contrary to expectation, that slum children are apparently more advanced than suburban children at first grade in terms of paradigmatic responses." This is on a test measuring the ability to form concepts, a process obviously essential to the development of cognition. Baratz reports similar findings from tests of the development of sentence types, using a developmental model based on the rules of a generative grammar: "Results indicated that the Negro Head Start child is not delayed in language acquisition. The majority of his utterances are on the kernal and transformational levels of Lee's developmental model."

12The article shows its age, here, in couching this stage of the argument in terms of transformational generative grammar. I leave this section, however, and retain its language, because the argument is still germane. The case for equality of dialects as instruments for the expression of thought is not a case based in mushy altruism but in empirical reality, once one puts aside (as if one could) biases and prejudice.

13Although I have reservations about the separate existence of a distinctly black dialect, I use the term here because it has been widely used by researchers in urban dialects and because it does point to real speech used by real groups. The illustration draws on data from several sources: notably, William Labov (1970, 1972a, 1973) and Ralph W. Fasold and Walt Wolfram (1970).

14The last example and much of the analysis is borrowed from Labov (1973).

15Further evidence of the systematic quality of the feature comes from Labov, 1973: "For core members of the [BVE] peer groups, we find that negative concord [that is, attraction of negative to indefinites without erasure of NEG from verb] operates not at a 95 or 98 percent level, but at 100 percent, in 42 out of 42 cases, 63 out of 63, and so on.

16Middle English, as everyone knows, permitted multiple negation for emphasis. A spectacular example occurs in the *Clerk's Tale* as Griselde expresses unbounded love and devotion:

> *Ne nevere, for no wele ne no woe,*
> *Ne shal the goost withinne myn herte stente*
> *To love yow best with al myn trewe entente.*
>   (IV, 971–73)

By the formula, the six negatives result in illogic, though not by the heart. The alert reader will apply the discussion of negative rules to this ME example.

17The example is from Labov (1972a).

18All teachers should at least skim R. Rosenthal and Lenore Jacobson, *Pygmalion in the Classroom* (1968), which reports an ingenious experiment into the operation of self-fulfilling prophesies. Briefly, a group of students in an elementary school were administered tests designed to measure growth in IQ. A number of students from this group were selected randomly, without reference to the results from an initial test, and designated as children who could be expected to "spurt" in IQ gain. When these children were retested, a year later, they were found actually to have made significant gains in IQ. The experiment strongly suggests that a teacher's expectations affect the accomplishments of pupils; in this case not because of halo effect, because the teachers did not administer or grade the test measuring IQ gain, but because of something that happened in the classroom between students and teacher to facilitate learning. These conclusions, however, must be considered in conjunction with the critique of the authors' experimental design by Robert L. Thorndike (1968).

19In the period in which we find ourselves, the linguists who sought to save minority children from themselves and their languages seem to have given way to those who would promote "effective schools" and those testers, especially of reading but also of writing, who seek to measure whether schools are effective. Literacy, of course, is what is measured; but one still suspects that the myths of a standard and standardized language are not far beneath the surface.

[20]There is little hard evidence to support claims such as this and the following: "studies of the language of the ghetto Negro child have shown that his language . . . is sufficiently different from standard English as spoken by middle-class Americans, that it poses serious communication problems"; "syntax (rather than spelling, pronunciation, or word recognition) constitutes the central reading difficulty" (Baratz and Baratz, 1969). As we have seen, grammatical analysis suggests more similarity than difference in syntax, and communication does not seem to be a serious problem for anyone with some acquaintance with nonstandard dialects. Other research, furthermore, has demonstrated that nonstandard speakers generally have passive control of standard and hence can understand it readily, even though they may not be able to reproduce its every detail. Certainly, basal readers should start with syntactic patterns familiar to children, and perhaps basal readers for slum schools should contain nonstandard patterns; but as readers mature, hearing standard and nonstandard, there is every reason to assume that tolerance for and receptive control of standard patterns will grow as well.

[21]See, for example, Goodman (1970).

[22]See, for example, several of the articles in Baratz and Shuy (1969).

[23]This particular argument is still a very live one, as all teachers know and the public, who holds strong feelings, senses.

[24]In the 1980s, when we know more, from Marxist and neo-Marxist critiques of schooling, about the costs to certain groups of socializing to hegemonic values, the phrase is even less harmonious. See note 2.

[25]The "natural law" argument is easily found in the work of bidialectalists. For example, Baratz, 1970a, 25:

> It would be nice to think that there are complex, socially stratified societies where the spectrum of standard language is so broad as to include all the different grammars and usages of persons speaking the many varieties of that language under the label of "standard." Sad to say, human behavior just doesn't operate like that. To date, wherever research has been done—in Europe, Asia, and Africa—this has not been the case. One variety of the language invariably becomes the standard—the variety that has grammar books written in it, the one for which an orthography is established, the one that is studied by the populace in school. Language standardization appears to be a universal aspect of language variation in a national context—particularly one involving literacy. There is standard English, standard Arabic, standard Yoruba, and standard Hausa, just to note a few. Standardization is not a political invention of racist whites to exploit the Negro, rob him of his heritage, and denigrate his language.

Standardization, especially of the written language, is a fact of the modern world. But so is the "political" use of language variety to maintain and perpetuate class and caste lines. Does that mean that as teachers we are obliged to accept and perpetuate it? Racial prejudice is at least as much a fact of human society. Do we teach that? Standard English may not be an invention of racist whites to exploit the Negro, but neither is its writing system an invention to record standard American English. The writing system we use developed, of course, from British English and a long time ago at that.

[26]One can easily tell that this essay was written in the early 1970s and not in the late 1980s. And yet, there do seem to have been changes in the willingness of Americans to listen to other dialects, if not read them.

5

Literacy and Conversation: Notes Toward a Constitutive Rhetoric

Prologue

There are questions that contain within them their own urgent imperatives. Demanding answers, when none seem apparent, when none can ever be fully satisfying, such questions still remain before us—urgent and insistent. Here is one such question, put in what seems to me an especially insistent formulation, a generative formulation, of the persistent question of what to do for the not-always-successful language learner whom we would help toward an effective literacy:

> How [do we] bring into a community an isolated individual who is now outside it[?] (White, 1984, 6).[1]

The essay that follows is my attempt to answer this question, no matter how tentatively, and to try to show the relevance of this particular formulation of the question for those of us who work with learners whom we would help toward literacy.

Those who raise insistent questions often help us to envisage the kinds of answers we should seek, the sorts of solutions to difficult problems we should prefer:

> Our practical and moral lives are radically communal—unless perhaps we live alone on an island—and this means that our thought about what we want and who we are must reflect the freedom and power of others, without whose free cooperation we can have nothing of value, be nothing of value (White, 1986, 25).

93

I thank my colleague James Boyd White for his guidance: both for his question and for ideas that I try to make use of in this essay. I thank, too, and especially, a high school student (whom I have named Fred Albright), whose first published essay you—my readers—will read shortly. Thanks are due as well to his teacher, Jane Denton, and to other teachers of mine, some of whom I have taught. Fred Albright, Jane Denton, and others of us who have tried to learn together have come to know how radically communal our lives are, and how hard it is to constitute a rhetoric that will make it usefully so. All who ask insistent and insistently generative questions know that none of them is ever definitively answered. Where contingencies are acknowledged, conversation is made possible, and as John Dewey is reported to have said when asked to sum up all he had learned, "democracy begins in conversation" (Lamont, 1959, 58).

I

Shirley Brice Heath and Amanda Branscombe (1985, 3) call attention to recent criticisms from social historians and other commentators concerning the teaching of communication in industrial societies:

> . . . formal education systems tend to teach and promote the learning of only the barest of rudimentary skills for communicating. Proper spelling and grammar, varied vocabulary, and topic-sentenced paragraphs are not sufficient to make cohesive intelligent whole narratives or expositions. Schools teach and test to insure that students "absorb the automatic response and rule-of-thumb techniques," but neither teaching nor testing touches "the higher, active sense . . . [necessary to] set up an interchange between ideas, needs, and external reality" (Calhoun, 1970, 130–31).

In America, the response of school planners to such criticisms has been a familiar one: test to find out if the criticisms are grounded; teach to ensure that the deficiencies are remedied. If teaching "lower-order" skills does not enable students to communicate in ways that society values, then teach "higher-order" skills.[2]

The model that produces this response is also a familiar one in American education. It reflects the basic assumptions underlying a perspective upon the world that has been called, by Donald Schön (1983) among others, "technical rationality." The assumptions are that events and behaviors are isolable from their contexts and causes; that once isolated, events and behaviors can be measured against norms established through theory building or by presumption; that problems are solvable through application of a means-ends rationality; that problem solving is the proper province and sole responsibility of experts whose expertise consists either in the possession of theories that delimit and define the disciplines they practice or in the possession of power that allows them to be presumptive. Like physicians, school planners (and especially those who plan from a place in the academy), when an apparent dis-ease arises, diagnose, prescribe or operate, turn the patient over to nurturing agents, and wait to test for the cure.

I want to suggest in this paper that the present emphasis upon the testing, direct teaching, and retesting of "higher-order" skills is likely to have the same effect on students' ability to *communicate* as the testing, direct teaching, and retesting of "lower-order" skills has had: lamentably little. If direct teaching of "lower-order" skills has little to do with "an interchange between ideas, needs, and external reality," neither does direct teaching of "higher-order" skills, for communication—by definition and in essence—is a matter of interchanges and interactions among people: people who *have* ideas, people who *have* needs, people who *want to express* their ideas and needs in response to, and must express them within, the various external realities that form the contexts for their communication. Communication, when it happens to take place, does so in a local habitation. In its full existential reality, communication is a matter of one human being talking and listening to other human beings, writing something that another may read, or reading what another has written. Talking, listening, writing, and reading are actions—actions in the world and upon the world. Like all other purposive human actions, talking and listening and writing and reading occur in context; and they are actions that are made meaningful by the contexts in which they occur.

In this essay, my primary arguments will be these: If we are teachers, we will have little effect upon our students' ability to communicate unless we seek to make our classrooms micro-worlds in which communication can have purpose and meaning. If we are educational researchers, we will say little that is useful unless we seek to understand the influences such micro-worlds exert upon our students' acts of communication and upon their ability to communicate. Micro-worlds, I will also argue, are best understood by teacher-researchers who live in them, and who wish to make sense of their own and their students' lives.

I begin my argument with an invitation to my own readers to read with me an essay written by an eleventh-grade student who is learning to communicate in a low-track classroom in the inner city of a north-central metropolitan area of middle size. The student was asked to respond impromptu to a bit of gnomic wisdom:

The wise man learns from others' experience; the fool learns from his own.

The student's response was untitled, but for ease of reference, I will title it "Learning from Experience"; to preserve the student's anonymity, but make it possible to refer to him as an author, I name him Fred Albright.

LEARNING FROM EXPERIENCE

I think that the statement that "the wise learn through the expe- (1)
rience of others, fools learn through their own experiences" (2)
means that a person who is wise see's someone else's experience (3)
and if its a bad experience for that person, the wise person will (4)
try not to have that same experience. Well the fool won't pay any (5)
attention to that and he might have the same experience as that (6)
person, and if he tryed to avoid he might not of been hurt. (7)

I think a example of this is getting pragnent befor you are (8)
married. Say Mary had a baby, she has a wise friend named Sue, (9)
and a foolish friend named Amy. Mary goes through alot of (10)
problems like desiding if she is to have a abortion, put it up for (11)
adoption, keep the baby, when to tell her parents, etc. Sue see's (12)
her having these problems, so when her boy friend want's to (13)
have sex she says no. But Amy say's it wont happen to her and (14)
she has a active sex life and she finally get's pragnent and she (15)
has to go through the same things that Mary went through (16)
because she didn't pay attention to Mary's experience. (17)

I didnt write that example to say you shouldnt have sex (18)
befor you are married, even though I don't think you shoud, and (19)
the Bible says you shouldnt, but because that was the first exam- (20)
ple that came to mind. I just that if you see thing's that happen (21)
to other people, and the thing effect their life negativly, maybe (22)
it will have a negative effect on you so you shoild avoid it. T.V. (23)
series often show people hitchhiking and getting picked up and (24)
molested, or other things to try to make people realize things to (25)
watch out for. If you pay attention to these things to you might (26)
have a happier life. (27)

There are as many ways to read this essay as there are readerly perspectives, but I want to sketch two as common teacherly readings, and then develop a third. The first reading is through lenses that liberal grammarians have provided (I include among that category C. C. Fries, William Labov, and Mina Shaughnessy)[3]; the second makes use of spectacles provided by one kind of higher-order thinker, the critical thinker, and is a search for "cognitive" competencies; the third—which is more congenial to the arguments of this paper—is a reading through the eyes of a rhetorician who is interested in the pragmatics of language acts. In each reading, I adopt the stance of a teacher good-willed and informed enough to ask two questions: What does this particular act of trying to communicate by making a written text tell me about the text-making capacities of this particular student? What does my reading tell me that will enable me to help this student and, perhaps, others like him?

Liberal grammarians have this much in common with their more conservative colleagues, the prescriptive grammarians: For both, student texts are less acts of genuine communication than opportunities for the students who write them to display their various competencies as sentence makers. But where prescriptive grammarians judge sentences and the usages within them as applications or misapplications of absolute rules, liberal grammarians, when they move from description to prescription, measure sentences against templates formed from the conventional usages and conventionalized expectations of favored groups—those with prestige and power. As liberal grammarians read student texts, others read over their shoulders and direct their attention; those others include such influential gatekeepers as admissions officers, grade givers in those inevitable "other" courses, personnel managers, and employers. Liberal grammarians will read in "Learning from Experience" the social implications for Fred Albright of the stereotypes that attach themselves to such departures from standard usage as the spelling "befor" (Line 8), the use of apostrophes in third-person-singular verbs (Lines 12, 13, 14), and the failure to use them in the expected places ("wont," "didnt," "shouldnt"), or the spelling "of" rather than "have" for the reduced auxiliary verb in Line 7. For liberal grammarians, correctness is not the proper application of right reason but a strategy for economic survival and social well-being.

Liberal grammarians have helped composition teachers read in texts more evidence of students' competence than is apparent without adopting their perspective. Liberal grammarians assume that students, like other human beings, are grammatical animals; on that assumption, they search for plausible explanations for the mistakes students make and for ways to categorize those mistakes. Mr. Albright's problems with the apostrophe, for example, most plausibly issue from systematic features of pronunciation in his dialect, which make it somewhat more difficult for him (especially in impromptu writing) to analyze the language he uses in order to mark it conventionally when he is writing it down. And if a reader-teacher studies Albright's mistakes and groups them by type, he or she will find out that he makes few, but repeats them often. Findings like these—readings like these—help both students and teachers, for they create a more accurately positive image of inexperienced writers as able language users, and they render errors less mysterious. But any pedagogy that issues directly from such readings is a severely limited and limiting one, for it takes the sentence as its whole domain of application and inevitably relies on exercises and drills. It is doubtless important to help some students gain control of the conventional features of the language of status and power, but doing so will never help them gain the sense that Calhoun calls for: "the higher, active sense . . .

[necessary to] set up an interchange between ideas, needs, and external reality."

Liberal grammarians concern themselves with the linguistic socialization of students to norms that privileged groups acknowledge, either in their usages of language or in their attitudes toward usages. Privileged users may split infinitives with abandon equal to that of nonprivileged ones, but they will hate themselves for doing so. Critical thinkers, on the other hand, or at least one school of them,[4] would socialize students to other kinds of norms: to norms of thought and its expression that have found permanent place in the intellectual traditions that constitute western culture; to modes of inquiry, demonstration, and argument that are valued in schools, in the various disciplines of the academy, in the professions, and in similarly organized ways of dealing with affairs of the world. Readings of student texts through lenses provided by critical thinkers reveal lines and patterns of argument and the strengths, weaknesses, and fallacies in them: hypotheses and evidential proofs; theses, restrictions, and illustrations; analogies and examples; presuppositions, assumptions, premises, claims, grounds, warrants, and inferences. For the critical thinker, humans are reasoning animals who use their language to express their thinking; to the critical thinker's chagrin, however, humans do not always reason well.

Read for its reasoning, "Learning from Experience" appears to begin and proceed logically enough, but to run into problems in the first sentence of its final paragraph. The thinking task demanded by the assignment appears to be this: "Reflect upon the meaning of the aphoristic statement you have been provided and articulate some of its implications." Mr. Albright provides grounds for his articulation rather deftly by glossing the statement in such a way as to make more concrete the notion of what it is to learn from experience: to learn is to pay attention—to see not only events but also their consequences in order to adjust behavior accordingly. The fool is one who refuses to pay appropriate attention. The fool may see an event as an event, but will nonetheless refuse to apprehend that its consequences may follow if he or she engages in similar behavior. The fool learns (if at all) only from personal, not from vicarious, experience. In his first paragraph, in short, Albright makes useful distinctions—ones that he can then develop further.

Albright does so by offering his readers a hypothetical example about premarital sex, its possible consequences, and the decisions that might be made when the consequences are seen or not seen: "Say Mary had a baby, she has a wise friend named Sue, and a foolish friend named Amy" (Lines 9–10). Mary's lot is to live through the consequences of her actions. Sue, the wise, "see's" her doing so and learns to say no. Amy, the foolish, sees too, perhaps, but denies the consequences as possible outcomes of her own actions, and thus must suffer through experiences similar to Sue's. We readers are offered a clear, concise illustration of what it means to learn and not to learn from the experiences of others in the world.

But then, at the beginning of his third paragraph, Albright seems to lose tight hold on his line of reasoning:

> I didnt write that example to say you shouldnt have sex befor you are married, even though I don't think you shoud, and the Bible says you shouldnt, but because that was the first example that came to mind (Lines 18–21).

There is plausible motivation for this move of thought of a sort that might please critical thinkers: Albright points his readers toward the intended application of his example by blocking other possible applications: his is not an argument against premarital sex as such, but an argument about learning from experience. But for him to say that his example just happened to come to mind is a near fatal move when judged by critical thinkers. For them, lines of reasoning must be carefully preplanned, and examples carefully chosen for their pertinence and force. What prompts this move, we wonder: a lapse in attention? a relapse into a precritical mode of thought? a reversion to some earlier stage of cognitive development?

When we discussed Albright's paper with the teacher-researcher who had assigned the writing task, she provided the piece of information needed to understand his seemingly errant move: Albright was writing in a classroom in which discussion is encouraged; in that classroom, students share what they write with other students, who are encouraged—in fact required—to respond. In talking with one another, in writing to one another, the students inevitably take on identities that define their stances toward issues under discussion. Albright had come to be known by his listeners and readers as deeply religious, tagged "fundamentalist" in his approach to questions of human conduct.

Knowing who this writer is—what his identity is perceived to be in the socially constructed interpretive community in which he writes and reads and speaks and listens—enables us to see and to understand what he is doing in the sentence that begins his third paragraph. But to see and understand the move, we must take off the spectacles critical thinkers provide and put on those worn by rhetoricians.

II

James Boyd White uses the term "constitutive rhetoric" to name "the art of constituting character, community, and culture in language" (1985, x). For White, a language is "a set of terms and texts and understandings that give to certain speakers a range of things to say to each other"; when humans *share* a language they share not

merely a set of terms and texts and understandings but "a set
of intellectual and social activities." These activities, and the language that makes them possible,

> . . . constitute both a culture—a set of resources for future speech and
> action, a set of ways of claiming meaning for experience—and a com-
> munity, a set of relations among actual human beings (1985, xi).

"Whenever you speak," White writes, or whenever you write, I
would add, "you define a character for yourself and for at least one
other—your audience—and make a community at least between
the two of you; and you do this in a language that is of necessity
provided to you by others and modified in your use of it" (1984, xi).

What "character" does Albright seek to define for himself? What
"community" would he make of himself and his readers? What set
of relations would he have among himself and the actual human
beings who will be his readers? And to ask the question that will be
addressed in the last section of this chapter: What might answers
to questions such as these tell us about what is important in language learning if students are to learn how to communicate?

Albright defines a character for himself that will protect his
argument against a dismissal based on *ad hominem* grounds. In
doing so, he shows himself sensitive to the expectations of his
audience in the form of their preconceptions of his character: "You
may *expect* I did," he says to his audience, "but

> I didnt write that example to say you shouldnt have sex befor you are
> married, even though I don't think you shoud, and the Bible says you
> shouldnt, but because that was the first example that came to mind."

"I have my own convictions," Albright acknowledges, "and they are
part of my character. But in this act of communication, I invite you
to join with me not in a community formed of believers and nonbelievers but in a community where reason, not faith, defines the
modalities of our shared language." In constituting his character,
Albright writes for the actual human beings who will read his
argument—those who in fact comprise his community; but he
defines for himself and for them a new set of relations that will
govern their social and intellectual interactions as thinking beings.

To read Albright's essay with understanding of his messages as
well as appreciation for his accomplishments, a teacher-reader will
have to know the writer and the writer's readers as social beings in
the contexts in which they are seeking to form community. For
some readers who write about literacy and its development, to say
so is to say that Albright is not yet adequately schooled, not yet
adequately socialized, not yet adequately literate, for the movement from orality to literacy—from talking and listening to writing and reading—is often characterized either as a movement from
contextualized uses of language to decontextualized ones or as a

movement from the use of language in personal contexts to language use in impersonal ones.[5] From either of these perspectives, Albright could be faulted for failing to recognize that the appropriate audience for his essay does not know him—should not be expected to know him—as well as his classmates and teachers do. His writing, it might be said, is ego-centered, is egocentric, or is at best ethno-centered in his apprehension of the nature of the primary relations that connect him to members of a group with whom he shares frequent face-to-face contact. But I want to argue—in urging readers (and researchers) of student writing to put on lenses ground by rhetoricians—that all effective writing is similarly centered in a writer's anticipation of the needs and interests and expectations of real or imagined individuals whose readings will count for something in the writer's system of values. Writing and reading are always interactive processes, and as such are social activities, even when performed by individuals in lonely silence.

The development of literacy, we are finding out, is not well characterized as a movement from orality to literacy, or as a movement from language use that is context-bound to language use that is context-free.[6] Rather, developing literacy is more accurately characterized as a movement from one range of contexts for language use in which speaking and listening predominate to other ranges of contexts in which writing and reading predominate. Each range of contexts for language use, however, is essentially social, for each—whether the dominant medium is speech or writing—has as its defining characteristic human intentions expressed by actual human beings who use language to constitute character, community, and culture in order to make meanings that are expected to be meaningful to others. In certain kinds of writing, of course, the relation of writer to reader or reader to writer may be a distant one, but even then it is still a human relation, a social relation.[7]

Most kinds of writing, reflective readers know, and most kinds of reading—perhaps all kinds—are essentially conversational. Writing and reading are nothing more and nothing less than attempts undertaken by human beings to form community with other human beings whose real needs and expectations and understandings are imagined when not known. In a rhetorical gesture toward the real human beings who make up his audience, a move very similar to one he might make in conversation, Albright demonstrates both a willingness to change his rhetorical context—his character as perceived, his community as it has existed, and the culture in which both exist—and the capacity to do so. Albright's move invites his audience to revise their preconceptions of his character and, in doing so, to join with him in a community that requires of him and them new uses of language, new modes of speaking with one another. His move takes him from a world of certainty—from a culture defined by a single perspective on human behavior—into a world of uncertainty, into a culture that admits of multiple perspectives, of contingencies, and of contingent choices—a culture where paying attention, listening, learning, and choosing take the place of obedience. Albright is learning his lesson.

A reader-teacher-researcher may guess that talking has informed Fred Albright's writing—that his gesture in this essay has been rehearsed in conversations with his classmates. No guess is necessary, when his move is understood and appreciated for what it is, to conclude that Albright has learned. He is making strides toward becoming literate in ways that both school and society will value.[8] Albright's move is a conversational one, made in anticipation of the reactions of other potential conversants who share his social space; but he gets it down on paper.

To speak of literacy as conversation—to say that writing and reading are conversational—is to speak metaphorically, of course, for the forms and modalities of written and spoken language exhibit obvious and easily describable differences. But to use the metaphor and mean it is to force oneself to look for deep similarities between these two realizations of language that may be masked by differences in the mediums. To write and read, to speak and listen, are all ways to use language in order to do something with it: that is what speech-act theorists have told us; that is what rhetoricians (and some literary critics) are telling us. We use language to make meanings, of course, but we make meaning in language only when our intent in doing so is perceived by those whom we address, or is at least perceptible to them. To know my meanings, my reader or my listener must know what to do with them; and to know what to do with my meanings, my reader or my listener must know me—or at least that particular construction of me that functions and counts in the community I am trying to constitute with my audience through my saying of what I am saying.

Fred Albright's argument will be misperceived, simply misread as a reflection of his intention, if his character is read as who he was and not as who he would be in order to make meaning with his readers. His is a rhetorical move like others frequently found in texts produced by published writers, whose literacy is more readily credited because of the fact of publication: it is a move to place oneself in relation to what is past and what may be future; it is a move to clarify one's stance by contrasting it to alternatives—either one's own previously taken, or those adopted by others; it is a move whose primary aim is to constitute character, and by doing so, to guide a reader toward an appropriate response—toward a mode of apprehending that makes it possible for readers in the community to question with purpose, to answer pertinently, to object cogently, if questions, answers, or objections are to be invited into the conversation.

III

I want to compare Albright's move to a similar one (or at least I will argue so) in the preface to a text titled *Discourse Analysis* (Brown and Yule, 1983), a volume in the series "Cambridge Textbooks in Linguistics."[9] The authors' general aim in the preface is to identify their particular approach to, and their particular perspective on, a field of study that has been variously delimited and defined:

> In this book we take a primarily linguistic approach to the analysis of discourse . . . (ix).
> Throughout the book we have insisted on the view which puts the speaker/writer at the centre of the process of communication. We have insisted that it is people who communicate and people who interpret. It is speakers/writers who have topics, presuppositions, who assign information structure and who make reference (ix).

What is interesting in these two assertions (which are separated by several sentences and an intervening paragraph) is that for many linguists—especially those who practice in the United States— what is said in the second assertion denies the claim made in the first: For linguists who delimit their discipline as concerned with *langue* and not *parole*; for linguists who center their discipline in formal systems and not in actual uses of language; for linguists who find their data in texts and not in the human activities involved in the production and interpretation of texts—to insist on a "view" that "it is *people* who communicate and *people* who interpret" (emphasis mine) is to choose to leave the community of linguists, to resign from the profession of linguistics. Brown and Yule must make a move to constitute character in such a way as to save themselves from exile or excommunication; they must find a way to insinuate their view into conversations that linguists have with one another about linguistics. Doing so is the only means they have to reconstitute that community and change the culture called linguistics—to raise new questions and introduce new perspectives, to change the "set of terms and texts and understandings"—to change, in other words, the language that linguists use to provide themselves "a set of ways of claiming meaning for experience."

Here, much elided, is Brown and Yule's three-page preface (what I have retained are those portions that support my own interpretations of their rhetorical moves):

PARAGRAPH 1

The term "discourse analysis" has come to be used with a wide range of meanings which cover a wide range of activities. It is used to describe activities at the intersection of disciplines as diverse as sociolinguistics, psycholinguistics, philosophical linguistics and computational linguistics. . . . Sociolinguists are particularly concerned with the structure of social interaction manifested in conversation, and their descriptions emphasize features of social context which are particularly amenable to sociological classification. . . . Psycholinguists are particularly concerned with issues related to language comprehension. . . . Philosophical linguists, and formal linguists, are particularly concerned with semantic relationships between constructed pairs of sentences and with their syntactic realizations. . . . Computational linguists working in this field are particularly concerned with producing models of discourse processing. . . . It must be obvious that, at this relatively early stage in the evolution of discourse analysis, there is often rather little in common between the various approaches except the discipline which they all, to varying degrees, call upon: *linguistics* (viii–ix).

The authors' move in this first paragraph is to establish character by showing their familiarity with the field and its related disciplines. This move allows Brown and Yule, in their second paragraph, to assert more directly their claim for a place in the discipline, for their character as linguists. Discourse analysis, they explain, is a term covering a wide range of activities; those they name in the first paragraph, however, are activities carried out in a variety of disciplines that have in common two things—the discipline they each call upon (linguistics) and their interdisciplinary character. One may be, the implication is, both a linguist and something other as well without changing character. That *linguistics* is the same thing, no matter how applied or practiced in the hyphenated disciplines, is strongly stated in the last sentence of this first paragraph.

Brown and Yule's next moves are clearly ones designed to establish community—to claim common ground—with those who profess linguistics by claiming common character with them:

PARAGRAPH 2

In this book we take a primarily linguistic approach to the analysis of discourse. We examine how humans use language to communicate and, in particular, how addressers construct linguistic messages for addressees and how addressees work on linguistic messages in order to interpret them. We call on insights from all of the inter-disciplinary areas we have mentioned, and survey influential work done in all these fields, but our primary interest is the traditional concern of the descriptive linguist, to give an account of how forms of language are used in communication (ix).

Brown and Yule's approach is "primarily linguistic"; their "primary interest" is the "traditional concern of the descriptive linguist," which is to "give an account of how forms of language are used in communication." They will examine " . . . how addressees work on linguistic messages in order to interpret them," not *how listeners or readers interpret texts they encounter*—alternative language that would associate the authors more closely with other communities of scholars who practice other disciplines. The authors' move is crucial to offset the riskier one they will make in paragraph four: the move cited and discussed above in which Brown and Yule identify their own particular perspective on the field of discourse analysis. The moves in paragraph two seem more obviously aimed at the professional linguists who might adopt this text than at the students who will be assigned to read it.

PARAGRAPH 3

[I omit all of this paragraph, which mentions mainly constraints on breadth of coverage, save for two sentences, which again seem to function to claim community with other linguists]:

. . . We try to show that, within discourse analysis, there are contributions to be made by those who are primarily linguists, who bring to bear a methodology derived from descriptive linguistics. We have assumed a fairly basic, introductory knowledge of linguistics and, where possible, tried to avoid details of formal argumentation, preferring to outline the questions addressed by formalisms in generally accessible terms (ix).

Here Brown and Yule associate themselves with the community of descriptive linguists by alluding to a particular methodology employed by practitioners in the community and a particular mode of discourse characterized by formal argumentation. Should members of that community take note of the absence of formalisms in the book they are about to read, they should draw no unwarranted inferences from that absence. The authors imply their control of the special languages of the community even though they may choose not to employ them.

The riskier move then follows (emphasis mine):

PARAGRAPH 4

Throughout the book *we have insisted on the view which puts the speaker/writer at the centre of the process of communication. We have insisted that it is people who communicate and people who interpret. It is speakers/writers who have topics, presuppositions, who assign information structure and who make reference. It is hearers/readers who interpret and who draw inferences.* This view is *opposed* to the study of these issues in terms of sentences considered in isolation from communicative contexts (ix).

In fact this view, especially as it is expressed, puts Brown and Yule in opposition to powerful figures in contemporary linguistics, including some who do discourse analysis. Another move to preserve community is in order, and in fact comes.

In appealing to this pragmatic approach, we have tried to avoid the dangerous extreme of advocating the individual (or idiosyncratic) approach to the interpretation of each discourse fragment which

> appears to characterize the hermeneutic view. We have adopted a compromise position which suggests that discourse analysis on the one hand includes the study of linguistic forms and the regularities of their distribution and, on the other hand, involves a consideration of the *general principles of interpretation by which people normally make sense of what they hear and read.* ... [emphasis mine] (ix–x).

Mention of such "general principles of interpretation" that people normally use "to make sense of what they hear and read" is saved for last, save only for a concluding quotation not cited here. Although Brown and Yule try to distance themselves from a view that is clearly divergent from those commonly adopted in the community (the "hermeneutic view"), their reference to "general principles of interpretation" is, in fact, anathema to many linguists,[10] and the best hope these authors can have is that they have constructed for themselves a character as legitimate members of the linguistic community that may save them from charges of blasphemy.

IV

It is no more possible to read Brown and Yule's preface as if it were a context-free text than it is to read Fred Albright's essay as if it were. Brown and Yule's preface has meaning only when it is recognized as a contribution to the conversations linguists have had and do have among themselves, on paper and face to face, in the culture they have formed through the language they employ with its particular "set of terms and texts and understandings," its particular "set of intellectual and social activities." To become a linguist is to learn how to use the language of linguistics—to learn how to employ its "set of resources for future speech and action," to learn how to position oneself, as a character, within the set of relations that the discipline constitutes through its language. Brown and Yule share with Fred Albright a common problem: Given who they are and who they would become, to say something novel in the communities in which they speak, and to have it heard and credited, they must each constitute a character that is not alien in the communities they inhabit. Otherwise, they cannot act to change it, save through means where language serves other functions than persuasion. A true believer can no more engage nonbelievers in productive conversational interchanges about problems of ethical behavior in which both can participate as equals, than can a nonlinguist engage with a linguist in productive, that is *professional*, conversations about language. To speak in community in a way that promises to change both the community and the language its members speak requires that one be accepted as at least a potentially eligible member of the community. Conversations change communities from within; outsiders must employ other modes of discourse—or remain where they are. *Language* must mean something else when it cannot be used in conversation.

Language, no matter who uses it, is much more than a code, much more than a set of terms and expressions for the conveyance of concepts and logical relations. Language as a human possession, a human construction, has potential to provide ways for humans to do things in the world as active agents, to act upon the world as social beings. To learn language is to learn how to use it, and to learn to use language is to learn about one's self and one's place in the world—about what is possible and what is potential. Language learning is crucially influenced by context, but yet the learning of language enables one to change contexts by remaking them through language. Fred Albright has learned this, even though he may not be able to say that he has. His moves with language show us that he can use his language to reconstitute his character—to remake himself— and in so doing, to reconstruct the community in which he lives in such a way as to make it possible for him to enter it as a participant without necessarily renouncing deeply held convictions. Knowledge of the sort Fred Albright has gained, because it is expressed as appropriate and intuitive action in response to demands in his context, may even be transferable to other contexts. Given opportunity, Fred Albright can become more expansively literate.

Moves with language of the sort we have been observing are not likely to be learned through direct instruction. Rather, they are more likely to be learned through active participation in a community of language users who use their language to communicate with one another about matters that concern them. The classroom is sometimes said to be an artificial environment—a community in which school language, not real language, is spoken and written. As various recent experiments in pedagogy have shown,[11] it does not have to be so; and to encourage the kind of language learning that leads to the ability to communicate, it must not be so. The implication for teaching of the arguments I have been making is that classrooms must be constituted as environments that encourage interactive uses of language in real acts of communication. It is only in such environments that students can learn to constitute character, community, and culture; it is only in such environments that students can learn in such a way as to enable them to use their knowledge in critical and creative response to the situations they will encounter as they grow and change.

Learning environments for the development of literacy must resound with talk, for it is in face-to-face encounters with others that language users first and most readily learn to negotiate the relations of self to others, character to community, that lie at the roots of meaning-making through language. The sets of relations that link writers to readers in the worlds of written texts grow out of and reflect social roles and their functions in the worlds of everyday face-to-face encounters. The links between orality and literacy, between talking and listening and writing and reading, lie deep in the base of the language competencies that enable humans to function as effective communicators. It is commonplace, now, to talk of students gathered in classrooms with a teacher as communities. What we need to do now is to explore that metaphor for its concrete implications—for ways to translate the verbal trope into effective actions. If classrooms are communities, curricula become much less important than pedagogies: the ways students and teachers communicate among themselves—the sets of relations they establish among themselves—are the crucial issues in language development.

If language development is as sensitive to context as most researchers now seem to assume, and if the development of written language depends—as this chapter claims it does—on prior and concurrent developments in the ability to use spoken language in social contexts, the study of classroom discourse becomes imperative, and in such study there are new questions to pose and try to answer. It will not do as we ask new questions to accept a simplistic dichotomy between speech and writing or between home language and school language. It will not do as we grope for answers to our new questions to look at classroom discourse as a two-way interchange between a teacher and a single student, or as top-down management of discourse in which a teacher controls the responses of students. Nor will it do, even though their findings are genuinely useful, to stop with the studies of classroom discourse now being done from sociolinguistic perspectives, since most such studies take the character of classrooms and of the communities that inhabit them as fixed and unchanging, as givens rather than ever-changing social organisms. Because sociolinguistic studies treat the social contexts for language use as constants, in order to show the relations between language use and its social constraints, they cannot capture the implications of a move like that Fred Albright makes— a move that in fact changes the social context by changing the significant set of relations among the participants in the context.

For purposes of understanding the kind of language development Fred Albright exhibits in the moves he makes with his language, there are these requirements for research:

1. The services of competent and empowered teacher-researchers who are participants in the conversations, communities, and contexts that are being studied. Only someone who is continually present will be sure to be there to observe each critical moment; only someone who knows the users and who understands the nuances of their language use in the community will be able to see it.

2. The development and acceptance of new notions about what "experimental" might mean in terms like "experimental setting," or "experimental research." Laboratories are not the only environments in which experiments can be conducted, and when the object of study is language development, they are not likely to be the most appropriate ones. Effective language use is an effective human response to a particular situation; effective language use in the lab is just that—a response to that particular environment.

3. The development of more realistic theories of language learning—theories that treat language use as action in the world and that link language use to the real contexts in which interacting and conversing human beings use language to form community by making meaning together in actions upon one another and upon their world.

In short, the conversations between practice and theory, theory and practice, must become real and continuing ones as must the conversations between theorists and practitioners. If teachers are not made full participants in research, the accomplishments of a Fred Albright might never be heeded or his move toward a larger world ever remarked. If teachers are not encouraged and empowered to make use of what they are learning from their research to experiment continually with the contexts in which they are asking their students to learn, the Fred Albrights of this world might never make such moves.

The objections to the kind of research proposed here are the obvious ones, and they are familiar because they are often stated. They are objections that issue from deep-seated beliefs about the nature of research and of expertise. What happens to the ideal of scholarly objectivity if researchers are practitioners engaged in trying to change the very phenomena they are studying? If some factors are not held constant, or assumed to be so, how do you tell if change has happened? How do you determine whether it is beneficial or harmful? If research is not carefully controlled, if distance and objectivity are not demonstrated, doesn't research become mere rhetoric—a branch of the persuasive arts—especially when researchers are practitioners who have a vested interest in finding good outcomes for the experiments they undertake?

And then there are objections that issue from the institutionalization of beliefs about research and expertise (objections that are more rarely stated): Do teachers in fact have sufficient expertise to warrant their empowerment as researchers and hence authorities? Given who they are, and what they must do, and the settings in which they must work, do they have capacity or opportunity to acquire sufficient expertise?

Questions like the last two slide easily into others that are blatantly self-interested or crudely political: If teachers are admitted to have expertise relevant to the solution of educational problems, what will happen to the status of other experts whose expertise has been validated in the institutions they have built—experts in universities, in central offices, in state and national departments of education, in research and development institutes and labs? If teachers are empowered to make crucial decisions about educational aims and practices—or to have a participant's role in making them—how will administrators, politicians, and the public control the schools and make them subject to their own political wishes? These last two questions are almost never put openly, certainly not in conversations in which they might be taken as real and not rhetorical questions. And yet those who have them in mind exert a persistent influence on educational decision making.

More important than political or even professional questions are ethical ones, and all too often we forget to put these into words. Whatever our roles—as teachers, teacher-researchers, or researchers—and whatever the modes of the experiments we conduct, we are experimenting with children's lives, with their hopes and expectations for the future, even, perhaps, with the possibility of a future.

What is our concern and what should it be for those children who are assumed to be the beneficiaries of schooling? Which kinds of formulations of our insistent questions about unsuccessful language learners should we prefer? This one: How to raise test scores across a district on critical thinking skills? Or another one: How to bring into a community an isolated individual who is now outside it?

What we know about what language is and how language and thinking develop—our best theories—will help us decide. But so, too, will our answers to other questions, answers that go beyond theory to implicate other kinds of issues. Which formulations of the insistent question, which answers, promise most benefit to Fred Albright and to others more or less like him? Which formulations, which answers, best match our best hopes for the kinds of communities and cultures we would help our students constitute?

Maxine Greene, in a recent article (1982), asks a question that should concern us more than it does: "Literacy for what?" And as she suggests, such answers as we give have everything to do with our own political and ethical commitments as teachers and researchers. They have everything to do with the kind of world we wish to live in with others.

All questions that involve the lives of children are serious ones. Those of us who are not children, and especially those of us who are obliged to ask them because of our choice of profession, bear a special responsibility to recognize that as professionals "our practical and moral lives" can be nothing other than "radically commu-

nal," for we do not "live alone on an island" nor can we seek to
insulate ourselves as professionals from the communities we have
chosen to serve. Questions about learning are perhaps best formulated as questions about *children* learning; such questions can be
answered only in conversations among all those who hold vested
interests in their learning and in their language development: theorists, researchers, teacher-researchers, children and older learners,
and members of the larger community in which language learning
takes place and in which the outcomes of learning will be put to
use. In matters of teaching, in matters of learning—and especially
in matters of the teaching and learning of language—all choices
are inevitably contingent, all findings inevitably tentative. If we
admit that, conversation becomes possible, and as Dewey said,
"democracy begins in conversation."

As a teacher and as a researcher, I know that there are no contexts that are not socially constructed through the interactions of
human beings in the institutions that other human beings have
constituted in history. If I take the contexts in which I work as given
to me—as not subject to my acting upon them—I abdicate my
personal responsibility as a professional and misuse such power as
accrues to that role. In our own professional communities we must
make our own choices, but we must learn to ask others to help us
to understand their limitations and consequences, learn to listen to
answers so that our "thought about what we want and who we are"
will "reflect the freedom and power of others, without whose free
cooperation we can have nothing of value, be nothing of value."

In conversations with others, we can insist on our own choices
if we know that others will insist on theirs, test theirs against ours,
negotiate with us as together we all seek to make choices that may
benefit us all. Through such conversations, language changes and
develops, and literacy expands; through such conversations, education can play a role in helping to constitute a democratic society.

We are, finally, rhetorical animals, for when we use our language we have no other choice than to constitute character, community, and culture. But we do have some choice about who we
would be, and in making choices, we might have some effect on the
communities we help constitute and on the culture that binds
them. If we wish to make it so, constitutive rhetoric can be an art
that helps us sustain human freedom even as we seek to understand
what freedom is and how it is constituted through the ways we use
language to talk with one another and to write for one another.

Notes

[1] I have wrenched White's question from the context in which he poses it.
In his use of it, it is the central question to be worked out in the conversations that comprise the action in Sophocles' play *Philoctetes*. In that

context, it is a question that Odysseus and Neoptolemus must answer, for their task is to persuade the banished Philoctetes to rejoin the community of Achaean warriors who had banished him. They must do so, not because Philoctetes is important to them, but because he possesses a bow and arrows given him by Heracles. Without these weapons, a soothsayer has said, the Achaeans cannot capture Troy; hence the urgency of the question in this context: " . . . how to bring into a community an isolated individual who is now outside it." The situation White describes is very different from the one I describe. And yet when one thinks of how communities might be built, and for what purposes—if one thinks only about present debates about what education is for—similarities between the two situations are not hard to find.

[2]Frank Smith comments usefully on our faith in the efficacy of direct teaching and the causes of that faith. See Goelman, Oberg, and Smith (1984):

> Although it is widely accepted that education and its institutions are primarily sociocultural in origin and purpose, educational research during the past 2 or 3 decades has turned almost exclusively to psychology for theoretical support of its practices and solutions to its problems. Not that other disciplines have been reluctant to make statements about education. Cultural anthropology has a long history of observation of educational practices in many cultures and of direct attempts to influence policies in prevailing systems. Sociologists have taken an increasingly vocal role, not just in claiming their relevance to educational theory and policy-making but in striving to achieve change in particular directions.
>
> Nevertheless, educational theory and practice have traditionally been dominated by psychology. The reason for this seems clear enough to me. The logistic triumphs of space exploration and of information management systems generally, added to an earlier respect for the standardized achievements of mass production, consolidated the belief among educators in authority that success would result from delivering to children the right amounts of the right instruction at the right time, with constant monitoring and quality control. The belief still has not been totally discredited that learning is a simple matter of individual ability and effort applied to appropriately organized and presented subject matter. Thus for literacy, educators occasionally turned to linguists to ascertain what should be taught but primarily to psychologists for how the instruction should be delivered. Success has not been conspicuous, but the failures of managed instruction continue to be attributed to the child or teacher rather than to the philosophy. Improvement still is sought through better and more extensive programs. The persistent underlying conviction is that if reading and writing are analyzed into component elements of basic skills and knowledge which are presented and rehearsed under appropriate conditions of incentive and reinforcement, then every relevant factor has been attended to. From this perspective, learning is essentially a series of inevitable psychological processes (vii–viii).

[3]I am thinking here especially of Fries' *American English Grammar* (1940), Labov's *The Study of Nonstandard English* (1970), and "The Logic of Non-

standard English" (1972), and Shaughnessy's classic *Errors and Expectations* (1977).

4The so-called "high-order reasoning movement" includes a number of streams, and among them are approaches to thinking and the teaching of thinking that treat these activities as essentially context-free. Participants in the critical thinking movement tend to acknowledge that thinking has much to do with cultural traditions and with the conventions and constraints of the languages used to express thought. See in particular Toulmin, et al. (1984) and Meiland (1981) for textbooks representative of this movement.

5Related perspectives are taken by those who would claim that thinking itself can be abstracted from the contexts in which it takes place. That perspective is also alien to the arguments presented in this essay.

6This seems to be a clear implication of recent work on early literacy development and on the relations of oral and written uses of language in literate societies. For illustrative work on early literacy, see Ferreiro and Teberosky (1982), Goelman, Oberg, and Smith (1984), and Graves (1985); for illustrative work on speech/writing relations, see Tannen (1982, 1984).

7This argument is developed at length in this book in the essays of Part III.

8Thinking of criticisms raised against developmental schemes such as those proposed by Lawrence Kohlberg, William G. Perry, Jr., and others, one wonders if changes like those exemplified here toward forms of relativism are not better characterized through rhetorical explanations than cognitive/psychological ones. Rhetorics are, of course, a form of art, not science; but they have been hospitable to consideration of contextual factors and socially constructed human values in attempts to account for human uses of language.

9I choose this example because I am a member of the "linguistics" community, and thus can act as a reader-researcher in trying to identify the rhetorical moves in this particular text.

10A well-known linguist colleague of mine at the University of Michigan submitted an article to a well-known linguistics journal on the contextual factors involved in the construction of meaning in language—a contribution to our understanding of "general principles of interpretation." The article was rejected on the grounds that it was more like literary criticism than linguistics.

11Illustrative merely is the work of Shirley Brice Heath (1983), Heath and Branscombe (1985), and Luis Moll (1986) and Moll and Diaz (1987). There are now, fortunately, many other workers in the vineyard who have found ways to ground language learning in activities that are real to children, adolescent, young adult, and adult learners.

6

Talk as Text: Students on the Margins

Carol Lea Winkelmann

For the past two years at the University of Michigan, several teachers have joined together to teach and research a course that reflects a social theory of the way language works, an introductory composition course based on the theory that a community forms its own language and that language forms the community.[1] In the world of the university, this means that students must acquire a metalevel perspective on the configurations of meaning and meaning-making that are currently valued in academic communities in order to enter the ongoing conversations that constitute a field of expertise. It means they must be aware that language communities create their own patterns of discursive practices that new members must become familiar with and eventually master. As teachers of reading and writing, we considered it our responsibility to facilitate this kind of rhetorical awareness so that we might help our students more easily enter into the scholarly conversations taking place in the academic communities across the university.

We also understood that it is human beings who constitute the very contexts in which their discourses unfold, grow, and change. Communities change through the conversations people have with one another. Thus the view of literacy cradling the course, in itself more important than the specific design, is one that recognizes the making of meaning as being always social, functional, and generative. Discursive practices are not static patterns, but dynamic configurations of meaning-making. Students then are asked not only to think about how they might enter into ongoing conversations with a knowledge of the conventions and configurations of meaning-making; they are also encouraged to think about how they might enter into their own futures as responsible adults who act meaningfully and ethically in their own contexts, sharing and shaping patterns of meaning-making.

To nurture these kinds of awarenesses—rhetorical and ethical—we began with our lived experiences, the backgrounds of students and teachers. In particular, we created opportunities in the first part of our course for students to rediscover their own family language. We wanted to show students that even their own families formed small language communities with special words and ways of interacting. In the second part of the course, we created opportunities for students to reflect on the common language and on the community as these were created in their attempts to compose in and for peer groups. We invited students to write about four different aspects of a topic of their own choice, thus becoming experts on their individual topics. Our intention was that the students would come to realize the significance of negotiating meaning as they attempted to share their expertise within their peer groups. In the last part of the course, we asked our students to research the language of the academic communities across the university that they anticipated joining. Small groups of students with shared academic interests interviewed professors across the university, shared their findings with the class at large, and wrote collaborative papers about the discursive practices in their field of research. Professors were also invited to speak to our joined classes about the discourse in their fields. Through these activities, we hoped that our students would develop an awareness of how knowledge is socially constructed through sets of discursive practices, particular configurations of meaning-making, then rendered significant and given value in the various institutional settings of the academy.

In keeping with the view that knowledge is socially constructed through language, the first decision on the part of the four instructors was to create a "conversation-centered" course[2] that avoided the dichotomizing of possibilities current in pedagogy: teacher-centered or student-centered courses. We teacher-researchers took inspiration from the words of Maxine Greene, recognizing that both students and teachers share knowledge in the classroom:

> Working in this fashion with students, liberating them to understand that the social reality they inhabit is a constructed one, educators ought to avoid, if possible, the high-sounding voice of expertise. They and their students might well enter a conversation with one another, the kind of conversation that allows a truly human way of speaking, a being together in a world susceptible to questioning. Each one, including the one who is the teacher, might articulate his or her particular themes of relevance, might speak truthfully and simply about backgrounds and foregrounds, and what it means to be present, what it

means to reach out and to question and to learn. It is indeed the case—or it ought to be the case—that formal inquiry, scientific thinking, and the rest are significant to the degree they nourish human conversation (1978, 69).

The reconceptualizing of the role of the teacher as an experienced participant in the community rather than sole authority and the reconceptualizing of learning as conversation, we believe, led students to feel more comfortable about being innovative and taking risks with their language as they articulated their own themes of relevance. They researched topics in which they had a personal interest and became the experts about these topics. They spoke and wrote about the topics in ways that they seemed to find personally meaningful, sharing their words with other participants in the classroom community and negotiating their way to common understandings of words spoken and written. This was made possible especially through the use of small peer groups in which students could read and write for one another and reshape their words in response to the reactions and contributions of others. They became experts on the discursive practices of the discipline or area of specialization they chose to research and shared their new knowledge with the large group. This meant that both teachers and students were learners in the classroom, sharing and shaping knowledge through conversation. Such a nontraditional learning situation itself called for risk-taking, both for teachers, who were unaccustomed to sharing authority, and for students, who were unaccustomed to having authority in the classroom as we all joined in conversation about the ways in which language communities function.

As teacher-researcher in my own classroom and participant-observer in the classrooms of my colleagues, I became aware of several implications of the metaphor "learning as conversation" as we attempted to implement this experimental conversation-centered course in Introductory Composition. One is that descriptions of classroom language as institutional language are inadequate to describe the dynamics of a classroom where the redistribution of power and authority is a priority. The frameworks for analyzing classroom language developed by early classroom researchers and discourse analysts[3] in which the teacher is seen, for example, as sole authority—initiating, responding to, and evaluating student responses—cannot describe the language practices in this context. Rather, the language of a conversation-centered course shares characteristics of ordinary conversation—cooperation and conflict, improvisation and ritual, constructions and breakdowns of meaning. Indeed, the goal is to engage in "ordinary" conversation.

To the experienced and sensitive teacher, this is perhaps not an extraordinary revelation. Perhaps those among us who always responded to our students as human beings rather than as vessels to be filled with knowledge did sense the problematic in the early findings of the discourse analysts at the same time as we could appreciate the warnings against the mechanical treatment of students implicit in the work of those researchers. Yet to recognize that the language in classrooms is more complex and dynamic than patterns suggested by early research such as "initiation, reply, evaluation" is to open ourselves to new vulnerabilities. This is especially true for teachers who base their curricula on emancipatory pedagogies such as the one the University of Michigan teacher-researchers attempted to shape.

Thus, the second implication that has become clear to me has to do with the ideal notion of the classroom as a community in conversation. In the scholarly articles about classroom communities, in the humanistic approach to language as a social construction, in the optimistic rush to rehumanize the role of the teacher lost in the behaviorist view of learning, the notion of the classroom as community, it seems to me, is misperceived as too idealistic. The notion of community in current theory and pedagogy should be extended to account for the workaday realities that include, for instance, breakdown of communication, fringe community students, lack of commitment. The teacher-researcher of the classroom as community would do well to focus carefully on those instances where the language disintegrates, communication fails, meaning breaks down. Philosophers of language and linguists have, for some time now, realized the significance of those spaces between intended, literal, direct, and nondirect speech, the meaning between the words that makes understanding the complex process that it is. They, along with others from diverse areas of study, have recognized the significance of miscommunications and misunderstandings.[4] In the classroom, the teacher-researcher might look at the spaces in communication, at apparent and real failures in the construction of meanings in community.

I have three students in mind from my language and community course: Julie, David, and Matt. For various reasons, on some level, each student can be labeled a "fringe community" student, a student on the margins of the classroom community in process of formation. Each was a student with whom my ability (or the community's ability) to communicate was either temporarily or perhaps permanently destroyed. Julie was a students' rights activist; ironically, she was forever opposing the opinion of the majority of students in the classroom community. She skipped class, opted out of collaborative work, rejected access to modes of communication (computer conferences, teacher-student conferences, peer critiquing). David, on the other hand, seemed to be fully integrated into the community. Well liked, articulate, bright, and a witty, resourceful writer, David guarded a not-so-well-kept secret: in his perception, the community was a failure; the teacher was not an equally contributing participant; the freedom of students to construct their own personal meanings was a farce; the grading system undercut the whole premise of the course. David also temporarily opted out of the course by refusing to submit written work that was to be analyzed, critiqued, and graded. Finally, there was Matt, a young man whose view of Colonial American history (his writing topic for the semester) was so thoroughly at odds with my own that we agreed to use an intermediator to critique his work, a crushing blow—it seems to me—to the notion of negotiation and shared meaning. (Was it a conservative/liberal conflict? A battle of wills, of sexes, of class?)

In a classroom where midsemester student evaluations and journals revealed satisfied participants, where conversation seemed strikingly honest and productive, where the grade book revealed a motivated, hard-working group of writers, these three students flitted around the fringes and impinged on my happy notions of the classroom as a cohesive community. An excerpt from David's journal is etched into the space between the pedagogy and the practice:

> If I could radio Edna [a baffling pseudonym for me] across the incredibly vast distance between our two planets, I would suggest that she put Dave in a noose when she takes off the shackles—that way he will understand that the restraints of the system are only being loosened—not removed. I'm sure he'd appreciate the additional freedom. After all, being taken for a walk on a leash with a choke chain is better than being cooped up in a box.

David teleports me to the "zone of proximal development," a possibility that Vygotsky ignores.[5] On my way, I probe at various rationalizations to salvage my happy notions of "community" in the face of the behavior of these students: the threat of grading was removed by the possibility of revising and resubmitting papers; the construction of meaning is two-way—if they could not negotiate meaning, it was not my fault; commitment to the course is primary; maturity is an expectation, and so on.

In the case of Julie and Matt, I can almost complete the rationalizations. Both students recognized, at some point, that they often did not wish to pursue shared meaning. Julie once admitted to me in a conference: "I have to be honest; I know that I put people on edge." And during a particularly tense conference with Matt about his paper on Colonial America, he said to me: "I know that I'm a stubborn ass." At the same time other members of their peer groups articulated, in conference or in journals, their own discomfort with the apparent self-alienation of the two. In their journals, a handful of students wrote in exasperation about Julie's uncompromising attitude. Pete, a member of Matt's group, often worried about the fact that their relationship was not as mutually beneficial as the relationship between himself and the third member of their peer group.

Julie's and Matt's actions, then, seemed to me to fit rather neatly into the the radical educator's category of "oppositional" behavior (Giroux, 1983; Chase, 1988). Oppositional behavior is disruptive behavior without radical significance, that is, it does not characterize intentional actions aimed at resisting dominant ideologies. It is directionless disruption that marks only the student's inability to enter into enabling conversations. The answer to these failures of communication, the oppositional behavior, seemed to lie somewhere in Matt's and Julie's personal histories and personalities, something that interfered with their entering the inner circle of meaning constructed by the group.

Julie, for example, newly situated in the largely upper middle class of the university, took pride in her own background. Her experiences in a predominantly black working-class high school were markedly unique contributions to the community, contributions that were not always understood and appreciated. Her recent involvement in a students' rights organization also provided her with a critical perspective unlike that of the other students. Although Julie's experiences and opinions were rich in potential for the community, she defeated herself with her own combativeness. She could not negotiate a common language with which to share her experiences with others. Jennifer, a member of Julie's peer group, eventually became exasperated with Julie's antagonistic behavior, as did many other of the class members, and—for a time—gave up initiating conversation with her. My own sympathetic overtures to Julie were generally ignored, although she eventually complied with the standards of our community in her written work, apparently to avoid failure in the academy. Within the brief span of a semester-long course, her integration in the community was functional and ultimately incomplete. In view of her presentation of self, then, I managed for a time to name the problem with Julie as a "student-centered" problem.

If Julie's stance was one of opposition against the entire community, Matt's stance seemed one of opposition against the notion of emancipatory pedagogy. His "oppositional" behavior took the form of an apparently needless needling, a testing of my endurance as a teacher. Matt's first move in the classroom was to test the meaning of "choice" of topics. Would it be acceptable to write about nude beaches in Rio de Janeiro? In the face of my full unflinching support of that topic, his second move was to saturate his written work with taboo words, barely masking his extremely conservative view of his final choice of topics: Colonial America! In this case, it seemed that no negotiation was possible. In two moves, and a few elaborate sidesteps to indicate that he wasn't interested in the meaning of "critical thinking" and "shared understandings" with his peer group, he had discovered the limits of my endurance! A mediator was called in to bridge the gap between the socially conservative, politically radical instructor and the socially radical, politically conservative student. A conjoined teacher and student failure to arrive at shared understandings?

To this day, however, the image of David chattering away with his peer group weighs on my mind. If I could relegate Julie and Matt to the margins of the community because of what I viewed as their oppositional behavior, David had me relegated to another planet, hanging out in the zone, waiting to recover from Maxine Greene's "experience of shock" (101). If this student was not at the center of the voices of the community, no student was. He was a well-liked, bright student who was always involved, making significant contributions to the classroom conversation. In an attempt to untangle the mystery of his temporary refusal to submit written work, I focused on the obvious weakness of the course that purported to distribute power more evenly in the classroom and so empower students: grading. I thought about some well-known options to mitigate the negative effects of this apparently last constraint: elaborate student self-evaluations, Anne Gere's notion of student formative evaluation, Andrea Lunsford's call for peer evaluation of collaborative work,6 my own negotiation with students of the relative weights of paper grades and revision options. I decided that, despite my students' overwhelming affirmative response on a class survey indicating that grades affected their writing, everything reasonable had been done to mitigate negative effects within the confines of this institutional constraint.

Mystified still, I returned to David's last words before he decided to temporarily opt out of the writing community by refusing to submit papers for grades. He is describing his paper (on which he did not get the grade he wanted) to the large group. He had just discarded an unsuccessful rough draft and changed his topic:

DAVID: I was getting frustrated so I decided just to write a nice short paper that got rid of all the hostilities I was feeling. I didn't try to make it fair. I didn't try to make it objective. I just wrote the paper and got it all out and I put in a few creative layers.

STUDENT: He's just showing how he feels.

DAVID: I was in a hostile mood. I was feeling frustrated about this class because I've never been forced to write before. All the other classes, I just cranked out papers and that's that. And in this class, it isn't working out like that.

TEACHER: How is it working out?

DAVID: After twelve years /is it?/ of easy education, I resent a little bit anybody trying to make me work. I will admit that. But ah I do see I know it's good for me. While I complain, I can see what's going on. I'd rather be in a class like this where I'm going to get something out of it.

I searched for ways of analyzing David's words for a key to the miscommunication. Some of the frequently useful ways of explaining miscommunications seem inadequate here: crossing of discourse boundaries, suspension of cooperative principles of conversation, a failure to follow the "cultural syntax" of the language of the community, different universes of reference.[7]

Transitivity is a concept that, for me, proves useful for understanding how miscommunication and conflict might occur in a community. The concept of transitivity is at the center of Michael Halliday's functional theory of language (1985). Briefly, Halliday views language as a system of choices. He recognizes three metafunctions of language—ideational, interpersonal, and textual—operating simultaneously through language structure. Theoretically, various configurations of these metafunctions reflect the world views of speakers/writers. Transitivity, in particular, has to do with the ideational function of language, the function of language as a means of representation. It is a way of thinking about how participants, processes, and circumstances relate to one another within language structures. If different language users are configuring different patterns of relationships, it is perhaps an indication of different world views in effect. It is also perhaps an indication that miscommunications might be forthcoming.

The conflict between David and me, barely masked by his oral text, perhaps had something to do with the configuration of, in particular, process relationships. Halliday has defined various types of processes that function within clauses such as material, mental, relational, existential, behavioral, and verbal. The names of these processes capture, to a degree, how language users define themselves or their subjects of consideration in relationship to other participants or circumstances. It seemed to me that David foregrounded the mental process in this text and others: the processes that have to do with feeling, sensing, and perceiving. I thought back to fragments of conversations with Matt: "This is how I feel about the history of Colonial America. . . ." I thought of Julie's words: "I know this description is overexaggerated, but I feel sentimental about it. . . ." In representing their experience of the world, my students frequently chose to use mental processes: they felt certain ways about their topics, they positioned themselves as subjects, as sensers, in relation to their topics.

I finally realized that I had valued certain *transitivity* patterns in their written work over others, certain patterns of representing self in relationship to others. I finally had to reckon with the truth that, as the evaluator of David's written texts as well as of my other students' written texts in an academic setting, I had valued certain ways of knowing over other ways of knowing.

Now this is a fairly ironic state of affairs. In an effort to create community, I had certainly valued mental processes in oral texts emerging in classroom discussions. In order to avoid the "high-sounding voice of expertise," I had valued students' accounts of their own experiences and feelings, especially those that spoke to their engagements in the processes of schooling. Yet, taking my cue from the conventions of the various discourse communities we had researched, I had valued other processes over Halliday's mental processes in students' written work. Despite the emphasis on conversation and community in our course, despite all the talk about the aim of emancipatory pedagogy and constructing meanings together, despite all the discussions of the "implicit manipulativeness of classroom life"[8] in the hopes of eradicating it, the valued product of this classroom community, like the academic community at large, was a product stripped of the emotive, a product restricted to certain ways of knowing about the world. Although the conventions of our own community had allowed for the expression of feeling and the development of communal relationships in the oral texts of the classroom, the transformation of such expression to the written text had been, to a degree, censored. If the conventions of the discourse community disallowed personal knowledge to surface in a piece of scholarship, our community disallowed it as well.

This is perhaps why Julie, Matt, and David opposed the social obligations of community building in their various ways. Perhaps they understood the contradictions between the oral texts and written texts that were being composed in our community. Julie resisted in her contributions to the oral texts that were in process of formation: as she perceived herself in relation to others, she concluded that the community could not or would not understand experiences of her own that were markedly different from their own. Her classmates' inability to understand earned them her contempt. She became hostile and uncompromising. Matt resisted in the making of the written text: he resisted decorum and convention by choosing to use taboo words to color his texts and by choosing to emphasize extremely conservative viewpoints in a community and a peer group that were very obviously striving for liberal, emancipatory goals. David simply opted out of an evaluation process that he believed was contradictory to the stated emancipatory goals of the course. He chose not to submit his feelings to evaluation.

The contradiction between my expectations for language use in the oral and in the written text of the community has forced me to reconsider my standards for what may constitute "evidence" in the texts of my students, both written and spoken. Although students must come to terms with the discursive practices of the various intellectual communities across the university, the intellectual communities that understand language as a social, creative phenomenon must come to terms with different ways of knowing. The old notion of the modes of writing dies a slow death in the English Language and Literature community, as slow as the dichotomy between objective and subjective evidence in the disciplines and professions at large. The validity of the personal narrative, and of the foregrounding of the expressive, conative uses of language, must be reckoned with—reckoned with necessarily by those who wish to keep theory and practice consistent, those who wish conversations in classrooms both to nourish the formation of community and to affect the ways writers behave in literate communities.

This is not to say that David, Julie, and Matt don't have something yet to learn about the concept of negotiating meaning and about the expectations of language use in various academic and real-world communities. Language functions as exchange between human beings as well as representation: the interpersonal function of language is also mapped onto language structure. Julie chooses to structure her messages as either commands or offers, statements or questions. She sends signals to her audience about probability, obligation, and inclination. Thus she positions herself in relation to those who seek to interpret her texts, written and oral. In view of the adverse reaction of the class to her oral texts, it would seem that she frequently miscalculated the consequences of her choices.

In thinking about how she might enrich the oral text of the community with accounts of her own experience, Julie might do well to understand the notion of "saving face" in social encounters. Erving Goffman suggests that the main principle of ritual conversational order is not justice, but face-work: the diplomacy and courtesy tactics participants are called upon to use in order to save the face and feelings of others present in an interaction (1967,10,44). Perhaps it might also be useful to consider the possibility that without allowing other conversational participants to save face, there is no justice.[9] Julie might think about the fact that the personal feeling she finds appropriate for her written text is also the underlying component of the spoken text of the classroom and, in order for her to expect others to be sensitive to her feelings, she must also be sensitive to theirs in the give and take of classroom dialogue. There is also a lesson here for Matt and me: perhaps the avoidance process[10] that we engaged in could itself have been avoided if we had both recognized that the social theorist's concept of "negotiating meaning" presupposes a degree of conflict as normal in a language community. We might have then chosen a more fruitful type of diplomacy without surrendering deeply held convictions.

Most important, however, I believe that Julie, Matt, and especially David would do well to consider a distinction that Michael Polanyi makes between "personal knowledge" and "subjective" states (1962). A subjective state is one in which a knower merely endures feelings: the knower is subject to his or her own condition. In a subjective state, a knower is uncommitted to sharing feelings in an effort to transcend his or her condition. Personal knowledge, on the other hand, is neither subjective nor objective. It is committed, passionate, active knowing that is open to transformation through community with others. It presupposes that previously acquired meanings will be modified through present uses. In the negotiation of meaning, conflict is to be expected; yet, opting out is not an option. In the context of the emancipatory classroom, personal knowledge entails intentional effort to strive for transcendence of subjective states and for a common language with which to reach for our ultimate liberation.

David, Matt, and Julie still have something to learn about the concept of negotiating meaning and about expectations of language use in various communities, but so do I. Teachers and students (like Gramsci's ordinary people: philosophers in their own right) who research the rhetorical strategies of the various academic communities might do well to focus on the concept of resistance in communities. Questions that will be thematicized in my composition course next semester include these: What does critical thinking mean in a community that owes its existence to the fact that it values certain unique configurations of meaning-making? Is the ability to speak and write critically valued in all communities? Or is it actually risky business? Does resistance to conventions and rules have a place in reading and writing "successfully"? What is (or should be) the relationship of the individual to the community? The presuppositions underlying these concerns are informed by a more realistic notion of language communities and by the notion of "learning as conversation." Becoming a fully participating member of a discourse community means successfully learning the language of the community. It means learning appropriate ways of doing, speaking, and writing. But it finally must also mean learning to negotiate the limitations of a community's guidelines and rules, learning to push at the contours of certain configurations of meaning. So it must also take into account the fact that conflict, as Bakhtin noted, is constitutive of the very dynamics of a living discourse.

In the classroom, a focus on conflict legitimizes—to an extent—the various responses students may have toward even liberatory pedagogies. It also provides the opportunity for teachers to rechannel individual student reaction that might not always be the most efficient response to the challenge of critical thinking. At the same time, as helpful as the distinction between oppositional and resistant behavior may be, I intend to problematize the simple dichotomizing of these reactions in my students. Although it may be true that not all oppositional behavior has radical significance (Giroux, 1981,101), I would suggest that conflict is more complex than the dichotomy allows. One might contest by pointing out that these three students engaged in resistant behavior that was misinterpreted as oppositional. Yet it seems to me that Julie, Matt, and David, as well as the rest of the community, had varying, shifting degrees of awareness of the significance of their own behaviors.

Just as the meaning of language changes with situation, the meaning of conflict changes with situation. Whether or not any behavior can be viewed as oppositional or resistant depends not only on all actors involved and the conditions under which actions are produced but also on how the actions are interpreted by others. The multi-accentuality[11] of words guarantees that the significance of conflict will change with situation. For example, Julie's reactions may be viewed as alternately oppositional or resistant, both for herself and for others. Opting out of the community at various points during the semester may have been unfruitful for her own development as a writer; at the same time, others in the community interpreted and counterreacted to her reactions in various ways. Jennifer, the young woman in Julie's peer group, was initially frustrated by Julie's oppositional behavior. She wrote about Julie frequently in her journal, making astute observations about the role of the individual in the community. Her own interactional moves were influenced by what she learned from Julie. Thus, Julie's oppositional behavior took on radical significance for Jennifer. Later in the semester, Julie and Jennifer developed a friendly working relationship as together they researched the language practices of the Social Science community. Jennifer was instrumental in transforming Julie's oppositional behavior to resistant behavior as together they critiqued the conventions of discourse in that field, the field they both anticipated joining at the university. In short, their actions took on shifting degrees of significance as their discourses intersected at different points during the semester-long conversation. Far from neutralizing radical behavior, community made it possible. As Maxine Greene emphasizes, "praxis cannot be viewed as the project of any one single individual" (1978, 99).

The meaning of all these observations to me is this: If I conceptualized David and Julie and Matt as marginalized students in my classroom, I intend to reconceptualize them and students like them at the center of the text of the community. Julie's reactions, like David's and Matt's, are part of the whole text of the community—a complex conversation that, like ordinary conversation, includes conflict as well as cooperation as part of its very ordinary dynamics. As in interpersonal relations, the classroom community sometimes breaks down in the face of seemingly disparate discourses that perhaps cannot be negotiated. The conversation of the composition community is bound up in larger discourses—for instance, the emerging discourse that debates different ways of knowing and meaning. One effect of the converging of different discourses is contradiction. These contradictions—inherent in any conversation as participants seek to orient themselves as individuals within wider social discourses—results (quite normally) in conflict that can be variously or simultaneously interpreted as opposition or resistance depending on the positions of participants within the shifting patterns of discourse itself. Thus, the metaphor "learning as conversation" presupposes conflict as individuals—both teachers and students—struggle to make sense of a polysemic world. It must also depend on the commitment of individuals, a commitment to add to human conversations that foreground ethical existences and emancipatory ends.

Notes

[1] The course was initially developed by Patricia Stock, our mentor at the University of Michigan, who invited us to both share and shape her original course design. The number of teacher-researchers has varied over the two years from four to nine. I myself have been a teacher-researcher of the course throughout the two years.

The view of literacy as social, functional, and generative, informing our thinking, is one that has been shaped through conversations especially with Jay Robinson.

[2] I wish to thank Jay Robinson for suggesting the name "conversation-centered" to describe the dynamics of a classroom in which both students and teachers contribute experience and talents to the community in class discussion. Shared understanding and common language are the goals in a classroom where all participants contribute, avoiding the type of discourse imbalances often made evident in transcriptions of earlier classroom discourse analysts. For example, in data collected by Britton to show how students shape one another's discourse, the voice of the teacher is often markedly absent. In the data collected by Bellack, on the other hand, the voice of the teacher predominantly figures while initiating, responding to, and evaluating student contributions.

[3] Examples of early research are well known: Britton (1969); Barnes (1976 and et al., 1969); Bellack et al. (1966); Flanders (1970); Mehan (1979); Sinclair and Coulthard (1975).

[4] The scholars I particularly have in mind are: Austin (1977); Searle (1979, 1983); Grice (1975, 1978); Leech (1980, 1983); Goffman (1967, 1981); J.B. White (1983); Gadamer (1975, 1976).

[5] Vygotsky defines "zone of proximal development" as "the distance between the actual developmental level as determined by independent problem solving and the level of potential development as determined through problem solving under adult guidance or in collaboration with more capable peers" (1978,89). In other words, good learning takes place in advance of level of development. For Vygotsky, as for most educators, learning in the classroom is, at least explicitly, a child process only. A teacher-researcher in a conversation-centered classroom, however, sees the learning process as shared by both students and teachers.

[6] Anne Ruggles Gere presents the notion of "formative evaluation" to refer to the type of evaluation that occurs during the writing process between students commenting on one another's work and that affects the quality of the final product. This type of evaluation is contrasted to "summative" evaluation, which assigns a value to the final product.

In a discussion of the "The Pedagogy of Collaboration" at the 1987 Conference on College Composition and Communication, Andrea Lunsford noted that assignment design in a collaborative-based course should provide for both peer and self-evaluation of writing.

[7]Discussions of these perspectives on miscommunication can be found in H. P. Grice (1975, 1978); J. B. White (1983); Geoffrey Leech (1980, 1983).

[8]In a discussion about creating the opportunity for sympathetic dialogue with students, Maxine Greene suggests discussing the "implicit manipulativeness of classroom life" with them (1978, 106).

[9]My thanks to James D. Winkelmann for suggesting this rather enlightening turn of Goffman's statement in a conversation we had about "facework."

[10]Goffman describes the avoidance process as a basic kind of face-work in which participants prevent threats to their face by avoiding contact in which threats will surely occur. He notes that go-betweens are often used for these "delicate" transactions (1967, 15).

[11]Volosinov posits the notion of the multi-accentuality of words to explain the social accenting of words in discourse. Words do not have one meaning; rather, they are arenas of struggle in which certain meanings foreclose others. For a concise explanation, see Threadgold et al. (1986, 30). For a fuller discussion, see also Clark and Holquist (1984).

Part Three

Literacy and Learning

The two essays in this section, each by itself long enough to test a normal reader's endurance, carry on conversations with researchers as well as with teachers. And in the frequent and extended quotations that precede, follow, and are embedded in the lines of exposition and argument that I and then we offer in the essays, they carry on conversations with texts that Patricia Stock and I were having together with other colleagues. The essays owe much to many people in the University of Michigan who have found time to talk with us about issues that range in their implications from classrooms to the wider worlds we inhabit separately. Our thanks for conversations are especially due to a group of faculty who met for several years, calling themselves the English Composition Board Advisory Committee: Rudolph Arnheim (Psychology and Art History), Richard Bailey (English), Loren Barritt (Education), Alton Becker (Linguistics), Elizabeth Douvain (Psychology), Thomas Dunn (Chemistry), Daniel Fader (English), Bernard Galler (Mathematics and Computer Science), Wilbert McKeachie (Psychology), Jack Meiland (Philosophy), Barbra Morris (English Composition Board), Patricia Stock (English Composition Board and English), Thomas Toon (English and Linguistics), Bernard Van't Hul (English), and James Boyd White (Law) were the more enduring members of the group.

Special thanks to David Bloome, now of the University of Massachusetts, for organizing two conferences that brought to the University of Michigan people of diverse perspectives to speak in diverse voices in conversations about literacy and learning. Both essays in this section began as contributions to those conversations; offering them there in that context gave us a chance to learn how others as unlike us as cognitive psychologists would react to what we thought we had to say to them.

The first essay offers a model for a way of characterizing the notion "text" that might make it possible to say something, perhaps sensible, about reading and writing (like speaking and listening) as social activities, not as isolated activities but as group work. Both essays try to deepen the notion of literacy as social activity as that notion is presented earlier in this book, and both treat more explicitly the question of what learning is when the focus is upon an individual not as an isolated but as a social being. Both essays too ask and try to answer questions about pedagogy: how it is and should be conceived; what its relations are to theories of literacy and theories of learning; and what its relations are to social, political, and ethical conceptions of schooling and of society.

The essay titled "Literacy as Conversation," in which I join Patricia L. Stock as coauthor, attempts a convergence of theories drawn mainly from sociolinguistics and rhetoric to account for literacy development among students working together to complete a remedial writing course. Its principal arguments are two: that discourse analysis, richly conceived, is a powerful means for studying students' language learning, and that teacher-researchers are crucially positioned to study and account for literacy learning and learning in general when these two processes are conceived as socially situated engagements with others and with the world. The essay is finally intended to open up and open out conversations about classroom learning by treating it as crucially involving the kinds of conversations and other social interactions that are common to classrooms and to other settings in the world. The essay serves, we hope, as an illustration of what it also argues for: the power of interdisciplinary inquiry and the inevitability of mixed genres as means for looking into something as complex as human learning.

7

Literacy in Society: Readers and Writers in the Worlds of Discourse

Prologue

Writing is distinct from most other forms of communication in that its basic skills—putting words into a conventional material form and being able to read them—do not come necessarily as parts of the basic process of growing up in a society. A spoken language, in terms of an ability both to speak and to understand, comes as part of the normal process of growing up in a particular society, unless there are some individual physical disabilities. Writing, by contrast, has been from the beginning a systematic skill that has to be taught and learned. Thus the introduction of writing, and all the subsequent stages of its development, are intrinsically new forms of social relationship. There has been great variation in making these skills available, and this has had major effects on the relationships embodied in writing in diverse historical and cultural conditions.

RAYMOND WILLIAMS

When I first began to learn to read, during the late years of the Great Depression, the process appeared neither complex nor difficult: the text was easy to locate—it was right there on the page in black print. Decoding the text seemed perfectly straightforward—a matter of matching sounds to letters until several came together to form a recognizable whole, an echo of what had been heard from the lips of parents and teachers. And interpretation was quite easy: Most stories had obvious morals for middle-class children, and those that didn't (and even many that did) had a moral or two printed at the end.

133

When I first learned to read critically, as a literature student at Berkeley during the late years of the Korean war, the process was a bit more—but only a bit more—complex and difficult. The text was still there, tangible and unchanging; and since our critical skills were honed on lyric poetry, it still made sense to think of letters as associated with sounds. Though interpretation was more problematic, because taste and apprenticeship to its dictates were involved, the text was still authoritative—it held its own meanings—and any context necessary to interpretation could be assumed to be bounded by the text's initial capital letter and its final period. And when the text was not authority enough for the apprentice critical reader, the critic-teacher was. His (and I use the pronoun deliberately) reading could be presumed at least to approximate the single meaning sometimes hidden in the authoritative text.

How things have changed since the 1930s, since the 1950s. Reading and writing—activities at the root of the more complex set of human developments comprehended by the term literacy, activities that are seen alike by professional educators and by the lay public as the most basic of the basics old and new—are now being seen, at least by professionals, as the complex phenomena that they really are. As professionals, our research agendas become not only ever more lengthy but also ever more difficult because, when our research is into literacy, our very topic becomes problematic.

Take reading, for example, as currently conceived. Reading is not, as was assumed in my day, a matter of a single reader decoding graphic symbols and then verbal cues to derive a determinable meaning from a fixed text. Reading is not a reactive process but an interactive one in which a reader brings at least as much to a text as the text offers. Readers are less well described as decoders than they are as co-creators of texts, since they are impelled by a need to find consistency and pattern in what they are comprehending, in which process they draw upon their own attitudes and feelings, their own knowledge of other texts and of the world, in order to construct satisfying wholes. Nor is reading a cumulative inductive process in which bits of information are linked together to form a single, unifying interpretive hypothesis once the text has been read through. Rather and crucially, reading involves prediction, since it proceeds through the formulation of expectations about where the text is going, then through expansion, modification, or negation of the expectations formulated. And readings are never final or texts ever fixed. Rereadings produce not necessarily more accurate, but certainly new readings—different interpretations, since human beings change between readings; different interpretations, since readings can be modified in group discussions that negotiate the meaning of a text both for the group and for the individuals who comprise it.

To take present theories of language and language use seriously is to place ourselves as students of language use in a far more difficult world than most of us have occupied before. When some reader-response theorists assert that texts do not really exist, except as physical objects—that texts are really created by readers—they are only reflecting other trends in twentieth-century philosophy. All philosophers have rejected absolutes, and language philosophers argue that while language is referential, it does not refer to something tangibly real so much as to something rather more like itself, that it is a system of signifiers that signal other signifiers. The more philosophical of literary critics argue that literature refers only to itself, and other certainties go. Walter Ong (1977) finds that a "writer's audience is always a fiction"(74)—something that the writer makes up as she goes along; and Michel Foucault (1979) claims that authors are things society makes up to limit and control discourse. A writer, a text, a reader: these used to be concrete identifiable points for those mapping communication. But the twentieth-century intellectual map cannot be drawn with fixed points; it has only constituents that keep changing shape and relations that keep shifting.

The dominant metaphors for research in our time are metaphors of interaction; they are in almost every domain of serious intellectual inquiry ecological metaphors capturing the notions of system and of systematic, symbiotic interrelationships of organisms. The emergent research focus in our time, when the topic is literacy, reading and writing, or any other human uses of language, is upon individuals and their interactions as participants in social groups—as participants in neighborhood activities or the activities of a classroom, or as members of discourse communities and intellectual communities, which are also, of course, social groups. The impulse behind the development and flourishing of ethnographic description of face-to-face interactions is not finally dissimilar to the impulse that produces reader-response theory, speech-act theory, or certain forms of the so-called new rhetoric: All deal with interaction and with the various contexts in which interactions take place.

It will no longer do, I think, to consider literacy as some abstract, absolute quality attainable through tutelage and the accumulation of knowledge and experience. It will no longer do to think of reading as a solitary act in which a mainly passive reader responds to cues in a text to find meaning. It will no longer do to think of writing as a mechanical manipulation of grammatical codes and formal structures leading to the production of perfect or perfectible texts. Reading and writing are not unitary skills nor are they reducible to sets of component skills falling neatly under discrete categories (linguistic, cognitive); rather, they are complex human activities taking place in complex human relationships.

These ideas are revolutionary in the field of pedagogy, we must recognize, just as they have been in the more abstruse domains of philosophical speculation, and just as they should be in the more conservative domains of academic inquiry and research.

On the occasion when the ideas published here were originally presented[1], I was asked to address two main questions: What, from my perspective as a humanist—a linguist trained also in literature, a student of writing and its teaching—is it important to know and say about literacy and especially about "print literacy"? And second, what would I recommend as an appropriate research agenda for other students of literacy, especially those interested in the functions of language in schooling? I will deal first with some notions of literacy and then make suggestions about research.

The Dimensions of Literacy

> The place of language in the cultural life of each social group is inter-dependent with the habits and values of behaving shared among members of that group (Heath, 1983, 11).

The range of meanings attaching themselves to the term *literacy* in our culture and to the related terms *literate* and *illiterate* is at once an interesting semantic phenomenon and a barrier to clear thinking about the topic. In some of its uses, literacy is equatable with the terms *education* or *being educated,* especially in socially valued ways, as when we speak of a colleague whom we admire as "highly literate," by which we seem to mean well read in respected texts and able to discourse about them articulately. Such uses of the term literacy seem to offer tacit justification for what, when examined from a distance, seem to be rather questionable educational arrangements: for example, the assignment of sole responsibility for teaching literacy to English departments in high schools and colleges or the assumption that literacy is taught in those departments, even though teachers in them most often teach only literature.

Related meanings for the term *literacy* may be found in the increasing usage of compound terms like *computer literacy, scientific literacy, media literacy, mathematical literacy,* even—may the good Lord help us—*musical literacy,* in which literacy seems to mean either being knowledgeable about or adept in some domain, and, in some cases, being able to think critically about issues in that domain. Thus the report of the Commission on the Humanities (1980) asserted that:

> Our citizens need to become literate in a multiple sense. We all need to understand the characteristics of scientific inquiry and the reper-cussions of scientific research. We must all learn something about the

use of the media and of new technologies for storing, transmitting, and expanding knowledge. Without this sort of literacy, our society as a whole will be less able to apply science and technology to humanistic needs, less able to measure the human effects of scientific achievements, less able to judge the information we produce and receive (18–19).

Two significant lessons can be drawn from the range of usages I have discussed: Something called literacy permeates the culture we inhabit—in fact, to a large extent constitutes that culture; and second, whatever literacy is, our culture values it, and highly. The term *literate* is awarded in our culture as a badge of honor, but *illiterate* stigmatizes, and, in fact, is often applied to persons who know perfectly well how to read and write for perfectly useful personal and social purposes.

It is tempting to say, especially when our concern is language and schooling, that we must restrict the term *literacy* to its involvements with language in print, to discussion only of the activities of writing and reading scripted and printed material, and for certain purposes we probably should. But doing so, if the broader contexts of human interactions with texts are ignored, invites a reductive approach to literacy and its uses, a focus upon code and text that has bedeviled the teaching of reading and writing, the measurement of their acquisition, and the study of both. It is also tempting to assert that we must, at least for purposes of study and description, treat *literate* and *illiterate* as quasi-technical terms and strip them of their laudatory and pejorative overtones. But doing so will result in inadequacy, if our aim is to describe accurately the place and functions of literacy in society; doing so is unrealistic if our aim is to prepare students for a place in the society they will inhabit as adults. We must not lose sight of two well-established findings: The possession of fully functional literacy, a term whose meanings will be explored later, correlates with economic and social success in our culture, in spite of the fact that exceptions can be found; the terms *literate* and *illiterate* are reflective of how our society views and values people and how people in our society value themselves. Feelings and attitudes constitute a significant dimension of the contexts of literacy and cannot be ignored.

Restrictive definitions of literacy, fascination with the codes and forms of written communication, and failure to see reading and writing as interactive processes involving individuals and texts in context have all led to educational practices that have disadvantaged many students and left many ill-equipped as users of written language in academic and workaday settings.

Social historians and critics of the development and role of formal schooling in industrialized nations have increasingly reexamined the content and methods of teaching and learning communication skills.

Bourdieu (1973) and Graff (1978) point out that formal education systems tend to teach and promote the learning of only the barest of rudimentary skills for communicating. Proper spelling and grammar, varied vocabulary, and topic-sentenced paragraphs are not sufficient to make cohesive intelligent whole narratives or expositions. Schools teach and test to insure that students "absorb the automatic response and rule-of-thumb techniques," but neither teaching nor testing touches "the higher, active sense ... [necessary to] set up an interchange between ideas, needs, and external reality" (Calhoun, 1970, 130–31). Through mechanistic linguistic tasks, such as spelling tests and grammar drills, schools claim to impart communication skills. Yet, the academic discourse forms which lie at the heart of success in the higher levels of schooling—oral and written extended prose, sequenced explanations, and logical arguments—[rarely] receive explicit identification and discussion (Heath & Branscombe, 1985, 3–4).

Similar findings issue from other more recent reports on school practices (see, e.g., Goodlad, 1984, chaps. 5, 7).

To study literacy and its uses is to commit oneself to the study of contexts and relations. Literacy exists only as human activity in context, and our job as students of literacy is to decide which activities and which contexts are worth studying and what relations we must seek to establish between literacy, language, learning, schooling, and life both before and after schooling.

Worlds in the Universe of Discourse

If the critic wishes to produce new and subtle readings, he is at perfect liberty to entertain himself in this way, but he should not do so in the belief that he is thereby making important contributions to the study of literature. An understanding of literature, both as an institution and an activity, involves an understanding of the conventions and operations which enable works to be written and read (Culler, 1981, 124).

It is genuinely difficult for someone who has spent a working life with print, and has had access, through it, to writing in societies quite unlike his or her own, to take seriously the idea that the conditions the reader shares with those available writers, through the common property of the texts, are socially specific conditions, which cannot be simply read back as the central truths of all active writing and reading (Williams, 1980, 4).

It is common in the literature on the acquisition and development of literacy to find written language and writing described as depersonalized and decontextualized when compared to spoken language and speaking. Even a scholar so sensitive to context as Shirley Brice Heath used the terms to describe contrasts between speech and writing and degrees of familiarity among writers and readers of letters:

> Writing to Shannon had bridged the highly contextualized letters of the upperclassmen [who attend the same school as their correspondents] and the more decontextualized, nonpersonalized letters to Heath and ultimately the standard classroom assignments of interpretive essays (Heath & Branscombe, 1985, 22).

When compared to the functions of speech in face-to-face interactions, the functions of writing are sometimes less personal, though not inevitably so. Some kinds of writing function to connect a writer with an audience of unknown others, but other kinds of writing—love letters, for example, or letters of condolence, or notes of reminder—presume far more personal relations and rely more heavily upon personally shared contexts between writer and reader than even those that obtain in face-to-face interchanges, especially those among speakers and hearers who do not know one another well. But even in the instances where it makes sense to talk of writing as depersonalized—when, for example, a writer and his or her readers do not know one another, or share contiguous geographical space (or ever intend to)—it is still misleading to think of written texts (or written language) as decontextualized, especially when that term is used by scholars less cautious than Heath to name an absolute, invariant quality of written language.

All texts exist in context. And while it is quite obvious that some written texts, like love letters, depend for their meaning upon shared contexts built through personal relationships, it is less obvious that all texts depend for their meaning either upon shared contexts or shared contextualization. Without sharing, there can be no communication between a reader and a writer. The problem for us professionals in understanding this notion lies in the appearance of texts—especially printed ones—and in our unconscious behavior as professionals who are literate. There is an appearance of stability in printed texts, and because they are objects, neatly packaged into what always appear as neatly bounded wholes, we are tempted to think that texts contain all context necessary for their interpretation. And because we are professionals like those pointed to by Williams, who have spent a working lifetime with print, gaining access through printed texts to societies unlike our own, we have sometimes been led to think—because of the stable appearance of texts and our uses of reading—that texts are all we need: that we can understand societies unlike our own as would citizens of those unlike societies.

I want to argue in this and the following section that written texts are always richly and complexly contextualized. Some written texts—love letters, for example, or notes of reminder—are contextualized in the same ways as intimate conversations are; other written texts—essays, for example, or lab reports—are otherwise contextualized. But all texts have contexts; and communication, if it is to be successful, requires on the part of writer and reader either the pre-existence or the construction of shared contexts. I will also argue, in this and following sections, that learning to write and learning to read are not movements from personal, contextualized uses of language to depersonalized, decontextualized ones but rather movements from one set of contexts to other sets of contexts. Writing and reading, like speaking and listening, are social acts: literature, Culler tells us, is both an institution and an activity.

To begin the argument, I will ask and then sketchily answer this question: What besides the code, the language used by the writer of the text, does a reader need to know in order to read a text successfully—to comprehend or construct a reading that is reasonably consistent with meanings constructed by other readers of the text and the meanings intended by the writer? Figures 7–1 through 7–3 sketch the categories of requisite knowledge that I will treat.

THE DOMAIN OF TEXT Simple models describing writing and reading as communicative activities place heavy emphasis on code as the means of contact between writer and reader, and code is taken essentially as a signaling system; in the simplest models, *code* and *text* are taken as essentially the same thing. In the model of figure 7–1, the notion of text is represented by the circle and its five elements: code, writer-in-text, reader-in-text, text-as-argument, and text-as-structured-language. All five are to be taken both as textual elements and as constructs on the part of a reader. The status of the elements is probably best described as a response to these questions: What must a reader minimally perceive and construct in order to know that what s/he is reading is a text and not some random gathering of language? What must a reader perceive and construct to know that a reading for meaning is appropriate?

The term *code* is familiar, but it is used here in something other than its customary sense. *Code* is not a signaling system capable of conveying meaning; rather it is a mode of contact capable of being invested with meaning by a writer and a reader. The terms *writer-in-text* and *reader-in-text* are adaptations from various sources: text grammar, semiotics, the less easily classified work of Walter Ong. As used here the terms refer to text functions in the sense that they can almost always be connected with code and its structured use or with isolable characteristics in the argument; they are reader constructs in the sense that they are created by a reader to help guide both his or her sense that the text coheres and his or her interpretation of the text. *Writer-in-text* is similar to the familiar notion of *persona* and is an element of what is perceived and constructed as stance or style; *reader-in-text* is perceived and constructed as a set of instructions for response: it is also an element of style.

The term *argument*, in *text-as-argument*, is used not in its current meaning but in one of its more common earlier meanings: the

FIGURE 7–1   THE NOTION OF TEXT AND ITS ELEMENTS

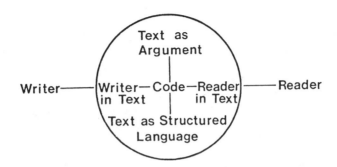

subject matter of discussion or discourse in speech or writing; theme, or subject. The term refers to a reader's perception that a text is about something—that its messages cohere and are intentionally organized into a unified and potentially meaningful whole. The term *text-as-structured-language* refers both to formal aspects of organization and to the various links and connections that are described by linguists as grammatical and semantic elements of cohesion, as that term is used, for example, by Halliday and Hasan (1976).

Taken together, these terms are a specification of interconnected elements that comprise the notion *text*. They refer, and their presence can be illustrated by reference, to features of language and thought in a bounded stretch of written language; but they also refer to a reader's responses to constructs formed by a reader interacting with a text, bringing knowledge and experience to bear in the task of reading it. The claims made here are these: that when a reader perceives that a text is present and thus that interpretation is possible, s/he sees in the text evidence of an author's control (writer-in-text), suggestions for how to respond to the text (reader-in-text), the presence of cohesive devices (text-as-structured-language), and the presence of propositions and assertions that are at least potentially connectable and thus meaningful (text-as-argument). These are reader percepts and constructs as are several other features customarily taken to be purely textual features: meaningfulness, unity, coherence, organization, for example. In talking about texts and the reading of texts, it is quite impossible to separate reader responses from the linguistic "facts" of a text and equally impossible to separate language from thought. A reader's judgment that a text is unified, coherent, well organized, is just that—a judgment; and it is as much a reaction to text-as-argument, to the perception that a text is about some one meaningful thing, as it is a reaction to the formal features of the text.

And what does a reader bring to this point of judgment? At least those categories of knowledge and experience named in the next concentric circle drawn in figure 7–2.

TEXT IN THE DOMAINS OF THOUGHT AND FORM   How does a reader perceive that an argument is present in a stretch of written language? It is possible, of course, to analyze a text, identify and isolate its propositions and assertions, and then describe their connections with reference to some system of inference and entailment. In order to do so, however, it is necessary to impose upon a text some abstract scheme, and then to extract from the text those features that seem to fit it. To perform such operations, in order to be able to claim that arguments are logical structures and that readers perceive them as such, relying when they do so upon general or specific cognitive capacities, it is necessary to make another abstraction: The structure must be abstracted not only from the text and the verbal context the text provides, but also from the context of a real reader interacting with a text for some purpose in some particular community of writers and readers. The counterclaim made here (see figure 7–2) is rather that readers perceive the presence of an argument in a text when they find similarities to other arguments they have read, or heard, and have remembered, arguments that were offered in some likewise remembered domain of inquiry or representation.

Arguments are instances of discourse in some clearly or ill-defined *field*; they are instances of discourse that are recognized as arguments because they employ some clearly or ill-defined *mode* of inquiry or representation. The argument of "Rose White, Rose Red" is recognizable and potentially interpretable because it, like other fairy tales, is narrative employing agents and events that are fanciful and implausible; the text you are now reading is inter-

FIGURE 7–2.   TEXT IN CONTEXT: THE NOTIONS OF THOUGHT AND FORM

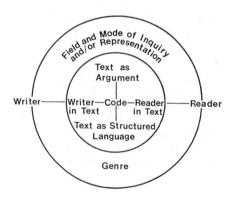

pretable because it, like other essays, shapes speculative assertions into informal arguments, reminds its readers of pertinent arguments offered in commonly read texts, and tries to push for synthesis of thoughts and systems of inquiry not before connected. Arguments, in short, exist in history—in a reader's memory of other arguments, in a reader's knowledge of human domains and modes of inquiry and representation. Logic, too, is a matter of history.

Text-as-argument is a term in the domain of thought but not in the domain claimed by cognitive psychologists. Text-as-structured-language, obviously a term in the domain claimed by linguists, reaches past that domain to other ways of characterizing the human capacity to create and recognize form. A text is perceived as structured language, as organized, in part because of its linguistic features of cohesion but also because it is recognized as a text of some one kind—as an instance or realization of a genre: as a letter, or an essay, or a technical report, or a sonnet, or a recipe for baking a cake. Recognition of form is in part a matter of responding to linguistic signals, to features of code; but it is in larger part also a matter of memory, of seeing in a presented instance of organized language a resemblance to other instances similarly organized, a matter of having formed something like a gestalt that allows one to find resemblances in otherwise nonrelatable presentations of texts. A reader's sense of form, as referred to by the term *genre*, operates in concert with that reader's sense of field and mode of inquiry to create the notion that a meaningful text has been offered; both operate in concert to help a reader know what to do with a text, to guide, to the extent they can be guided, that reader's interpretations. A single text comes into existence, for an individual reader or an individual writer, in the context of similar texts, prior in history and stored in memory.

TEXT, THOUGHT, AND FORM IN THE DOMAINS OF KNOWLEDGE AND DISCOURSE   Finally, in the outermost circle of figure 7–3, which completes the diagram, are placed two notions: both the notion of "accumulated human knowledge and imagination" (*the universe of discovered and represented meanings*) and the notion of "functional forms of human expression" (*the universe of discourse*).

An argument is recognized as such and gains value, in a reader's eyes and mind, as it fits into one or another field or mode of inquiry; and that field or mode is valued and validated as it fits into or adds to or modifies those meanings that constitute human knowledge.

Peter L. Berger and Thomas Luckmann put a similar point this way:

What is taken for granted as knowledge in [a] society comes to be co-extensive with the knowable, or at any rate provides the frame-work

FIGURE 7–3.   TEXT IN CONTEXT: THE NOTIONS OF KNOWLEDGE AND DISCOURSE

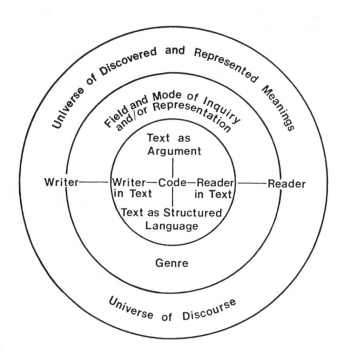

within which anything not yet known will come to be known in the future. This is the knowledge that is learned in the course of socialization and that mediates the internalization within individual consciousness of the objectivated structures of the social world (66).

Berger and Luckmann are talking here about the construction of knowledge about everyday reality through interactive, intersubjective, social processes. But similar processes are involved in the construction of knowledge and representation as these are presumed to be stored in texts. All knowledge, or at least that which is judged to have human value, is socially constructed, through material and describable social mechanisms.

Similarly, a text is recognized as an instance of some one genre, e.g., sonnet, and thus gains value as one contribution to human expression in that world of human discourse called "poetry," which world along with all others so far created and discovered constitute the universe of discourse. A sense of what is or may be known and a sense of form make thought and language meaningful for readers and for writers, because they enable them to find, validate, and make use of meanings: to act, in short, as human beings, as social beings, in communities made possible and, in fact, constituted by language written down and read. Community is established not merely through a code, not merely through the existence of texts as organized language, but through the common understandings, intuitions, experiences, and memories that readers and writers bring to the negotiations we call reading and writing.

And what of the two terms so far not described—writer and reader? Each of us, whether a 13-year-old ninth grader in Ms. Callisher's remedial reading class or an English professor in an elite university, finds existence in a universe bounded by language and made interpretable only through language, made manageable only through interchange of meanings where language is the coin of exchange.

Readers and writers are also human beings, of course, and as such have their own particular and unique material existences in the world as well as their own individual and unique complexes of impulses and intentions. But the terms *reader* and *writer* do not name solitary physical and psychic existences but rather social roles, for the terms have meaning only in reference to interchanges within the social institutions of written language.

In the next section, I want to make more explicit three arguments that have already been suggested: (a) that the communities formed by writers and readers within the universes of knowledge and discourse are essentially social in their character (to argue otherwise is to misunderstand the functions and importance of written language and literacy in modern societies); (b) that the links formed by written language in creation of these communities are in some ways the same kind and fully as functional as those formed in face-to-face interaction in communities created through speech; and (c) that education is usefully thought of as a movement from community to community, better thought of in this way than as a quasi-maturational process, as something akin to growing taller or developing secondary sexual characteristics.

Interpretive Communities and How to Join Them

Student writers must, however, learn for written communication—just as they have learned for oral language—that communication is negotiation. When direct response is not possible through a return letter, the writer must play the role of writer *and* reader, anticipating and hypothesizing the kinds of information the reader will bring to the text and the questions which, therefore, the writer must explicitly answer. This social interaction is similar to the process through which children acquiring oral language move as they learn to handle discourse topics—to adjust, clarify, expand, or abandon their efforts to communicate with listeners. Crisis in communication is a natural part of this learning process; at some point in learning to write, students must have the experience of an audience which responds, "I don't understand you. What do you mean?" (Heath & Branscombe, 1985, 26).

One should stress that the whole institution of literary education depends upon the assumption . . . that one can learn to become a more competent reader and that therefore there is something (a series of techniques and procedures) to be learned. We do not judge students simply on what they know about a given work; we presume to evaluate their skill and progress as readers, and that presumption ought to indicate our confidence in the existence of public and generalizable operations of reading (Culler 1981, 125).

To begin my arguments, I will use concepts identified in figure 7–3 and apply them to a text, Lewis Thomas's essay "The Medusa and the Snail" (1979), as "operations of reading." Then I will ask how such operations might be both learnable and learned. The concepts I will use primarily are those of writer-in-text and reader-in-text.

READERS AND WRITERS AS PARTICIPANTS   Walter Ong (1979), a critic and a cultural historian, claims that "the writer's audience is always a fiction," and is so in two ways: First, "the writer must construct in his imagination, clearly or vaguely, an audience cast in some sort of role—entertainment seekers, reflective sharers of experience . . . inhabitants of a lost and remembered world of pre-pubertal latency (readers of Tolkien's hobbit stories), and so on" (60–61). Second, readers must consent to fictionalize themselves in a way that corresponds to the writer's imaginative construction of their role: "A reader has to play the role in which the author has cast him, which seldom coincides with his role in the rest of actual life" (61). Reader roles are best thought of, I will argue, as essentially social roles, mirroring those of everyday life.

A specialist writing for a general audience undertakes difficult problems of exposition. Because he is a specialist, he has knowledge that his readers do not have, and he cannot presume their interest in his topic. Lewis Thomas (1979), biologist and physician, begins his essay on uniqueness and symbiosis in nature in the following way:

We've never been so self-conscious about our selves as we seem to be these days. The popular magazines are filled with advice on things to do with a self: how to find it, identify it, nurture it, protect it, even, for special-occasion weekends, how to lose it transiently. There are instructive books, best sellers on self-realization, self-help, self-development. Groups of self-respecting people pay large fees for three-day sessions together, learning self-awareness. Self-enlightenment can be taught in college electives.

You'd think, to read about it, that we'd only just now discovered selves. Having long suspected that there was *something alive* in there, running the place, separate from everything else, absolutely individual and independent, we've celebrated by giving it a real name. My self.

It is an interesting word, formed long ago in much more social ambiguity than you'd expect. The original root was *se* or *seu*, simply the pronoun of the third person, and most of the descendant words, except "self" itself, were constructed to allude to other, somehow connected people—"sibs" and "gossips," relatives and close acquaintances, came from *seu*. *Se* was also used to indicate something outside or apart, hence words like "separate," "secret," and "segregate." From an extended root *swedh* it moved into Greek as *ethnos*, meaning people of one's own sort, and *ethos*, meaning the customs of such people. "Ethics" means the behavior of people like one's self, one's own ethnics (1–2).

Thomas's form of address is the inclusive pronoun "we," a form of address that involves and implicates both himself, as writer, and all of us, his readers, in a single perspective on the subject matter he will treat. The role he creates for us is a role identical to his own: Both he and we are to look at things in the world, muse about the implications of observable phenomena, and try to find messages hidden in them. We as his readers are not fictionalized as his pupils, nor is he as our teacher; Thomas as writer does not play the expert, nor are we imagined as lacking expertise in a collaborative search for things and their meanings. Rather, we and our companion who gently guides us are fictionalized as alert to our environment and curious about its meanings. In company with Thomas, "we" have read about "self" in popular magazines and instructive books (even if we have not); he and "we" are implicated alike even in the *naming* of the phenomenon: "Having long suspected that there was *something alive* in there, running the place, separate from everything else, absolutely individual and independent, we've celebrated by giving it a real name. My self."

By including his readers in his musings and assuming their curiosity, by reminding them of things familiar, and by treating difficult concepts in common language (there is "*something alive* in there"), Thomas prepares his readers to play the role *he* is playing as the author of his essay: an observer who tries to find meaning in what he sees—meaning that is personal but also shared, because it applies to all humans. The role Thomas assigns us is a flattering one. We are his colleagues, not his pupils; we are assumed to be as able as he is in identifying significant observations and in drawing important conclusions.

The role Thomas assigns *himself*, as writer, is as fictitious as the one he creates for his readers. In fact he is an expert, and in fact he must teach us because he is a biologist and we are not; in fact he must point us toward important phenomena and help us to see them, since that is his function as a biologist and teacher. But when Thomas instructs, he does so as one would inform a colleague:

> Beans carry self-labels, and are marked by these as distinctly as a mouse by his special smell. The labels are glycoproteins, the lectins, and may have something to do with negotiating the intimate and essential attachment between the bean and the nitrogen-fixing bacteria which live as part of the plant's flesh, embedded in root nodules. The lectin from one line of legume has a special affinity for the surfaces of the particular bacteria which colonize that line, but not for bacteria from other types of bean. The system seems designed for the maintenance of exclusive partnerships. Nature is pieced together by little snobberies like this.
>
> Coral polyps are biologically self-conscious. If you place polyps of the same genetic line together, touching each other, they will fuse and become a single polyp, but if the lines are different, one will reject the other.
>
> Fish can tell each other apart as individuals, by the smell of self. So can mice, and here the olfactory discrimination is governed by the same H_2 locus which contains the genes for immunologic self-marking (3).

Thomas does not pause in these three paragraphs to define terms that only a biologist might be presumed to know (glycoproteins, lectins, polyps, immunologic self-marking). Were he to do so, he would risk causing us to step out of our role as his companions and colleagues. And if as his readers we were to step out of this role, we might forget that we are engaged with Thomas in a search for something more important than mere detail: some sense of our place in nature and of our oneness with nature's many detailed manifestations. To enkindle this sense in his readers is Thomas's central purpose; and his creation of a role for his readers—the role of colleagues, fellow humans, who observe and wonder and try to find meaning—is essential to the achievement of his purpose.

Thomas's own musings are about manifestation of self in nature (beans, polyps, fish as distinct selves) and about opposite phenomena—symbiotic relationships in which self becomes a problematic concept. To illustrate symbiotic relationships between individual selves, Thomas tells a story about a snail and a jellyfish:

> Sometimes there is such a mix-up about selfness that two creatures, each attracted by the molecular configuration of the other, incorporate the two selves to make a single organism. The best story I've ever heard about this is the tale told of the nudibranch and medusa living in the Bay of Naples. When first observed, the nudibranch, a common sea slug, was found to have a tiny vestigial parasite, in the form of a jellyfish, permanently affixed to the ventral surface near the mouth. In curiosity to learn how the medusa got there, some marine biologists began searching the local waters for earlier developmental forms, and discovered something amazing. The attached parasite, although apparently so specialized as to have given up living for itself,

can still produce offspring, for they are found in abundance at certain seasons of the year. They drift through the upper waters, grow up nicely and astonishingly, and finally become full-grown, handsome, normal jellyfish. Meanwhile, the snail produces snail larvae, and these too begin to grow normally, but not for long. While still extremely small, they become entrapped in the tentacles of the medusa and then engulfed within the umbrella-shaped body. At first glance, you'd believe the medusae are now the predators, paying back for earlier humiliations, and the snails the prey. But no. Soon the snails, undigested and insatiable, begin to eat, browsing away first at the radial canals, then the borders of the rim, finally the tentacles, until the jellyfish becomes reduced in substance by being eaten while the snail grows correspondingly in size. At the end, the arrangement is back to the first scene, with the full-grown nudibranch basking, and nothing left of the jellyfish except the round, successfully edited parasite, safely affixed to the skin near the mouth.

It is a confusing tale to sort out, and even more confusing to think about. Both creatures are designed for this encounter, marked as selves so that they can find each other in the waters of the Bay of Naples. The collaboration, if you want to call it that, is entirely specific; it is only this species of medusa and only this kind of nudibranch that can come together and live this way. And, more surprising, they cannot live in any other way; they depend for their survival on each other. They are not really selves, they are specific others (4–5).

In telling his story, Thomas ultimately becomes our teacher—inevitably, because he must tell us about unfamiliar things and make his point: The two creatures "are not really *selves*, they are specific *others*" (italics added). But he stops well short of explicit didacticism: "It is a confusing tale to sort out," he confesses, "and even more confusing to think about." And he refuses to identify himself as an expert biologist. What he gives us is not evidence, data, but a "story," a "tale"—"the best story I've heard about this . . ." Other experts, "some marine biologists," may search the waters for "earlier developmental forms"; for Thomas, it is enough to hear their narratives about what they have found.

In the concluding paragraph of his essay, Thomas in effect invites us to form our own conclusions:

The thought of these creatures gives me an odd feeling. They do not remind me of anything, really. I've never heard of such a cycle before. They are bizarre, that's it, unique. And at the same time, like a vaguely remembered dream, they remind me of the whole earth at once. I cannot get my mind to stay still and think it through (5–6).

The writer is now "I," but still part of the community of the inclusive "we." Because "we," as Thomas's readers, have seen what he has seen, have heard the same tales, have shared his concerns, have pondered and mused and wondered with him, each of us as an individual reader understands the task: to act as a companion "I," to recall our own "vaguely remembered dream," and to find a meaning that is personally significant. "They are bizarre, that's it, unique" is a sentence that invites us to choose our own words, tentatively, knowing that they are replaceable by better ones should we find a surer truth. There is no final meaning in Thomas's essay, no sure and certain message, if Thomas's readers do not act the role he has created for them.

Lewis Thomas's essay is deliberately artistic, and it might be argued that the reading offered here is one appropriate only to belletristic texts; and in some respects it is, since operations of reading must to some degree be sensitive to the requirements of genre and argument. But I would argue that sensitivity to writer-in-text and reader-in-text is perfectly generalizable: that the systematic absence of personal address in scientific prose, for example, defines its reader's role as certainly as Thomas's personal address does in "The Medusa and the Snail." Explicitness, objectivity, and distance typically define the terms under which a negotiation for meaning may take place in scientific prose as certainly as tentativeness, subjectivity, and familiarity do in Thomas's essay. The textual domain, as identified in figure 7–1, is a society in miniature with fictional writers and readers represented in familiar social roles. To enter that small domain writers must project for themselves a social role, for only by doing so can they convey their intentions and with them their proffered meanings; in agreeing to play a complementary social role, readers enter the same domain and in doing so consent to control their own particular intentions in order to negotiate a meaning for the text that approximates the meaning intended. As James Boyd White (1984) puts it: "Whenever you speak [whenever you write], you define a character for yourself and for at least one other—your audience—and make a community at least between the two of you; and you do this in a language that is of necessity provided to you by others and modified in your use of it" (xi). Text analysts, even literary critics, are coming to use a language familiar to those who describe face-to-face interactions mediated by language; some sociologists and sociolinguists even read literary criticism.

STUDENTS AND TEACHERS AS PARTICIPANTS Classrooms, of course, are the larger and more tangible social environments in which the roles of writer and reader must be learned if they are to be learned functionally. If in reading, a text is mediative between the intentions of the writer and reader so that meaning may be negotiated, in a classroom texts are even more importantly mediative as apprentice readers share their changing and enriching constructions of meanings with one another and with the teacher, reaching beyond their present conceptions of arguments, modes of inquiry, their present stores of knowledge—beyond their present sense of structure and form, their limited acquaintance with genres, and their present worlds of discourse toward the wider universe. Learning is finally social, and not only because it involves face-to-face interactions of students with students and students with teachers; it is social, because students interact within the larger historical contexts and structures made possible through written language.

The process that leads a serious though young student of literature to ever more satisfying readings of texts is at base similar to that which leads a marginally literate student to a more functional literacy. Both processes begin in the acquisition and use of spoken language; both proceed through stages in which meanings of texts are negotiated—stages in which formal education is vital; and the acts of reading and writing always imply, finally, a community of interpreters—even though that community may be (though it rarely is) entirely imaginary. Heath and Branscombe say this about the connections between the development of oral and written language:

> We maintain that just as the development of oral language depends on the context of the rich interaction between child and adults, so the development of written language depends on a rich responsive context. This context is especially critical for older students who have reached high school without opportunity to participate in any extended inter-active writing. Young children acquiring language *search for units of symbolic behavior, construct systems of elements and relations, and try to match their production to those of selected others in recurrent situational contexts*; the new writer must follow similar steps to generate internal rules for writing to communicate. Responsive, interactive writing frequently occurring over a period of time provides the data from which students may search out meaningful units and systems in writing (1985, 29–30).

In the early stages of learning to write, personal, direct, immediate response is certainly necessary and may differentiate the needs of an apprentice from those of an experienced writer. But all writers require a responsive context, all seek to participate in extended interactive writing and reading (What are learned journals for?), and all try to match production with that of selected others (What are style manuals for?): Literate societies, after all, devote a major share of their resources and modes of production to the maintenance and control of literate discourse. Literate communities are real communities, not imaginary ones, and they are rooted in social practices even if not always in person-to-person contact. Janice Radway's (1984a, 1984b) pioneering works describe in detail one such community composed of readers of romance; hers is important work in its description of institutions and forces binding a literate community together in a social compact formed by readers who have not necessarily even met one another.

The model of reading and writing touched upon in the immediately preceding discussion and treated more fully in the explanations of figures 7–1 through 7–3 implies these things about the development of reading and writing: (a) Once the rudiments of decoding are managed, part of the process of learning to read is reading—in an ever widening array of genres—so that memory may begin to apply functionally in the process of text interpretation; (b) Part of the process of learning to read is the accumulation of knowledge and experience so that these may be brought to bear in the comprehension and interpretation of texts; (c) Essential in learning is the opportunity to discuss with others what has been read, so that the social relations implicit in texts may be made explicit as readers share with others their own particular perceptions of their places in the textual world. Writers must have equal opportunity to have their works read and then discussed as contributions to communal knowledge, and to have their works reacted to by readers who share their social space and will grant them their intentions. In designing curricula for the teaching of reading and writing we have been all too eager to search for isolable constituent skills and to teach these as somehow basic: spelling, vocabulary building, grammar, problem solving, word-attack skills, semantic analysis—activities of a sort that are easy to translate into drills and worksheets, activities that are easy to teach and to test.

The matter is a serious one. Goodlad (1984) reported, on the basis of perhaps the most comprehensive survey of schools and schooling done in recent years, that in elementary schools, junior high schools, and senior high schools:

> The dominant emphasis throughout was on teaching basic language use skills and mastering mechanics—capitalization, punctuation, paragraphs, syllabication, synonyms, homonyms, antonyms, parts of speech, etc. These were repeated in successive grades of the elementary years, were reviewed in the junior high years, and reappeared in the low track classes of the senior high schools.
>
> Reading instruction in the junior and senior highs appeared to be a matter of remediation involving mechanics of word recognition, phonics, and vocabulary development. In English, there was still a substantial emphasis on the basics of grammar and composition—punctuation, capitalization, sentence structure, paragraph organization, word analysis, parts of speech. *In line with the findings* [all emphasis mine] *of our analysis of tracking in Chapter 5, lower track classes tended to emphasize the mechanics of English usage, whereas high track classes were likely to stress the intellectual skills of analysis, evaluation, and judgment, especially through literature. The low track classes were unlikely to encounter the high status knowledge dealt with in the upper tracks and normally considered essential for college admission* (205).

Do we, either unknowingly or deliberately, design for failure in the curricula we offer certain of our students?

To read and to acquire through reading (and other means) knowledge and experience *is* the crucial thing in the development of a reader; to write and to acquire through writing the capacity to convey both personal intention and what can be known or experienced by others is the crucial thing in the development of a writer. In some sense these are "natural" developments in the academic world and in the literate world. Part of our job as teachers is to design and put in place contexts in which the processes of development take place naturally. If we want to intervene, we might do so more effectively by paying less attention to skills and mechanics and using the time saved to help our students perceive the various moves and strategies employed in the various fields and modes of inquiry and representation, and then to practice them.

James Boyd White (1983), lawyer, legal scholar, and rhetorician, claims that the layman's difficulty in understanding legal discourse does not result from an ignorance of legal language—its vocabulary, its sometimes peculiar syntax—but rather from ignorance of what he calls the "invisible discourse" of law: "the unstated conventions by which [legal] language operates" (48).

> Behind the words, that is, are expectations about the ways in which they will be used, expectations that do not find explicit expression anywhere but are a part of the legal culture that the surface language simply assumes. These expectations are constantly at work, directing argument, shaping responses, determining the next move, and so on; their effects are everywhere but they themselves are invisible (49).

Each domain of inquiry and expression, each domain of endeavor, no matter how modest, is held together by a system of invisible discourse. And in each case, it is this system of invisible discourse that binds together readers and writers into an interpretive community, into a cohesive social group able to use language to find meaning. Our job as scholars is to make the invisible visible, just as our job as teachers is to do the same and thus invite our students to join our groups as full participants.

Some Imperatives for Research on Literacy

Nevertheless, educational theory and practice have traditionally been dominated by psychology. The reason for this seems clear enough to me. The logistic triumphs of space exploration and of information management systems generally, added to an earlier respect for the standardized achievements of mass production, consolidated the belief among educators in authority that success would result from delivering to children the right amounts of the right instruction at the right time, with constant monitoring and quality control. The belief still has not been totally discredited that learning is a simple matter of individual ability and effort applied to appropriately organized and presented subject matter. Thus for literacy, educators occasionally turned to linguists to ascertain what should be taught but primarily to psychologists for how the instruction should be delivered (Smith, 1984, vii–viii).

It has come to be recognized, in recent years, that St. Augustine was an astute developmental psychologist, and in the *Confessions* he has something to say about language learning that is relevant here. He is contrasting the learning of Greek, which was for him a second language, with the learning of Latin, his mother tongue:

> Time was also (as an infant) I knew no Latin; but this I . . . (came to know) without fear or suffering . . . for my heart urged me to bring forth its own thoughts, which I could only do by learning words not of those who taught, but of those who talked with me; in whose ears also I gave birth to such thoughts as I conceived (Donaldson, 1984, 177).

The multitude of human activities in developed societies that are comprehended by the term *literacy* permeate every aspect of life—even the lives lived by those who are or are called illiterate. For the researcher this means there are rich fields to plow, but it means other things as well. Because literacy is so all-pervasive, it has been and continues to be studied from a wide variety of perspectives; but because literacy is merely a term used in general reference to a complex of very complex human activities, no single perspective seems to reveal very much. Written language can be viewed as an artifact, or as a tool, or as a code, but it is more than any of these because it *is* language and because, in a real sense, as humans so are we, for humans are social beings. Reading and writing can be viewed as skills, but because they are human activities linked to social existence and the processes of coming to know, they are far more than that. To study literacy seriously is to commit oneself to interdisciplinary work—to the risk of stepping beyond one's comfortable academic domain. And to study reading and writing, because these are complex human activities taking place in some complex of real circumstances, is to commit oneself to a study of contexts and relations. Literacy is impossible to define, for whatever purpose, without reference to its nature and use in some one context—in some one delimited and clearly defined social context: To drive this point home has been a major contribution of ethnographers to the study of literacy in school and society. But to remind ethnographers that "literacy events" occur in the wider social contexts of literate communities linked together by the institutions of written language is the joint responsibility of sociologists of culture, social historians, rhetoricians, and certain kinds of literary theorists.

Raymond Williams (1981) employed the term *convergence* to speak of a coming together of different interests and methods applied to increasingly common issues and problems in formation of something approximating a new academic discipline (9–32). Those of us who study literacy have not yet reached convergence of this kind, but increasingly we are dealing with similar issues, similar problems, and learning from one another in the process. High on our agendas for study and research, even as we follow our own interests and employ our own methodologies, should be a search for new ways to share information about literacy. The amount of work coming out in books and journals is staggering, and some of it is even good and useful. Given societal needs and a proper, ethical sense of professional obligation, we cannot afford disciplinary parochialism; neither can we afford wasteful territorial disputes. We need to learn from speculative studies, from those scholars who rely on insight, from those who do careful analyses of historical documents, from those who propose general, integrative, and abstract theories as well as from those who go out and look, digest, and interpret. If as teachers we must construct classrooms in which reading and writing can happen, as researchers and scholars we must create forums for fruitful exchange.

To reach toward convergence as scholars in separate disciplines who would be interdisciplinarians we must meet three challenges of theory. The first is to engage in rigorous critical analysis of the methodologies that are dearest to our hearts and minds—the kind of analysis, for example, that Clifford Geertz (1983) offers in several essays in his collection *Local Knowledge*. In such analysis, I believe, outside and even alien perspectives can be useful. When I teach English grammar, as I sometimes do, I teach my students at least two systems of grammatical description, because I want them to see that grammar is not something given by God but rather something human beings construct as a system of discourse about language. I suggest that we will learn more about literacy if we apply multiple perspectives and explore differences and similarities among the discourse systems we construct, looking for their limitations and strengths. We need forums in which widely divergent positions can be stated and examined: forums, for example, in which ethnographers—with all their commitments to the particular—can talk fruitfully to cognitive psychologists—with all of theirs to generalization.

If we are to make further progress toward convergence, we will need to overcome the mutual unintelligibility of the discourse systems—the very languages—that we employ in our work. We badly need, if not theories of translation that may prove to be too abstract, at least methods or operations for translating one set of claims into another, for talking sensibly about similarities and differences between disciplinary approaches, some of which differences are sometimes exalted into a claim that different epistemological assumptions are at work. If they are, we need to know it; if not, we need to know their status. Committed sociologists can easily claim that the language used in earlier sections of this essay is far too figurative and fuzzy; but I would want to ask them if their language is less figurative, and if so on what theory of referentiality: and I would want to ask whether or not figurative and fuzzy language is a better or worse kind for describing indeterminate events and their relations to changing situations.

Third, and I think the most important of our theoretical tasks: If we are finally to reach convergence in the study of literacy, we will recognize that we are jointly engaged in the study of context and that we are rapidly moving toward, in our several disciplines, a usable general theory of context. In saying this, I am thinking about ethnographic work, much of it indebted to John Gumperz and Dell Hymes, which for all its particularity implies some generalizations about what counts as relevant context in descriptive work on interaction (Fetterman, 1984; Gilmore and Glatthorn, 1982; Goelman, Oberg, and Smith, 1984; Hymes, 1974; Wagner, 1983); I am thinking about work in conversational analysis and the analysis of other forms of talk (Goffman, 1981); I am thinking about work in speech act theory (Bach and Harnish, 1979; Coles and Morgan 1975; Searle, 1969, 1979, 1983), and in reader-response theory and semiotics (Culler, 1981; Eco, 1979; Iser, 1978; Tompkins, 1980); about work in rhetoric (White, 1984; Knoblauch and Brannon, 1984; Winterowd, 1975); and about sensitive new work by my colleague Alton Becker (1982, and in press) drawn from linguistics, rhetoric, and philosophy. References provided can be only suggestive, which is itself a measure of the volume of activity in study of this problem. Context is becoming, for those of us who study language and its uses, less a garbage-can term, a useful receptacle for the inexplicable, than one that we can use in principled ways to explain what needs explanation. We need, I think we all recognize, to explore the multiple contexts of literacy; we may, before too long, be able to explore together as a community of participant observers informed by theory and able to communicate intelligibly and usefully. It is right, and will be useful in future research, to treat literacy as a set of differing but related social phenomena, embedded in history and involving for individuals both linguistic and cognitive capacities. The challenge for us is twofold: Make sense of this notion and then apply it rigorously to understand such pressing social problems as school failure, high rates of illiteracy, and the relations between illiteracy and poverty.

Some Imperatives for Research on Functional Literacy

What then is "English literacy" for professional students and teachers of English? Is it their own condition and that of people much like them, currently and retrospectively applied? Or is it the diverse and changing conditions of their whole nominal people? To approach two

centuries of English literacy means restricting our account to a bare
majority. General literacy has a bare century, and within that many
are still disadvantaged. In relation to what is seen as "our" literature,
where then do students and teachers of English stand?

I have made my own awkward stand. By my educational history
I belong with the literate and the literary. By my inheritance and still
by affiliation I belong with an illiterate and relatively illiterate majority. It is said that as a whole society develops, and has for the past
century been developing, these inherited problems and contradictions
resolve themselves. I do not think so. Beyond our local and diverse
histories there are major intellectual issues, of a fully objective kind,
which need to be traced to this radical unevenness between literature
and general literacy. Underlying them, always, are the complex general problems of language, and it is in how these problems are dealt
with, in the coming years, that the success or failure of English studies
will, in my view, be decided (Williams, 1980, 212–213).

The problem of a "radical unevenness between literature and general literacy" is one not only for those who think of literature as
a particular body of imaginative writings. It is the problem of
expertise in all complex modern societies, in which ever more specialized intellectual elites produce theories and information inac-
cessible and unintelligible to the general public while continuing
to influence public policy. It is the problem of media control and
access to the various media controlled by economic conditions as
print sources become ever more expensive, leaving the less affluent
dependent upon the more easily controlled electronic media. It is
the problem of decisions made by those in control about the wishes
and wants of the illiterate and relatively illiterate that lead to
debased entertainment and to political debate that finds its most
influential forms in one-minute television commercials or ten-
minute film biographies that resemble either the lives of saints or
those of movie stars. The problem of the radical unevenness of
general literacy and literature is as much these things as it is the
more familiar problems associated with the term *functional literacy*: denial of access to jobs that demand an increasingly higher
level of literacy, denial of access to training programs for such jobs
because entrance tests demand a relatively high level of literacy. In
thinking about the more obvious problems associated with literacy, we should keep somewhere in our minds the less obvious ones
of access to something beyond economic sufficiency. Not to do so is
to render ourselves as teachers and researchers into mere function-
aries in a society we may not wish to leave unchanged; not to do so
is, perhaps, to limit access through literacy for our students. I do
not think, in our culture, that we can maintain that illiteracy per se
is not necessarily a problem just because some illiterates manage
to get money.

Ethnographers of literacy and of schooling have made important contributions to our understanding of functional literacy by exploring the uses of reading and writing in particular social contexts,

giving substance to such definitions of the term as UNESCO's—definitions that emphasize the relativity of the term. It is certainly right to say that the terms *literate* and *illiterate* find meaning only with reference to specific social contexts; it is no less right to say that the problematicality of illiteracy is contextually determined. But who delimits the contexts that determine access to other contexts? Do we merely observe and describe, or do we act as participant observers? And in what roles should we participate?

I want to offer two simple and complementary definitions that may be useful in talking about functional literacy:

> *Writing is the ability to employ written language to create texts that are valued by one's self and by readers in particular contexts.*

> *Reading is the ability to act upon written texts to create meanings that are valued by one's self and by other readers joined in community in particular contexts.*

And to these definitions, I would add one other dimension, borrowed from James Boyd White (1983):

> Literacy is not merely the capacity to understand the conceptual content of writings and utterances, but the ability to participate fully in a set of social and intellectual practices. It is not passive but active; not imitative but creative, for participation in the speaking and writing of language is participation in the activities it makes possible. Indeed it involves a perpetual remaking both of language and of practice (56).

But to participate, of course, one must gain or be granted access; and because literacy, reading and writing, are as much group activities as individual ones, to exercise them fully—to develop "ability"—requires opportunity. Our instructional programs often fail because we fail to provide opportunities for our students to make best use of their abilities with written language; and our society in fact creates functional illiterates by denying many citizens the opportunity to participate in a broad enough range of social and intellectual practices. There is little purpose in urging high literacy upon a person with dismally low prospects.

Ethnographers studying language and literacy in schools and schoolrooms have quite properly and usefully focused upon teacher-student face-to-face interactions, and sometimes—now increasingly—upon written texts as mediative in such interactions, an even more promising line of research. But because many such studies have produced negative results, there is growing reluctance in schools to having them done and increasing skepticism about their usefulness. Courtney Cazden (1983) reported having been told in Alaska that somewhere in the Alaskan State Department of Education there is a sign that says:

WE DON'T NEED ANY MORE
ANTHROPOLOGICAL EXPLANATIONS
OF SCHOOL FAILURE (33)

I think we do, when schools in fact fail, so that we may come to understand why. But more important, I think we need wider understanding of the reasons for failure; and to get this, we will have to study schoolrooms and schools in their various contexts. Along with Cazden (1983), I believe we need

> a broader view of research relevance. Exclusive concern with translating the outcomes of research into improved skills of the practitioner is too narrow; practitioners have not only skills, but also a view of reality, a vision of reality, a vision of the achievable, and a commitment to act; and social science knowledge can influence all four (33).

Humanistic knowledge can also influence all four, and perhaps even social scientists as well.

One of the more exciting developments within ethnography, and one that seems to promise productive change in practice, is the joining of teacher-practitioners with researchers in a model now known as "teacher-as-researcher." But after reading impressive reports of new curricula and student achievement (Moll and Diaz, 1987; Heath, 1983; Heath and Thomas, 1984; Heath and Branscombe, 1985), one is left with a nagging question: Will these changes and gains last? The gap between research and educational practice is very wide, even when the research is into practice and even when it is done in schools; and for those who read history, even very recent history, the gap between research and educational policy often appears unbridgeable.

In these circumstances lie new opportunities for ethnographers interested in questions of education. Why is it that useful findings are so rarely used, while obviously trivial ones are so readily adopted and applied? Who and what forces control the flow of information from researchers to teachers? What are the impediments to information flow? Why are our institutions so impervious to change—even when change would seem to support and sustain their very continuation? Using various theories, we can offer various generalizations in answers to such questions, but we do not know very much in detail—perhaps because such study is inevitably depressing. I suggest that our first need in studying literacy, its uses, and its acquisition is an ethnography of power and its uses, the kind of study that identifies agents and their actions rather than forces and their operations, and in doing so, perhaps makes change more possible. We need an ethnography of power at least as much as we need more of the useful studies now appearing that treat continuities and discontinuities between home and school, community and school, and work and school, important though these are.

I am struck by what we do know and believe that suggests what should and should not be looked at. Even granting that individual differences exist in the intellectual equipment of individual children, we do *know* that insofar as linguistic competence is involved in the acquisition of literacy, all people have a sufficient measure of such competence, as a birthright, to escape illiteracy, unless some kind of pathology intervenes; we do *know* that insofar as cognitive competence is involved in the acquisition of literacy, most people have that, and for the same reason. Given these articles of our mutual faith, we should be able to frame pretty good guesses about where to look for the causes of illiteracy. Students are often all too easy to blame when we focus upon the linguistic and cognitive competencies involved in writing and reading to the neglect of social interaction and the larger social forces that affect interaction and language use. Teachers are also all too easy to blame when we isolate their interactions with students for study while ignoring contexts that limit what they can say and how they can say it.

A final imperative for those of us who do research on questions in education is to meet a challenge made by Stephen Cahir of NIE to students of literacy who attended a conference on research in literacy at the University of Michigan in 1984: Append, he said, to all research papers a statement saying "This is what our findings are good for." He added, jokingly, what many others who fund research say seriously: It would also be good if we could later show results in upward changes of test scores. As researchers, we do have the responsibility to state the relevance of our research and to involve ourselves in making it work in practice. But in so doing, we must also have a voice in determining the means by which results will be evaluated. Test scores have contexts too.

When testing is the topic of research or the means of measuring outcomes of its application, what we should be after, in my view, is not always changes in test scores but as often changes in tests. If I understand the findings of ethnographic research about literacy, they lead to the conclusion that standardized tests are poor instruments for measuring such things as writing and reading: Certainly this is true of those national tests that are completely insensitive to local contexts of need and opportunity.

Let me speak briefly to a case. The University of Michigan has a writing program that offers some students who need it remedial preparation for an introductory course; the introductory course then leads in turn to a more advanced content-based course that all students must take. This final course is offered in each department in the College of Literature, Science, and the Arts and is intended to instruct students in how to write effectively in the discipline they are studying. Chemists teach chemistry students how to write as chemists do; art historians introduce students to the art of describing art; and economists teach acolytes the mysteries of economic discourse.

Those of us who work in the program and are responsible for it think it is a good one but would like to find out whether or not it produces results—for better reasons than to save our funding. But how do you test for learning and development in a complex and loosely organized program that is deliberately designed to produce diverse outcomes? We could easily test common mechanical features like spelling or verb agreement, but the results would be trivial; we could test writing correlates, but we would not be certain that, in fact, the correlates correlate; and if we were to build into the instructional program, for purposes of testing, constant tasks for purposes of comparability, we would waste our students' time and irritate them with irrelevancies while contradicting the program's major assumptions and subverting its aims.

The simple fact is that although we are working on the problem, we do not know how to test for real rather than apparent growth in our program. (I would feel worse about this confession if I thought that anybody did.) We do not know how to test for real growth because we cannot reconcile prevailing assumptions about testing with these two definitions:

> Writing is the ability to use written language to create texts that are valued by one's self and by readers in particular contexts.

> Literacy is the ability to participate fully in a set of social and intellectual practices.

As we grope our way toward an adequate means of evaluation, we know these few things: We will not be able to decontextualize our tests; we will have more use for variables than for constants; and we had better be ready to involve human beings and to trust their informed, if sometimes subjective, judgments.

Note

[1]The occasion was a conference at the University of Michigan in 1984 organized by David Bloome and sponsored by the Horace H. Rackham School of Graduate Studies and the School of Education. The conference brought together scholars and researchers from a variety of disciplines, all of them interested in the study of literacy. The papers from the conference have been published: see Bloome (1987).

8

Literacy as Conversation: Classroom Talk as Text Building

Patricia L. Stock and Jay L. Robinson

Introduction

A number of things, I think, are true. One is that there has been an enormous amount of genre mixing in intellectual life in recent years, and it is, such blurring of kinds, continuing apace. Another is that many social scientists have turned away from a laws and instances ideal of explanation toward a cases and interpretations one, looking less for the sort of thing that connects planets and pendulums and more for the sort that connects chrysanthemums and swords. Yet another is that analogies drawn from the humanities are coming to play the kind of role in sociological understanding that analogies drawn from the crafts and technology have long played in physical understanding. Further, I not only think these things are true, I think they are true together; and it is the culture shift that makes them so that is my subject: the refiguration of social thought.

This genre blurring is more than just a matter of Harry Houdini or Richard Nixon turning up as characters in novels or of midwestern murder sprees described as though a gothic romancer had imagined them. It is philosophical inquiries looking like literary criticism . . . scientific discussions looking like belles lettres *morceaux* . . . baroque fantasies presented as deadpan empirical observations . . . histories that consist of equations and tables or law court testimony . . . documentaries that read like true confessions . . . parables posing as ethnographies . . . theoretical treatises set out as travelogues . . . ideological arguments cast as historiographical inquiries . . . epistemological studies constructed like political tracts . . . methodological polemics got up as personal memoirs. . . . Nabokov's *Pale Fire*, that impossible object made of poetry and fiction, footnotes and images from the clinic, seems very much of the time; one waits only for quantum theory in verse or biography in algebra.

Of course to a certain extent this sort of thing has always gone on. . . . But the present jumbling of varieties of discourse has grown to the point where it is becoming difficult either to label authors . . . or to classify works. . . . And thus it is more than a matter of odd sports and occasional curiosities, or of the admitted fact that the innovative is, by definition, hard to categorize. It is a phenomenon general enough and distinctive enough to suggest that what we are seeing is not just another redrawing of the cultural map—the moving of a few disputed borders, the marking of some more picturesque mountain lakes—but an alteration of the principles of mapping. Something is happening to the way we think about the way we think.

CLIFFORD GEERTZ

It is teachers who, in the end, will change the school by understanding it.

LAWRENCE STENHOUSE
Memorial plaque on the grounds of the
University of East Anglia

In this essay, we offer an exploratory sketch of a model we are developing to analyze talk and its relationship to writing in composition courses that are deliberately designed to treat talk and writing as seamless uses of language and to treat language as the fabric from which communities and their constitutive meanings and values are fashioned. We have undertaken the research that has led us to develop the model for three related reasons. First, as teachers of such composition courses, we are concerned about how effectively they serve our students; therefore, more and less formally, we continually conduct research into our teaching and our students' learning. Second, in conducting such research, we have come to believe that the analysis of classroom discourse is a powerful means for understanding the processes of students' learning. Third, because we believe that teacher-researchers are uniquely positioned to observe and understand the talk and writing that students compose in their classes, we also believe that they are uniquely able to contribute to scholarly conversations about the relations between classroom interactions and learning. We argue—if only by implication—that the perspective of the teacher-researcher is essential if the analysis of classroom discourse is to be sufficiently sensitive to capture the nuances and to explicate the complexity of individual students' learning.[1]

We begin our discussion by describing a composition course that Stock designed and taught and to which we will refer in our analysis, briefly contextualizing our description with reference to theories that guided its construction; then we explicate the model we are developing, illustrating its possible uses by analyzing stretches of talk among students and teacher in this composition course. As we discuss the course and the model, it will be apparent that both are grounded in similar theories: both are indebted to process theories of learning; both are indebted to social constructivist theories of knowing and of knowledge. In conclusion, we talk about the implications of our work for understanding language learning and for understanding learning through language.

One Composition Course in Context

"Literacy," or "liberal learning" is often taken to refer to a fixed, isolatable concept. Actually, those terms would not be intelligible at all were it not for their relationship to other terms like "language," "education," "tradition," "science," "humanities," "rationality," "scripts," "criticism," even "freedom." It seems evident enough that the concept of literacy or the concept of liberal learning (or any other concept) can only emerge with some degree of clarity for us when we begin moving back and forth through one of such networks, allowing one signifier to play upon another. We become conscious of this, I think, even as we become conscious of the ways in which our very thinking is constituted by such signifiers, and of the choices we are bound to make— choices having to do with the kinds of persons (or thinkers) we intend to be. I am suggesting ... that literacy and liberal education and higher learning and the rest are not to be conceived as single or fixed ideas. I am suggesting as well that how they mean and what they mean ought not to be dissociated from what Michael Oakeshott has called the "conversation" that civilized human beings have inherited, a conversation "begun in the primeval forests and extended and made more articulate in the course of centuries" (1962, 199), just so long as that great conversation is understood to include not only the voices of disciplinary scholars, but the voices of ordinary people across the years writing or speaking the scripts of their lives (Greene, 1986, 232).

"How We Construe Is How We Construct" (Berthoff, 1981).

Persuaded that language development is a process in which students must study not only the forms of language but their functions as well, in order to learn, think, and communicate in various contexts; persuaded that this process is one in which context influences both language functions and language use; and persuaded that talk and writing are in fact seamless uses of language, we have developed and taught several composition courses like the one we describe below. With many of our colleagues, we have shaped our teaching practices to make them consistent with principles of language learning like the following ones outlined by Angela Jagger:

1. *Language learning is a self-generated, creative process.* ...

2. *Language learning is holistic.* The different components of language—function, form, and meaning—are learned simultaneously. ...

3. *Language learning is social and collaborative.* . . .

4. *Language learning is functional and integrative.* . . .

5. *Language learning is variable.* Because language is inherently variable, the meanings, the forms, and the functions of [individuals'] language will depend on their personal, social, and cultural experiences (1985, 4).

Because we believe that language learning is *self-generated, creative, holistic*—not a matter of learning forms as items but rather a matter of learning forms and their functions and their meanings and all three together in contextualized acts of making meaning— in composition courses we have designed we have invited our students to talk and write as well as to listen and read their way to understanding (see also Bartholomae and Petrosky, 1986; Berthoff, 1981a,b; Elbow, 1973; Fader, 1976; Fulwiler, 1987; Graves, 1983; Knoblauch and Brannon, 1984; Macrorie, 1980; Stock and Wixson, 1983); furthermore, we have allowed our students a measure of choice in the subjects about which they read and write (see also Birnbaum, 1982; Graves, 1985; Hansen, 1983; Heath and Branscombe, 1985; Murray, 1982). Because we believe that language learning is *social* and *collaborative*, as teachers of composition we have joined with our students in a community of language users, not only to model effective language use for students but also to demonstrate that it is only in community that the functions of language use find their values (see also Bazermann, 1983; Bloome, 1983; Emig, 1983; Milz, 1980; Robinson, 1986, 1987; White, 1983). Because we believe that language learning is *functional* and *integrative* only in a community bonded by common language and by the systems of values reflected in that language, as teachers of composition we have asked students to speak and listen, write and read, for one another to dramatize and thus come to understand how common language is constructed—how common worlds and their values are made, how "local knowledge" is constituted (see also Fader, 1983; Fish, 1980; Greene, 1978; Macrorie, 1970, 1980; Robinson, 1986; Stock, 1986, White, 1983).

The course we describe was designed as an enactment of these beliefs and practices in a particular setting: it served as a pre-introductory college composition course in a two-course sequence intended to prepare students for entry into the several discourse communities that comprise the modern academic world.[2] This particular course was designed to enable students both to talk and to write their way toward membership in those communities by becoming composers, as Ann Berthoff defines *composing*:

> Composing—putting things together—is a continuum, a process that continues without any sharp breaks. Making sense of the world is composing. It includes being puzzled, being mistaken, and then

suddenly seeing things for what they probably are; making wrong—
unproductive, unsatisfactory, incorrect, inaccurate—identifications
and assessments and correcting them or giving them up and getting
some new ones. And all these things happen when we write: writing is
like the composing we do all the time when we respond to the world,
make up our minds, try to figure out things again (1981, 11).

Because the subject matter of this composition course was conceived not as a body of content but rather as the discourse students
can and do produce, students were asked to bring their own subjects to the class and then were provided opportunities to talk
about them and to write about them, both for each other and for the
teacher. They were also provided a model composer—the teacher—
someone who struggled to make meaning just as they did.

We reproduce the following excerpt from the course outline,
not only because it describes the content of the course but more
importantly because it describes the conduct of the course: both
the means by which the teacher and her students might explore the
theories of language learning and use that would guide classroom
activities, and the modalities of social interaction through which
she and her students might form themselves into a productive
learning community. This excerpt serves as necessary context for
the analyses of classroom talk that we will provide later. It also
serves as base for one of the points that will emerge in our analyses:
that a teacher's beliefs about learning, as well as her political and
ethical commitments, will have much to do with how a community
is constituted through the interactions of its members. In the syllabus, the teacher projects a social self for others to emulate, react
to, or reject; modes of social interaction are preferred and encouraged, just as means of composing are.

THE SYLLABUS

In this course, we will study some of the uses of spoken and written
language. The subject of our study will also be the means of our study.
That is: we will use talk and writing as our means of learning about
the powers and limitations of spoken and written language.

Since most people don't spend their time talking and writing
about talk and writing, I am not going to ask you to do that. What I
am going to ask each of you to do is to identify a subject you know
something about and you are trying to learn more about. Then, I'm
going to ask you to talk about that subject both with members of this
class and with me and then to write about that subject (1) for yourself
in a *journal*—a place to "think on paper," (2) for members of this class
and me in *dialogue papers*—informal written conversations, and (3)
for members of this class and me in *essays*—attempts to communicate
your unique understandings of a topic to others.

I will be a fully participating speaker/writer in this class. That
means that I, too, will talk with you, keep a journal, write dialogue
papers, and write essays about a subject I know something about and
want to learn more about.

Earlier I wrote that most people don't spend their time talking and writing about talk and writing. Most people don't. But I do. The subject of my talk and writing for myself and for you this seven weeks will be talk and writing, especially writing. In my writing for you, I will try to teach you some of the things I know and am learning about writing. At the moment, by dividing my subject—Talking and Writing, Especially Writing—into six topics, I plan to complete six essays for you. My tentative topics are the following ones:

1. From Talk to Writing, or Why Was Plato So Afraid of Writing?
2. A History of *Literacy*, or Why Does the Meaning of That Word Keep Changing?
3. Learning to Speak, or How Do Those Kids Do It?
4. Learning to Write, or Do Kids Really Have to Be Taught?
5. Talk and Writing in Classrooms, or Does Filling in the Blanks Make You a Blank Filler?
6. Writing across the Curriculum at the University of Michigan, or Are You Ready?

The essay topics I have listed for you are subject to change because I will be writing one of them each week just as you will be writing one essay each week on an aspect (topic) of your own subject. On my way to writing each of these essays, I will be keeping a journal, "thinking on paper"; I will be writing "dialogue papers" to you and you will be responding to me about them, letting me know where I am clear and unclear, letting me know what about my topic is of interest to you, what—from your perspective—is not worth reading about.

My own writing and your comments to me about my writing may help me realize I need to learn something about another topic if I am to fully understand the one I am writing about; therefore, I may change the essay topic I had planned for a given week to allow myself the opportunity to form my thoughts on a new issue or problem I have discovered. For example, when I am writing about topic (4) on my list, Learning to Write or Do Kids Really Have to Be Taught? I may convince myself that they do, and then, I may want to write my next essay on the best ways to teach them. Instead of (5) Talk and Writing in Classrooms or Does Filling in the Blanks Make You a Blank Filler? I might instead write another essay (5) The Best Way to Teach Kids to Write, or If You Put a Microcomputer in the Crib Will Your Baby Teethe on It? What I am saying is that when you or I write in order to learn about a subject and in order to teach other people about that subject, it is best to be flexible and let the process of discovery involved in our writing guide our individual inquiries and writing projects. We've got to complete an essay each week, but it does not necessarily have to be the one we originally thought we were going to write.

The primary benefit to us in a course such as this one is that we will become more practiced and more expert writers. The secondary benefit asks some things of us: we will each learn about a wide variety of subjects and topics because we are the audience for one another's writing. As such an audience, we have to help one another just as listeners help speakers by laughing at good jokes, by asking questions like: "Excuse me, I must have missed something because I didn't understand that. Could you explain what you meant by that remark?" Or "Wait a minute. How did you get there from here? You lost me." Or "No kidding, Babe Ruth hit 714 home runs. How many did Hank Aaron hit? 745! Why don't you include that figure here? It gives me a picture of the gap between Ruth and Aaron." And by saying things like this about what we read in one another's writing: "I never knew that. That's interesting. Thanks for teaching me about it." Or "I never thought about these things in that way, but from what you say, I see that is a way to think about them." In other words, we have to be a responsive audience to one another's writing—we have to praise, approve, question, and even disagree to help one another form strong arguments, coherent essays.

In a writing class like ours, each of us can learn from one another. Writers are always teachers. They teach because they are authors, *authorities* about their subjects. I teach this course this way because I believe that the best way to become an expert writer is to write about subjects that interest you, for audiences and purposes that are real to you. And I can promise you that by doing the work of this course, you will grow as both a writer (an author) and as a scholar (an authority).

I will meet with each of you individually to talk about the subject you would like to write about for the next seven weeks and to help you divide the subject into six topics for six essays. During the course of our seven weeks together, I will meet with each of you individually for a one-half-hour to a one-full-hour conference each week. You may also feel free to schedule other appointments with me to discuss papers you are writing for other courses if you wish. Because our class is too large for each of us to help every other member of the class, we will divide into Writing Groups. I will do my best to form the Writing Groups by interests. In other words, depending on the subject you decide to write about for the seven weeks, with your advice, I will place you in a group with other people who share your interests and, therefore, who will make a good audience for your writing.

The people in each writing group will serve as the primary audience for one another's work. Each of us will talk with the members of our Writing Group about our topics, and we will circulate our dialogue papers and the first drafts of our essays among them. As members of a Writing Group, each of us is primarily responsible for responding to the writings of the others in the group. IT WILL BE OUR JOB TO HELP ONE ANOTHER WRITE EFFECTIVE ESSAYS.

With her syllabus the teacher opened the conversation of the course this way: We shall write the text for this course—you and I together. We shall all be inquirers in this course, teaching one another from the range of experience and knowledge we each bring to the course. As I am able, I expect to teach you what you need to know to build our common text; as you are able, I expect you to teach your classmates and me what we need to know to build our common text. If we are to become authors who are also *authorities*, then we must write "the book"—individually and together.

It was the teacher's plan that when the students in the class wrote for one another and for her, and when she wrote for and with them—all of them about subjects they brought to each other— the class would dramatize the tension that is both inevitable and essential for all who would be readers and writers in any new social community: the tension between one's own and the community's forming and formed languages. The teacher knew well that in time her students must come to be familiar with the broader academic community's various languages—their peculiar conventions and vocabularies, their different ways of introducing discussions, shaping questions, forming problems, posing solutions, expressing concepts; but she also believed that students must speak and write their various ways toward such familiarity, not merely listen and read their ways toward it. She believed that any community worth that name must include individuals as active participants, thinking their own thoughts, speaking them in their own languages.

When the students who enrolled in the course described here joined their teacher in composing from a variety of social perspectives, they began to shape a common language that would serve as means to form community among themselves. As they sought to do so in the broader social settings in which they found themselves— the university communities—they encountered languages that had already been created and shaped in those wider communities. But as they encountered those languages and sought to use them for their own purposes, they renewed and changed them. The message of the course design and conduct was twofold: the social worlds of conversation and letters are ones that continually make and remake discourse and shape and reshape knowledge; the perspectives and expressions that students bring from the worlds of their prior experience have place and purpose in them.

The work of James Boyd White, Professor of Law, English, and Classical Studies at the University of Michigan, has contributed much to our own understanding of the relations of talk to writing, of the relations of the literate acts of composing and comprehending to similar acts in spoken language, and of the uses of language in the formation of community by human beings of diverse origins who seek to come to understand one another. White discusses reading and writing as if they were, in fact, the same as talking and listening. And by discussing these activities as similar means "of claiming meaning for experience and of establishing relations with others," he gives encouragement to our own attempt to try to understand the interconnections of talk and writing and the interconnected contributions of both to the construction of a community of language learners.

In introducing a way of reading that he is urging in his book *When Words Lose Their Meaning*, White writes:

the premise implicit in the title of this book [is] that language is not stable but changing and that it is perpetually remade by its speakers [among whom he would include writers], who are themselves remade, both as individuals and as communities, in what we say. The basic question asked of each text [in the series of exemplary readings he provides in his book] is how it performs as a response to this situation. We shall thus be interested less in what differentiates the genres represented here—poetry and philosophy and history and moral essays and fiction and politics and law—than in what unites them, in the tree of which they are several branches. For they are all species of the more general activity that is our true subject: the double activity of claiming meaning for experience and of establishing relations with others in language. Each of the texts we shall read proceeds by working upon a world it defines and leading its reader to a position within it. To put it in a single word, I would say that our subject is rhetoric, if by that is meant the study of the ways in which character and community— and motive, value, reason, social structure, everything, in short, that makes a culture—are defined and made real in performances of language. Whenever you speak, you define a character for yourself and for at least one other—your audience—and make a community at least between the two of you; and you do this in a language that is of necessity provided to you by others and modified in your use of it (1984, x–xi).

The model we are developing to analyze both talk and writing in composition courses of a particular kind might better be termed a rhetoric, in White's sense of the term, although it draws its shape and content, quite deliberately, from other disciplines as well. In developing our model—our rhetoric—our aim will be to suggest how, together, speakers and listeners, writers and readers, constitute communities, if they do; and if they do, how they invest specific forms and practices with meanings and values as they do. Our description will be of language learning in a particular context. But our argument will be more globally this: that in constructing community, writers and readers behave in much the same way as speakers and listeners do; that individuals who speak and hear, write and read, for and with one another over a period of time in a given context come to constitute what Stanley Fish might call an "interpretive community"—a community of individuals with shared expectations and values. For an interpretive community to take shape, it is essential that members enact publicly and communally the constitutive hermeneutics of the forming community. To rephrase our claim in White's terms: members must enact with and for one another "motive, value, reason, social structure, everything, in short, that makes a culture."

What we will try to show is that the requisite hermeneutics— patterned negotiations over meanings and values—are enacted in the interactive uses of language employed by members of the forming community as they converse with one another. In doing so, we will explore the notion that an illuminating model for an analysis of classroom discourse might well take root in a metaphor that Clifford Geertz offered all of us who seek to understand how human communities form themselves: Communities are texts in the process of formation.

Models and Methods for Describing Interactions in Classrooms

The various disciplines . . . humanistic, natural scientific, social scientific alike, that make up the scattered discourse of modern scholarship are more than just intellectual coigns of vantage but are ways of being in the world, to invoke a Heideggerian formula, forms of life, to use a Wittgensteinian, or varieties of noetic experience, to adapt a Jamesian. In the same way that Papuans or Amazonians inhabit the world they imagine, so do high energy physicists or historians of the Mediterranean in the age of Phillip II—or so, at least, an anthropologist imagines. It is when we begin to see this, to see that to set out to deconstruct Yeats' imagery, absorb oneself in black holes, or measure the effect of schooling on economic achievement is not just to take up a technical task but to take on a cultural frame that defines a great part of one's life, that an ethnography of modern thought begins to seem an imperative project. Those roles we think to occupy turn out to be minds we find ourselves to have (Geertz, 1983, 155).

For those like us who are interested in investigating the exchanges and interactions that take place between teachers and students and between readers and writers in classrooms, several models for study already exist. They have emerged from various fields and disciplines: from research into curriculum and instruction and into effective teaching; from discourse and conversational analysis as done in linguistics, sociology, and anthropology; and from studies of various kinds done in the field of English education.

For the most part, models of teacher–student exchanges and interactions proposed by curriculum designers and researchers into effective teaching have been intentionally constructed ones. In most cases, they have not been descriptive of actual classroom practice so much as prescriptive of what researchers have offered as models of effective practice (see, for example, Taba, 1967; Good and Brophy, 1978). Since our purpose was to describe actual exchanges in the composition classes we have been teaching and studying, we turned to descriptive models to guide us.

Recent studies that employ a sociolinguistic approach to the description of teacher–student exchanges and interactions have been influential upon our own work (see Wilkinson, 1982, for a representative collection). Particularly useful to us have been the ideas Frederick Erickson develops in a study of a mathematics lesson in a first-grade classroom (Erickson, 1982). In this study, Erickson reacts against the oversimplification and unreality in some studies of classroom talk that rely exclusively on formalisms (see 167–8). Erickson's own work grows, not only out of his belief that teachers and students who interact in classrooms "can be seen as drawing on two sets of procedural knowledge simultaneously; knowledge of the *academic task structure* and of the *social participation structure*" (153), but also out of his belief that even though some formal models of teacher–student exchanges take account of constraints of the *academic task* in which participants are engaged and rules for *social participation* of adult teachers and student learners with one another: "Formalization, taken by itself, misleadingly cleans up . . . messiness, ambiguity, and suspense in the moment of enactment" (168). Hence his claim that classroom discourse is best characterized as "improvisation"—a claim that we find substantiated in our own work.

Yet, while the work of sociolinguists like Erickson effectively demonstrates that teacher–student exchanges cannot be described satisfactorily in terms of the three- or four-part moves outlined in earlier work of researchers into curriculum and instruction and conversational analysis (see, for example, Bellack et al., 1966; Flanders, 1970), the models that emerge from it—in spite of the fact that they are based on studies that reveal much of the complexity of social interactions in the classroom and the diversity in students' patterns of learning and development—focus attention too selectively among the range of exchanges and interchanges that do take place in classrooms and can take place in classrooms. They do so, perhaps, because of central assumptions built into such an approach: "that the classroom is a unique communicative context" (Wilkinson, 1982, 4); that to succeed in classrooms, students need similarly unique communicative competencies; that there is inevitable conflict between communicative competencies developed outside the classroom and those required in it for learning to take place. Even Erickson, who reminds us that "outside influences do impinge" on the social interactions in classrooms (1982, 155), maintains that the "action inside the encounter [the social interaction in the classroom] takes on, to some extent, a life of its own" (155). Perhaps this reasoning explains why he and other sociolinguists who have reacted against formalist studies have not undertaken to develop models that account for how the prior knowledge and experiences of teachers and students figure into and complicate their exchanges and interactions, even as they make them meaningful.

If knowledge existed apart from individuals as a preformed body of verifiable information and concepts, largely transferable from one individual to another, formalist research of the kind that we join Erickson in criticizing—research into the dialogic interchanges between teachers and students that take forms like question–answer, topic–comment, statement–response, and so on—would tell us much, if not most, of what there is to know about "educational" talk. However, contemporary epistemology suggests to many scholars that knowledge does not exist apart from individuals. Most contemporary epistemologists agree that objects and events in fact have existential reality apart from individuals' "knowing" them, but that knowledge itself is constructed by individuals as they make meaning of existential realities. (For just one thoughtful early account of this epistemological movement, see Langer, 1942; for the relevance of this philosophy of learning and knowing to composition curricula, see Knoblauch and Brannon, 1984.)

Furthermore, based on research in the areas of memory, perception, thought, language development, and language comprehension, current theories of psychology that account for how individuals come to know support current theories of epistemology. (For just one thoughtful argument by a psychologist for this theoretical position, see Kelly, 1955; for a thoughtful application of this position in a study of reading development, see Bussis, Chittenden, Amarel, and Klausner, 1985.)

Anne Bussis and her colleagues, summarizing the work of contemporary psychologists, remind us of the following tenets of this position:

- The brain constructs perceptions and thought (as opposed to behaving like a sponge).
- The brain's central function is to create meaning.
- Meaning arises through the perception and interpretation of patterns, or relationships, in events.
- Anticipation and intention exert a direct influence on the brain's activity (12).

Educators who subscribe to contemporary epistemological and psychological theories; who believe that individuals create their personal meanings and knowledge primarily through the use of thought, language, and image; who believe that individuals build bodies of generally valued knowledge as they communicate their personally constructed meanings to one another in a language they share—a language grounded in objects and images of their common world—generally do not believe a teacher's most fruitful functions are to examine, monitor, and evaluate a pupil's command of information. Rather, they believe with Ann Berthoff—who borrows her terms from I. A. Richards—that a teacher's most fruitful functions are realized when she offers her students "assisted invitations" to learning (1981a,b).

Teachers and researchers who recognize the primary role of the teacher as that of assisting students in their own learning have also been interested in "educational" talk, although for somewhat different reasons than curriculum designers, researchers of effective teaching, linguists, sociologists, and anthropologists. Because they assume that individuals create their personal meanings and knowledge through their thoughts and perceptions—both of which individuals make explicit to themselves and apparent to others primarily in the form of language—these teachers and researchers have investigated the "talk of learning" in order to trace the way individuals make sense of things.

It is not surprising that researchers of teacher–student interactions who subscribe to the modern constructivist theories of epistemology and psychology and to the pedagogical principles that follow from them offer different models for documenting and investigating "educational" talk in classrooms—and beyond classrooms—than those we have just sampled. Many of these researchers have chosen to record and gloss fairly complete transcriptions of exploratory talk, usually as it occurs among students organized into small groups, in order to demonstrate that exploratory talk is a powerful resource for learning. Consider, for example, the following glossed transcript offered by Douglas Barnes in his book *From Communication to Curriculum* (1975).

Barnes introduces the transcript with a description of the context in which this talk undertaken by 12- and 13-year-olds occurred:

> The children were asked: "What would a Saxon family first do when they approached English shores in order to settle?" They were also told that the discussion was a preparation for individual written work, in which they would write as if they themselves had been one of the invaders.

DIALOGUE	COMMENTARY
B: The Saxons used er timber didn't they to . . .Yes B: (cont.) to build houses?	Betty begins the sequence with what at first glance appears to be a statement. It functions however as a hypothesis inviting further exploration. (Implicitly: "How should we take this into consideration in choosing a site for the village?")
T: They cleared a . . . Say they found a forest and you know they're probably all forests near the . . . [inaudible]	Theresa takes up the implicit suggestion of the need for a site with a plentiful supply of timber. The "Say" formula and the "probably" invite the others to regard this contribution not as final but as open to qualification.

B: Yes. They cleared it all . . . and then built all the little huts and brought all their animals and . . .	Betty accepts the invitation and develops the idea further.
C: . . . All the family and that. They'd have to be pretty big huts.	Carol has not been following this line of thought, and now interrupts Betty with a dogmatic assertion which could lead in another direction.
T: Yes.	This is politely acknowledged but taken no further.
B: Why did they live in valleys? [Long pause] Aarh.	Betty rescues the group from the dead end by raising a new question (provoked by the textbook illustration).
T: I suppose so . . . so they . . . they'd be sheltered.	The tentativeness with which Theresa eventually offers an answer is expressed both by her hesitations and by "I suppose . . ."
B: Yes, for shelter . . . and so er . . . so there was less risk . . . of being attacked I should think.	Betty accepts Theresa's answer but puts an alternative one of her own beside it; her hesitant delivery and the phrase "I should think" disclaim any pretension to firm knowledge and implicitly invite further additions or qualifications.
T: Yes.	Message received.
C: Because they could only come from two directions. (52, 54–5)	Carol accepts the invitation and extends Betty's suggestion a leap further.

Researchers like Barnes interested in the relationship of language use to learning have transcribed and reflected upon a fair number of exchanges like this in which teachers have self-consciously withdrawn themselves from the conversations in which students learn what they think as they hear what they say (to cite a few: Barnes, Britton, Rosen, and The L. A. T. E., 1986; Barnes, 1975; Bleich, 1978; Britton, 1970; Britton, Burgess, Martin, McLeod, and Rosen, 1975; Elbow, 1973; Emig, 1977; Gere and Stevens, 1985; Graves, 1983; Macrorie, 1980; Martin, D'Arcy, Newton, and Parker, 1976). Perhaps the reason these researchers most commonly offer transcriptions in which teachers are noticeably absent is that teachers whose practices are shaped by constructivist theories of learning subscribe to discovery methods of teaching and learning; perhaps they conceive their professional function as best fulfilled not by their dissemination and verification of information and concepts but by their provision of occasions through which their students can learn independent of teachers' authority if not of teachers' guidance.

In the essay "Talking to Learn" (Barnes et al., 1969), James Britton, reflecting on the exploratory talk among a group of students and a teacher, describes the teacher's role and language in this way:

> The teacher is occasionally drawn into the ding-dong, but more often comes in as a kind of chairman—trying to get sharper definition ("Well, what do you mean by that?"), or to untangle particular knots ("Yes, well, what's the other counter to C's argument?"), or to broaden the perspective ("You're still seeing it in terms of jobs"), or occasionally to sum up the position (102–3).

In his discussion of exploratory talk, Britton implies that the teacher stays out of the "ding-dong" of the talk purposely, coming into it only when her presence might give better direction to students' exploration of the subject matter being discussed. Apparently, the teacher recognizes her role not as authority but as a sympathetic adult participant, more familiar with the issues imbedded in the discussion, whose function in the community is to help direct exploratory talk toward the construction of satisfying meanings as she presses for definition, calls for extension and amplification, and summarizes.[3]

Although researchers like Britton who have transcribed and glossed extended chunks of exploratory talk have not prescribed that all "educational" talk should sound or read like the examples they offer, a number of English educators have found prescriptions in their research, prescriptions such as these, for example: teachers should not be the primary spokespersons in interchanges with students; teacher's talk should direct students toward processes of learning rather than toward facts about the subject matter under discussion. Sensitive as Britton and his colleagues have been to the influences of context upon learning and teaching, they would be the first to question such prescriptions as applicable in all situations and for all subjects.

A Sketch of a Model for Describing Interactions in Classrooms

Meaning in Context—Is there Any Other Kind? (Mishler, 1979)

The rhetorician . . . begins not with the imagined individual in imagined isolation, as political philosophers who think in terms of a social contract do, and not with the self isolated from all of its experience except that of cogitation, as metaphysicians in the Cartesian tradition do, but where Wittgenstein tells us to begin, with our abilities of language, gesture, and meaning. This knowledge is itself not reducible to rules, nor subject to expression in rules, though many analysts wish it were; rather it is the knowledge by which we learn to manage, evade, disappoint, surprise, and please each other, as we understand the expectations that others bring to what we say. This knowledge is not provable in the scientific sense, nor is it logically rigorous. For these reasons it is unsettling to the modern scientific and academic mind. But we cannot go beyond it, and it is a mistake to try. In this fluid world without turf or ground we cannot walk, but we can swim. And we need not be afraid to do this—to engage in the rhetorical process of life—notwithstanding our radical uncertainties, for all of us already know how to do it. By attending to our own experience, and that of others, we can learn to do it better if we try (White, 1985, 40).

Given the questions we wanted to ask about the exchanges and interactions that took place in the course described above, neither the more formalist nor the more holistic models of interaction offered us fully adequate means either to meet our wish to characterize classroom language use as a mode of learning or to account for the complexity and variety we have found in our data.[4] The formalist models would not serve for two reasons: they are designed to account for "what ethnomethodologists term 'local production' . . . the action situated in its immediate locale" (Erickson, 1982, 155); the analytic procedures derived from them focus too narrowly on what Erving Goffman calls the system constraints governing teacher–student interchanges.[5] In doing so, they fail to account adequately either for the idiosyncratic and dynamic interplays among individual human beings that can take place in classrooms or for the influence of broader contexts upon the composition and comprehension of those exchanges and interchanges that do take place in classrooms. Taking as data for analysis and illustration small chunks of conversational exchanges stripped of their contexts (save for occasional notations about local situations), the most formalist of these models characterize educational interchange as static, game-like, removed from the world of ordinary human conversation. The holistic models of interaction, on the other hand, while able to capture idiosyncrasy and some of the influences of context, are inadequate in other ways, for they fail to account for what is in fact conventional and systematic in classroom discourse, as if historically constructed patterns of social action did not exist in interactions among human beings. These models also usually fail to adequately characterize the teacher as participant in the exploratory talk they report, leaving unaddressed such important questions as these: What—if any—are the differences between teachers' contributions and students' contributions in exploratory talk that is undertaken for the purpose of learning? Do teachers who engage in exploratory talk with students do so as systematically as teachers who solicit, respond, and evaluate the talk of their students? How do teachers and students establish and maintain their "footing"—to borrow a rich term from Erving Goffman that we will make use of in our analysis—in classroom conversations in which all parties are identified as "learners"?

For reasons like these, we are working to develop a model that allows us to find and to describe what is systematic in classroom discourse while still capturing the fluidity and individuality of verbal interchanges, whether in talk or writing or talk about writing; we want a model that will allow us to capture the contexts (both linguistic and extralinguistic) that participants draw upon in managing their verbal interactions. With the model, we are seeking to answer these two major questions: How do students and their teacher form themselves into a productive learning community through their uses of language? What do their uses of language tell us about what and how they are learning?

Initially in thinking about our study, we were attracted to the work of Erving Goffman because such system as he employs in describing talk is always an open-ended one, always subject to revision when he or it comes up against a surprise. In particular, we were and continue to be intrigued by Goffman's claim that conversation may be "a sustained strip or tract of referencings, each referencing tending to bear, but often deviously, some retrospectively perceivable connection to the immediately prior one" (1981, 72). Before this study, less systematic observations of our own students engaged in exploratory talk had led us to appreciate not only the conversational nature of their efforts to think and learn but also the fact that we—their teachers—were parties in their conversations and that these teaching–learning conversations were not particularly different from other conversations we might have had with our students about topics that might be of interest or significance to us. Watching our students and listening to them, we have become convinced that any useful description of what it is they are doing as they talk about the topics of discussion in our classes—whether they talk with us in the group or not—will have to be able to account for their "referencings." One of us was particularly struck by this while watching a two-hour-long videotape of four of her students moving from the act of reading together an assignment she had given them, to discussing it, to writing a first draft of the assignment in preparation for their final papers, through discussing the assignment again in light of their drafted ideas. She concluded from her viewing and reviewing of the tape that the students' conversations about the assignment and about their individual pieces of writing were not only rich with imbedded meanings and references to one another's unique ideas and experiences and to the personalities they presented in their class, but also with references to her as a teacher whose predispositions and values they knew very well. Their knowledge of each other and of her as members of a community was as significant a part of their individual efforts to negotiate toward understanding—to think about the assignment and to satisfy it—as was their knowledge about the subject of their writing.

Our experience coupled with Goffman's insight convinced us that to understand teacher–student interactions, the researcher must understand a great deal about the discourse of the community in which teachers and students talk. The researcher must have access not just to the apparent forms of talk but to the forms imbedded in allusions and in other references that the community invests with meaning. Just as attorneys understand and use "the invisible discourse of the law" because they are actively participating in a community that invests it with meaning (White, 1983), teachers and students understand and use "invisible discourse" in the educational communities they constitute, whether these communities be as small as one teacher and one student or as large as The University of Michigan.

Of the "invisible discourse" of law, James Boyd White writes:

> Behind the words ... are expectations about the ways in which they will be used, expectations that do not find explicit expression anywhere but are part of the legal culture that the surface language simply assumes. These expectations are constantly at work, directing argument, shaping responses, determining the next move, and so on: their effects are everywhere but they themselves are invisible (1983, 49).

So, too, is the discourse of a teaching–learning community "invisible." To have access to it, to be able to analyze what is behind the words, what expectations are at work, what culture lies under its surface, one must be a participant in the community and a self-conscious observer of it.[6]

The Problem of Units and the Problem of Context

Analysts of conversation who seek for system in human interchanges have expended much time and energy trying to find satisfactory answers to two fundamental questions: What are the basic units that function in conversational interchanges? What are the effects of context on the composition and comprehension (i.e., the rendering meaningful) of these units? For the purposes of our analysis, which we wish to make as sensitive to context as possible, we find something like Goffman's "interactional unit" most satisfactory of those that have been proposed:

> What is basic to natural talk [and we will argue to talk that is natural in educational settings] might not be a conversational unit at all, but an interactional one, something on the order of a mentionable event,

mention, comment on mention—giving us a three-part unit, the first part of which is quite likely not to involve speech at all (1981, 48).

What is most important in this definition of an interactional unit is the insistence that the unit cannot be isolated from its contexts that exist in space and time or from its linguistic contexts, all of which also exist in space and time. And since language use takes place in human interactions, neither can such a unit be isolated from the expectations, perceptions, thoughts, and intentions of those who engage in "natural talk." Context is crucial even in the identification of basic units.

Here is a verbal interchange, for example, that occurs in the beginning of a teacher–student conference that we will describe in greater detail later:[7]

(TEXT 1)

| T(EACHER): | I walk around shivering all the time in Michigan winters, I think. | (1) |
| Y: | Oh. | (2) |

A strange opening for a writing conference, one would think, unless one had access to the teacher's purposes, and unless one were there to observe the mentionable event that provoked the teacher's mention:

(TEXT 2)

When Y entered the room, the teacher and another student, J, were concluding their writing conference. As J was putting on his large down coat, he and the teacher were complaining about the cold in Michigan and celebrating the warmth of the down coats that they as Michigan residents found comforting in the cold. The teacher was remarking that a down coat changed her life for the better when she first moved to Michigan several years before.

Interactional units are characterizable, we will note below, both by their referencings[8]—what they pick out and point to in their contexts of use, and by the intentions of the participants in them as these take shape in patterns of social interaction.[9] The teacher's intention in this exchange was to put the student at ease by making reference to the immediate social situation; but her references are both to the immediate past action—the putting on and taking off of coats while talking about doing so—and to a piece of personal experience—shivering in Michigan winters—that she presumes might be a shared one.

The teacher's second reference—a reaching toward some imagined common experience—is an exploration of ground upon which "footing" might be established so that the developing interaction can take place. Footing, which in Goffman's use of the term is a matter of stance, or perspective, or "projected self"—"the alignment we take up to ourselves and the others present" (128)—is a functional element in the context for any given interchange.[10] It is crucial to the establishment of the social roles and relationships that will enable participants in an interchange to accomplish any "coordinated task activity" (143) that may be at hand. [11] Footing works within a coordinated task activity to help shape a complex interactional unit, in this case a writing conference—one that exhibits features both of an "academic task structure" and a "social participation structure." What we are finding, however, is that these two structures are not easily distinguishable from each other.

This particular writing conference, for example, continues as a negotiation for the informal, familiar footing that the teacher was trying to establish in her initial moves:

(TEXT 3)

T:	Are you from Michigan?	(1)
Y:	No, Princeton, New Jersey.	(2)
T:	Is that right?	(3)
Y:	Yeah.	(4)
T:	My mother and father live about 45 minutes from Princeton, farther south in New Jersey, toward ... in one of those retirement communities, you know, down around Lakewood?	(5)
Y:	Yeah.	(6)
T:	Ah, we used to live on Staten Island, and when they retired they moved down there, so I might be going there tomorrow.	(7)
Y:	Oh really?	(8)
T:	Um hmm. Did you have a chance to think about the subject you might want to write about for the next, ah ...	(9)
Y:	Um ... yes, ah, Chile, South America. Because, um, like, I was accepted for an exchange program ... [T: Really!] and I was supposed to leave July the ninth, eighty-four, for one year ...	(10)

In turn 9, the teacher's informal "Um hmm" seems to signal suspension of the footing she has been seeking to establish, thus closing the first series as a unit. And her question ("Did you have a chance to ...") seems to shift footing toward another that will more efficiently permit accomplishment of a task activity that is among the purposes of the conference. In short, a unit boundary seems to fall between the teacher's "Um hmm" and the teacher's question. But as Y's response shows, the boundary is not a clearly demarked one.

For one thing, the teacher does not complete her question in turn 9, yet Y has no trouble providing an appropriate response: "Um ... yes, ah, Chile, South America." What this suggests is that the teacher's question neither initiates the task activity nor serves as a beginning point for the construction of an academic task structure. Even though this is a first writing conference between T and Y, prior contexts give it shape and meaning: T's and Y's mutual but differing expectations about what a writing conference is; the course syllabus and the teacher's explanations of it in class; Y's prior conversations with other students who have already attended a conference. In something of the same way as the action of putting on coats (Text 2) serves as the mentionable event mentioned in turn 1, Text 1, these "events" give shape and meaning to interactions in the conference. They serve as tentative characterizations of the coordinated task activity—a writing conference—whose fully functional shape can be negotiated only through the interactions that take place in the conference.[12]

For another thing, the footing that T was seeking to establish in the exchanges before her question seems to carry over into Y's response to the question (turn 10). Y offers a reason for her interest in "Chile, South America," and it is a personal reason (". . . like, I was accepted for an exchange program . . ."). In trying to put Y at ease, the teacher has invited personal responses—among them, personal reasons for Y's interest in the academic task they are negotiating together. As we shall show in later discussion of this conference and of other interactions, echoes of social relationships established in conversation continue to have resonance, even as footing shifts to other ground; when they do, they often take on "academic" functions as tasks are accomplished and learning occurs.

For purposes of analysis, it is useful to view the flow of talk as composed of units, but the units that do compose it are not freestanding, independent ones; they are not closed but open. If educational talk, like conversation, is at all accurately described as "a sustained strip or tract of referencings," the units that compose it are open to memories of the lived and living lives of participants in the talk. Since educational talk, like conversation, is improvisation in which human beings project a self to establish relationships with other selves, it is subject to all the fluctuations and misapprehensions of human intention and human perception, even as it progresses toward the constitution of satisfying meaning. Footing is always on an unstable ground in a world made of words and actions; that world exists only in a universe similarly composed. The boundaries between the moves that constitute the larger interactional units are never easy to identify, for they always involve not only the intentions of the human beings who make them (which are often complex) but also the modalities in which those human beings elect to make them.

The problem of context for the analyst is essentially the problem of identifying among the myriad features that may be isolated those that in fact function to shape a unit and render it meaningful and significant. It is relatively—but by no means always—easy to specify relevant features in the spatiotemporal contexts of utterances; it is another matter, however, to find in those features what is in fact functional and to tie that to features in the utterance. Once again, however, Goffman is helpful by suggesting that the notion of *speech act* may provide a productive link: "contexts," he writes, "might be classified according to the way they affect the illocutionary force of statements made in them" (67).[13] If we add to this notion the notion of referencing and the fact that only human agents refer, we have some chance to see how interactional units, or rather the persons who realize them, construct contexts that make the units significant. In human interactions, functional contexts are not merely preexistent; to be functional, they must be constituted through the verbal exchanges that community members engage in.

Schematically, the domains of context that we have identified in our work are represented in figures 8–1 through 8–4. The basic *interactional units* in figure 8–1 (a,b,c, . . . n) are those interchanges that can be segmented (if not always neatly) from the ongoing interchanges that constitute a class—in part by familiar procedures in interactional analysis (rhetorical analysis; grammatical and phonological analysis; noting of paralinguistic and extralinguistic cues; anticipation of patterns; wild guesses). *Class* is an interactional unit as well, though a composite, complex one— one that has characteristics of a unit of the sort that Erickson, following Goffman, calls an *encounter:* "a partially bounded social occasion, influenced by social norms and having within its frame something of a life of its own" (1982, 165).[14] For our analysis it is

FIGURE 8–1.

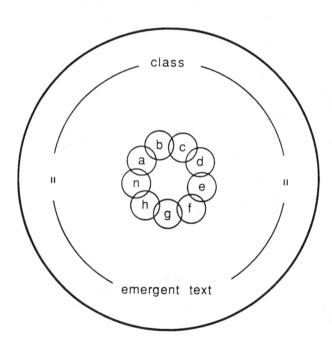

important to think of *class* as providing the most immediate spatiotemporal and linguistic context for the basic interactional units. One distinguishing feature of the basic units, as we have said, is their referentiality: each unit serves to draw upon and/or to construct context so that an in-forming text—what we call *emergent text*—may be constituted from the conversational and other kinds of verbal interchanges that take place during the time allotted to the class.[15]

The class, however, exists in other contexts and these are outlined in figures 8–2 through 8–4. It is obvious that a class exists in the context of a *course* and functions, or should, as part of a total plan. It is less obvious (and denied in much of the literature on curriculum as well as in some forms of educational practice) that course plans, like lesson plans, are collaboratively developed, whether intentionally or not, and take reality only in the interactions of teachers and students. What is real in student learning is the *emergent text* that is constructed and drawn upon by students as they learn. The emergent text is composed by the interactions of members of the classroom community and from their transactions with written texts, and it is written in memory. To some extent the text that emerges will be a common one for all members of the community, but each will have a personal version; such commonality

FIGURE 8–2.

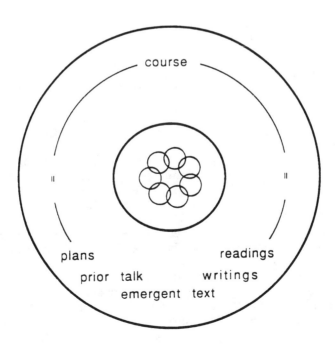

course

plans   readings

prior talk   writings

emergent text

FIGURE 8–3.

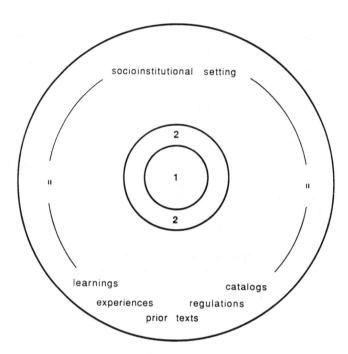

as does come to exist will do so only through negotiation in classes over the meanings and values of the texts that are emerging.

We use the term *emergent text* to distinguish it from the texts that students and teacher bring with them to the course—prior texts that have been constructed in other domains:

One set of "prior texts" (see figure 8–3), constitutes a library in memory of a student's experiences and learnings in the socioinstitutional setting she inhabits as a student: Y's notions about what a writing conference is, for example (see pp. 182–83 and note 12), and her expectations as to what will emerge from the particular conference she is about to enact with her teacher, are prior texts of the sort identified in figure 8–3.

Other sets of prior texts record a student's knowledge and experience accumulated in the historical settings of a lifetime. This last domain is represented in figure 8–4.

The referencings that function centrally in the talk that constitutes the interactional units of classroom discourse may be to any one (or to more than one) of the four contextual domains: the arrows in figure 8–5, which is a summary of the model, show this.

FIGURE 8–4.

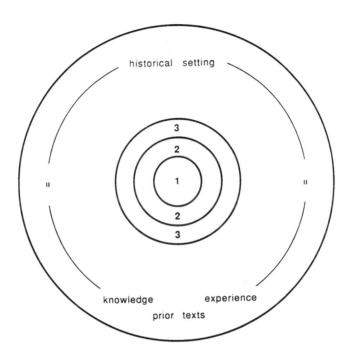

There may be references as well, of course, to the persons as perceived—to the "projected selves"—of those who are participants in the interactions. What seems to characterize classroom talk of the kind we recorded in the composition class we are discussing here is the wealth of referencings to the various contexts that surround individual interactions. Such referencings typify the teacher's talk as she seeks to build verbal contexts for classroom interactions, but referencings are fully as common in students' talk. If one wishes to characterize teaching as the construction of a community for a teacher and other learners so that knowledge might be constituted and shared, referencing is the means for community building.

References in Language Learning Actions

Influenced by Goffman's claim that "contexts might be classified according to the way they affect the illocutionary force of statements made in them" (see pp. 183–84), we have sought to identify what we will term *language learning actions*: actions in language that

FIGURE 8–5.

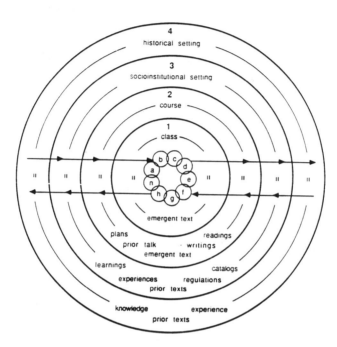

function referentially either to draw upon preexistent contexts or to fashion verbal structures that will come into being as context.[16] We have named six: *recollection, allusion, exposition, exploration, enactment, reenactment.* While the first three—recollection, allusion, and exposition—typically call up prior texts and bring content from those texts into focal attention as emergent texts are being constructed, and the latter three—exploration, enactment, and reenactment—are typically moves for building toward imagined texts, all six refer both to the past (prior texts) and to the future (emergent texts). It is this characteristic of certain educational interchanges—their simultaneous referencings to the past and to the future—that prompts us to identify them as language learning actions. In them, we have observed students and their teacher using language to reclaim prior texts as they form in their imaginations the emerging texts they are composing individually and in common for and with one another.

But these texts are emerging, of course, in a present that includes among its realities both the selves—real and projected—of those persons who make up the community and the social relationships among those selves as these are projected and perceived: thus the references of language learning actions are always to a social present, even as they are simultaneously to past and future. Because they are characterized by dual references to a recalled past and an imagined future, and because they are realized in an enacted present consisting of the relations among a set of actors presently engaged, we find these actions, realized in language, to be dramatizations not only of individuals' processes of learning but also of the community's emerging hermeneutics—its informing and patterned processes of negotiating meanings and values. With Goffman, we "make no large literary claim that social life [including the life of learning in community] is but a stage," but we find with him "that deeply incorporated into the nature of talk are the fundamental requirements of theatricality" (1981, 4). As the work of Vygotsky and his followers reminds us, however, theatricality in the social domain of learning is not mere play acting; rather, it is a matter of trying out new roles and relationships that will inevitably affect the development of so-called "higher mental functions."[17]

Language learning actions, of course, because they are actions in language, are accomplished through the moves with language that other analysts have described: moves to meet the requirements of system and ritual constraints, moves to meet the constraints upon speech acts, moves to meet the institutionally imposed requirements of a task. But the moves within language learning actions are also influenced by the beliefs and plans of a teacher who is seeking to enable the constitution of a learning community, as are the overarching modalities that give classroom interactions a particular character in the constitution of community. In the data, for example, initiating and soliciting moves more often take the form of invitations than that of directives; the dominant modality for interactions, which is realized through selection and employment of particular forms for various moves (invitation rather than directive to initiate exchange, for example), might best be named *negotiation*— collaborative work among equals to accomplish a goal that is modified in the reaching of it. The forms and the resulting modalities that do emerge in the classroom interchanges we will now describe do so at least in part because of the course design (rooted as it was in constructivist epistemology), which called for students to initiate talk as frequently as the teacher did, and in part because of the style of social interaction that the teacher modeled. But with Erickson, we recognize the limits of plans and models on the shape talk takes in actual time and real circumstances. In the last section of the essay, we return to the issue of plans, accidents, and modalities.

RECOLLECTION, ALLUSION, AND EXPOSITION   *Recollections* are language learning actions prompted by invitations that offer a floor for the recital of past personal experience (there are several such invitations in the teacher's turns in Text 3, most of which are declined). With their *recollections*, members of the class enrich and expand the context within which the emergent texts of the class and the emergent co-text of the course may be constructed. Recollections take on some nameable forms: items of information ("so it's quite a primitive land ..."; see Text 5, turn 11), anecdotes, descriptions, personal narratives.[18] References in recollections are typically to personal prior texts in the domain that we have called the "historical setting" for the course (see figure 8–4), though they may also be to prior texts constructed in the more immediate domains of socioinstitutional setting and course.

Text 4 contains a typical recollection: a calling up of personal experience (as in turns 14 and 18) in response to invitations. In the encounter from which Text 4 is excerpted, recollection serves as a means to help Y, assisted by J and E, to resolve a problem of focus and coherence in an essay she is in process of writing; at issue is why and how a personal interview is important in the selection process for a foreign exchange program, and why Y had anxieties about the interview based on her relations with her family:

(TEXT 4)

J: Was it this hard a process also?   (1)
Y: What? The interview?   (2)
J: You get applications, right?   (3)
Y: The interview?   (4)
E: Where the decision is based, isn't it?   (5)
Y: Yeah.   (6)
E: Okay, you can do it. . . .   (7)
Y: That's what I want to ... that's what I want to say about the   (8)
    interview.
E: That's what you want to say, okay. That has nothing to do   (9)
    with the family and stuff. You can say later on—that they
    asked you the questions on that. But if—I mean ...
Y: Okay, so this should be a totally different paragraph.   (10)
E: Well, you said ... you could—keep the end on what you guys   (11)
    talked about. You know, during the interview, but you've got
    to explain why it's important, how much it becomes in the
    decision.
Y: Oh—how much my responses to what my family relationships   (12)
    are count in ...
E: Oh! Did it?   (13)
Y: Very, yeah ... because if I were to say, well, like during the   (14)
    interview, I probably wouldn't tell her, well, my family and I
    don't really get along, you know, we don't do too many activi-
    ties together, et cetera et cetera—I doubt if I really would have
    been accepted, because like I said, if I don't fare well at home,
    how will I fare well in a foreign country?
E: Did you know that before you went into the interview?   (15)
Y: No, I didn't.   (16)
E: Okay.   (17)
Y: She didn't tell me until the last words. [laughs] But all right, I   (18)
    see what you're saying, so wait. Say that again? After all of
    this, I just lost it.

When it is recalled, the prior text of this experience provides for E explicit links between what Y had written about her relations with her family and her anxiety about the outcome of the interview—links that Y had not provided in the first draft of her essay. In turn 11, E expresses his confusion: "... you ... could keep the end on what you guys talked about"—i.e., Y's relations with her family, "but you've got to explain why it's important, how much it becomes in the decision." "Oh," Y replies, "how much my responses to what my family relationships are count in ..." "Oh! Did it?" E responds. Through recollection, the link has been found, and in E's response, which means "now I see," Y is offered guidance for expansion and revision of her essay.

In Text 5, a record of an exchange during a Writing Group meeting that is slow to form toward purposeful collaborative action, the actions of recollection are more complicated. The action is initiated by TS, a newcomer to the United States, who has chosen to write his six essays about Malaysia, his homeland. By referring to prior texts known to them individually (and guided by references to the co-text emerging in the course as it directs their task activity), E, TS, and Y recall for one another information and interests that serve to advise TS about the topics he might productively develop in his essays.

(TEXT 5)

TS:	Um, I think I'm going to write about the country I came from.	(1)
E:	Yeah.	(2)
TS:	I'm from Malaysia.	(3)
E:	Yeah.	(4)
TS:	And I think most of you don't know about it.	(5)
E:	No.	(6)
Y:	[Laughs]	(7)
TS:	Have you heard about it?	(8)
Y:	Yeah, I heard about it.	(9)
E:	Yeah.	(10)
TS:	You've heard about it. So, the particularly ... one of the largest ... [inaudible] So it's quite a primitive land ... [inaudible] and some regions and some deep big jungles, thick jungles ...	(11)
E:	Yeah.	(12)
TS:	And, so, it's ... I just don't know where I should start on, if I should start on the geography, like where is it on the globe....	(13)
E:	Well, do you know what could be interesting is ... I'm sure not all the kids, you know, have the chance, I mean, can come to the U.S. like this. Ah, well, I don't know, it's a lot of them do. Do you have some friends that did that, the same thing that you did?	(14)
TS:	You mean to come over here?	(15)
E:	Yeah.	(16)

TS: Yeah, they've come over here.   (17)

E: Is it, is it hard or is it ...   (18)

TS: Hmmm, it's not hard, but it mainly depends on the financial   (19)
     ability of the family.

E: Yeah. Yeah.   (20)

TS: Cause it costs quite a lot for us, and so currency, the exchange   (21)
     rate is ...

Y: Is there a limited number of students from Malaysia that are   (22)
     allowed into the U.S. or is it just ... ?

TS: No.   (23)

E: Yeah.   (24)

Y: Some countries are like that.   (25)

TS: Yeah.   (26)

E: Hmmm.   (27)

TS: So we can come here if financial ...   (28)

E: Yeah in this country. I don't know, it's weird because it seems   (29)
     so far away that ...

Y: [Laughs]   (30)

TS: [Laughing] Yeah, only three thousand miles away.   (31)

E: Are you a freshman?   (32)

TS: Yeah.   (33)

E: How old are you?   (34)

TS: Hmmm?   (35)

E: How old are you?   (36)

TS: Pardon?   (37)

Y: How old are you?   (38)

TS: I'm nineteen.   (39)

E: Nineteen?   (40)

TS: How old are you?   (41)

Y: Seventeen.   (42)

E: I'll be eighteen next month.   (43)

Y: So will I.   (44)

E: Yeah?   (45)

Y: [laughing] What day?   (46)

E: Eighteenth.   (47)

Y: [laughing] Tenth.   (48)

TS: So, I don't really feel like I know about it. . . .   (49)

E: Oh, it's pretty ... if you ask me I wouldn't be able to tell you   (50)
     where—exactly where Malaysia is, so ...

TS: Yeah?   (51)

E: I guess you can kinda point out ...   (52)

Y: Start out with like a description of your country, you know.   (53)
     Some of the ...

E: Yeah. But I'd be careful if I were you because if you start talk-   (54)
     ing about your country, you know, your country, there's a lot
     to talk about. You know, I think you should talk, you know,
     talk, okay, where it is, what kind of governments they have,
     umm ...

Y: Particularly the school system ...   (55)

E: Yeah.   (56)

Y: You could talk like, you know, the school system in Malaysia   (57)

compared to that in the U.S. Umm, how you fit in there, and
how you fit in here maybe. Ummm . . .

E: I don't know, how did you think you were, do you want to talk   (58)
    about . . .

TS: Yeah, because I've heard that most of you don't know any-   (59)
    thing about it, so maybe I should start something about what
    is happening, and where is it—what is the governmental orga-
    nization. . . .

For purposes of our analysis, we found it useful to view turns
1 through 57 of Text 5 as dividing into three related basic units,
each of which is initiated by an invitation for a recollection. In the
first unit (turns 1–12), TS invites E and Y to share with him their
knowledge of and interest in Malaysia. With brief statements in
turns 1, 3, 5, and 11 and a brief question in turn 8, TS tries to
initiate a discussion of his subject but is unable to do so. E and Y
apparently have no prior texts to bring to the topical invitations TS
is extending; they are unable to build a text with the introductions
they have been provided.

Recognizing that E and Y are unable to respond purposefully
to his efforts to initiate discussion, in turn 13, TS tries another tack.
He invites them to offer some specific advice (TS: "And so, it's . . .
I just don't know where I should start on, if I should start on
geography, like where is it on the globe. . . ."). Working from this
new starting point, E invites a recollection from TS. As he does so,
E not only indicates that he is interested in why and how TS
himself came to be a Malaysian student in the United States but
also that his interest might serve as a topic for TS's writing ("Well,
do you know, what could be interesting is . . . I'm sure not all the
kids, you know, have the chance, I mean, can come to the U.S. like
this. Ah, well, I don't know, it's a lot of them do. Do you have some
friends that did that, the same thing that you did?"). Starting in
turn 14 with E's invitation to TS, E, TS, and Y engage in a series of
interchanges in which they provide one another information about
themselves recollected from prior texts. In this second unit of
exchange, turns 13–48, E, TS, and Y begin to shape a social context
within which they can build a text; they begin to build—no matter
how tentatively—a community of common interests and values
within which they may communicate.

After their context-building interchanges in turns 14–48, it
is interesting to note how E and Y take up TS's invitation to them
to return their attention to the subject about which he is seeking
their advice. In turn 49 (in reference to the co-text that defines the
task), TS initiates the third unit (turns 49–57) when he says: "So, I
don't really feel like I know about it. . . ." E and Y take up the
invitation immediately and purposefully. E, with reference to TS's
initial invitation to share what he knows about Malaysia (turns 1,

3, 5, 8), now confesses his lack of knowledge; Y, referring to the first information TS provided them (turns 11 and 13), advises TS to "Start out with like a description of your country, you know. Some of the . . ." (turn 53). And even before Y can finish her thought, E interrupts her to offer his advice: "Yeah. But I'd be careful if I were you because if you start talking about your country, you know, your country, there's a lot of talk about . . . " Taking her turn again, Y interrupts E to suggest that TS write about the school system in Malaysia. E quickly concurs with Y's suggestion, whereupon Y amplifies the suggestion, indicating how TS might build a text about education in Malaysia (turns 54–57).

The move realized in turns 55–57 serves in the conversation re-corded in Text 5 as a collaboratively constructed invitation that E and Y are extending to TS: an invitation to recollect and share with them information about a subject that is particularly interesting to them, an invitation whose import can be recognized only by par-ticipants in the classroom community (including the participant observer). To recognize the significance of their invitation to TS to recollect information about the school system in Malaysia, one has to know that both E and Y are planning to write essays about edu-cation—E, a native Frenchman, plans to write for students in the United States about the French educational system; Y plans to write about her preparation to be an exchange student in a school system in Chile. When E and Y invite TS to write about the subject they will be addressing, they are inviting him to conjoin his text-build-ing activities with theirs so that they might work together in ways they anticipate as mutually interesting and mutually beneficial.

In a gracious move in turn 58, however, E redirects the conver-sation. As if he is unsure whether he and Y have exceeded their appropriate role in the conversation, E changes footing in order to "table" the implicit invitation he and Y are offering TS—to join them in writing about a subject that interests them—in order to offer another invitation: he asks a question that places TS in con-trol of the recollection once again ("I don't know, how did you think you were, do you want to talk about . . ."). In turn 59, TS takes up E's invitation and begins to talk about the topics he would like to write about. At this point in the conversation, E and Y seem to want to hear what TS has to say about his subject, and he seems to want to tell them. Few as their recollections for one another have been, the information they have gathered—coupled with the good will established through their exchanges—appears to have pro-vided them sufficient ground upon which to establish footing for taking on the task at hand.

Allusions refer to the same contextual domains as recollections, but differ from the latter in both form and function. Through recol-lection, members of the classroom community reconstruct for one

another, in explicit language shaped for the occasion, prior texts
that are stored in their individual memories. In doing so, they
enrich and expand the context within which the emerging texts
of the class and emergent texts of the course can be constructed;
they make common ground. Through allusion, on the other hand,
members of a classroom community call attention to texts that are
presumed to be common ones—already stored in memory and
available to all. The texts referred to may be those that have already
become part of the emerging text of the course, or they may be prior
texts that can reasonably be assumed to exist in the separate memories of all present (e.g., Chile is a country in South America; The
Axis powers and the Allies were mortal enemies in World War II).
Unlike recollections, however, which must be explicit in their treatment of prior texts, allusions leave explicit language to memory.
Below is a typical allusion: it is embedded in a complex teacher
turn, some small part of which we give (the context for this excerpt
may be found in Text 12, pp. 206–207). The allusion is italicized:

(TEXT 6)

[Five sentences precede]

T: . . . As a reader—I want you to know what readers do. They go   (6)
       along and they try very hard to fill in the blanks. They try to
       make meaning with the writer. *Remember I gave you that circle
       with the writer in the text?* Okay. *This is the writer in the text and
       now you're trying to be the reader in the text.* And you're trying
       to help the writer out.

Here the allusion functions to remind students of a previously ex-
plicated framework for responding as readers to a writer's text. The
allusion functions to connect a present task to the set of learnings
that constitute the emergent co-text of the course.

Allusions are common in our records of classroom interchanges.
They serve two important functions: pointing to and highlighting
organizing concepts in the emergent co-text of the course, and providing a base upon which new concepts and constructs can be elaborated.[19] Allusions serve to remind students that both emergent and
seemingly finished texts exist in rich contexts of prior knowledge.

Like recollection and allusion, *exposition* serves to bring pertinent information into focal attention as emergent texts are being
constructed. In expository actions, and in recollections, too, one
speaker assumes a role as principal speaker and presumes that his
or her listeners will take on receptive postures: listeners may also
speak, but only to confirm understanding or to question. The character of the principal speaker differs, however, in recollections and
expository actions (which is to say that they operate on different
footings). In recollections, a speaker is an *author* with responsibility only to his or her own personal knowledge as he or she seeks to

reconstitute for others a prior experience; in expositions, however, the principal speaker is an *authority* and bears a responsibility to knowledge that is presumed either to be common or to be capable of becoming so.[20] In our data, exposition is not a teacher move only: in part this is the result of the intentions of the teacher in planning and conducting the course.[21] Texts 7, 8, and 9 are records containing typical expositions: in 7, by the teacher in a discussion involving the whole class, and in 8 and 9, by students in small-group discussions:

(TEXT 7)

E: I was going to say he expects us to know . . . I mean World   (1)
     War II—you know—the people who were fighting the Rus-
     sians . . . I mean . . . he expects us to know that it's the Ital-
     ians, and the . . .

T: Probably the most common shortcoming of writers anywhere,   (2)
     not just writers at the University of Michigan, but probably
     the most common shortcoming is that we expect the reader to
     know something the reader doesn't know. In other words, we
     have a whole world of experience and we start to write it
     down. We make a lot of connections that our readers can't
     make. It is part of why I asked you to work in groups and why
     I ask you to ask each other questions. I am trying to have you
     demonstrate to one another—my reader isn't there with me.
     The biggest problem with writing is the absent audience.
     When we talk, the audience is present. I say this. You answer
     me. We try together to work it out. In common, in a commu-
     nity. In writing, you can't do that. You write it down, you
     send it off in the mail, a letter, the person gets it on the other
     end. [The move continues for several more sentences]

(TEXT 8)

Y: Okay. The subject I'll be writing about for the next six weeks   (1)
     is my experience with Youth for Understanding. And YFU is a
     foreign exchange program of which I was accepted to spend
     one year in Rancagua, Chile. Ah . . . my first topic is how I
     became interested in Chile. And actually I don't know where
     to begin. I guess I could start with a conversation I had with a
     friend of mine who spent one year in Chile with AFS or I
     could begin with the presentation that the YFU representative
     gave in our school. Or actually, you could do both of them.
     [laughs]

E: How did you decide to go there?   (2)
Y: Um, well, you know—a representative came to speak to our   (3)
     Spanish class and—like—I picked up one of the little post-
     cards to mail in and then I received a phone call from YFU
     and then they conducted an interview in my home, and later I
     found out I was accepted.

E: You a sophomore? Junior?   (4)
Y: Freshman.   (5)
E: A freshman?   (6)

Y: I started in the winter.   (7)
E: Oh . . . okay.   (8)
TS: I'm not quite sure what is . . . what YFU really is . . .   (9)
Y: It's a foreign exchange program where students from America   (10)
     choose . . . like they list a few foreign countries where they'd
     like to go visit and they go . . . you know . . . they go through
     an interview process and then if they are accepted they . . .
     get . . . you know . . . they go to one of the countries and then
     foreign students come visit America for a time. Either a sum-
     mer term of a full year. And I was chosen for the full year.

                              (TEXT 9)

C: What's a blind? You sit in the blind?   (1)
M: I sit in a blind, it's smaller than a chair. It's about like the (2)
     seat that the tape recorder is on. And it's got metal things
     going down and it's got a little platform to put your feet on
     and it straps to a tree, you can put it up in a tree, climb up
     and you sit on it. The deer walk underneath you.
F: How long do you stay in there?   (3)
M: Usually, at a time, about 3 or 4 hours.   (4)
C: Drinking, eh?   (5)
M: No, just sitting.   (6)
F: I'm just kidding there.   (7)

The teacher's expository move in Text 7 functions as a contribution to the emergent text in the domain *course:* it is a section that
might be titled "The Problem of the Absent Audience" in the textbook about writing that she hopes her students are constructing in
their memories. The students' expository moves in Texts 8 and 9
are in some ways similar to one another. In Text 8, Y is in process
of building a text for her listeners, who will help her revise it as she
speaks; but in turn 10 she must pause in that process to explain
for TS the meaning of a term that she had presumed as common
knowledge. In Text 9, while engaged in a similar process, M is also
defining for his peers a word he had used—*blind*—that also closed
them out as collaborative composers of his text. C's question (turn
1) calls to M's attention the fact that language intimately familiar
to him from his past experience is not necessarily common language. To build a new community of understanding, M must explain, as Y was obliged to, and he does so adeptly by "pointing to"
an object in the concrete context they share—"the seat that the
tape recorder is on." In this interchange, M learns something about
the problems that can exist when an audience is absent; he learns
something as well about how to respond to that problem—by
recognizing that while language familiar to him can be unfamiliar
to others who have grown up in other communities, familiar verbal
strategies can be used to overcome the problem of the unfamiliar.
Through the exchanges in Texts 8 and 9, other contributions are

made to the emergent co-text of the course. Y and M are learning, and because they are enacting their learning in language for a community, their personal learnings may be shared.[22]

In the teacher's plan, small-group discussions—such as those recorded in Texts 8 and 9—were designed to provide practice in text-building. It was the teacher's hope that text-building through talk would carry over into writing so that students would become more adept in dealing with such problems as the "absent audience"—the one that must be imagined in order to write well; that as they built the emergent texts of the course, students would learn how to communicate their personal understandings in common terms. Y's exposition is an enactment of her learning, and it provides a text whose meanings and values can be negotiated. M's exposition in his community of three is the translation of private information into common knowledge. In Writing Groups, students enact the role of audience for those who are speaking and writing, and in so doing give an author or an authority some sense of the questions that might be asked, the puzzlements that might arise and need to be spoken about, if an absent audience were present.

EXPLORATION, ENACTMENT, AND REENACTMENT   While individuals involved in the language learning actions of recollection, allusion, and exposition focus on prior texts as new texts emerge, those involved in the language learning actions of exploration, enactment, and reenactment focus on imagined texts as they remember prior texts. Typically *exploration* begins as recollection, allusion, and exposition do: someone offers an invitation—a request for information or clarification, a confession of puzzlement. But conversations that realize exploration are more problematic than those that realize the other acts we have described. In explorations no one in the conversational group has "the answers" that are being sought; in fact, often the individual who extends the query that launches exploration has not even formed or stated an answerable question. Explorations are characterized by talk that stops and starts, talk that aborts, talk that edges its way toward meaning.

As they engage in exploration, students and their teacher are doing more than recalling necessary knowledge to advance the construction of emerging texts; rather, they are about the business of making knowledge, seeking ground familiar to them all, ground upon which to explore concepts. In explorations, the action is further complicated because the individuals who undertake them are trying to make sense to others even as they are trying to make meaning for themselves. As individuals grapple with a concept that is emerging in a piece of writing that they are composing or with a concept essential to the study of composition, they must find not only words to explain the concept to those engaged in the exploration with them but also prior texts they may share with their colleagues to illustrate their words. The action of exploration is not unlike the action Paulo Freire reminds us individuals must undertake if they are to make ideas their own: within explorations, individuals must "name" their worlds in order to make them theirs, and they must name them together, in common language, in collective action (Freire, 1970). When exploring, members of a community must project themselves as equals, for all must talk and listen and no one may claim the authority of principal speaker. To do so is a move to shift footing to other ground.[23]

Text 10 is a record of exploratory actions undertaken by three students during their first Writing Group meeting. In the text, E begins by reading from her dialogue paper. She quickly leaves her written text, however, to frame a series of questions she believes she needs to address in preparing to write her first paper for the course.

(TEXT 10)

E: Ok, just rough? It just sounds so funny, cause it's involved in (1) fashion merchandising, who selects the materials, where they are bought, when and for what season, and how it's all done. I don't think I will use general fashion merchandising topic. By depicting a few related designers I could explain the process thoroughly. And perhaps using two from Milan or Paris would be foreign to the reader and make it more interesting. This will probably end up being a research paper for me. I just don't want it to come out reading like one. And then—let me see—I didn't even write that much. But then I wrote, you know: Where to start? Magazines? Fashion pages in newspapers? Should I use a specific designer or keep a general topic? Do I want this to sound like an essay or a magazine article on fashion merchandising? What kind of reader do I want this to appeal to? So, I mean it's like—help . . . [laughs]

C: Oh, you don't want it to be a research paper? You know, I (2) mean, like . . .

E: I want to, you know, have a paper, but I sort of want it to (3) sound different. Not like "Here is my essay on fashion merchandising"—or . . . you know?

C: Then, why don't you say something about should I—um— (4) [inaudible] magazine or should I go to a fashion . . .

E: Yeah, do I want this to sound like an essay? Or a magazine (5) article on fashion merchandising? Okay, my general, complete topic is fashion merchandising. And then I broke it into six groups. And I'm going to write a paper on designers, advertising part of it. You know—the art, buying—um—fashion illustration. And this one is on fashion merchandising. So I'm just trying to figure out . . .

C: Oh, in general, it's . . . Are you going to combine it like all six (6) things?

E: No, this is just going to be complete fashion merchandising, (7) like . . .

C: Oh, okay. (8)

E: ... how do people go and get it, and so on and so forth. But   (9)
     I'm just trying to figure out if I should use—maybe ... Let's
     say I wanted to use—um—like Perry Ellis and Calvin Klein,
     for example. How do they go about it? Or do I just want to
     have completely ... How does anyone go about it? You know
     what I mean? I don't know if I should just use a couple ... or
     if I should just use a general topic?

M: Well what kind of example would you use?   (10)

E: Do you ... ?   (11)

C: Yeah me too. I think I'd use at least, at least one.   (12)

E: Yeah ...   (13)

C: And you can go about it in general, but you can also give   (14)
     examples. Like write about it in general and then say—well,
     for example, you know, Calvin Klein does blah, blah, blah,
     blah....

E: Does this, and where does he ... okay.   (15)

C: Yeah, I think, I think that's what I would do.   (16)

E: See I have all these ... I love collecting magazines. Ever since   (17)
     I was little I always ... It's like they're my pride and joy—
     collecting foreign magazines. So I have a lot of—um, you
     know... yeah [laughs] international. So I was going to look
     through them, the ones that are in English—cause a lot of
     them are in, either in Italian or French or something—and see
     if they say anything about ... I was trying to figure out where
     all ... I could find information.

C: Okay, I think they would probably have books, just plain ...   (18)

E: Fashion.   (19)

C: Do they have a major here? They don't have one in ...   (20)

E: No they don't, cause that's what I wanted to do.   (21)

C: That's what I want to go into for a while.   (22)

E: Really?   (23)

C: Yeah, and um, I took this ...   (24)

E: It's real expensive to go to New York.   (25)

C: They don't ... they don't have it here.   (26)

E: Yeah, so.   (27)

C: But, um, I'd probably ... I'm not sure there's, like, if you go to   (28)
     the grad or undergrad libraries or something, I'm sure there's
     just general books on fashion merchandising which should tell
     you about ... You know ... that.

E: Well, that was my main question. I just wanted to know if,   (29)
     um, if I should make it ... you know, if I use a couple of
     designers and if I should make it sound like it's an article
     instead of just an essay. You know what I'm saying?

C: Well, I think you could do both, um, well I think if you did   (30)
     it in general I really don't think it can be an article, you
     know ... it's gonna have to be an essay. But I think that if you,
     if you used like a person then I think it could be more or less
     an article.

E: Yeah. I'm going to experiment.   (31)

C: Like if you act like you're that person or something, like you   (32)
     act like you're Calvin Klein you know, then I think you could
     use it in a magazine or something, but maybe you ...

E: But I don't think I . . . [laughs]   (33)
M: You know it's against the rules for this class. She probably   (34)
      wants essays cause that's our main purpose.
E: Yeah. Right. Well.   (35)

When E, a student in the School of Art, asks the members of the Writing Group her series of questions in turn 1 ("Where to start? Magazines? Fashion pages in newspapers? Should I use a specific designer or keep a general topic? Do I want this to sound like an essay or a magazine article on fashion merchandising? What kind of reader do I want this to appeal to?"), she invites them to explore with her the rhetorical problems she believes she needs to solve as she begins to compose her first essay. C, the only other woman in E's Writing Group, initiates the group's exploration of E's rhetorical problems by testing her understanding of them. C: "Oh you don't want it to be a research paper?" In a move to confirm C's initial understanding and to extend it, E responds: "I want to, you know, have a paper, but I sort of want it to sound different. Not like 'Here is my essay on fashion merchandising . . .' or . . . You know?"

Having focused her attention on only one of the rhetorical issues E has identified as problematic for her, in turn 4, C suggests that E restate her original questions: "Then, why don't you say something about should I—um—[inaudible] magazine, or should I go to a fashion . . ." If E were to allow C to finish her move and to reframe the four rhetorical problems E has posed—from what sources should she draw the information she will write about? How specific/general should she be in her treatment of her topic? What genre will best serve her? What audience should she address in her writing?—into one problem—What genre will best serve her as she writes about fashion merchandising?—the conversation would be unproductive for E. Therefore, before C finishes her turn, E interrupts. In turn 5 she graciously confirms C's sense of the one of her concerns that C had taken up by restating the issue in her original language: "Yeah, do I want this to sound like an essay? Or a magazine article on fashion merchandising?" However, because she wishes C and the others in her Writing Group to understand—as she does—that the problem she faces in choosing a genre is complicated and related to other problems she imagines herself facing as the writer of a text about fashion merchandising, she shifts the focus of the exploration from the genre of her writing to the topic of her writing: "Okay, my general, complete topic is fashion merchandising. And then I broke it into six groups. And I'm going to write a paper on designers, advertising part of it. You know—the art, buying—um—fashion illustration. And this one is on fashion merchandising. So, I'm just trying to figure out . . ." (turn 5).

At this point, C calls for clarification: "Oh, in general, it's . . . Are you going to combine it like all six things?" Alluding to the requirement that each of the students in the class choose a subject to write about for six weeks and divide that subject into topics, each treated in one essay, C, in turn 6, is asking E to clarify whether fashion merchandising is her "general subject" or the topic of her first paper. As E responds to C's inquiry, she elaborates on another of the rhetorical problems she faces as she thinks about the essay she plans to write on fashion merchandising—How specific/general should she be in her treatment of her topic?

E: No, this is just going to be complete fashion merchandising,   (7)
     like . . .
C: Oh, okay.   (8)
E: . . . how do people go and get it, and so on and so forth. But   (9)
     I'm just trying to figure out if I should use—maybe . . . Let's
     say I want to use—um—like Perry Ellis and Calvin Klein, for
     example. How do they go about it? Or, do I just want to have
     completely . . . How does anyone go about it? You know what I
     mean? I don't know if I should just use a couple . . . or if I
     should just use a general topic?

M, who stands out in the Writing Group because he is a large young man, a football player, enters the conversation at this point with a focused question: "Well, what kind of example would you use?"[24] Although E tries to initiate an exploration of M's question in turn 11 ("Do you . . . ?"), C interrupts her. Assuming that she understands what M had in mind with his question, C means to support the observation she believes he is making: "Yeah, me too. I think I'd use at least one." M has introduced as an issue the question of the kind of example(s) E might use in her writing; C has heard him suggest to E that she must use examples, that she must be specific. In turn 14, while wanting to reinforce the suggestion she has heard in M's question, C seeks to assure E that including specific examples of fashion merchandising in her writing need not keep her from writing generally about the topic: "And you can go about it in general, but you can also give examples. Like write about it in general and then say—well, for example, you know, Calvin Klein does blah, blah, blah, blah. . . ."

Her sense that her group believes she should include specific examples in her writing encourages E to recall some information about herself and her interest in "fashion" for her colleagues (turn 17):

E: See I have all these . . . I love collecting magazines. Ever since (17)
     I was little I always . . . It's like they're my pride and joy—
     collecting foreign magazines. So, I have a lot of —um, you
     know . . . yeah [laughs] international. So I was going to look
     through them, the ones that are in English—cause a lot of them
     are in, either in Italian or French or something—and see if
     they say anything about . . . I was trying to figure out where
     all . . . I could find information.

The information E shares provokes C to suggest that "books, just plain" on the subject of fashion merchandising are probably available in the library. Although C fails to confirm for E that E's fashion magazines are an appropriate source for her research (and apparently the source E would like to investigate), C responds to E's personal anecdotes with some of her own. With their exchanges, in turns 20–27, E and C begin to build the community their Writing Group will become. As they share their interest in fashion, and their regret that Michigan does not have a major in the subject, they begin to enrich the social context within which they can explore, dramatizing for one another that all texts are embedded in a context of shared interests and values.

By the time the members of E's Writing Group have finished discussing her first writing project, they have begun to explore the first three of the four rhetorical problems about which she asked them for advice: the problem of sources, the problem of degree of specificity, the problem of genre. And even the fourth, the problem of audience, which appears to remain unexplored, is implicitly raised in M's comment in turn 34: "You know it's against the rules for this class. She probably wants essays cause that's our main purpose." While M may be recalling the course syllabus, which named the teacher and students in the class as the audience for the writing produced for the class, he is certainly indicating that at least the teacher will be the audience for the writing, and he believes "she probably wants essays."

It is important to note that even as they explore the concrete questions about the shape her writing should take that E has raised, the Writing Group is about the business of exploring the abstract concept of *genre*. Although neither names the concept they are discussing with the term *genre*, both E and C are nonetheless "naming" it. E names the concept metaphorically in turns 1, 3, 5, and 29, when she questions whether her writing should "sound like" a research paper or an essay or a magazine article. C names the concept in terms of how "specific" or "general" the piece of writing E will compose should be. Implicit in C's statements in turns 14, 28, 30, and 32 is her conception of an essay as a *general* piece of writing and a magazine article as a piece of writing that may be composed of *specific* facts and details exclusively.

In this first meeting of her Writing Group, while E appears to realize that what her writing will *sound* like is related to the other questions she has posed—where she should seek the information she will write about, how specific or general she should be in her writing, what kind of reader she should appeal to—she seems to be unable to make the relationships between and among the questions explicit for herself or for the others in her group. In her contributions to the exchanges in the meeting, C appears to suffer from the same inability: While she appears to sense that a piece of writing can treat a subject generally but still contain examples (turn 14), that different relationships can be established between general and specific material in a piece of writing (turn 30), and that a writer can assume one among a variety of "voices" as she composes (turn 32), C, too, seems unable to express effectively her understanding of the relationship of her contributions to one another. Yet in turns 29, 30, and 32, although they are still exploring for an appropriate vocabulary with which to express themselves, E and C are beginning to discuss their notions of genre in each other's terms—to find a way toward a common understanding, to build a text that will integrate their various understandings of a concept they sense is important for them to learn to manage. If at some point they find and find useful the technical term *genre*, they will do so because it names for them a rich conceptual structure of issues and their relations that they have already explored.

As a result of another exploration undertaken by the same Writing Group, E subsequently writes an entirely different essay on the subject of fashion advertising than the one she had planned and then described for her group in a dialogue paper:

(TEXT 11)

M: It sounds like you are going to cover all aspects of advertising.   (1)

E: Yeah. That's why it's going to be so long. Like the part where I   (2)
put "the billboards, newspaper captions, store window dis-
plays. . . ." I'm just going to do little things about that. Just little, like, touch them, but not going into them full. Is there . . .
I don't know . . . is there anything I left out, or anything I
should include or something? Do you see what I'm saying?
You know about . . .

C: I think it sounds, you know, I think you're going to pretty   (3)
much . . .

E: Cover it all?   (4)

C: Yeah.   (5)

E: It's just going to be long.   (6)

C: I think it's going to be . . . yeah.   (7)

M: I think you should go into each one. It might not be that long.   (8)

E: I mean this is just like, I just felt like, when I just—even   (9)
explaining what I wanted to do and I wrote four pages you
know, and I didn't even touch into it like the designers and
stuff. . . .

C: You know what you might probably want to do is, because there (10)
will be a long paper and stuff, is maybe do each one, but . . .
and explain it clearly, but not go into depth, into depth . . .
into so much detail that we couldn't really understand it.

E: I'm going to use examples so people know what they can see   (11)
and stuff. Cause I'm doing fashion advertising not just like
there's only going to be . . . this is sort of specific, like billboards, you know, I wasn't even going to put that, but I
thought, Oh—there's a couple I think of. So I don't want to use

that as too big of a topic because they're, you know, billboards
are more for like car ads and you know that . . .

D: Cigarettes.   (12)

E: Right, cigarettes and alcohol and everything. A lot of   (13)
    magazines, I mean, if you look in a *Vogue*, half of it is advertis-
    ing, and the other quarter, little fourth of it, is the captions,
    and the feature stories.

D: A lot of it's on TV too.   (14)

E: Yeah, well, well there's a . . .   (15)

D: Different jeans anyway.   (16)

E: Well yeah, for fashion like that . . . so . . . yeah I didn't even put (17)
    commercials on, I don't know why, but it's so much I was
    thinking of that I was trying too hard to think of, like, the out
    of the ordinary. . . . So I should put commercials, how they
    were . . . and then . . . is there anything on radio? I never
    really . . . cause you can't really describe on the radio, it all
    has to be visual.

M: Most advertising is visual.   (18)

E: Yeah. Thanks.   (19)

Text 11 shows that as E has recollected examples of fashion
advertising, she has overlooked advertising on television. After D
calls her attention to the omission, E begins to explore whether she
has also overlooked other electronic media (". . . and then . . . is
there anything on radio . . ."). Her own exploration causes her to
give voice to musings: "I never really . . . cause you can't really
describe on the radio, it all has to be visual." When M confirms this
observation with his comment that "Most advertising is visual,"
E responds: "Yeah, thanks." The first sentence of the essay E submitted to the class that week was this one: "Advertising for the
fashion industry needs to be broadcast visually." Her essay, an
argument for the thesis stated in that sentence, is directly indebted
to the text building talk (Text 11) that occurred as she explored
her ideas for her essay about fashion advertising with her Writing
Group.

In the composition course to which we refer, while exploration
arises naturally out of conversations in Writing Groups that begin
with students' writing—their conversation papers, their drafts—
exploration is also intentionally planned by the teacher to be the
customary form of talk during whole-class conversations. In Text
12, the students and their teacher are discussing one student's
completed essay. Because the writer of the essay—the authority
on the subject—is absent from the class, students and the teacher
are relying on their own ingenuity to answer for themselves questions they have about an ambiguous allusion in the absent student's essay. The writer's absence was not part of the teacher's
plan, but turned out to be one of the "fortuitous circumstances"
(the term is Erickson's, 1982) that we talk about in the last section
of this essay.

(TEXT 12)

T: M is confused about the reference to the battle. All right. Can   (1)
     anyone else? Now, let's try to play H [the author] as much as
     we can. Can anybody answer M, and tell him which battle?
     Does anybody feel secure enough from having read it, that
     you know: Gee, it's this battle. Most of you were confused
     about that?

C: It's World War II. [Embarrassed] Oh. Wait.   (2)

T: ... particular battle ... [Sympathetic laughter among mem-   (3)
     bers of the class.] Lot of battles in World War II ...

J: [Inaudible talk of students with one another.] Wouldn't that   (4)
     be the ... uh ... title?

CM: What was the title?   (5)

T: The title of the paper was "The Russian Seaborn Invasion of   (6)
     the Taman Peninsula." So, your first thought would be, since
     there is a reference here I don't know, my logical thing is to
     go back and what's the title, it's "The Seaborn Invasion."
     Good point. Okay. Could it be—now I'm going to suggest
     some answers for myself—could it be the Seaborn Invasion.
     Okay? Is that a possibility? As a reader—I want you to know
     what readers do. They go along and they try very hard to fill
     in the blanks. They try to make meaning with the writer.
     Remember I gave you that circle with the writer in the text.
     Okay? This is the writer in the text and now you're trying to
     be the reader in the text. And, you're trying to help the writer
     out. That is what all readers do. You try to go along with the
     writer. You try to play the role he wants you to play—and
     where you are a little bit unsure, where reference isn't really
     clear, you try to fill in the answers for him. And what J is
     saying is one potential answer: "Since I am a little confused, I
     will look at the title. I think that is what he [H, the author]
     wants me to be thinking about and I will try that out." So he
     is going to read with that in mind. Okay, E, what are you
     going to suggest?

E: What—it may be Stalingrad. I don't know. The way he really   (7)
     brings it up it may be this. I don't think it is ...

T: Okay. Stalingrad. The first reference to it comes in line ten.   (8)
     And why do you suggest it? Do you know there was a battle
     there?

E: Yeah, but see, he goes in this battle along the Donets to the   (9)
     Don and then out of ...

S: Yeah ... the City of Stalingrad ...   (10)

T: So, you are inferring, do you know what I mean by the word   (11)
     inferring? You are putting two and two together and getting
     four, and you are saying there must have been a battle at
     Stalingrad, cause look at all of the people that got killed there.

D: See, since you don't know when you read through this battle   (12)
     what it is, you are looking for it, and then ...

CM: Well, it seems like he is saying that that is where all the peo-   (13)
     ple got killed. So you would think that that is where the bat-
     tle was.

T: That's your reasoning for getting to that one. Okay. Jeff's rea-   (14)
     soning is: It is an unclear reference and therefore I am going
     to try the place where I know all those people got killed.
     Okay. Both are darn good ways to go.

After studying transcriptions of the talk in this class, we have
observed that the teacher uses occasions of exploratory talk that
she has intentionally initiated to invite *recollections* (turn 8: "Do
you know there was a battle there?"); to make *allusions* (turn 6:
"Remember I gave you that circle with the writer in the text."); to
offer *expositions* (turn 11: "So, you are inferring, do you know what
I mean by the word *inferring?* You are putting two and two together
and getting four. . . ."); to dramatize *enactments* (turn 6: "And what
J is saying is one potential answer: 'Since I'm a little confused I will
look at the title. I think that is what he [H, the author] wants me to
be thinking about and I will try that out.' "); and to encourage
reenactment (turn 13: "Well, it seems like he is saying that that is
where all the people got killed."). Language-learning actions embed
themselves within one another to compose the rich texture of the
language of teaching and learning. Exploration, with its relaxed
structures of social roles and relationships, is particularly open to
the embedding of other actions in language; exploration, more than
any other language-learning action, serves to establish the dominant modalities for interacting in this particular class.

With *enactments* (like that in turn 6, Text 12) and with her encouragement of *reenactments* (like that in turn 13), the teacher
demonstrates for others to observe the different thought processes
by which students might solve problems in composing and comprehending. Enactments and reenactments have this in common: both
are ways to make tangible in talk mental actions that are crucial to
the construction of oral and written texts; when such operations
are dramatized in language they become subject to human interaction and hence subject to modification and change.

The language-learning action that we name *enactment* figures
more largely and more centrally in the patterns of teaching and
learning through classroom interchange that emerged in the conduct of the class than either of us had suspected or imagined before
studying the data. Even more surprising to us was our discovery of
reenactment—an action in which members of the classroom community "imitate" enactments first performed by other members of
the community. For the most part but certainly not exclusively,
enactments are actions performed by the teacher, reenactments
those performed by students. An enactment is both a teaching de-
vice and a way of building community, if these two can in any way
be separated; reenactments are both demonstrations of learning
and ways of signaling membership in a community that is in process of formation. Text 13 contains typical enactments performed

by the teacher; unlike the equally typical enactments in Text 12, in which the teacher refers to mental actions already completed by students, the references of enactments in Text 13 are to future mental operations that might usefully be undertaken by a student in carrying out an assigned task:

(TEXT 13)

[We pick up a first writing conference, parts of which have been provided before as Texts 1, 2, and 3.]

T: ... [seven sentences precede] ... Now how do you think ...   (27)
Y: How will I break it up?   (28)
T: Exactly.   (29)
Y: I was thinking about that. I'm not really sure, um ... I'd prob-   (30)
     ably start off with the first topic ... of, ah ... maybe when the
     representative came to our school and spoke to our class ...
     you know ... I picked up information then.
T: Okay. So you would almost do it like a, um, a narrative, a   (31)
     story....
Y: Yeah.   (32)
T: That's a nice way in. That's a nice way in. *That this person*   (33)
     came and told me these things and therefore I ... and so the first
     thing to all of us could be a paper on really, how you got inter-
     ested in Chile.
Y: Okay.   (34)
T: I think that sounds very nice.   (35)
Y: Okay.   (36)
T: Okay ... now you realize what you've got to do over the week-   (37)
     end, is get notes for yourself in a journal.
Y: Um hmm.   (38)
T: Ah ... and that would be a good way for you to try to recall   (39)
     those things. You know, just sit down and try to remember just
     what the representative said, and how you happened to get
     interested, and then the kinds of things you did after that to
     maybe even try to go ...
Y: Okay.   (40)
T: And then for Monday, for your group, you've got to have a dia-   (41)
     logue paper, which is literally just about like a letter to the
     group saying, *this is what I'm going to do. I'm going to write to*
     you about when this representative came, and these kind of things
     that he said, that were interesting to me, and then how I started
     to get ... and that—what that really does is it starts that sub-
     ject, that topic, as a conversation in the group. And they'll ask
     you questions, like I just did. You know—*and did you take a*
     year off, or whatever. The stuff they ask you—if you'll take
     notes on it—that will be a real key to you as to what you ought
     to include in your papers. It's, ah ... And then on Wednesday,
     and you bring in—when you've seen what they suggest and
     you've got your own ideas and you write a rough draft and you
     bring it in ... then they'll give you a lot of help on ordering
     information, organizing it, where this information ought to
     come ... *"There ought to be a couple more examples here, or—or,*

Why don't you tell more about that? That was fascinating when
you told us about that the other day and you left it out.... "
Okay ... It's that kind of stuff that'll be helpful. So over the
weekend, get your notes down and recall, and that stuff.... So
the first paper is, you know, how I became interested in Chile.

Y: Um hmm.   (42)

We have italicized those parts of this complex interchange that
have the most obvious feature of enactments referring to future
mental actions that must be undertaken: placing oneself as one
who has done such a thing before in the place of someone who is
presumed to be about to do the thing for the first time.[25] In enactments, the speaker may adopt either the persona of an individual
who has carried out a mental action (as the teacher did in Text 12,
turns 6, 11, and 14) or the persona of an individual who must carry
out an assigned mental action (as the teacher does here in text 13,
turns 33 and 41). In Text 13, the teacher is exploring various ways
to help Y begin a first paper on the topic Y has chosen. In turn 31,
T invites Y to think about doing it "like a ... narrative, a story"; and
then she enacts her advice (turn 33): "... this person came and told
me these things and therefore I ..." In the series of exchanges that
follows, this enactment is echoed in the language used by the
teacher (see turn 41) to give Y particular advice about how to meet
the directive to begin a journal (turn 37). What results is a quasi- or
near-enactment: "You know, just sit down and try to remember
just what the representative said, and how you happened to get interested, and then the kinds of things you did after that to maybe
even try to go ..."

The teacher's advice and directives, coupled with her enactments of how they might be carried out, serve as emerging glosses
on the course syllabus to help to construct the emergent text that
defines and describes objects and actions that will count as meaningful and valuable in the context *course*. In Text 13, for example,
and in other texts in our data, the directives, which often take
the form of invitations, usually combine with expository or other
explanatory moves (e.g., "... for Monday ... you've got to have a
dialogue paper, which is literally just about like a letter to the group
saying this is what I'm going to do"). The particular contribution
of enactments, however, when coupled with directives, is to give
students ways to imagine how their private mental actions might
fit through verbal interactions into the social construction of the
course, which was designed to facilitate the social construction of
knowledge. In Text 13, the teacher enacts not only imagined activities attributed to Y as she goes about constructing a text that can
be shared, but also the activities of the members of her Writing
Group whose obligation it will be to read and respond to her text
(turn 41): "... then they'll give you a lot of help on ordering information, organizing it, where this information ought to come ...

'There ought to be a couple more examples here, or—or, Why don't you tell more about that?' ..." Enactments serve to prefigure in words a learning environment that is intended to be realized in the verbal exchanges of human beings negotiating their understanding of the texts each is composing.

In *reenactments*, students sometimes adopt quite literally the persona taken on by the person who dramatized the original enactment and even the very language in which the enactment was first realized.[26] Y, for example, takes her assigned dialogue paper to her small group session and begins the series of interchanges with the reenactment below (she is partially reading in her opening move):

(TEXT 14)

Y: Okay. The subject I'll be writing about for the next six weeks is   (1)
my experience with Youth for Understanding. And YFU is a
foreign exchange program of which I was accepted to spend
one year in Rancagua, Chile. Ah ... my first topic is how I
became interested in Chile. And actually I don't know where to
begin. *I guess I could start with a conversation I had with a
friend of mine who spent one year in Chile with AFS or I could
begin with the presentation that the YFU representative gave in
our school. Or actually, you can do both of them.* [laughs]
E: How did you decide to go there?   (2)
Y: Um, well, you know, *a representative came to speak to our*   (3)
*Spanish class, and ... like ... I picked up one of the little post-
cards to mail in and then I received a phone call from YFU and
then they conducted an interview in my home, and later I found
out I was accepted.*

Y's reenactment is met with a response that she could easily anticipate because of the teacher's initial enactments: E asks a question about her announced topic, and Y is able to reenact what served in her writing conference as a recollection. But because the interchange is now a real one among human beings who must construct a community in which they can participate as themselves, E's next question is not about the topic but about the person behind the persona:

(TEXT 15)

E: You a sophomore? Junior?   (4)
Y: Freshman.   (5)
E: A freshman?   (6)
Y: I started in the winter.   (7)

And the third member of the group, TS, who as noted before is an international student, asks a question about the topic that was probably not anticipated by those either enacting or reenacting:

TS: I'm not quite sure what is, what YFU really is.   (9)

His question invites Y's expository move reported in Text 8, turn 10—her explanation to TS of what the term YFU means. In making an expository move, Y speaks with an authority she cannot have in performing a reenactment. And because her expository move is made in response to a question, Y is assured of the value in her community of the knowledge she already possesses—her personal knowledge gained from experience. In a community like this Writing Group, prior texts have value because community members must come to know one another—to know what each knows—in order to converse meaningfully. A dialectic is established between roles that are already familiar and others that are new, and thus must be tried out through enactments and reenactments, or in explorations.

Enactments and reenactments bridge between prior actual interpretive communities and those in formation by prefiguring new social roles and relationships in an imagined world. Our analysis seems to be telling us that fictions—moves made in the imagination, moves explored and enacted in language—are vitally important in helping us work with our students toward a literacy we all might want, a literacy James Boyd White defines for us. According to White, literacy is not merely a competence or capacity to make or read texts, but "the ability to participate fully in a set of intellectual and social practices" (1983, 56).

But for such an ability to develop, two conditions must exist: one that provides an opportunity for participation, and one that provides for the possibility of a common language in which participation may be enacted. For students whose past experience is varied, whose prior texts read differently from one another's, a common language can come into being only if it admits of diversity, only if it can be constituted as a means to form community among diverse beings who would retain a rooted sense of self—one connected to personal knowledge—even as they seek ground to stand on with others in search of common knowledge. A common language finds its origins in a set of attitudes and dispositions that enable the social formation of a language that can be used in common, in community—a language that does not provide, but rather provides for the possibility of, "a set of terms and texts and understandings that give to certain speakers a range of things to say to each other" (White, 1985, xi). A common language is always in process of its own formation, its own constitution, in the things its users do say to one another in language-learning actions that foster its formation.

A common language might be contrasted to a single language—a "school" language or a Standard Language.[27] Single languages rarely admit of diversity and, through some means, are almost always imposed. A common language cannot be imposed; rather it can be found only in the communal processes of its own formation, and it can never be fixed. Political economies and political commitments, and the historically constituted institutions that express them, lie deep in the origins of these contrasting notions that lead to attempts to enable the human impulse toward and capacity for language. Each language—the common and the single—implies a set of roles and social relationships assigned as an expression of a distribution of power. In a single language, all may speak, but some do better when they only listen—or parrot; in a common language those who must listen find ways to talk back. A single language is a lecture in the making; a common language is conversation.

The Character of Educational Interchanges: Minds, Modalities, and "Matters Arising"

Up to this point I have been considering wolves from three fairly distinct viewpoints: as objects of scientific inquiry, as objects of interest to people bound up in the natural world with them, and as objects of hatred for livestock raisers. But the points of view are not quite so distinct. And the intimation that the wolf can be objectified is one that must ultimately break down, even for science.

We create wolves. The methodology of science creates a wolf just as surely as does the metaphysical vision of a native American, or the enmity of a cattle baron of the nineteenth century. It is only by convention that the first is considered enlightened observation, the second fanciful anthropomorphism, and the third agricultural necessity.

Each of these visions flows, historically, from man's never-ending struggle to come to grips with the nature of the universe. That struggle has produced at different times in history different places for the wolf to fit; and at the same moment in history different ideas of the wolf's place in the universe have existed side by side, even in the same culture. So, in the wolf we have not so much an animal that we have always known as one that we have consistently *imagined*. To the human imagination the wolf has proved at various times the appropriate symbol for greed or savagery, the exactly proper guise for the Devil, or fitting as a patron of warrior clans.

How did people arrive at all these notions? The wish, of course, is to uncover some underlying theme that synthesizes all perceptions of the wolf, all allusions to him, in one grand animal. I will suggest some themes below, some ways to organize the visions so that when a human being suddenly confronts a wolf there can be both a sense of richness of ideas associated with the animal and a sense that an orderly mind has been at work. But I am not hopeful that a feeling of integration will be forthcoming. And even if it is, I don't think it should be trusted. It seems important to be kept slightly off-balance through all this. Otherwise the temptation is to think that, although what we are examining may be complex, it is in the end reducible. I cannot, in the light of his effect on man, conceive of the wolf as reducible.

> We embark then on an observation of an imaginary creature, not in the pejorative sense but in the enlightened sense—a wolf from which all other wolves are derived (Lopez, 1978, 203–4).

The course we have described was deliberately constructed to encourage a particular set of modalities for social interaction through language: collaborative exploration of experiences and understandings; negotiations among equals over meanings and values; personal empowerment not through competition but through social cooperation in a context in which every voice was to be heard, every message attended and responded to. The reasons for encouraging these modalities are rooted in beliefs about what language is and how it works and about how language and language use are learned; they are also rooted in political and ethical commitments—in beliefs about what institutions should be like in a democratic society, in images of their shapes and how they should function.[28] Because language and its uses are radically social, normative values are always involved in acts undertaken to encourage their learning.

The model of research we have described was also deliberately constructed, not only to capture these modalities of social interaction through language, but also to see, if possible, whether in fact their employment can be shown to have some effect on students' language learning. Because we are teachers, we wanted such answers as we could find to the pragmatic questions: Does this teaching work? Does it work in institutional terms? Does it work in ways that satisfy students? Does it work in ways that satisfy us, given our beliefs and aims and hopes?[29] But because we are teacher-researchers as well, we wanted answers to other questions too: Can we make our theories fit with the best beliefs and commitments of other researchers, both teacher-researchers and the unhyphenated kind, and especially with those of other researchers whose work has informed us? How might we best describe what it is that we think we do, and what we think we see, and hear, and read? What have we created in this vision of ours of classroom talk and classroom learning? What have we not seen? Which conventions have we followed and which have we challenged? What genres have we blurred, and to what purpose?[30]

Whether we have seen anything at all is for others to judge—those who have had patience to read our interpretations of our students' spoken texts. And we know full well that some judgments will have to await our analyses of our students' written texts, even though we will try to suggest in this section, even as we have tried to suggest both in our model and in our analyses of talk, what these might look like. But we think we see this much, for now, from the perspective we have adopted. Our visions might even be stated as axioms, much like Erickson's axioms "regarding the nature of classroom work by teachers and students" (1986, 139–40); ours, however, regard the learning of language in classrooms with special reference to the development of literacy:

1. In attempting to characterize language and learning through language it is not helpful to separate what is "social" from what is "academic." Our usual dichotomies—social versus individual, common sense versus scientific, affective versus cognitive, contextualized versus uncontextualized, subjective versus objective—have not served us well in our various attempts to come to grips with the nature of language learning and of learning through language. In fact this last division—which we have named in our own essay—is doubtless a wrong one: learning language *is* learning through language. Given the way we have organized ourselves into academic disciplines, genre blurring may be our only hope to capture what learning through language is.

2. Students' uses of language are ineradicably rooted in the concrete details of personal experience and in concepts that constitute their own personal knowledge—most of which are also rooted in personal experience. And yet these details have been selected and the concepts formed under the influence of others in community: they exist in prior texts shaped by social actions carried on in other contexts. Perhaps this is what gives them their remarkable durability.

3. Students seem to know, and not only instinctively, that the private worlds of personal experience and personal knowledge must be explored if they are to form themselves into social communities in which the acts of text building—composition and comprehension—are made possible and enabled as something other than mechanical exercises. In the interchanges we have studied, it is quite impossible to identify something that might be called "off-task talk." Talk about persons and personal experience, even when it appears to be far from the immediate task at hand, is purposeful: not only does it build community among those who must learn to communicate, but it also provides common ground to which references may be made when students are working to make meaning of concepts already named and invested with meaning in the public world.

4. Students negotiate toward common understandings expressed in common language, and both must be formed in particular negotiations in order to prove useful. Sometimes, the common language will be that of wider social communities; other times, its currency will extend no farther than the membership of a Writing Group. Both stages appear to be necessary for fully functional language learning to take place. Literacy is inevi-

tably a movement into widening communities—into communities written texts make possible; but it has its roots in social engagements with present others and in personal knowledge and experience shared with others and thus modified.

5. In an obvious sense, acts of text building—when they are literate acts, actions with letters—are "solo performances."[31] But solo performance does not seem possible unless the internal actions that enable it have been enacted—have been practiced and modified—in society with others, in attempts to establish communication, in community, with others. The constitutive hermeneutics of an interpretive community must be made public, not remain hidden; and they seem only to be able to be made public in interactions among others in a learning social group. Absent audiences remain such if actual audiences have not dramatized their possible responses for a writer who must learn to imagine them.

Our hope is that we have provided some tentative proofs of these axioms in the analyses of classroom interchanges that we have offered. Because these analyses are our best proof—in fact, because our axioms derive from them—we want to offer a final one. Its points are two: that teaching and learning are rooted in the "now" of present engagement and thus have much to do with "matters arising"; that teaching and learning involve essentially the individuals engaged in them, informing those individuals—through their engagement—with a sense of themselves in relation with others and in that way with a sense of values and meanings of their prior texts.

Text 16 is another excerpt from the writing conference cited above in Texts 1, 2, 3, and 13. As we present and comment on this interchange between teacher and student, we do so with reference to Frederick Erickson's description of "Talk among teachers and students in lessons" as "the collective improvisation of meaning and social organization from moment to moment" (1982, 153). When he argues that "school lessons, considered as environments for learning and teaching, are social occasions that are distinctively characterized by fortuity" (161), Erickson says well part of what we want to say; when he describes "improvisation" as "strategically adaptive action in lessons" that enables a teacher and students to make use of the opportunities for social action that arise "in points of fortuitous happening that are not amenable to formal modeling," Erickson invites us to explore the relationship between his observations and insights and our work and what we are learning from it. We, too, are interested in "the collective improvisation of meaning and social organization," but see these two outcomes of classroom interaction as more closely linked than perhaps he does; we are tempted to reject the distinction (at least

for analyzing courses of this kind and for characterizing language
learning) between "academic task structure" and "social participation structure" as "two sets of procedural knowledge" (153). In
classrooms of the kind we are describing, meaning is socially constructed and socially validated as an inherent component in social
participation. In this course, meanings and values are at the cohesive core for emerging social relationships. Because the composition
course we have described was deliberately designed to encourage
exploratory talk among all members who formed its community,
fortuitous happenings are the rule rather than the exception. Therefore, in the following discussion of a teacher–student interchange,
we will explore what "strategy" might mean in Erickson's characterization of "improvisation" as "strategically adaptive action."

We begin Text 16—an excerpt from the teacher–student interaction we will discuss—by repeating the last two turns of Text 3:

(TEXT 16)

[Texts 1, 2, and 3 precede.]

T: Um hmm. Did you have a chance to think about the subject (11)
you might want to write about for the next, ah . . .

Y: Um . . . yes, ah, Chile, South America. Because, um, like, I was (12)
accepted for an exchange program . . . [T: really] . . . and I was
supposed to leave July the ninth, eighty-four, for one year . . .
[T: um hmm] . . . til July eighty-five, but I—my trip was can-
celed financially. They had awarded me a scholarship and then
they had to retract it because they overextended their scholarship fund. So they expected us to pay, like, a couple thousand
dollars in two weeks' time, and we couldn't do that, so . . .

T: Right. So are you going to apply again? Or are you just . . . it's (13)
just that you . . .

Y: No, I'll be eighteen late next month. And it won't work out (14)
now because I'm in school.

T: I see. (15)

Y: You know I graduated as a junior. And I did that mainly (16)
because, you know, it'd be hard for me to transfer credits back
over here to America, you know, to graduate, so . . . I had
enough credits anyway so they let me graduate in three years.

T: So—then did you start school right away or did you do some- (17)
thing else for a year?

Y: I worked for the first semester and then I . . . I'm coming here (18)
in the winter.

T: So you're entering now, brand new for you. That's hard, isn't (19)
it? Cause other people have congealed already.

Y: Yeah. (20)

T: Um, have you moved into a dorm? (21)

Y: Um hmm. I'm into——and my roomate's a nice . . . in a triple. (22)

T: Nice. That's going to help. Yeah. (23)

Y: Yes. I met a few people in my dorm, um, during orientation (24)
Sunday and Monday. That was really good. . . .

T: Good, okay . . . Well, that's, you know, that's a fascinating topic. (25)

Readers of Texts 1 through 3 will remember that this conference begins with the teacher's invitations to Y to offer personal experiences as a way to put Y at ease. In this excerpt, although the teacher has changed the footing by referring to the task at hand ("Did you have a chance to think about the subject . . ."), she hears Y's extended responses after the brief naming of her subject (". . . Chile, South America . . .") not as talk about the topics Y will develop on her subject but as recalled personal experience proferred as a way of both explaining her interest in the subject and building toward a personal relationship. Consequently, the teacher shifts back to the original footing by asking personal questions ("So are you going to apply again?" "So, then did you start school right away . . . ?"). The teacher reads in Y's recalled prior texts information that will enable her to know Y better, but she does not yet read in them the substance of a text that will emerge in talk and writing for the class. So once again she changes the footing as the conference continues:

(TEXT 17)

T: Good, okay . . . Well, that's, you know, that's a fascinating (25)
topic. In fact of the people this morning that I talked to, the topics are extraordinary, or the subjects that they're going to, you know, divide into topics. And we have a number of the people in the class who are . . . who have lived or were born in other countries.

Y: Oh, yeah? (26)

T: Ah, E is from France, and F is from France, and SW is from (27)
Korea . . . and HS is interested in Russian history so he's going to be writing about that. So we have a lot of these international . . . You know, in fact, I was worried a lot when I thought about making groups. I thought, oh, how will I get people with the same interests? And now if I put you all who have similar interests in the same group, the group would be the whole room. So that's great . . . that's a wonderful subject, Y. I love it. Now how do you think . . .

Y: How will I break it up? (28)

T: Exactly. (29)

[Text 13 contains the continuation of the conference to T's next utterance]:

T: Where do we go from there? (43)

Y: Maybe . . . the process of what I went through to be accepted, (44)
you know, like the interviews, and [unintelligible: Y is speaking very softly and tentatively].

T: Okay. (45)

Y: And [unintelligible]. (46)

T: All right. What was the program? The . . . (47)

Y: Ah, YFU. Youth for Understanding. (48)

T: Youth for Understanding. Right. So the way I'm seeing this (49)
shaping up, it's not just Chile, so much as, ah . . . an experience

with Youth for Understanding. You know, cause first of all the representative for Youth for Understanding comes, and you become interested in this country. And the second is how you go through the process of applying to YFU to go to Chile. The process of application. Then what next?

Y: Ah [unintelligible].   (50)

T: Yeah, that would be six different papers.   (51)

Y: The process of application, then I'll do interviews. Then it was   (52)
like waiting, organizing everything, and then orientation . . .

T: Is that all one paper? Or should it be several?   (53)

Y: I think the orientation should be somewhat separate.   (54)

T: Okay. The application and the interviewing and all that, and   (55)
then the orientation which would be another one. And was it
orientation to, um, to Chile? Or to living in a foreign country
generally, or . . . ?

Y: Um, just general orientation for living in a foreign country.   (56)
And then the other exchange students . . . in my group I was
the only person in my group going to Chile, or actually I was
the only other person in the mid-Atlantic going to Chile, but
there were other students coming from California. But . . .
ah . . . like, everyone was going to Japan, but we still talked
about how to survive in a foreign country, getting used to
speaking nothing but Spanish around the clock. And the different way of living, culture shock and that. It was really interesting, though . . .

T: Did you go someplace special for it? Were you all in . . .   (57)

Y: Um, we were . . . I can't remember where we were, somewhere   (58)
in northern New Jersey. I had no idea of where it was. We had
never heard of the place before then.

T: Did you stay overnight or . . . ?   (59)

Y: No.   (60)

T: No?   (61)

Y: This was a one-day thing, like 9 to 5. People had overnight ori-   (62)
entation, but I couldn't make that. That was prom night.

T: Oh [laughs] all right. Priorities . . . okay. . . . so it's the repre-   (63)
sentative in the introduction, the process of applying, then orientation . . . um . . .

Y: [unintelligible] . . . getting ready for the trip, packing and   (64)
preparing . . .

T: Yeah. . . . You mean you got to the stage of doing all *that* before   (65)
you found out you weren't going to go?

Y: Yeah, I tell you I got all the way up to the stage of arriving at   (66)
the airport. [T: You're kidding!] I had to drive all the way up to
Kennedy for me to find out that I couldn't board the plane,
and you know, so I told them when I arrived, he said I recognized your name but I don't have the airline tickets here with
me. So he called his supervisor in Washington, that's where
the central office is, and he said yeah, I'm holding her tickets
right here, I don't know why I still have them, but you know,
I'll send them out with our next representative, and she can
leave, you know, on the next flight to South America. And they

were willing to put us up in a hotel and everything. And two days, this was on Monday, two days went by and we didn't hear anything, so my mother called. She talked to the people down in Washington, and the lady she talked to couldn't . . . she was vary vague. And like that Thursday, my mother received a phone call and they told her—you know—the circumstances. . . .

T: Ohhh.   (67)

Y: She had to . . . be the one—to break the news to me . . .   (68)

T: Umm . . . Well, that's going to be, um . . . that in itself sounds   (69)
as if it could be one of the papers. The, um, arriving maybe, what happened, and not going. The whole, the story of the—of the disappointment really. Except preparing for the trip is, could be four and then the fifth one could be the surprise at the airport. Because it's a big story really. The details that you'll have to handle in there to communicate exactly what that was. Maybe in the sixth you could do something by way of recommending to Youth for Understanding or any or all of these programs, um, a way not to get into that kind of a fix. Ah, do you think there could be more communication earlier on, or do you, you know, what do you, in other words you went through a pretty . . . [tape ends and talk is lost while it is turned over] . . . how to avoid this kind of thing in the future . . . or maybe you want to make a comment about programs like this in general. Or maybe, you know . . . I think as you're writing this, frankly you'll work your way toward what that last statement's got to be. But it could be you've got something significant to say. And the truth of the matter is, when you get this all written up, maybe this will be a very valuable thing to send to Youth for Understanding.

Y: I was thinking about it. See, because, ah, in my last English   (70)
class we had to keep a journal . . . um . . . see I started, I reenrolled as a postgrad. I started teaching at my old high school, ah, Pre-Algebra and Algebra One, and to make up the time I took an English and a history class and she had us keep a journal and I wrote about that, a lot about my South American experience, and, ah, she was really shocked . . . like five pages long . . . She didn't know, you know, all my teachers, they knew that I didn't go, but no one really knew all the details.

T: Um hmm.   (71)

Y: She told me that I should speak about it, and collect it, and   (72)
send a copy of it to them.

T: Do you still have that journal?   (73)

Y: I do, it's at home. I was going to have my Mom mail it to me.   (74)

T: I was going to say, you know what would be a fascinating   (75)
thing, go through all this stuff five weeks from now. Five weeks from now read through your journal and read through this stuff. And take a look at who you were writing about it then and who you are writing about it now. In other words you'll read your own material like a reader. Immediately after the experience my reactions were blank. At this point in time my

reactions are blank. And if you discover that they're different that'll be interesting. If you discover that they're the same, that'll be interesting. Um, and you can write about that. What it means to have had an experience like this and over time to reflect on it and come to terms with it. And I think all of this will be interesting stuff for Youth for Understanding. That sounds really good. So let's hold the last topic up, until you see, going through these, where you want to go with it. You may want to write a really long and interesting letter to Youth for Understanding to cover, you know . . . I'm writing, I'm writing to you because of blank, and I'm going to send you a series of things I've written over time to try to come to grips with this experience. You know, that kind of thing. But a letter to them saying this and this and this . . . and, ah, and they need it, because they really do rely, those organizations, on people to keep them informed. When I first graduated from college, my college roommate became representative for the American Friends, and she worked for two years—ah—with kids on exchange programs going back and forth. And she would take American youngsters to Europe and then to all the various countries to the sites and she was seeing all the contacts, and she'd bring the kids from Europe back and then she'd follow up on how their experiences were going. And I was a teacher in a high school near——at the time. And this was twenty years ago, and that high school happened to have one of those students . . . a young man from Italy, who had a really horrendous experience. And so I was in close in that I was a good friend of hers, and she would keep contact through me to try to find out what was going on with the family, you know, what was going on and stuff. So it's, it's . . . tricky.

Y: Yeah . . . really.   (76)

T: Yeah, that moving into countries and families and stuff . . . it's   (77)
tricky. That's great. Okay. Do you have any questions other than that? That sounds good to me. I think that's going to be fine. And I'll try to put you with other really interesting kids who've had some good international experiences. So far, I don't know anybody who's been on an exchange, but I've got a lot of people to talk to tomorrow so maybe there might even be an exchange person.

Y: Good.   (78)

   The teacher's general strategy in this conference for accomplishing her aims—making the student comfortable, helping the student with the first set of writing tasks (a journal entry and a dialogue paper), explaining directives in the syllabus, helping the student divide her subject into topics about which she can write— is to have the student talk about what she can imagine herself doing. To accomplish these aims the teacher assists her with questions and other invitations, offering expositions, exploring with her, making allusions, engaging in enactments. But because Y is being encouraged to think about *her* subject—to think about how she will develop *her* topics by exploring and offering knowledge that only she possesses—it is finally quite impossible in analyzing this conference to distinguish between an "academic task structure" and a "social participation structure." In urging Y to speak content stored in her own memory, in prior texts, the teacher both strengthens the social ties that she is establishing with Y and engages Y in text-building activities. Even though certain moves may clearly be identified as contributing to the development of an academic task structure ("T: . . . Now how do you think . . . Y: How will I break it up?") and others as contributing to the social participation structure ("T: . . . so are you going to apply again? . . . Y: No, I'll be eighteen late next month . . ."), what is task and what is social participation mingle inextricably in the interchanges of talk. The teacher's very uncertainty about the footing for any given series of exchanges, a fortuitous happening that is commented on above in the discussion of Text 16, proves to be one of the most generative features of this particular conference, for it allows Y's real topic—her real subject—to emerge fortuitously in a form that is hers. Her subject is not "Chile, South America," a typical "school" subject, but her experiences in being chosen as a YFU representative and then having her wishes and expectations frustrated, a personal topic that will allow her to do more than rehearse names and places and dates. The topic that has emerged from the conversation undertaken by Y and her teacher turns out to be one that may finally serve the best aims of schooling: Y has the opportunity to shape her personal understanding into public knowledge, knowledge with the potential to inform—even influence—the experience of others. In this conference, the teacher seizes on "points of fortuitous happening" not merely to make use of "opportunities for social action" but also to work collaboratively with Y to help her accomplish academic tasks. But her collaborative work is always social action.

The teacher's sympathetic and encouraging response, when she becomes fully aware of what has happened to Y to make her want to write about her experience (". . . You mean you got to the stage of doing all *that* before you found out you weren't going to go?"), validates that experience as content worthy of development in the work of the course: composing texts that are meaningful and valuable for self and others. The teacher's response puts into words, for Y to hear, her own genuine interest in hearing and reading about what Y may have to say. And in her talk that closes the conference (see especially turns 69 and 75), the teacher makes clear not only that others may be similarly interested but also that certain others might find use and value in the texts Y will compose for the course (". . . they really do rely, those organizations [like YFU], on people to keep them informed")—a comment that is given force by recall of a prior text from the teacher's own personal

experience ("When I first graduated from college, my college roommate . . ." see turn 75).

   Interestingly, a similar response is offered to Y as she reenacts
this conference in subsequently offering her dialogue paper to the
other two members of her Writing Group (the first portion of this
conference is recorded in Text 8, which is context for Text 18):

(TEXT 18)

E: What, what . . . what do you want to do exactly? I mean . . .   (11)
    talk about . . . you mean . . .

Y: [Laughs] Um, like I talked to Ms. Stock and she said that I   (12)
    should just start with Chile as my topic, I mean as a subject,
    and then the first topic should be how I became interested in
    Chile and then follow that with the process of application and
    interviewing, then the orientation, preparing for the trip, and
    then the surprise at the airport, because, as it turned out, I
    never went. [Laughs]

E: You never went there?   (13)

Y: No . . . because they had awarded me a scholarship, and they   (14)
    had overextended their scholarship fund, so they had to retract
    some of the money, so they actually expected us to pay over
    two thousand dollars within two weeks' time, and, like, we
    couldn't do that. And I didn't find that out until I was at the
    airport, ready to go.

E: Oh, wow! That could be some story all right.   (15)

   Through talk undertaken with members of her community, Y
is learning how to build a text: how to tell a story to others that she
will later write for others to read—what to put in and what to leave
out, what to expand and what to compress, what to connect and
how. In social interaction, however, she is learning other lessons as
well: not only what she must write for others to understand, but
also—and perhaps more important—how others will value what it
is she offers to their understanding. Y learns about the value of her
emergent text in face-to-face interaction; having learned through
such a means, she may presume similar responses from absent
others. A sense that what one has to say is valuable—which is part
of a sense of self—seems an essential component in the range of
attitudes and competencies that enable text building; it is a sense
that can only come from others through interaction when those
others enact their interest and speak their evaluations.

   It is this sense that students seemed to bring to their writing
when they composed essays that were judged successful: both
among themselves and by the teacher and others. While it has been
our primary purpose to examine the talk that emerged in this composition class, we want at least to illustrate the apparent impact
of students' talk upon their writing even if we can merely touch
on one instance. In doing so, we believe we are able to demonstrate something of the influence students' conversations had

upon their composition of written texts: both when these conversations appear to have direct influence upon their writing and when conversation, as remembered engagement, appears to influence the character and competence of their writing. We take the talk and writing Y engaged in as our instance.

The direct influence of conversations upon students' writing is evident in almost all essays students composed for this course. It would be surprising if this were not the case: students were asked to write for those to whom they were talking and they were advised to make use in their writing of the ideas their classmates and their teacher were offering them. For example, after E's question to Y (Text 4, turn 13), in which E makes it clear that Y will have to demonstrate how her relationships with her family played a part in her YFU interview, Y goes on to expand and revise the essay she is composing to include this demonstration.[32] In her final essay that week, which she entitled "Process of Application and Interviewing," Y included this passage:

> The representative and I set up a convenient date and time for an in-home interview. The interview was the most important step in the process because it was the basis on which the representative wrote her recommendation. During the interview, the representative asked me several questions about my relationship with my family and how our household has been run. To the representative and the Youth for Understanding admissions committee, the family was the most important aspect of the exchange because they felt that if I could not get along with my natural family, I would not fair [sic] well with a host family in a foreign country.

The indirect influence of talk upon her writing is evident when one compares two essays composed by Y—one before the course began, and one at its end. The first, which is the entrance essay Y composed during her orientation to the university, caused the teacher-evaluators of the essay to place Y in the preintroductory composition course we have described. The second, the exit essay Y wrote upon completion of the course, caused teacher-evaluators other than the teacher of the course to place Y in an introductory composition course. In each case the essay examinations required Y to write on a given topic of presumed general knowledge to a simulated audience for a specified purpose assumed to be real or realistic to students entering the University of Michigan. The examinations asked Y to begin writing with two given sentences that signaled to her the tone, level of diction, and language conventions to be used in the composition. The entrance-essay prompt asked Y to write an essay for the National Student Association, which was sponsoring an essay contest on the subject of "cheating" by students in college; the exit-essay prompt asked Y to write an essay on the subject of high school preparation for *The Michigan*

Daily, the student newspaper at the University of Michigan, which would publish her opinion.

Y'S ENTRANCE ESSAY

A large number of students report that cheating is widespread in their colleges. Although most students believe that cheating is wrong, many do it nevertheless. Because of tough competition, some students feel that in order to be successful and to be recognized, they have the cheat their way through life. Everyone wants to achieve a great deal, but they may not have the will-power to go out and do things on their own. Many students realize that when they cheat, they are only cheating themselves, but at the same time, they do not think they have the knowledge or potential to achieve the success they are seeking, without the help of someone or something. It is true that some students cheat because of poor study habits, or just plain laziness, but success is always the key. If competition was not as tough as it is, then the need to cheat would not be as widespread as it is in our colleges today.

Y'S EXIT ESSAY

Many young people in the United States feel that their high schools have not prepared them adequately for higher education or for career employment. If public school education is to succeed, its importance must be stressed in the home so that students are motivated to prepare themselves for the future. That is also true of private school education. I attended a private school for four years, from sixth to ninth grade and I feel that is when my education was most complete. In private school, emphasis is put on the academic courses such as English, Math, Science, & History and not on the practical arts. The teachers felt that the academic education was a very important asset to prepare the students for higher education.

While in private school my teachers often stressed the importance of seeking outside help from parents and other relatives. They felt that the key to a successful education began in the home. It is important for parents to involve themselves in the students education. Parents must stress how important it is for a student to complete long and short term assignments, no matter how tedious they may be, put every effort into the assignment to make it the best paper the teacher will receive, and most importantly, parents should stress the overall importance of a good education. My private school education was more complete than the education I received in public school.

After my freshman year I transferred to a public school. Because of my strong academic background in private school, I was placed in several accelerated and advanced courses in public school. My sophomore year in public school was successful, but afterwards I sensed a severe change in my study habits, as well as, my attitude towards school. Because my mother was somewhat disappointed at my decision to transfer from private to public school, she no longer kept after me to complete my assignments on time, nor did she give me the incentive and the help needed to do well as she had done in previous years. That is when I slackened up altogether. By my junior year I made a complete change for the worse. I filled my schedule with only the required academic courses, such as English and Math, and the remainder was filled with practical and creative arts courses. Although I graduated at the end of my junior year, because I met all academic requirements for graduation and because I had more then enough credits, I do not feel that my secondary education was as complete as it would have been. If I had remained in private school I would probably have received a much better education. There the emphasis in a good education was much greater which motivates the students to want to do well.

From personal experience it is true to say that the successfulness of public school education begins in the home. The parents must continue to motivate students to do well to prepare themselves for the future no matter what type of academic setting they are in. The stress should really be applied to students in the public schools because it is very easy for a student to slip out of the academic state of mind because of the many curricular and extracurricular options that are offered, and into the nonacademic.

A reader of these two essays is struck at once by their difference in length: Y's exit essay is more than three and one-half times as long as her entrance essay, although both were composed in the same amount of time. What is more significant for us is the character of the expansions in the exit essay. In her second attempt, Y does what is so difficult to do when writing in fifty minutes to an essay prompt designed to allow every student who enters The University of Michigan to respond to it: She appropriates the "general" topic (critics of this and other writing assessments would say the "impossibly general" topic) and makes it her own. In doing so, she provides access for herself to personal knowledge that she may recall in order to ground and elaborate her argument.

Recollection serves Y well in making her argument concrete, but her very act of claiming ownership and authority over the topic gives Y a problem in composing her essay. While the prompt requires her to argue a general position—that the importance of public education needs to be stressed in the home if students are to be successful—she clearly wants to argue for a position that is at once more complex and more specific: private education is more successful than public education, and for reasons that include—but are not restricted to—parental involvement.

In developing her argument, Y offers pertinent and elaborated evidence. First, she establishes that in her case private-school education motivated her to prepare herself for the future; then she begins her argument in earnest. From her own experience, she documents that private-school educators are successful, in part, because they stress to students that students must turn to their parents and relatives for support and encouragement as they study. Then she claims that her own parent was less supportive of her studies (though for reasons she does not connect to her argument) when she attended public school than when she attended private school. Finally, she argues that because there are more distractions in public school from academic studies—the primary purpose of schooling—support and encouragement of public-school students by their parents is more—not less—necessary than support and encouragement of private-school students by their parents. To move the argument to a more fully coherent one than that she produced in fifty minutes, Y needs only to make explicit that hers is indeed a more complex and specific argument than the one provided in the second sentence of the prompt and to suggest the limits of her argument because it is from personal experience.

We would argue that Y's ability to construct in so short a time the elaborate—albeit flawed—argument is in part a result of her sense that her own personal knowledge is both pertinent and valuable and in part a result of her learned ability to imagine herself in conversation with her readers—her ability to anticipate her readers' interests and questions. We would also argue that Y's ability to bring to bear upon a question of public concern lessons learned from her personal experience—her ability to speak in a public voice about the relevance of personal understandings—is evidence that she is finding her way as a grounded self into the wider conversations in which literate communities engage.

Y's essay written in response to an assignment to write an impromptu essay on an arbitrarily assigned topic suggests that the mental actions in which she engaged as she composed the essay were much like the language-learning actions she undertook in the course. In her essay, she composes recollections, allusions, and expositions into an argument that might well be characterized as exploration, enactment, and reenactment. Furthermore, her strategy for turning the impromptu essay and the assigned topic into a "fortuitous happening" is in some ways reflective of the teacher's strategy for turning points of "fortuitous happening" in classroom interactions into "strategically adaptive action": it is a matter of aims and beliefs and commitments.

The teacher's strategy in planning and conducting the course, her strategically adaptive actions, are quite directly products of her informed beliefs about the nature of her subject, about learning and how it happens, about literacy and its functions: of commitments to a way of being in the world and to a way of being in the world with others. Practice always implies some form of strategy, and strategies always imply some form of theory—good or bad, closed or generative, tied to practice or abstracted from practice or indifferent to practice. Furthermore, practices and strategies, because when adopted are always ways of interacting with others (or of refusing to interact), always imply as well political and ethical commitments—even when a practitioner is not aware of or self-conscious about such commitments, and especially when those commitments are not a practitioner's own. No course can be planned or conducted without a system of governance being enacted—some scheme for the distribution of power; no course can be planned or conducted without a system of human relationships being enacted—a set of roles for the participants and a set of rules for their relationships with one another. When commitments are made public and understood by all, they can be negotiated; when commitments are invisible, they can easily (because subliminally) be imposed.[33]

We would also press the more obvious point that no research can be planned or conducted without a viewpoint from which what is observed may be looked at—may even, in fact, be constituted. Our perspective is that of teacher-researchers whose commitments we have named as clearly as we are able, in order that our readers may evaluate our observations and interpretations by being mindful of the inevitable biases in the way of looking that has shaped them. As we have observed and sought to understand the classroom interactions emerging from a course one of us designed and taught, we have tried to be mindful of Barry Lopez's attempt to come to terms with the wolf as a creature "consistently imagined," for so has been the object of our study. As we worked, we have looked for "themes . . . some ways to organize the visions" so that, when other teachers, researchers, and teacher-researchers read our words, they will have a sense not only of the complexity of the educational interchanges we have observed but also of "an orderly mind" trying to make sense of those interchanges. In inviting others to look with us—to confront the object of our study—we, too, have tried to give "a sense of the richness of ideas associated with the animal."

As Barry Lopez believes it is "important to be kept slightly off-balance" when observing a creature of the natural world, we believe it is even more "important to be kept slightly off-balance" when observing human beings engaged in educational interactions: "Otherwise the temptation is to think that, although what we are examining may be complex, it is in the end reducible." Teaching and learning are not reducible. The more perspectives we have on them the richer our understanding of them will be.

Like Barry Lopez, we "embark[ed] . . . on an observation of an imaginary creature, not in the pejorative sense but in the enlightened sense." The observations we made, filtered through our imaginations, make us bold to draw this final conclusion from them: If we observers of educational interaction are to discover something of value about what students are learning and how, we will need to look for evidence of the meanings students' learnings have for them in the social worlds they inhabit. We will need also to look for evidence of the meanings students' learnings may come to have for them as they imagine how they will use those learnings in social worlds they can now only imagine. Learning, like language-learning actions, looks to past and to future, even as it is enacted in present realities. It is not so much like a thing found as it is like a creature at least in part imagined.

Notes

[1]It might be more accurate to name the perspective we take in this essay "collaborative teacher research." While both of us are teachers of writing and have taught and done research together, giving us a base of shared assumptions, knowledge, and values, in this instance one of us was the teacher of the course we describe, and thus could bring to the data the perspective of a participant-observer, while the other of us was not, and thus could bring to the data a more distant perspective. We found the dialectic between the two ways of looking especially generative: we had to "tack," as Clifford Geertz argues that all interpretive researchers must, between experience-near and experience-distant concepts (Geertz, 1983, 57).

[2]In the large university in which it was taught, the course functioned institutionally as "remedial": as a course required to be taken by students whose performance on a writing test indicated that they might profit from writing instruction before entry into a required introductory composition course. This particular classroom community was a diverse one, composed of students from differing ethnic, socioeconomic, and linguistic backgrounds.

[3]For an excellent illustration of the uses of exploratory talk in a college writing classroom, see a videotape "Language, Literacy, and Local Knowledge: Literacy as Conversation," prepared by three graduate student teaching assistants in the Department of English, The University of Michigan (Carol Lea Winkelmann, Victor Macaruso, and David Schaafsma).

For an excellent description of young children's exploratory talk and their teacher's guidance of it, see Vivian Paley's account of her classroom conversations with her kindergarten students in *Wally's Stories* (1981).

[4]The body of data for the study we are undertaking includes all writings students produced in the seven-week course described in this essay as well as tape recordings of classroom sessions, Writing Group meetings, student–teacher conferences, and the teacher's descriptions of classroom activities and interchanges. Because we wished initially, and continue to wish, to explore the relations of talk to writing in the development of the competencies of literacy, we noted and recorded the interactions and conversational interchanges in teacher–student conferences, as well as in small-group and whole-class sessions so that we might analyze a range of the kinds of interactions and interchanges that took place in the enactment of the course design. And because one of us was the teacher of these students, we are able to rely upon her memory (prompted by the records) as an invaluable source of data even if, in the eyes of some researchers, it is a problematic source.

5See Goffman (1981, 12–15). System requirements and constraints are "the sheer physical requirements and constraints of any communication system...." In specifying such constraints, which can be formalized quite successfully, analysts are addressing this issue: "Given the possibility and the expectation that effective transmission will occur during talk, we ask what conditions or arrangements would facilitate this and find some obvious answers" (12). In dealing with talk in this way, "we would... be dealing with talk as a communications engineer might ..." (14). One advantage of this for the analyst is that "... the role of live persons in the communication system can be very considerabiy reduced" (15); but that is hardly an advantage to those who seek to understand the uses of language by teachers and learners who are trying to teach one another and learn from one another.

6Erickson frames the issue of informed observation well in a set of "axioms regarding the nature of classroom work by students and teachers":

> The choices of teacher and student are made in the context of lived history—such diachronic information is not available to the intermittent observer who can only take a synchronic look at any point in time. Teachers need to ask, "What do we need to know from outside this classroom and this point in time in order to make sense of what we see going on now?" (1986, 140).

7The transcripts we offer in this and all subsequent "Texts" are verbatim ones, but we have not constructed them, save in isolated instances, to capture phonological or paralinguistic information. This decision reflects our interest in capturing the flow of talk and the content in the flow. When used, *dashes* mark pauses long enough to call attention to themselves; *dots*[...] mark still longer pauses. Other punctuation marks follow the conventions for written English.

8We are using notions of reference and referring in noncanonical ways to call attention to the indexing of texts not merely to extralinguistic (spatiotemporal) contexts but to linguistic contexts as well—some of which are only in process of coming into being and others of which exist only in the imaginations of those who are conversing their way toward construction of linguistic contexts.

9We use intention in something of the same way we understand other students of speech-act theory to use it: as a name for a disposition, publically enacted in language or gesture, to indicate how utterances or gestures are to be taken, i.e., what they are to "count as." Intention, in other words, is a social as well as a psychological phenomenon; a matter of language as well as a matter of nervous system.

Stanley Fish offers a useful gloss of the term *intention* as used by speech-act theorists:

> "Count as" is the important phrase ... because it gets at the heart of the speech-act position on intention. Intention, in the view of that theory, is a matter of what one takes responsibility for by performing certain conventional (speech) acts. The question of what is going on inside, the question of the "*inward* performance" is simply bypassed: speech-act theory does not rule on it. This means that intentions are

available to anyone who invokes the proper (publically known and agreed upon) procedures, and it also means that anyone who invokes those procedures (knowing that they will be recognized as such) takes responsibility for having that intention (1980, 203–204).

[10]Goffman summarizes the characteristics of footing in this way:

1. Participants' alignment, or set, or stance, or posture, or projected self is somehow at issue.
2. The projection can be held across a strip of behavior that is less long than a grammatical sentence, or longer. . . .
3. A continuum must be considered, from gross changes in stance to the most subtle shifts in tone that can be perceived.
4. For speakers, code switching is usually involved, and if not this then at least the sound markers that linguists study: pitch, volume, rhythm, stress, tonal quality.
5. The bracketing of a "higher level" phase or episode of interaction is commonly involved, the new footing having a liminal role, serving as a buffer between two more substantially sustained episodes (1981, 128).

We are tempted to argue—and do in other terms later in the essay—that in educational talk of the kind we find in our data, "bracketing" does not occur in the way Goffman suggests; very often, for example, personal exchanges—while involving a change of footing from that of other exchanges more obviously linked to the "coordinated task activity"—nonetheless serve to advance that activity. What is important for our uses of the notion of footing is expressed in these words of Goffman's:

A change in footing implies a change in the alignment we take up to ourselves and the others present as expressed in the way we manage the production or reception of an utterance. A change in our footing is another way of talking about a change in our frame for events (128).

[11]These words of Goffman's gloss the term: "One clearly finds . . . that coordinated task activity—not conversation—is what lots of words are part of. A presumed common interest in effectively pursuing the activity at hand, in accordance with some sort of overall plan for doing so, is the contextual matrix which renders many utterances, especially brief ones, meaningful" (143).

[12]There is an even more compelling example of the collaborative setting of "task" (showing the influences of prior contexts) in later exchanges in this writing conference (see Text 17 for the context of this exchange):

T: . . . so that's great . . . that's a wonderful topic. I love it. Now   (27)
   how do you think . . . ?
Y: How will I break it up?   (28)

The teacher and the student are working their way together toward accomplishing the "academic" aims of the conference as specified in the "institutional" rules for the course: those that have been instituted by the teacher in her course design and in her classroom explanations.

13Goffman's notion of *speech act* (really, its illocutionary force) as an index to context doubtless refers, at its root, to the classical ambiguity of an utterance like "There is a bull in the field," when its context of utterance is not taken into account. Spatiotemporal context affects whether this is taken as a description, or as a warning, or as something else. But the contexts that seem to be influential in classrooms (and probably in other genres of interaction) are far more complicated than that. His notion, however, is a good place to begin as a way to tie intention and its perception to the contexts in which these two factors operate.

14Erickson's characterization of the term captures something of the flavor of classroom interchanges that we want also to capture in our model:

> This leaves us a place [he is contrasting deterministic and "radically contextual" theories of society and of socialization] for a theory of school lessons as *educational encounters*: partially bounded situations in which teachers and students follow previously learned, culturally normative "rules," and also innovate by making new kinds of sense together in adapting to the fortuitous circumstances of the moment. Students are seen as active participants in this process, not simply as the passive recipients of external shaping. Teachers and students are seen as engaged in *praxis*, improvising situational variations within and around socioculturally prescribed thematic material and occasionally, within the process of improvisation, discovering new possibilities for learning and for social life (1982, 166).

15We use the term *text* quite deliberately in our model to emphasize the hermeneutical character of classroom interchanges and of attempts to understand them. What we are about in studying texts is similar to the kind of study Michael Shapiro recommends for talking about texts in political science:

> The text identified in one's analysis of political thinking becomes not simply a document in the history of political theory but rather the sign of constitutive processes which give that text various meanings. Interpretation then becomes an analytic inquiry into the meaning contexts that produce the text—including the linguistic context of the speaker/author and a reflexive inquiry into the meaning context of the interpreter (1981, 168).

The terms *text* and *emergent text*, used to name both talk and writing and what both reflect of student learning, are used to emphasize our position that the analysis of conversation, and the analysis of learning as well, are no more and no less than interpretive acts. No matter the language in which they are expressed—formalist or holistic—such analyses are expressions in an art of interpretation.

16We intend an allusion to the term *speech act* in our term *language-learning action*, and for several reasons: (a) Because the language-learning actions we name recur in the interactions of members of the class, and can be connected to the descriptors in other accounts that focus upon the system and ritual constraints in conversation, it is clear that they are socially constructed—systematic rather than idiosyncratic ones; (b) The term allows us to treat intentionality (see note 12) as a factor in our analysis;

(c) It is clear that these actions have illocutionary force analogous to that captured in speech-act theory, since actions initiated by one person in an interchange are perceived and reacted to as such—proving they count as such—by those who are participants in the exchange. Language-learning actions can be felicitous or nonfelicitous, as teachers know, and for some of the same reasons that speech acts are or are not felicitous.

We use the term *action*, however, rather than act, to avoid some of the implications of speech-act theory. Our notion of reference is different, for example, as is our extension of the notion of pertinent context. An even more significant departure is our wish to claim that most language-learning actions, in order to have force, must be collaboratively undertaken and collaboratively accomplished, not merely initiated by one speaker and then "taken up" by another.

In doing our analyses we have been much aided by the identifications other scholars have made of speech acts and their functions, even though our conception of language-learning action departs from that of speech act. It is important to stress one similarity, however: language-learning actions, like speech acts, function in part to effect the building of social community among human beings who are using language in an attempt to come to understand the world they live in and to act upon it by engaging in social relations with committed and understanding others.

[17]Our thoughts about language learning, and especially about learning through language, have obviously been influenced by the work of Vygotsky and some other of his more recent followers. Vygotsky's notions, as exemplified in the following citation, have prompted us to take the study of classroom discourse more seriously than we might otherwise have done and have suggested emphases for such study:

> The very mechanism underlying higher mental functions is a copy from social interaction; all higher mental functions are internalized social relationships. . . . Their composition, genetic structure, and means of action [forms of mediation]—in a word, their whole nature—is social. Even when we turn to mental [internal] processes, their nature remains quasi-social. In their own private sphere, human beings retain the functions of social interaction (Vygotsky, 1981, as cited in Wertsch, 1985, 66).

As we shall show, something akin to dramatization is an essential stage in the movement from external social interaction to internal processes: there are roles and relationships to be learned when students are making their way into a new community, just as there are strategies for the employment of language in order both to play the roles and to make meaning. Trying out new roles and acting them out in language are essential steps toward learning.

[18]We have not yet carefully studied the *genres* of the oral texts students construct and the relations of these to identifiable *genres* of and in written texts, even though we feel it would be illuminating to do so. That some forms of talk in language-learning actions have the characteristics of recognizable *genres* testifies to two things: the social character of talk in language-learning actions (i.e., the forms are not unique but repeated) and the reality of such actions in social interchanges. They also testify to the influences of written texts upon talk in literate societies.

[19]In classroom talk, allusions seem to have some of the same functions as naming. By organizing a complex set of understandings and using a "symbol" for them, what is thereby collected can serve as a unit in another complex structure. Allusions may well be more important in processes of concept formation—and in the process of forming community—than our brief treatment of them here indicates.

[20]In trying to understand these distinctions, which we feel are necessary for a proper understanding of our data, we have found helpful Goffman's explication of the notions of *participation framework* and *production format* (see Goffman, 1981, 137–57). These notions will be the focus for a subsequent paper. Our notions are also indebted to Suzanne Langer's distinction between discursive and presentational modes of discourse (1942, Chaps. 4, 5).

[21]In the course we describe here, the teacher generally restricted her expository moves (save for task setting) to points in interchanges when she could seize upon an emerging issue in order to offer direct instruction about writing and its various demands.

[22]It is perhaps useful to note that expository moves by students are less common in the records of whole-class discussions than in those of small-group discussions, although the number of them increased as the term progressed. The uncertainties and hedges in Y's expository moves are in some ways typical of what all students do, and in other ways particular to Y and to the relationship that developed in the small group during the course between her and E—a young man with a French-accented voice (Text 8).

The question F puts to M in Text 9—"Drinking, eh?"—and his tacit apology for the question—"I'm just kidding there"—after M sincerely responds to his question, is illustrative of students' moves to build and preserve the fragile communities they are constructing when they realize they have prejudged—stereotyped. During this half-semester course, F's initial disdain for M's explanations of how and why a young man from rural Michigan hunts deer developed into open curiosity and finally into what might be called cautious respect.

In doing analysis of this kind, one is forcibly reminded always of the overlapping of what Erickson calls the academic task structure and the social participation structure.

[23]This is an important characteristic distinguishing exploration from other language-learning actions, most especially recollection and exposition. Social roles and relationships figure crucially in language-learning actions, to some extent similarly to how they do in speech acts. Issues of authority and power are central in learning communities, as much recent work on education emphasizes (see for pertinent references note 28). In a very real sense, "footing" is exploration of political ground.

[24]We noted with interest that until M's question, E and C, the two women in this four-person Writing Group, appear to be talking to one another. We suspect that E and C might have thought the two males in their group were less interested in E's subject—fashion—than they. M's question to E in Text 10 suggests not only that he will be a participant in discussions of E's planned writing, but also that he promises to be a valuable contributor to explorations E invites. Text 11 indicates how much influence M actually comes to have on E's act of text-building.

[25]We find purpose for our own studies of enactments and reenactments in ideas that Jerome Bruner has explored, in order

> to follow the spirit of the Vygotskian project to find the manner in which aspirant members of a culture learn from their tutors, the vicars of their culture, how to understand the world. That world is a symbolic world in the sense that it consists of conceptually organized, rule-bound belief systems about what exists, about how to get to goals, about what is to be valued. There is no way, none, in which a human being could possibly master that world without the aid and assistance of others for, in fact, that world *is* others (1985, 32).

We want to include among the "tutors" and "vicars of . . . culture" all of those social beings in learning communities who are "aspirant members of a culture," for all of our sakes. Teachers as well as learners aspire. We also want our work to reflect the humane spirit characteristic of Bruner's:

> If tutors are seen not as partners in advancement, but, as reported in some recent research . . . as sources of punishment, then it may have disastrous consequences for the candidate learner. That problem has not been at the center of my attention, although I know how desperately important it is (1985, 32–3).

That problem is at the center of our attention; and from work we have done in various settings, especially with failed and failing students, we, too, know how desperately important it is.

[26]Reenactments might be a particularly interesting instance of movement into Vygotsky's "zone of proximal development." For a helpful discussion of this notion of Vygotsky's see Wertsch (1985, 67–76).

[27]In some of the sociolinguistic literature on the problems nonmainstream students encounter in schools, and in almost all of the literature on the problems of basic writers, there may be found a hidden assumption (though it is not always hidden) that something called "school language" is an invariant language. The pedagogies recommended in these literatures almost always call for the culturally divergent to accommodate themselves to the norms of school language. Since these norms are rarely described, save with reference mainly to features of Standard English— which is also often taken as invariant—it is almost necessary to hide the assumption.

[28]Although the course we have described was designed to enable newcomers to a university's several communities to find confidence enough in themselves as language users to imagine a place for themselves in the various languages used by those communities, the teacher embarked on a broader aim: the empowerment of newcomers, the freeing of their voices, so that academic discourse communities might be changed from the excluding societies all too many of them have become. With Maxine Greene, this teacher wanted "to see the means of achieving literacy made continuous with the end in view, which for both is the achievement of social communion by an articulate public" (see Greene, 1982). Both confess commitment to the kind of world John Dewey envisioned:

Half a century ago John Dewey expressed the need for an articulate public and linked its emergence to a "subtle, delicate, vivid, and responsive art of communication." Only when we have achieved such communication, he said, will democracy come into its own, "for democracy is a name for a life of free and enriching communion. . . . It will have its consummation when free social inquiry is indissolubly wedded to the art of full and moving communication (1982, 326).

It was along the road toward such a society that these aspirants to membership in "an articulate public" sought to make their way, formulating for one another, through talking and writing, through listening to one another and through reading what others had written, as "subtle, delicate, vivid, and responsive art of communication" as they could manage together at that time in their lives and in the community they inhabited.

In short, the course aimed for a form of empowerment: one rooted in notions formed by Dewey (see, especially, 1916) as interpreted by Maxine Greene (see, especially, 1978, 1982). In having such a political aim, the pedagogy we describe manifests its allegiance to the movement that has come to be called "liberatory" or "emancipatory pedagogy." Our notions of what pedagogy should be, but more our notions of what pedagogy should be for, have been much influenced by the work of others who see learning as appropriately aimed at *praxis* (see, especially, Aronowitz and Giroux, 1985; Everhart, 1983; Freire, 1970; Greene, 1978, 1986; Shor, 1980, 1987).

[29]In our society at this time, even in that part of it called "academic," bottom-line questions are always asked: Did this course and its conduct achieve its aim? More concretely, did this course and its conduct improve the writing of students who were obliged to take it? Some answers are available: Among the 15 students who took the course for credit (one student audited the course), only one student failed to pass the exit examination—an essay sample read by others than the teacher; 13 students entered introductory composition and one student was exempted from introductory composition. The student who "failed" the course, as it happened, had been misplaced in it. New to the United States and to English, he had not taken a prerequisite course to which he had been assigned, a course offered in the University's English Language Institute for students whose knowledge and usage of English is as limited as his was.

Other questions about the course may also be asked: Did students perceive that the course served their needs? Did they find it useful to them? Again, some answers are available: In their responses to the following key questions on a survey which the Center for Research on Learning and Teaching in The University of Michigan asks students to complete at the end of each of their courses of study, the 15 students who completed the course offered the following evaluations on a five-point Lickert scale (SA equals Strongly Agree, A equals Agree, N equals Neither Agree nor Disagree, D equals Disagree, SD equals Strongly Disagree)—Q: I developed greater awareness of my writing abilities (R: SA equals 7, A equals 8); Q: I improved my ability to analyze my writing (R: SA equals 7, A equals 8); Q: I improved my ability to revise my writing (R: SA equals 9, A equals 6); Q: I improved my ability to develop my ideas (R: SA equals 6, A equals 9).

And still other questions may be asked: If invited to describe their experience of the course and the conception(s) of literacy they gained from it, what would students have to say for themselves? And again, some answers are available. The teacher asked the students to write her brief letters, telling her what they "thought" of the course. Students were not anxious to please the teacher with their "thoughts" because they believed their success in the course might be affected by them, for they knew the teacher would not determine if they "passed" or "failed"; but it would be foolish not to realize that in a teaching-learning setting in which much emphasis was put on respect for one another's ideas and concern for one another's feelings, the students would be concerned for the teacher's feelings as they wrote. As the teacher read students' "thoughts," written to her in letters, she was particularly interested in those aspects of the course and their learning that students chose to comment on. It is interesting to note what "counted" as literacy learning for three representative students whose thoughts we reproduce here, omitting only personal messages of appreciation.

E: This class has been for me, one of these classes to which one wants to go to everyday, and it is not due to the fact that I never had a class in which I could get coffee in the middle of the class. It was a very enriching class for different reasons.

 One of these reason was the diversity of the people. I learned a great deal from the Asian cultures and laughed at the numerous adventures of a young women went through, preparing for a year trip in a country she would never get to see. Being open to many cultures, it kept me very interested. But the most enriching part of the course was for me the different perspective I got on writing. I made it out a lot more complicated than it can be at a student level. I needed improvement and still do but I feel a lot more able to write impromptu essays than before. This class should be taken by more freshman because the ECB workshop ends up being an advantage after all.

TS: At the beginning of this class. I don't even know what is the purpose of our lessons or what I am suppose to achieve. I just enjoy reading some other people's essay. I like those essays on hunting and wind surfing. As time passed, I knew that I am suppose to write an assessment essay in order to be exempted from this tutorial class, where as I have written my 1st assessment essay during the orientation which I don't even know the purpose of writing it.

 Sometimes I feel a little bored in the class, especially when discussing some essay topic which I am not interested at all. But most of the time I did enjoy the class.

 I think I've learned most from those individual conferences, where I discovered my weakness in writing, when I have my own paper interpreted more deeply.

D: This class was a new experience for me. I became close to many of my classmates and the instructor. You have a wonderful way of making me write my best and making me feel good about my writing. . . .

What I liked the most about your teaching was the personal touch you gave to the class. You made writing an enjoyment and a challenge. The ideal of writing on one subject the entire course truly helped me to develop my skill. Also, look at other people's writing help me to see some of the common mistake in writing and also some of the creativise of my classmates. Over all this was a positive experience for me and will help for in my college writing in the future.

Of course nothing can be said as yet about the larger aims of the course, for, as Maxine Greene says, "literacy ought to be conceived as an opening, a becoming, never a fixed end" (1982, 326). It is the work of a lifetime to achieve a "subtle, delicate, vivid, and responsive art of communication"; and for that art to develop and have force as praxis presumes opportunities and actions that cannot be provided in a single course. Our inability to measure achievement of the best aims we can imagine should not deter us from trying to reach them.

30The model we have described was also designed to be responsive to ethical and political commitments—to reflect the argument that normative values cannot be banished from work on learning that any one of us does as a researcher. Our own perspective is unashamedly that of the teacher-researcher self-interested—though we hope not selfishly interested—in the outcomes the research seeks to demonstrate. Our object is to study what we do with others in order that we might do better for the benefit of all: do it more self-consciously and, with work and luck, more humanely with reference to ethicopolitical aims that can be made explicit and thus become subject to objection and negotiation. Our aim is to study practice, not in order to fix or prescribe it, but to change it.

Good classrooms, we want to show and argue, are those in which worlds to be made are imagined and enacted so that they can come into being—even, perhaps one day, outside the classroom; in such classrooms, we hope to show, knowledge has real value—to those human beings who are constituting a world in order to live in it with others. Good research, we want to argue, is that research which imagines worlds as well, from knowledge that is communally constituted, so that whatever *is* might have some chance of becoming what *might be*. It is in this sense—that it aims at change with reference to what might one day be—that our research is intended to contribute to what Maxine Greene calls "knowledge as praxis" (1978, 95–110), and Patti Lather, "Research as Praxis" (1986, 257–77).

31The term *solo performance* is now much in the literature of cognitive science. We have been made to reflect by Bruner's reflections upon the term and its use in cognitive science:

> I would like to comment in passing on one point that has usually been overlooked or given second billing in our own achievement-orientated Western culture. It is inherent in [Vygotsky's] conviction that passing on knowledge is like passing on language—his basic belief that social transaction is the fundamental vehicle of education and not, so to speak, solo performance. But alas, he did not live long enough to develop his ideas about the subject. I believe that it was his eventual

hope to delineate the transactional nature of learning, particularly since learning for him involved entry into a culture via induction by more skilled members. But though he did not live long enough to carry out his program, it seems to me that it remains an important one to pursue. Too often, human learning has been depicted in the paradigm of a lone organism pitted against nature—whether in the model of the behaviorist's organism shaping up responses to fit the geometries and probabilities of the world of stimuli, or in the Piagetian model where a lone child struggles single-handed to strike some equilibrium between assimilating the world to himself or himself to the world. Vygotsky was struck, rather, with how much learning is quintessentially assisted and vicarious and about social conventions and intellectual prostheses in the manner of Popper's World Three (1985, 25).

[32]We mentioned another example earlier in the essay in our discussion of Text 11. After M's remark to E in turn 18 ("Most advertising is visual"), E went on to compose an essay that argued for M's observation, an observation that gave focus and coherence to the ideas and materials with which she had been working that week.

[33]We would argue that there is at least as much need for teachers to become self-conscious and reflective about the political and ethical implications of their stances and actions as some researchers argue that students must become about their own processes of learning. If metacognition is important for students, teachers need a metapolitics. Ways of being and behaving that are taken as neutral with reference to systems of political and ethical values can be perceived and hold status as givens: objects in the nature of things, not processes constructed by humans in history. It is perhaps useful to remember that effective schools, like wolves, are in part imagined; we need to learn to become critical inquirers into what it is that causes us to see the images we do, and what the imagined object might look like to others.

Part Four

Literacy and Our Institutions

A large share of my professional life, more than two decades of it, has been devoted (if that is the word) to administration, mostly at the program or departmental level. It is from my own experiences in English departments and in writing programs that the arguments in the first two essays of this section emerge; it is from quite other experiences that the last does, although it, too, touches on institutions as they affect what we are able to accomplish as teachers and as researchers and scholars. All three essays might as well have the title of the last, "The Politics of Literacy," for they all explore the implications of social roles and relationships, the way we make our institutions and they us, and the implications of all of these for the teaching of literacy.

The first two essays return to themes and questions raised particularly in the first section of this collection: What is literacy? How in our culture is literacy institutionalized? How well or how ill in our culture do our institutions serve real and perceived needs for literacy, actual and imagined uses for literacy? And whom do we, who conceive of literacy, seek to serve and end up not serving, through the ways we think of literacy and act to enable it? "Literacy in the Department of English" has been read as an attack on English departments, but it is not that (or not only that). Rather, it was written in an attempt to invite English teachers and departmental administrators to extend conversations about what English departments might be if recognition were given to where we are situated and what our obligations are in our intellectual worlds and in the larger societies in which we live our intellectual lives. The essay takes up and talks about whether our various conceptions of our professional and intellectual roles separate us; and it asks whether these roles should separate us, given present chasms between composition teachers and literature teachers, rhetoric and literary criticism as practiced and institutionalized. The argument in the essay is not finally a separatist one, however, even though it does describe de facto separation between composition and literature in many academic settings and raise the possibility that separation may be inevitable, may be one way in which the inertial forces in our separated pasts may work themselves out. In a number of academic settings, bridges between composition and literature have collapsed; in others, would-be engineers have given up on the task as not worth the expense of energy, spirit, or money.

"Constitutive Literacy," the second essay in the section, glosses and expands upon a handful of issues raised in the first and becomes more explicit in the recommendations it makes about ways in which a split might be avoided, ways in which bridges might be built. In doing so, it seeks to connect a view of literacy to a view of liberal education, and both to a vision of a just society made just by its discursive practices—its means of determining who gets to say what to whom, in what language and in which human settings. It connects literacy to politics, to issues of the distribution of power; but it connects it, too, to visions of a politics that might enable the formation of community through informed and critical conversation.

It is that kind of a politics of literacy that Patricia Stock and I try to describe in the final essay of the section and the collection. Ours is a vision that has been called idealistic: in this essay, however, we try to show that ideals have some hope of being realized and, when worked out into pedagogical practices, of changing present realities. We describe work done in inner-city classrooms with teachers and students who know well the emptiness of ideals that never seem to change their lives or their worlds. Because of their courage to try yet once more to imagine worlds different from their inherited ones and translate ideas and ideals into something like *praxis*, some changes have been made in the political structures that govern their literacy and its development: changes in social roles and relationships, changes in structures of schooling that affect roles and relationships for students and teachers, changes in perceptions and conceptions of self and others in a literate world that is in part of their own making. A politics of literacy must confront present realities, but it will offer little hope if it cannot transform a past into a future worth having. Literacy develops only in a language of possibility.

We would like to think of this final essay as complementing the one that ends Part III: "Literacy as Conversation." And we would like to think of both as contributions that may turn theories of instruction and learning into sensitive and liberating theories of the politics of instruction and learning: theories that ask and speculate about the social relations among those who teach and those who learn; theories that ask and speculate about the real-world contexts of teaching and learning and the social purposes of these activities in real and imagined worlds. Theories of instruction and learning have often been constructed and offered as apolitical, as exempt from issues of power, ends, and the aims of people who do and do not hold power. To claim that one's stance is apolitical is, of course, a political speech act; and it is an act available only to an agent in the world who enjoys a place among those who hold power.

We think it will be liberating, for ourselves and for our students, when we recognize that we act as political agents when we act out our roles as teachers, researchers, scholars. If we do recognize that, then as teachers of reading and writing we may help contribute to the development of literacy as a language of real possibility.

9

Literacy in the Department of English

Over the past ten years or so, I have had the mixed pleasures of being rather deeply involved in academic administration, at a level low enough to be able to look at the landscape close at hand. From 1974 to 1981, I was chairman of Michigan's Department of English Language and Literature; from January 1983 through June 1985 I was chairman of Michigan's English Composition Board—the unit charged in our institution with administering and conducting some parts of a college-wide writing program, a program, by the way, *not* housed in an English department. In these ten years, I have had a chance to stand at each side of the great divide that separates the home of literature from the home of composition, and I have gazed into the space between them, wondering not so much about ways to get home as about where home is or should be.

In the quieter moments of my two chairmanships, I have explored some other territory. I have looked at linguistics at Michigan from the perspective of a chairman of a review committee. And I have looked at an Education School—Michigan's—as a member of a transition team charged with reorganizing Michigan's School after another review committee (on which somehow I did not serve) imposed upon it a 40 percent budget cut.

That sounds like my own biographical headnote, but that is not why I begin with personal history. Rather, it is to say that quite by chance I have had an unusual opportunity to think about some of the issues now being actively discussed in the profession, an unusual opportunity to view from several perspectives what might be involved in trying to bridge the gap between literature and composition as some of my colleagues now want to do. From my various perspectives, I see at least these questions as necessary ones for bridge builders:

1. Is the gap between literature and composition bridgeable?
2. Should the gap be bridged, and if so, for whose benefit? Who should bridge to whom? and why? and from which side first?
3. Is it probable or possible that the gap will be bridged, and if so, who will be the engineers?

The questions suggest at least three avenues of approach to the bridge site:

1. One is through theory, with students of literature and students of composition leaving their separate homes to find a place for candid, critical discussion of whether synthesis of their now separate theories is possible or potentially useful.
2. The second is through careful consideration of what we do in our separate classrooms, and whether what we do meets the needs of our students and the legitimate expectations of society.
3. The third is through sober reflection on the performance and potential of various institutions, such as academic departments, with special attention to their histories, to what in other contexts is sometimes called a "track record."

Thinking about these questions and about possibly useful approaches to them led me to my own topic: "*Literacy* in the Department of English."

Literacy is a wonderfully ambivalent term, its meaning dependent upon the contexts in which it is used. Thinking about how the term is typically used in English departments led me to another question: Will instructional programs in reading and writing—the two main activities most often associated with the term literacy—continue to be housed in English departments as they have been in the past? Or will such programs find another home—one less subject to domestic strife, one not divided into separate spaces with no sure and safe passage between them? The question, I would suggest, is not an empty or academic one. You as well as I can read statements like this:

> Writing instruction was for years a stepchild of English departments, who have always dominated it. As recently as fifteen years ago many colleges dropped composition altogether—partly on the basis that the high schools were handling the job, and mainly to give still greater emphasis to literary study. That development should make us hesitate about trusting that English departments, as they are presently constituted, will solve the problem [of ineffective instruction in composition].

Now there has been a resurgence of active involvement by English faculty along with others. Writing instruction could be a boon for underemployed humanists, a large and influential group. But teachers trained in literature may not necessarily be well situated to work with beginning students, or to prepare students for the kinds of writing tasks they will likely face after school. English professors are not even necessarily good writers themselves, and their commitment to specialization has been at least as strong as any other discipline's (1981, 56).

The author of these paragraphs is Richard Hendrix, who at the time he composed them was associated with the Fund for the Improvement of Postsecondary Education; his paper was prepared for a conference sponsored by the National Institute of Education. Among the thirteen papers published in the proceedings, only two were by members of English departments (one a rhetorician, the other a linguist); the remaining eleven were by education professors, anthropologists, sociologists, and linguists from linguistics departments.

There are, my point is, competitors to English departments for the tasks and rewards of teaching literacy. Funding agencies, my other point is, are not unaware of track records. Do English departments have the horses for what could become a very tough race? Do they really want to run in it?

I think we all recognize that there are both powerful and quite diverse social needs for the competencies referred to by the term literacy: reading, writing, comprehending, and communicating. There is need for programs that enable students to acquire these competencies—and especially for programs that make it possible for *all* students to acquire them, not just white middle- and upper-class students whose native language is English. There is need as well for research that will enable us to understand these competencies better, and thus make possible the construction of better programs. Need there is, and needs there are, but I do not see in our colleges and universities, certainly not in mine, despite our success with a good writing program, units deliberately designed or adequately institutionalized to meet present needs: neither needs for research nor needs for adequate instructional programs.

"Literacy in the English Department"? Maybe. But I doubt it.

I know of few English departments, and none in major research-oriented universities, that have deliberately made a comfortable home for those teacher-scholars who wish and are adequately prepared to teach composition and reading and do research in the various domains of literacy and its uses. English departments mean by the term literacy one particular and quite specialized thing: an easy familiarity with a certain body of texts, a particular attitude toward them, and special practices for reading texts so that they will yield the appropriate attitudes—attitudes that might lead a professor to call one student "cultured," another "urbane," and still another a "candidate for graduate school." It is literacy thus defined that English departments strive most energetically to institutionalize: through allocation of budget resources, through vigilant protection of the tenure track and of tenure itself, through always watchful graduate admissions, through exclusive course offerings, through careful limits placed on what counts as serious discourse in the discipline—on what one may say and where one may safely publish.

It is with help from this system of discourse that we in English departments find means to ignore the needs of our students, especially those of our most needy students, and yet feel good about it. Except when we are talking about our "introductions to literature," we characterize our students' difficulties with reading and writing as "deficiencies" needful of "remediation"; we characterize what students in composition courses do as practice in basic skills. We do so comfortably, because we do not teach the courses or the students. We do so the more comfortably because we tell ourselves that this is how composition specialists and reading specialists define literacy—even though we could find out, if we wished to read, that no knowledgeable and self-respecting composition or reading specialist would use the term skill, or more surely the modifier basic, to characterize the activities of writing and reading. Not in our time.

What I have learned from talking with my colleagues who teach and think about reading and writing are these lessons: reading and writing are complexly constituted and potentially enabling competencies that develop only when they are practiced: literacy that is worthy of the name, these practitioners tell me, develops only through the productive exercise of available and developing competencies with language—through the use of such competencies in composing and comprehending texts, through the use of language to make meanings that count for something in contexts where learning and sharing what is learned counts for something. Literacy is an outcome, not a skill, and not (even) a competency. It is something that is achieved when competencies are enabled through exercise of the human capacity to make meaning.

Exercise of that kind is a serious business, and should count for more than it does in English departments, or in the academy.

To think of literacy as a set of skills and to think of these skills as basic, as mere rudiments, is to misconceive it badly, perhaps maliciously. The misconception of the real competencies involved in achieving literacy has harmed all students much, but most of all those students whom we characterize as most needful of special help. John Goodlad, in his study of schools and schooling, found in the majority of language-arts classrooms in elementary and secondary schools a "dominant emphasis [on] teaching basic language use skills and mastering mechanics. . . ." The emphasis, he found, intensifies the farther down the ladder of tracks one looks:

> . . . lower track classes tended to emphasize the mechanics of English usage, whereas high track classes were likely to stress the intellectual skills of analysis, evaluation, and judgment. . . . The low track classes were unlikely to encounter the high status knowledge dealt with in the upper tracks and normally considered essential for college admission (1984, 205).

The myth of basic skills, when applied in classrooms, deprives students of what they most need. Those most frequently deprived, of course, are members of racial, social, and linguistic minorities, for their children most numerously populate our lower-track and remedial classes. And the myth operates another way: it allows those of us who teach advanced courses to look down our noses on those who teach lower-track and basic ones—allows us to say, because we view such courses as basic, that those who teach them need little knowledge, no special preparation, no particular expertise, and exactly such recognition as accrues to these absences. Tasks that are basic can safely be assigned to lesser mortals than those riding high on the tenure track: to graduate students, no matter what their preparation, or to part-time lecturers, no matter what their past or future.

Recent arguments for bridging the gap between composition and literature like those in a collection of essays sanctioned by MLA (Horner, 1983) can be seen, if one wishes so to see them, as attempts to enrich the intellectual content of composition courses, thus raising their status in the English profession—something that could benefit teachers of composition, though not so much as English departments themselves. But will such bridge building benefit students?

I do not think so. We will not meet the needs of our students— neither our current ones nor those who may come to us in the future—nor will we meet the expectations and requirements of our academies or of our society, unless we in English departments are willing to change—to challenge inertia, to alter the nature of English studies, to redefine what we think of as centers and peripheries, to reshape our departments and alter their priorities.

To change effectively we must begin with theory, thinking of the task of theory building in new ways. We will not prevail with quasi-theories that are mere apologetics for the teaching of literature as we have come to know and love it; nor will we prevail by trying to smuggle poems and novels into composition classrooms, by trying to impose our own preferences and our own wishes on a clientele with other needs and other interests. As we build theories, we must also try to build new departmental structures, structures designed as deliberately as our theories to rectify past inequities and inequalities. What we will need in effect is an affirmative-action program for at least three oppressed minorities: those many who have been excluded for reasons of color, linguistic background, or poverty from the attainment of literacy; those few who are seriously interested in theories of composing and comprehending; and those more numerous, yet still far too few, who do not suffer shock or burnout when they are asked to teach those many who would compose and comprehend, write and read, but don't know how to begin, or haven't yet found that they can.

When we look only at the surface of things, as some now do, it would seem that the time is ripe for at least a détente between the two hostile camps—the literati and the rhetoricians. I read, for example, in Horner's "Introduction" to the volume *Composition and Literature* a report of change in the profession that begins with the imperatives of social change:

> In the 1970s the situation in the English discipline changed drastically, again for a number of pragmatic reasons. As the post-World War II baby-boom babies grew up and graduated from colleges across the nation, enrollments at large universities dropped or leveled off, and, worse still for the humanities, students turned to more practical degrees that would ensure them a share of the dollar pie.
>
> At the same time that literature enrollments dropped, enrollments in writing courses increased. In many cases administrators withdrew funds from literature programs and added them to writing projects.

Affected were, she writes, those

> senior scholars who had not taught writing since their graduate-school days [and who now] were forced to teach composition when their seminars failed to "make."

Also affected were

> junior members of English departments. In most cases their entire Ph.D. training had been in literary studies, but, if . . . fortunate enough to obtain university positions, [they would find] all or a large portion of their teaching . . . in composition (1983, 7).

Familiar facts, though one might ask a stranger's question: Why were even these fortunate few hired if they didn't offer appropriate qualifications for the primary teaching task? But we know the answers to that question already, though it is rarely asked openly.

Horner finds, in what might seem to the stranger a rather bizarre and dismal situation, reason for hope:

> Since the inception of the Teaching of Writing Division [in MLA], I have attended most of the sessions. In talking with the members of the division, the second largest of the association, I discovered that most were persons whose first interests were in literature and critical theory, but they had chosen the Teaching of Writing Division because

they were, in fact, now seriously engaged in teaching composition. Most readily admitted that all their training had been in literature and that they attended sessions to learn about research in the teaching of writing (1).

Once more, a reflex of the pragmatics of history. But Horner wishes to claim more in the way of change than a shift of budget priorities, a matter of making a living, a matter of making the best of what has happened by undesign. "The size of the division," she writes, "reflects dramatically the changing nature of our discipline. . . ." But not only that, it is occasion for opportunity of another sort, for

> In reality, literature and composition cannot be separated either in theory or in teaching practice. Composition theory and critical theory are indeed opposite sides of the same coin, and the "teaching" of writing and the "teaching" of literature are applications of theories that are closely connected, often inseparable, and always fundamental to the study of language (1–2).

Now in reality, or at least in the one I occupy, literature and composition *are* separated, certainly in anything that can be called practice, and certainly in the way they are regarded and supported as practices. As I read the history of critical theory in my working lifetime, critical theory and composition theory have indeed been not "opposite sides of the same coin" but currencies as different as the pound and the yen. And as I read the institutional history of the thing called *English Studies*, with special attention to its dominant and dominating concepts, I see nothing that suggests complementary bonding, nothing to suggest more than a rather tenuous linking, like a plank thrown across a steep-sided deep creek. Those of us who would build bridges between composition and literature had better be good historians, and better theorists, or risk getting very wet indeed.

Raymond Williams writes instructively about the institutionalization of certain conceptions of literature in our immediate past and our inertial present in two works that I would recommend to all bridge builders: *Marxism and Literature* (1977) and *Writing in Society* (1980).

It is common in our time, Williams writes, to "see 'literature' defined as 'full, central, immediate human experience,'" and as such to find it privileged as an essential and unique way of knowing or coming to know (1977, 45). To have students study literature, we sometimes argue, is not merely to provide materials from which a past can be constructed, an identity found—something that historians, sociologists, anthropologists, psychologists do; rather it is to provide immediate experience of the past or of the present—"full, central, immediate human experience." Thus literary experience is conceived as unique; and as such, given its essence, it is thought essentially fundamental to the activity of being human. From this perspective, literature becomes its own epistemology: it is not a subject among many, not an alternative perspective on reality, but the preeminent way to apprehend it. There is literature, and through it, because it is experience, we apprehend the world as humans do; and then there is science, or worse yet social science, whose practitioners glimpse only partially, and then never centrally, either the world or the experience of humans in it. From this set of notions, it is so easy to make an argument for literature in the composition classroom: for just as writing is a means of coming to terms with experience, a means of coming to know, so literature *is* experience and a unique way of knowing what it is valuable to know. In literature is embodied all we need to know about composition, about language as it apprehends reality. "Shakespeare and Composition"—the perfect composer, the perfect composition. The bridge is built.

But Williams complains that this definition, or concept, of literature is

> a powerful and often forbidding system of abstraction, in which the concept of "literature" becomes actively ideological. Theory can do something against it, in the necessary recognition ... that whatever else "it" may be, literature is the process and the result of formal composition within the social and formal properties of a language (45–46).

The conception of literature as "immediate living experience," says Williams, suppresses "the very process that *is* specific, that of actual composition." From the privileged perspective, literature is a thing in and of itself, not a thing made through writing or remade through reading. Literature becomes, in this way of conceiving it, a self-justifying body of texts that in themselves constitute the literary experience and authenticate it as finer even than human experience itself, for real experience is embarrassingly rough and diverse. Through literature, a reader may refine and cultivate his own experience, remove himself from conflict and accident, and achieve a tranquil and civil sanity.[1] To read literature is to refine one's sense and sensibility; no further justification is either needed or warranted.

To conclude his argument about the ideological privileging of "literature" as a concept, Williams turns to semantic history, tracing development of the term from its early usages, in which its reference was often close to what we now mean by *literacy* ("a condition of reading: of being able to read and of having read") to its now more specialized one: a body of texts of a particular kind and quality. In tracing the history, Williams reminds us that the term "literature" once referred to more than imaginative works: histories, biographies, works of philosophy, political and scientific treatises were all works of literature and thus grist for the mill of literary study; literature was a condition of reading, of having read, not a set of special procedures for interpreting a body of specially privileged texts. Williams traces the specialization of the concept of "reading" to the narrower professional activity of criticism, a shift from reading as learning to reading as the exercise of taste and sensibility. To read is human; to criticize, professional (46–54).

We could retain our notion of literature as a particular body of imaginative works, and our special definition of reading and writing as criticism, if we were content merely to add writing assignments to our syllabi for literature courses, merely to smuggle composition into them just as some of our colleagues have smuggled it into history, political science classes, or even into biology classes. But we seem to want more than that: English departments still seem to want to teach *all* students, not just those interested or dabbling in literature; they seem to want to teach introductory composition courses; and they seem to want to keep hold of college writing programs. And they want to keep "literature" in introductory courses, and professors of literature in control of writing programs.

If we want such things, then I think we had better be ready to rethink what we mean by the term "literature." And we had better be ready to rethink what we mean by reading and by writing. As things are now in our intellectual world, literature (in its generally accepted meanings) and composition (in certain of its currently framed ones) *are* separated. Composition theory and critical theory can perhaps be *made* to be opposite sides of the same coin, but only if the coin is deliberately minted.

When literature was at the core of humane learning, which was some time ago, the very term meant something quite different from what it means today—it applied to a different range of texts and to texts of different kinds, to reading and to writing, not to specialized kinds and uses of these activities. University teachers of literature thought of themselves as teachers of reading and writing. When, in more recent times, literature—in its specialized senses—could still be taken as the core of humane learning, institutions were different. They were attended by a smaller and more homogeneous percentage of the population, biased in favor of the white and well-to-do. Sometimes these institutions were even headed and administered by professors of literature, for scientists and economists have come even more recently than we humanists to the halls of power and influence. But our academic world is at present a diverse one, and its diversity exists along at least two dimensions: the clientele to be educated and the intellectual world into which they are to be led. In our present world, privileged definitions of literature, of reading and of writing, will serve neither students nor the world of ideas. Such definitions cannot compatibly be wedded to emerging definitions and descriptions of composing and comprehending, or to emergent definitions and descriptions of literacy and its uses in the world. What one fears, of course, is that a shotgun marriage will take place, because it is clear in present circumstances who owns the key to the armory.

Richard Lanham, in an important contribution to the volume *Composition and Literature*, takes up some of the same history Williams does in tracing the development of English studies from the foundation of the Oxford English School in 1894 to what he calls its "maturation"—the achievement of "departmental and disciplinary status." Lanham traces the development toward maturity from its origins in an argument "that literature constitutes a reality apart from ordinary reality, [thus] deserving of study in and of itself"; he sees this argument coming into its own with New Criticism, and later "with the work of Northrop Frye and others"; then, Lanham writes:

> The maturation was accelerated by the two go-go decades of academic prosperity from 1955 to 1975, [when] a flood of students and money . . . released English studies not only from composition instruction, until then its historic base in America, but also from routine instruction in the lower division. The discipline was thus freed to draw in upon itself, become graduate- and professional-centered, and sponsor metalevel reflections upon literary texts and inquiry—upon, that is, itself (1983, 15).

The consequences of this? Two for Lanham: impressive achievement in the discipline—in philology, in criticism, but at considerable cost. "No knowledgeable person," Lanham writes, "would want to belittle, or to damage, this powerful maturity in the discipline. But, as we are now finding out, such maturity assumed a specific social base—the reigning society, in fact, when the Oxford English School was founded in 1894: white, literate, and at least middle class." "English studies," he concludes, "now provides a superb instrument to educate such a society. That society, alas, no longer exists" (15–16).

If our students are no longer similar in color, background, language, aims, or aspirations, the world of ideas they will encounter in the academy is no less diverse. "The felt center for studying man," says Lanham, the renegade Renaissance scholar, "is shifting from the traditional humanities to other disciplines in much the same way that the traditional European focus for Western thought has now diffused throughout the globe." He speaks of a "new humanist curriculum" constructed from sources of literature so wide as to include evolutionary biology (22). Clifford Geertz, an anthropologist who offers his own view of intellectual diversity, glimpses a similar redrawing of boundaries by calling our attention to what he calls "blurred genres"—works of scholarship and literature that drive typologists and librarians berserk by refusing to be either history or philosophy, linguistics or criticism, fact or fiction. Works of this kind now appear frequently, Geertz argues, and their appearance is more than accidental:

> ... it is more than a matter of odd sports and occasional curiosities, or of the admitted fact that the innovative is, by definition, hard to categorize. It is a phenomenon general enough and distinctive enough to suggest that what we are seeing is not just another redrawing of the cultural map—the moving of a few disputed borders, the marking of some more picturesque mountain lakes—but an alteration of the principles of mapping. Something is happening to the way we think about the way we think (1983, 20).

To write his own brand of cultural anthropology, Geertz creates his own blurred genres, adopting perspectives alien to the specialized social scientist, plundering the methods, concepts, and vocabularies of textual and literary critics to describe and interpret not texts themselves but cultural events, actions in the world.

And yet when Geertz looks to the academic disciplines, to discourse in the modern academy, to codes our young students must somehow crack and then learn to use, he is struck mainly by difference, by multiplicity:

> ... the various disciplines ... humanistic, natural scientific, social scientific alike, that make up the scattered discourse of modern scholarship are more than just intellectual coigns of vantage but are ways of being in the world, to invoke a Heideggerian formula, forms of life, to use a Wittgensteinian, or varieties of noetic experience, to adapt a Jamesian. In the same way that Papuans or Amazonians inhabit the world they imagine, so do high energy physicists or historians of the Mediterranean in the age of Phillip II—or so, at least, an anthropologist imagines. It is when we begin to see this, to see that to set out to deconstruct Yeats' imagery, absorb oneself in black holes, or measure the effect of schooling on economic achievement is not just to take up a technical task but to take on a cultural frame that defines a great part of one's life, that an ethnography of modern thought begins to seem an imperative project. Those roles we think to occupy turn out to be minds we find ourselves to have (155).

So how do we use discourse to lead our students from their diverse homes and minds to where they may want to go, through an academic world that we inhabit and they must somehow enter, a world that is itself composed of diverse homes and minds? How do we make our world, our discourse, meaningful to them, as they pass from there to here and beyond? These are questions bridge builders *must* ask, especially those who ask for the task, those who want to teach all students.

I would suggest that a proper aim for *introductory* composition courses in the modern academy is to help students learn to play the various roles that will lead to development of their minds, in so far as minds can usefully be shaped by the discourse and noetic systems of modern scholarship. Such is the aim and argument of the better informed of those who would spread writing across the curriculum, but still find place and purpose for a generally required introductory composition course. This aim and argument is better than that which argues for an introductory composition course based in "literature" that serves only as introduction to discourse about "literary" texts, and is better by far than introductory literature-composition courses that make no argument for themselves but merely presume a privileged place in the academy.

Yet even the better arguments do not go far enough. What we should aim for in college and university *writing programs* is not only capacity and competence in specialized discourse systems, but also capacity and competence in a common language, a generally available educated discourse: one that enables our students to move from mutually unintelligible or difficult academic jargons to talk and writing that they can share with other specialists and non-specialists, and to talk and writing that puts our students, and us, in contact with others who are differently educated and with our various selves, our mutually separated selves. What we really need is a discourse that puts us in contact with the resonances and echoes of the experiences that constitute our own separately lived lives and our all-too-often separated social identities, our ways of being in a world that we did not necessarily choose.

A proper aim for writing programs in colleges and universities, maybe even in schools, might well be to invite and help students to develop as ethnographers of thought—as careful and reflective participant-observers, critical thinkers of their own thoughts, able to reach beyond the constraints of discourse, able to escape from narrow perspectives, able to move from restricted and restricting ways of being and behaving in the world, able to assert and make a place for themselves as makers of meanings that are personally satisfying, no mater how constrained by the language they must use.

To reach toward aims like these will of course require much more than a bridge between literature and composition, much more than current talk even suggests about bridge building, much more thought and talk than the current uses of the terms "literature" or even "composition" begin to imply. What is needed is not talk about bridging from literature to composition or from composition to literature, but more serious talk about the human uses of language—the uses diverse humans make of language. We need talk not about "composition" and "literature," but about talking and listening and reading and writing as centrally human and humanizing activities.

Rudiments of theory that might make possible such serious thought about talk and writing and listening and reading are readily available for our use, if we have energy and will and opportunity to avail ourselves of them. Theories linking reading and writing are becoming the dominant ones among those who study either reading or composition—theories that reconceive reading as the active construction of texts and their meanings; theories that reconceive writing as an act of perpetual making, perpetual revision, with publication or submission for a grade an arbitrary stopping point. As readers of Cassirer, Langer, and Burke know, theories defining reading and writing as symbolic action, linking the written to the spoken word, have been with us for some time; and, as readers of Austin, Searle, Pratt, and Goffman know, theories defining talk and listening as intentional yet ordered actions in a social world, linking the spoken to the written word, have been with us for almost as long. Theories that re-place reading, as process and procedure, at the heart of literacy criticism—as central to interpretation—are readily adaptable to the classroom from the work of semioticians like Jonathan Culler and Umberto Eco, and from the work of reader-response theorists like Louise Rosenblatt and Stanley Fish. Those who have read Michel Foucault know how discourse can constrain as well as liberate; those who have read Paulo Freire and other theoretical Marxists know why it does, and what its potential is and isn't.

If the activity of reading and writing were defined as it is by modern workers in the field, who have knowledge not only of where they come from, but also of the consequences and constraints that attend upon their engagements with students, then we could worry less about the inclusion of "literature" in the composition classroom, inhabited as it is by those diverse students. When reading and writing are defined as activities then we come closer to something we can do for all students, with all students, for mutual benefit and enlightenment. We reach, I think, toward a common language when we put in practice what Raymond Williams tells us can come from a proper engagement with texts:

> A newly active social sense of writing and reading, through the social and material historical realities of language, in a world in which it is closely and precisely known, in every act of writing and reading, that these practices connect with, are inseparable from, the whole set of social practices and relationships which define writers and readers as active human beings, as distinct from the idealized and projected "authors" and "trained readers" who are assumed to float, on a guarded privilege, above the rough, divisive and diverse world of which yet, by some alchemy, they possess the essential secret (1980, 189).

Student writers, of course, are authors, too, and inhabitants of their own particular worlds; and their own works should be read in the same spirit and with the same rigor that we would have our students read the texts we assign them. What others have written, and what they write, are equally constructed as are their very selves from a "whole set of social practices and relationships which define writers and readers as active human beings." Our own teaching practices come out of a similar matrix, and we are disingenuous when we do not recognize and act upon that fact.

It will, in short, finally matter which texts we include in our composition courses—even in our literature courses—introductory or more advanced. For we have our students and the responsibility to prepare them for productive intellectual life.

In thinking about the texts I will choose for the next composition course I will teach, I will not forget Geertz's notion of blurred genres, his fascination with those works that refuse easy classification, those that fall in the empty spaces between the lines of disciplinary division, those that require some uneasy accommodation to what is comfortably categorized. At the same time, I will be plagued by his insistence that "the hallmark of modern consciousness ... is its enormous multiplicity," a result of sharp divisions among ways of knowing, ways of acting in the world. Geertz, like many in the world we now inhabit, worries about "where the 'general' went in 'general education,'" about the need for integration of cultural life, a concern of humanists as well; and with me, Geertz worries about the very possibility of reaching toward a common language. With him, I see no possibility for integration in "some kind of diffuse humanism," no possibility for integration in easy attempts to build bridges:

> The problem of the integration of cultural life [he argues] becomes one of making it possible for people inhabiting different worlds to have a genuine, and reciprocal, impact upon one another. If it is true that insofar as there is a general consciousness it consists of the interplay of a disorderly crowd of not wholly commensurable visions, then the vitality of that consciousness depends upon creating the conditions under which such interplay will occur. And for that, the first step is surely to accept the depth of the differences; the second to understand what these differences are; and the third to construct some sort of vocabulary in which they can be publicly formulated—one in which econometricians, epigraphers, cytochemists, and iconologists can give a credible account of themselves to each other (1983, 160–61).

To accept a depth of difference, to understand what the differences are, and then deliberately to construct a vocabulary in which they can be formulated so that we may talk intelligibly to one another, write what another can read, to "begin to find something circumstantial to say to one another again"—that, says Geertz, "would be that rarest of phenomena, a *useful* miracle" (160). That is the miracle we should seek in building bridges. It is, in my view, no unwarranted leap to see in composition programs the opportunity to try to find a common vocabulary, to establish a common means of discourse, to try to call into being and use a genuinely public language. But we must not be led to think of this task as easy, its achievement as anything less than miraculous, should we somehow achieve it. In the academy, we inhabit a complex world, and our separate languages create a multiplicity of thoughts and forms, of words and actions, and with them, worlds we cause ourselves to inhabit. And because, as composition teachers, we somehow inherit the responsibility to bring our students into the academy without insisting that they leave their own lives and worlds behind—for we *are* both humane and humanists—our task is more difficult than even Geertz imagines.

Yet were I to teach a composition course in which the founding of a public language was the aim—were I to teach a course including works of imagination—I would still take Geertz as my model and two works of his as my teacher's manual: "Blurred Genres: The Refiguration of Social Thought," and "Deep Play: Notes on a Balinese Cockfight." In these two essays, Geertz offers a meeting ground for humanists like me and social scientists like him, a meeting ground he and I can stand on to talk about our convergent preoccupation with interpretation, with using language to make sense of human actions, either in their forms as written texts or in their forms as cultural events. In "Deep Play," Geertz bridges the gap between writing and event by deliberately treating an action in the world, a cockfight, as if it were a text, written by actors, read by spectators, serving in its meaning as a tale the Balinese tell themselves about themselves to make meaning in their lives. I would begin with Geertz in my search for a public discourse because he gives me a place to stand in my attempt to understand his vocation as an anthropologist, because he has borrowed my vocabulary to talk about his subject. And he builds a bridge for my students because he gives them a vocabulary that is useful to them and to me for talking together about events in the world as well as events in the worlds made by texts, and about texts as events. And in building bridges like these, maybe I can find, or maybe my students can if I can't, ways to bridge toward other ways of seeing and saying that are less accessible to me or to them: how econometricians, epigraphers, cytochemists see and say. In building bridges, I want to begin first with something relatively easy—something with pontoons perhaps, certainly something with easy instructions.

If I can meet Geertz on his ground, and he me on mine, I will have something to offer my students, living as I do in an academy that they are venturing their young energies to enter. In trying to write about the meaning of actions in the world, and being willing to use a vocabulary that is familiar to me, yet wishing to be critical in his use of it, Geertz has reached out to me, opened the door from his department to mine. And I remember, as I think about the gesture, these words of his:

It is when we begin to see this, to see that to set out to deconstruct Yeats' imagery, absorb oneself in black holes, or measure the effect of schooling on economic achievement is not just to take up a technical task but to take on a cultural frame that defines a great part of one's life.... (155).

I do not want my students, especially those who write for and to me, to think of what they do as a technical task, to make of what they are learning and know some kind of meaningless exercise. When I teach a composition class, I must remember that their experiences are neither mine nor something I want to appropriate by investing them with my meanings. And yet, I want them to learn; and yes, I want to work with them toward common meanings, meanings that we can share, meanings that will make possible the possibility of a common language, a public discourse made of and constitutive both of self and of community.

In a language that allows me, as a member of the academy and a user of its discourse, and them as newcomers and learners to talk in the same terms both about events and about texts, I find a bridge: from their experiences to a way we can talk about them; and from there, with luck and patience, a way to say that all texts work like that—even works of "literature." Even great works of literature, after all, like experiences we comfortably or uncomfortably participate in and remember, are stories that people tell themselves to make sense of their lives. To engage in this kind of meaning-making excludes no one, no matter what their experiences, no matter what kinds of cultural frames they have constructed. A common language, a public discourse, must bridge not only from discipline to discipline, from the jargon of anthropology to the jargon of literary criticism, but from each equally to the discourse systems constructed for our students by their ways of being in the world, the discourse systems of self, family, and neighborhood. Community is made possible only when diversity and its expression are made equally possible.

And that is why it seems to me far too easy to talk in our time about building bridges between what we customarily call "literature" and what we have more recently learned to call "composition."

In his essay "Beyond Cambridge English," Williams writes of another gap, that between literature and literacy. It is this gap, or to use his metaphor this "unevenness" that poses the real challenge to the future of English studies:

It is often said that there are more than six centuries of English literature. It is not often said that there are less than two centuries of English literacy. Of course "English," in those two statements, has different meanings. The first refers primarily to the language, the second to the people. But then it is the ordinarily unexamined relationship between these meanings that can reveal a central problem in English studies. The idea of literature, throughout, has been so closely connected with the condition of literacy that it can hardly be said that this deeper relationship needs to be forced. Powerful social and cultural conventions control or displace what is otherwise an obvious connection. What then is "English literacy," for professional students and teachers of English? Is it their own condition and that of people much like them currently and retrospectively applied? Or is it the diverse and changing conditions of their whole nominal people? To approach two centuries of English literacy means restricting our count to a bare majority. General literacy has a bare century, and within that many are still disadvantaged. In relation to what is seen as "our" literature, where then do students and teachers of English stand?

I have made my own awkward stand. By my educational history I belong with the literate and literary. But by inheritance and still by affiliation I belong with an illiterate and relatively illiterate majority. It is said that as the whole society develops, and has for the past century been developing, these inherited problems and contradictions resolve themselves. I do not think so. Beyond our local and diverse histories there are major intellectual issues, of a fully objective kind, which need to be traced to this radical unevenness between literature and general literacy. Underlying them, always, are the complex general problems of language, and it is how these problems are dealt with, in the coming years, that the success or failure of English studies will, in my view, be decided (1980, 212–13).

As members of English departments, where will we make our stand? Will we continue to confuse literacy with literature, remaining insensitive to the needs of those who would move from the ranks of the relatively illiterate? Will we continue to believe that literature and literacy are synonymous terms? Will we refuse to see that literacy and literature are social constructions, the products of social and historical forces? Will we be open to new theories that offer new concepts and suggest new relations, and recognize that there are other gaps to be bridged, new techniques for building bridges?

When I think about my life in an English department, I have to shift to the cruder metaphors I have played with. What is our track record? A few questions, merely:

1. Have English departments been hospitable to interdisciplinary work, or competent in it?

2. How many critical theorists find colleagues to talk to? (Linguists don't count, because they're so lonely they will listen to anyone.)

3. When was the last time that an English professor thought of himself or herself as teaching reading?

4. How many English departments try to steal remedial reading and writing courses from support units?

5. Who gets to direct freshman composition? How much competition is there for the job?

6. Who gets to teach freshman composition? If the job market were good, how much competition would there be for that job?

7. Who plans freshman comp courses? The best and most experienced literary critics?

8. Who gets tenure, and how many composition and reading specialists are there nationally among the tenured ranks? Outside of Education schools, that is?

9. Who kids whom, and for how long?

The needs are there, the theories are emerging, and some few are seeing the question of bridge building as crucial to the development of the profession. Richard Lanham does, for example, as well as in his own way, does Raymond Williams: "The relation with composition," says Lanham, "stands at the center of the basic decisions for English studies" (25).

So what does the future hold?

Composition in the English department? Maybe—but what will it mean, and whose needs will it meet, and whose will it ignore?

Literacy in the English department? Maybe. It could be, but I doubt it.

And where will literature go; should we once again begin to think seriously about its uses for all students?

Note

[1]See the elaboration of this argument, much truncated here, in these essays of Williams gathered in *Writing in Society:* "Cambridge English, Past and Present"; "Crisis in English Studies"; "Beyond Cambridge English."

10

Constitutive Literacy: The Department of English Revisited

The previous essay, originally published in *College English* (1985) caused some consternation—at least within my own department—because in it I suggested that English departments, and the discipline the majority of their members profess, are not well constituted to meet society's needs for programs of instruction and research that will promote a fully functioning literacy for a broad majority of our society's citizens. I wrote that article out of years of experience trying to develop useful programs in English departments, and out of fewer years of experience helping to develop a college-wide writing program.

In the article, I directed my criticisms at English departments, because I know them best, and because in most institutions English departments are assumed to be responsible—in some cases solely responsible—for fostering literacy. (My severest critics, of course, would place my motivations elsewhere: in some form of the cuckoo syndrome—a matter of an old bird fouling his own nest.) Now, several years and some experiences later, I would direct my criticisms—if that is what they are—more broadly. I would do so because I think that such deficiencies in literacy that our students exhibit reflect much less failures of English departments than the absence of opportunities for students to use written language purposively in a sufficiently wide variety of settings. Failure to provide such opportunities cannot be blamed on English departments alone, or even on schools and colleges alone. Ours is a society that sometimes values wordlessness—especially from certain of its citizens, and more especially when wordlessness is the only alternative to the use of words that Paulo Freire calls "naming the world" (1970, see Chapter 3).

The practices we engage in—the ways we order our own and our students' lives—inevitably reflect conceptions we have inherited or those we have managed to form for ourselves. The heart of the problem we have as teachers of literacy, or would-be teachers of literacy, is that we have either inherited misconceptions of the nature of literacy or managed to misconceive it all on our own. Having done so, we have had marginal success in managing to design effective mechanisms for fostering it. We, with our colleagues in other departments and with our fellow citizens in the communities we inhabit, have thought of reading and writing— which is what most of us have in mind when we talk about literacy—as basic skills, as fundamental tools that will enable our students, when they reach higher, to have some assurance that their grasp will be in some proximity to their reach. Thinking of literacy—of reading and writing—in these ways, naming them with these names, we get stuck with the implications of the very metaphors we use. Whatever is *basic*, whatever is *fundamental* (when the domain for the metaphorical uses of those terms is something like "learning as construction" or "learning as architectural design"), must be built first before the more useful parts of the house can take inhabitable shape. A tool must be acquired before its uses can be explored, and a skill—when we think of it analogously to what we do when we learn to ride a bike or knit—once managed, lasts for a lifetime in usable form.

It's interesting to think about how these metaphorical usages— *basic, fundamental, tool, skill*—articulate themselves into institutional structures (another metaphor) and into the assumptions that support and sustain them. We have required *introductory* composition courses, save for those students who have acquired sufficient *skills* to be exempted from them; and the students whom we deem unprepared even for introductory courses we name *basic* writers, and we put them in *tool* courses. Deans who fund introductory composition courses (and who would prefer to fund courses in systems design or corporate management) often wonder whether it isn't the proper business of secondary schools to excavate and pour concrete—relatively poorly paid jobs in the building industry. And legislators balk at spending more money to re-fund the basics when the foundation doesn't seem to hold.

One of the reasons, perhaps, that these notions of reading and writing—of literacy—have had such permanence in English departments particularly (but in the wider academy as well) is that they fit neatly into the hierarchical systems into which we have arranged our disciplines and which reflect our hierarchy of values. We in English departments teach literature and linguistics quite comfortably at the graduate level, but rarely composition—even more rarely something called reading. And our hierarchy of values expressed in the system of discourse we employ makes us—and usually our deans—happy with how we staff and fund basic and introductory courses: graduate students and temporary faculty are sufficient there, since the courses are basic or introductory; and of course graduate students and temporary faculty cost less money. Questions of professional wisdom and cost accountability are raised if an accomplished and highly paid full professor is assigned to teach (or even to direct) introductory composition.

But what if our conceptions of reading and writing—of literacy—are wrong? What if they are inconsistent with our best notions of what it means to read literature well, or to write about it cogently? What if our conceptions are incompatible with what we know about how the discourse of various disciplines is best acquired? What if they do not match with defensible notions of liberal education, or with notions of the place and functions of liberal education in a democratic society?

Maxine Greene, a philosopher of education and a friend, whose notions of literacy I am only now beginning to understand because of my own previous misconceptions, objects passionately to prescriptions of educational means that do not contain within them the essence of the ends to be reached:

> ... I want to see the means of achieving literacy made continuous with the end-in-view, and I would also remind teachers that *literacy ought to be conceived as an opening, a becoming, never a fixed end* (1982, 326).

So much for exit examinations, and other forms of competency testing; so much for *introductory* composition courses that happen only once, and then only in the freshman year. The reasons behind Greene's insistence that means are as important as ends—that literacy must "be conceived as an opening, a becoming, never a fixed end"—are these: She is herself a reader and writer and knows that for readers and writers learning and learning-how-to never end; and she is herself an educational philosopher and, being one, looks to education and to the literacy it should make possible as means toward the same society John Dewey envisaged. For Greene, education and the activities we point to when we use the name *literacy* are important only as they model that society and provide students practice in the arts that constitute and sustain it.

Maxine Greene is a reader, and one reason she reads is to engage her *self* in conversation with other selves, who will raise questions for her. Reading *Billy Budd*, for example, whose hero "stutters when he is agitated" and who "can find no words to answer ... Claggart's charge of treason, and so ... strikes out," knocking him to the ground and killing him, she is "compelled once more to ponder the connections between speechlessness and alienation and violence" (1982, 326). For Greene, *all* of the forms of coming to know—"formal inquiry, scientific thinking, and the rest are signif- icant to the degree they nourish human conversation" (1978, 69). Human conversation is important because it is collective action, action in which one must reflect upon others' and one's own words in order to reach a common understanding, to reach toward reflec- tive action. For Greene, literacy is an opening to, a becoming of the only kind of knowledge much worth having—a "kind of knowing called *praxis*, a type of radical and participant knowing oriented to transforming the world" (1978, 13).

Reading in order that questions might be raised and a conver- sation started, trying to come to know so that a conversation may be sustained and nourished, are vitally important activities because they hold promise for overcoming "automatism, wordlessness . . . passivity" and powerlessness; they are important activities because they can lead to liberty—to freedom—to democracy:

> Half a century ago John Dewey expressed the need for an articu- late public and linked its emergence to a "subtle, delicate, vivid, and responsive art of communication." [Dewey. *The Public and Its Prob- lems*, 1954, 164.] Only when we have achieved such communication, he said, will democracy come into its own, for democracy is a name for a life of free and enriching communion. . . . It will have its consum- mation when free social inquiry is indissolubly wedded to the art of full and moving communication" (Greene, 1982, 326).

Late in his life, John Dewey put his case more succinctly: "Demo- cracy," he is reported to have said, "begins in conversation" (Lamont, 1959, 58).

What is basic to the *development* of literacy, I would argue, is the same as what is basic to its full exercise: the empowerment of individuals to speak freely in such voices as they have about mat- ters that concern them, matters of importance, so that conversa- tions may be nourished. The most debilitating suggestion in our dominant metaphors for literacy is this one: that a language must be learned, a voice acquired, before conversation can begin. When taken literally, as these metaphors often have been, means are devised that are radically discontinuous with the end in view if that end is the creation of communion and the nourishing of human conversation among readers and writers.

James Boyd White offers a definition of literacy that can be made consistent with the ends I am urging:

> . . . I start with the idea that literacy is not merely the capacity to understand the conceptual content of writings and utterances, *but the ability to participate fully in a set of social and intellectual practices* [em- phasis mine]. It is not passive but active; not imitative but creative,

for participation in the speaking and writing of language is participation in the activities it makes possible (1985, 72).

In White's view, reading and writing—like speaking and listening—are actions, and they are actions *in* the world and *upon* the world: they are participant actions that constitute a world in which still other activities can take place—a world in which free agents can negotiate and, in doing so, can construct the sets of social and intellectual practices they can profitably engage in. To exercise literacy, for White, is ultimately to engage in the active construction of a just society; in his view and mine, as many citizens as can be enabled should engage in that construction if justice is in fact to be attained.

White uses the term "constitutive rhetoric" to name "the art of constituting character, community, and culture in language."

> Whenever you speak [White writes, and whenever you write, I would add] you define a character for yourself and for at least one other—your audience—and make a community at least between the two of you; and you do this in a language that is of necessity provided to you by others and modified in your use of it (1984, xi).

Language, for White, is much more than a code—much more than the set of usages and conventions that are usually taught in "tool" classes. For him, a language is "a set of terms and texts and understandings that give to certain speakers a range of things to say to each other." When humans *share* a language, they share not merely a set of terms and texts and understandings, but "a set of intellectual and social activities." These activities, and the language that makes them possible,

> ...constitute both a culture—a set of resources for future speech and action, a set of ways of claiming meaning for experience—and a community, a set of relations among human beings (1985, xi).

The crucial questions for teachers of literacy are these: What sets of resources for future speech and action exist in the languages we share with the students whom we would engage in conversation? What ways of claiming meaning are possible in those conversations, and how can we extend their range? To what extent do the conversations we hold within our professional communities—the discourse systems that constitute the intellectual and social practices of our disciplines—exclude those whom we try to engage in conversation in classrooms?

The sum of my argument is this: The possibility for a just society is grounded in the uses we make of literacy and of liberal education. The possibility that the three of these—literacy, liberal education, and the just society—are all alike as means and ends is grounded in the possibility that human beings in society may find a common language that will bring them together in conversation, in community, ideally in communion. To find a common language—to found a common language—is to make it possible for writers to write and for readers to read, and for all to learn together in community in order to achieve some larger common end, to act together in community to build a better world. We now know well—from the work of Foucault and others—that language and its uses are intimately related to power and its uses: that is why concepts of literacy are ultimately related to concepts of the just society.

Michael Shapiro, in *Language and Political Understanding*, explores the links between language and power in these terms:

> If we recognize that among the conventions which give statements meaning are those that determine who must make the statement for it to have a particular meaning, we are in a position to relate the meaning of statements to the distribution of power in a society ... (1981, 151).

We should want our students to be meaning makers, but they can be so only if we deliberately seek to build literate communities in which their voices can be raised, in their own language, so that we may hear them and answer in terms they can understand. The literate communities we build—those that will encourage the constitution of a common language—must substitute an authority gained through experience or through learning shared in conversation for an authoritarianism that can only be gained through the exercise of coercive power and be sustained only when only the powerful speak and the powerless listen quietly.

Concerned with signs of cultural disintegration, many thinkers and writers have called for the creation of some means to pull things back together. E. D. Hirsch calls for cultural literacy, and many others echo him—William Bennett among them. Maxine Greene calls for creation of a public space in which serious discourse might be heard and responded to. I prefer the metaphor "a common language" for these reasons: If we think of "language" in terms like those employed by James Boyd White—as a set of terms and texts and understandings, as a means to constitute character, community, and culture—we force ourselves to engage in conversation with those others whom we would bring into community, into communion with us. To achieve community through a common language, we cannot *impose* our language on those others; to find a common language, those others' languages will have to change, of course, but so will our own.

To create a common language appropriate to a just society, we will have to find better ways to engage in conversation with those in our society who have been assumed to be wordless, and thus have been rendered so: the culturally and linguistically divergent, the economically depressed, and the politically oppressed. To

create a common language appropriate to the academy in an appropriately just society, we will have to find means to talk to one
another across the barriers we have erected around our specialized
disciplines. The way to do that, it seems to me, is not so much as
Clifford Geertz says—to find means for translation from one discourse system to another—but to ground our intellectual activities
in real human concerns, and to talk about them when we can in the
language of everyday life. It seems to me that if we can find ways
to talk productively, meaningfully, generatively, with the least well
prepared of our students—those least like us—we might even find
ways to talk among ourselves.

One thing I know: We will in no way achieve a just society if
we do not talk to those alien to us; nor will we do so if we continue
to encourage the fragmentation of educated language into mutually
unintelligible specialized jargons. A chemist friend of mine, Thomas
Dunn, spoke recently in a lecture about the jargonization of science;
that has come about, he said, because what scientists have come to
know has not passed into the common parlance of the educated. The
cost of this is twofold, he said: The common language is impover-
ished, but so too is the language of science.

When Carl Lovitt invited me to speak to the ADE Western
Summer Seminar on a panel titled "Literacy and the English
Department," he asked me to do three things: To outline my views
on the need to reconceptualize literacy; to elaborate on my call in
the *College English* essay for the development of a common language; and then to discuss how these changes could or should affect
English departments. Having tried to meet the first two charges, I
will now fall under the weight of the third.

The *could* is relatively easy: if such arguments as I am making
about the nature of literacy and the need for a common language
ever find force in the academy, English departments could lose their
hold on the teaching of composition, perhaps their hold on other
requirements as well. If literacy is acquired through purposive
action in a wide variety of settings, and if development of a common
language is an aim of instruction in writing, it makes far more sense
to institutionalize that aim and such instruction in a college, rather
than in a department, or else in a department that is deliberately
constructed to house experts in discourse and in the discourses
of various disciplines. I like Theodore Sizer's arguments in *Horace's
Compromise* for the reorganization of departments in schools from
the many to these four: Inquiry and Expression; Mathematics and
Science; Literature and Arts; Philosophy and History (1984, 132–36).
That kind of reorganization would force many of us to talk to one
another and render invalid at once the rarely spoken real justifica-
tions for keeping composition in English departments: support for
graduate students and cost-effectiveness.

The *should*, of course, is harder, and I will touch on it only more or less in list form. What should English departments do?

FIRST: Stop making deals with the devil. By that I mean, stop making false claims about what can be done in a basic writing class, or in an introductory composition class, or in writing courses that purport to prepare writers for action in the real world. As White says of "legal literacy" of the sort lawyers must have:

> ... "legal literacy" means full competence in legal discourse, both as reader and as writer. This kind of literacy is the object of a professional education, and it requires not only a period of formal schooling but years of practice as well. Indeed, as is also the case with other real languages, the ideal of perfect competence in legal language can never be attained. The practitioner is always learning about his or her language and about the world, is in a sense always remaking both, and these processes never come to an end (1985, 60).

SECOND: Stop discriminating against certain members of the department—those who research and practice in the various fields of literacy. No matter what we now say about the place of composition in English departments or in the profession, our actions speak louder than our words, and someday somebody is going to listen to what we do.

THIRD: Take the lead in knocking down the walls that separate departments and make the aims of liberal education unreachable. English departments will be able to do that when their members recognize that English is not a discipline but a historical accident. We might find it useful to redefine ourselves as engaged in an interdiscipline, and to begin talking about possibly common interests of the sort Raymond Williams calls convergences (1982, 9–14).

FOURTH: Reorient our research interests to the needs of all the constituencies we in fact serve, and especially to the needs of those whom we have most often ignored. If we want to study readers reading, for example, which is in fact what we do when we write criticism or articulate literary theories, we should pay attention to those who are beginning to read their way into the interpretive communities we inhabit.

FIFTH: Stop thinking of pedagogy as a four-letter word—as a topic not to be mentioned in polite company. *How* we do what we do is more important to read and write and think about than *what* it is that we do. What *are* our canonical pedagogies and how do these fit with the needs and aims of our students? With the character of the intellectual world we inhabit?

SIXTH: Look for new kinds of expertise in the hiring we do. Since resources are limited, few of us can afford lit specialists, and I'm not at all sure that comp specialists have the expertise we need should we seek to foster literacy and to found a common language.

Six simple commandments, none of them, of course, either controversial or difficult to put in action.

I will end this revisit to the English department more or less where I ended the original article, but with a slightly new twist. In a paragraph near the end of that article, I quoted Richard Lanham, who wrote in an important essay in *Composition and Literature: Bridging the Gap* that:

> The relation of [literary study] with composition stands . . . at the center of the basic decisions for English studies: the decision about its place in the humanist curriculum and the decision about its place in a multilingual America (1983, 25).

That is one of the centers, I think, but a perhaps more important one in the next few years will be the relation of English departments and English studies to the preparation of teachers. Our involvement with teachers is one of the ways (perhaps the most crucial in the sweep of its effects) in which we articulate our own concerns and interests as professionals—as professors—with the needs and desires of those outside the academy, both those who will enter it and those who will not. We can make a modest contribution to schooling in America by refusing to talk ever again about the *training* of teachers: *education* should be our aim, and the kind of education that liberates and empowers. We can make a less modest contribution if we recognize that there is need in public education for a language—a common language—that will express in common the aspirations and the understandings of all—professors and poor learners as well. We cannot leave the constitution of that language either to politicians or to the kinds of social scientists who now dominate decision making in the schools through construction and manipulation of a discourse that causes only certain voices ever to be heard, that ensures only decisions of a certain sort ever to be reached. A voice from the humanities needs to be heard in discourse about education—but it had better be a human voice, a humane voice.

11

The Politics of Literacy

Jay L. Robinson and Patricia L. Stock

Insofar as we account for our own actions and for the human events that occur around us principally in terms of narrative, story, drama, it is conceivable that our sensitivity to narrative provides the major link between our own senses of self and our sense of others in the social world around us. The common coin may be provided by the forms of narrative that the culture offers us. Again, life could be said to imitate art.

JEROME BRUNER

Things Fall Apart

CHINUA ACHEBE

It is easy to assert "The Right to Literacy." It is another matter, however, when literacy is defined nontrivially, to devise and engage in professional activities that have some possibility of aiding those who are not literate to become so. Literacy, we are told, should be thought of as "the ability to use language in order to become an active participant in all forms of public discourse" (MLA, 1988). Literacy involves, we read in James Boyd White, "not merely the capacity to understand the conceptual content of writings and utterances, but the ability to participate fully in a set of social and intellectual practices" (1983, 56). Abilities of these kinds presume opportunity, for they come into being only through their exercise; all human actions, in order to be realized, presume some measure of opportunity, some opening toward possibility.

   Paulo Freire is challengingly right when he advises those of us who teach in societies that produce large numbers of illiterates to link literacy and the possibility of its fruitful attainment with social

271

change—perhaps with change so far reaching as to deserve the modifier *revolutionary*. *Illiterate* is a name, he writes, a label, by means of which those near centers of power push others to peripheries, to function as "marginal men" or women (1985, 47). *Illiterate* does not name cognitive or intellectual or linguistic deficiencies so accurately as it does identifiable places at the outer reaches of society. To use other of Freire's own metaphors:

> Critically speaking, illiteracy is neither an "ulcer" nor a "poison herb" to be eradicated, nor a "disease." Illiteracy is one of the concrete expressions of an unjust social reality. Illiteracy is not a strictly linguistic or exclusively pedagogical or methodological problem. It is political, as is the very literacy through which we try to overcome illiteracy (10).

How might we conceive, for our time and place, a politics for a literacy through which we might hope to overcome illiteracy? And what might be the implications for educators of such a politics? And, if it is to be realized in this nation's schools, how might such a politics of literacy take shape in a pedagogy for literacy? And, finally, if they are realized, how might such a politics and such a pedagogy be received in a nation that defines its commitments in terms of economic well-being and social stability? These are the vexing questions we will try to answer, however tentatively, as we talk about collaborative work we are doing with teachers and students in a school district in Michigan.[1]

For Freire, whose work has been one influence on our own, the following generalizations identify characteristics of a literacy that may offer some hope:

> . . . the critical view of literacy does not include the mere mechanical repetition [of syllables and words and sentences]. Rather, it develops students' consciousness of their rights, along with their critical presence in the real world. Literacy in this perspective, and not that of the dominant classes, establishes itself as a process of search and creation by which illiterate learners are challenged to perceive the deeper meaning of language and the word, the word that, in essence, they are being denied (10).

A literacy that develops learners' consciousness of personal rights, literacy enacted as a process of search and creation, literacy that results in a learners' critical presence in the world, offers promise of changing the world even as it changes learners' ways of being in that world. But such literacy cannot find a place for development save through a politics of education that allows for origins and openings. And when the learners are individuals whom others have labeled *illiterate* or *marginally literate,* a critical politics of education must allow for diversity in origins and for openings into new places; the critical pedagogy such a politics implies must empower teachers and students to find substance in origins and to make of openings spaces in which together they might negotiate the meanings of terms like "rights" and come to realize a "critical presence in the real world." In a critical pedagogy, the openings students provide enable teachers to create from them places for instruction where students might learn for themselves "the deeper meaning of language and the word," and where the spatial location *margin* may be recognized for what it is—a generative site for making meaning, a generative site for building knowledge with the potential to benefit all of us wherever we reside.

A Politics for Critical Literacy

Language is not a neutral medium that passes freely and easily into the private property of the speaker's intentions; it is populated—overpopulated—with the intentions of others. Expropriating it, forcing it to submit to one's own intentions and accents, is a difficult and complicated process (M. M. Bakhtin, 1981, 294).

For the past three years, with university colleagues, we have engaged with colleague students, teachers, and administrators in Saginaw, Michigan, to search together for ways to find words, both for ourselves who would help students, and with and for students who have either been denied or have not been able to find them.[2] Saginaw is a mid-sized largely industrial city that has suffered many of the afflictions visited upon cities in the rust belt whose economies have depended upon ailing industrial corporations— save for those afflictions of apathy among the school district's leaders and leader-teachers or unconcern among its citizenry. Saginaw's schools have been consistently, if not always adequately, supported financially (no millage has failed in over ten years, not even in the time of the recent severe recession); committed and effective teachers may be found in all buildings; imaginative administrators have found both ways and means to support teachers and us in our work with them and in our joint work with students.[3]

We have all worked together, of course, within the peculiar sets of political and pedagogical constraints that are imposed by the larger contexts of schooling in the United States: standardized testing and the public's and politicians' faith in its results; state and national proposals for school improvement whose mandates are insensitive to local needs and possibilities; inequalities in purportedly equalized public funding; the politics and publicity of alleged school failure—the *Nation at Risk* syndrome that has been exploited by politicians, and especially by those politicians who see schools merely as the servants of corporations and of the corporate state. But within these constraints, and others more sensitive in the naming of them—those that inevitably arise in multiracial and multiethnic communities (53 percent of Saginaw's students are black, 32 percent white, 13 percent Hispanic)—we think we have made modest gains.

Because literacy and illiteracy are reflexes of the social environments in which students and citizens do or do not use written language for their own and the community's purposes, and because our aim was to increase the number of those who could meaningfully be named literate, we knew we had to work—as we worked together to build toward a critical literacy—to build as well toward a critical politics of education: we had to work to change the structures and the sets of social relations that sustain our work together and define for our students, at least to some extent, the range of their possibilities. As university teachers, we had to establish new relationships with our colleagues who teach in schools in order to enable free and critical dialogue. As teachers working together, we had to establish different relationships with administrators and schoolboard members to alter well-established structures of authority and equally well-established patterns of action. New relationships had to be formed among those of us who are black and those who are white and those who are Hispanic, if for no other reason than to find those common spaces in which we might negotiate over the meanings that attach themselves to language differences in communities that are socially separated along racial and ethnic lines.

And then, because there can be found among Saginaw's students, despite the district's committed efforts to serve them, the unforgivably customary number who are labeled illiterate or marginally literate—a number similar to that customarily found in other American cities of Saginaw's size and composition—we knew we had to strive for other changes: changes in ourselves as social beings in our relationships with our students; changes in the social roles allotted to students in interactions in the classroom; changes in the ways students see themselves as readers and as writers; changes in students' ways of relating themselves, as social selves, to the written word. Any critical politics of literacy must take into account the social identities of readers and writers, and the potential in these identities for origins and openings, for difference and even for resistance, in the socially constructed worlds constituted through written words. To those we label illiterate, the written word is all too often alien, a strange thing to be feared for its obvious power to render them marginal, to serve as still another token of failure, another symbol of powerlessness.

Interestingly, ironically perhaps, we found means to begin to come together as teachers and to alter our relations with administrators and board members by developing and carrying out a district-wide assessment of writing ability. The results of that assessment, when taken to be the scores raters assigned and when expressed in the numerical language that is now the dominant one for talking about educational achievement, are not much different from those of standardized assessments—those that measure isolated student performances against norms that are expressions of hegemonic values embedded in a prevailing ideology of literacy. Our assessments, like those kinds, distributed students—and probably the same ones—along a scale from high to low, separating those who apparently could from those who perhaps couldn't, those who did from those who clearly didn't. But because we were teachers who had taken on the task of assessment, these were not the results we cared much about or made much use of. Results important to us as teachers came from our attempts to find out from students the topics they would like to write about for an assessment and the forms in which they might comfortably shape meanings important to them. Results important to us came as we talked together, argued together, about standards and expectations that might fairly and equitably be applied to the writings of tenth-grade students in a school district like Saginaw's, in a city like Saginaw. What rights *do* students have to their own language? What rights do students have to a literacy that has to some extent, in their lives outside school, already enabled them in those systems of discourse in which they are active participants? Because we teachers were to be the readers and raters of the writings students composed in response to prompts and in situations that we had designed, talk about standards and expectations had to become very concrete, very much connected to those concrete everyday situations in which students do or do not learn to write and in which we do or do not teach them how.[4]

Still other results issued when the teacher assessors were treated as professionals responsible for reporting the results of the assessment to the Board of Education and to the community. Not only did this alter the teachers' roles and their place in the educational hierarchy (they became speakers and not merely listeners in talk among local policy makers about educational achievement), it also gave them a forum in which to raise professionally responsible questions about the whole enterprise of testing writing: crucial questions about what differences tests in fact reveal among those who apparently can and those who apparently can't, questions about the differences among those who clearly did and those who as clearly didn't. Questions, too, about the need for words like *apparently* in the language of educational evaluation. To say *can't*, without *apparently*, is to commit oneself to at least the connotations of a language of deprivation—a language that has meaning only in a system constructed through discursive practices that reify and enforce hegemonic values. *Can't* implies a deficiency in the student and expresses a stance that leaves little opening for questions about how well the student is served by the system, little space for the nuances and implications of difference. To say *didn't*, even *clearly didn't*, allows otherwise: both for the possibility of difference and for that of resistance—for unintentional or deliberate responses to imposed tasks that in their making offer to reflective and imaginative educators occasions for dialogic critique both of what they ask of students and of the values implied in requirements and actions.[5]

And then there were these other results as well, the most important of all: assessors who are also the teachers of the students being tested are not and cannot be carpetbaggers. They have to stay at home to face the implications of what they have done—to ask, if only themselves, why some students could and others apparently couldn't; why some students did and why some didn't; and to question values that identify some students as successful and others not. For over a year now, teachers in Saginaw, ourselves among them, have studied the texts students produced in response to the assessment, with special attention to those texts we identified as failures according to criteria we had devised—those texts that did not meet our expectations. What can such texts tell us, not only about the students but also about ourselves and our expectations? What did we see—when we scored it as such—as student illiteracy? Are texts that are labeled illiterate always or ever produced by illiterate students? Who would we have our students be and become as they enter worlds our words have made, in classrooms, and in the spaces outside classrooms?

And having assigned scores, sometimes with certainty, sometimes tentatively, sometimes grudgingly, what could our scores tell us about the ways we read student texts, about our capacity for what Bakhtin calls responsive understanding? What did our readings tell us about the ways we habitually engage students in processes of learning, in collaborative searches for meaning and understanding? Who had we been and who would or should we be as readers of student texts, as speakers who seek to engage students in talk about texts, as social beings in the oral and literate communities taking shape in our classrooms?[6]

As teachers who inevitably do make social communities with our words, these questions, the ways in which we have framed them, the answers we have posed for them, and the ways in which we have framed our answers, constitute for us not only a politics of literacy and a politics of education but also a set of principles to guide our pedagogical practice. Our assessments, the judgments we make every day, never result merely in seemingly innocuous ratings that we record in grade books, never merely in more noxious labelings from illiterate to literate; rather, our ratings and labels constitute a social world in which students find (or do not find) some place. Our ratings and labelings both constitute and reflect, for the students to whom they are assigned, our own stances as teachers—stances that always affect how we engage with students and they with us. And, of course, our stances and our students' perceptions of them are realities in the social worlds of the classroom: on such footing as they provide for our interactions with students are constructed the social and ethical relations among us that shape, in turn, both what is learned and the purposes for learning.

When we are thinking about the possibilities for origins and openings, for difference and for resistance, in our classrooms, our most important questions might be put this way: Who gets to speak? About what? To whom? And in what circumstances? Who has the obligation to listen or the right not to listen? Who assumes an obligation for responsive understanding and who refuses it? For whose benefit do we seek to promote literacy? And what kinds of social worlds do we seek to construct with the words we and our students use?

These questions are, of course, quintessentially political ones. They speak clearly to "our own sense of self and our own sense of others in the social world around us" and invite inquiry into that world as it affects our sense of self and of other. Language, as we know, always encodes both a sense of self and a sense of other, even as it makes the social worlds in which we do in fact live, whether we inquire about them or not. A sense of self in the word inevitably implies a sense of self in the world, even as a sense of self in the world shapes our words.

Self and Other in a Politics of Literacy: Critical Implications for Instruction

I believe too that Self is a construction, a result of action and symbolization. Like Clifford Geertz and Michelle Rosaldo, I think of Self as a text about how one is situated with respect to others and toward the world—a canonical text about powers and skills and dispositions that change as one's situation changes from young to old, from one kind of setting to another. The interpretation of this text *in situ* by an individual *is* his sense of self in that situation. It is composed of expectations, feelings of esteem and power, and so on (Jerome Bruner, 1986, 130).

So when I got to school I could not think in class. So I left school and all most got into a crash (Charles Baldwin, 1987).

The majority of students who responded to our assessment's prompts presented us selves we could recognize inscribed in texts that met our expectations sufficiently for us to assign them the ranking 2 (*Interesting but Flawed*) or 3 (*Proficient*). Another number of students, a customary one, impressed us enough by their control of their worlds and their words to enable us to assign their texts the highest ranking 4 (*Excellent*). The remaining texts, also a customary number, were ranked 1 (*Unsuccessful*). Given our hopes that we could design an assessment that would enable all students to compose as well as they could,[7] as assessors we studied the texts we had failed. Our hopes as teachers motivated continuing study for what these texts could tell us about why some students failed and where we might have failed them.

Below is one set of such texts. It is representative, we feel, at least in some of its characteristics, of the challenges failed texts offered us as teachers who would understand how we might have. There are four texts in this set, each one produced on a single day in an assessment that took four days to complete. On all four days, students were asked to write about teenage stress. First, in something we called "Free Writes," students were invited to relate, in whatever form they chose, instances of stress that they (or someone they knew) had experienced; then, in something we called "Tries," they were invited to draw, in a form closer to something that might be called an essay, such implications as they could from their own or others' accounts of stressful experiences. A tenth-grade student, a fifteen- or sixteen-year-old young man we will call Charles Baldwin, gave us these texts to assess and think about:

FIRST FREE WRITE

Stress is when you impell force like for example it was this certain person who hang out with this group of people who use to fight and get high and sale drugs And He was allways called a square or a nerd so he was allways thinking should he do it so he could be one of the boys in the crew. So he decided to do what ever they did. So one day they were throwing down at a party so they told him to start it off. So they smoked a joint and he smoked one to but he never smoked before and he started feeling funny. So he walked up to the boy and hit him then they started fighting so then he was given a gun and he shot the boy and then he went to Jail then he could handle it so he killed his self.

SECOND FREE WRITE

STRESS

Is when for about two week's I had a lot of things on my mind. It seem like every thing was coming down on me at once. So I went home and tried to rest for a little. But the thought's kept coming back So I got my jacket. Then on the way a guy said he will take my jacket So it seem like I just exploded and I broke his arm well I was in the police van. I was just thinking about my intire week. And the policeman said I looked like I had a lot of pressure on me. So when I got home I thought I was going to die but after I got all the problem off my chest I felt better. So the next day I seen my girl talking to the boy I got unto it with so then he started kissing So I just went over and they walk away. So when I got to school I could not think in class. So I left school and all most got into a crash.

FIRST TRY ... PROMPT

STRESS

One day I had called up a few of my cousin's to go to a dance. And
when we were on our way to the party we had seen a lot of boy's they
were looking at us like they wanted to fight so we first kept on riding
so we went to the dance. So as we got inside we were walking around
then we seen a few girls then we started dancing So when we walked
off the floor the boy's we saw earlier were following us so we went to
the bathroom and they seene us and we started to fight so the police
officer seen the whole thing so he put them out so we kept on dancing
and then the dance was over. When we got out side they had bats and
chains, knifes. So we all stept back and on of my counsins ran at the
boy with the bat and got his head bust. So we took him to the hospital.
Then the next day I felt hurt cause I felt like I should have help him as
I could have got hit then I could not even work I felt like life was
closing around me.

SECOND TRY ... PROMPT

STRESS

I remember when we were at the mall and there were 6 boys in the
sports store but when we went by the store they ran out and we started
fighting and one boy got killed. and that hole day I was thinking about
it and I could not work I was in my own world for a long time and we
had got locked up for allmost a year and when I got out I could not
deal with life.

As assessors, we failed Charles Baldwin. Almost unanimously
we gave his texts a 1, seeing them as *Unsuccessful.* We did so partly,
no doubt, for the customary reasons: Given the time he was provided to compose them, his texts were very short; he lacked consistent control of the conventions of standardized written English
(although he is a remarkably good speller); he refused (or could not
take up) our invitation, as prompters, to move from story to essay,
from narrative to reflection, at least not in an assessably successful
form. And although we rated only his fourth piece of writing during
our assessment evaluation session, in our subsequent research sessions, when we studied all four pieces of his writing, Charles Baldwin's narratives—taken as a whole—posed problems for us too:
most of us read them as incoherent.

More globally and perhaps justifiably, we could not conclude,
as assessors—even as ones who questioned our own judgments—
that Charles Baldwin's texts exhibited an "ability to use language
in order to become an active participant," not even in those "forms
of public discourse" that we were seeking to encourage and value
in our own classrooms and in the assessment we had designed. No
matter that, as other kinds of readers than assessors, we valued
Charles Baldwin's texts as powerful statements about the world
in which he lives, we failed them. We did so surely because we

feared for his future, in school and beyond, insofar as his future depends upon his own use of language and his tutored capacity to use language. We identified him clearly as one who certainly didn't, as one who perhaps couldn't—at least not without imaginative help.

And yet Charles Baldwin wrote, when others certainly hadn't. And later, as we reread his texts as teachers who wished to help him, we asked ourselves about the meanings of *Unsuccessful* applied to texts that offer us so startling a glimpse into the world Charles Baldwin occupies; we asked ourselves about the meanings of *Illiterate* if we were to apply that label to Charles Baldwin and risk marginalizing both him and his world. If Charles Baldwin in fact couldn't, what could we find in his texts that would help us to understand why he couldn't? Since he had written, and in so doing had provided origin, how could we make of his action an opening toward something more? Given his beginnings, no matter how different they were from our customary expectations, how might we talk with him in opening conversations—in expanding conversations—that might prompt him to make meanings of his world that would enlighten for him his possibilities in it, conversations that might prompt us to transform our expectations.

We looked in Charles Baldwin's texts for someone we might talk to, for a self with whom we might connect, but his texts about his experiences, when read in Jerome Bruner's terms as inscriptions of self, as inscriptions of "how one is situated with respect to others and to the world," are texts whose texture is defined by an absence of self. If self is conceived as consciousness both of how one is acted upon by others and of how one reacts deliberately toward others—if consciousness includes both a sense of one's "rights" and of one's "critical presence in the real world"—then Charles Baldwin's texts are remarkably absent of a self. In his texts violence happens, and its causes are not attributed to the human beings who act it out and suffer its consequences:

> I remember when we were at the mall and there were 6 boys in the sports store but when we went by the store they ran out and we started fighting and one boy got killed.

> So he walked up to the boy and hit him then they started fighting so then he was given a gun and he shot the boy and then he went to Jail then he could handle it so he killed his self.

Human agents, when their influence is implied, almost never speak:

> And when we were on our way to the party we had seen a lot of boy's they were looking at us like they wanted to fight so we first kept on riding so we went on to the dance.

And even when agents are represented as speaking, their words might as well be actions for they are almost always powerful performatives that leave little room for considered choice of any option other than reaction.

> And He was allways called a square or a nerd so he was allways thinking should he do it so he could be one of the boys in the crew.

> Then on the way a guy said he will take my jacket So it seem like I just exploded and I broke his arm

The only opening toward a reportable use of words comes, possibly, from a policeman's mouth:

> And the policeman said I looked like I had a lot of pressure on me.

But even then, events speak, too, for Charles Baldwin is in a police van.

The stories Charles Baldwin tells, which we assessed as incoherent, are not fictions, not in the usual sense, not in their reference to events that lie behind them. We learned that from talking with his teachers and his counselors. And the assessable incoherences in his accounts, after a more reflective reading, come rather to seem—to readers who know something about how Charles "is situated with respect to others and toward the world"—starkly representational and fully coherent images of a world in which violence is a feature of the natural landscape, in which forces overwhelm human agency and the actions it might make possible. This is a world about which reflection—when innocent of critical awareness, of some sense not only of personal rights but also of the very possibility of claiming personal rights—can produce very little but confusion or despair:

> Then the next day I felt hurt cause I felt like I should have help him as I could have got hit then I could not even work I felt like life was closing around me.

> I was in my own world for a long time and we had got locked up for allmost a year and when I got out I could not deal with life.

In a world like this, how does one move—as anything like a self—from incidents and instances to reflection upon them, from story to essay? What is Charles Baldwin's interpretation of self *in situ* and how does that interpreted self compose "expectations, feelings of esteem and power . . ."? As teachers who care about his future, we could feel more comfortable with Charles Baldwin's texts, perhaps, if we could persuade ourselves to imagine him, somehow, as an author—as one who makes and composes, and not as something quite other: as something closer to a marginal character in stories made by others than himself, stories narrated as wordless happenings. It takes little imagination to speculate that for Charles Baldwin, such sense of self in the word as he possesses is largely constituted by his sense of self in the world, or his lack of it. How could he possibly write coherently for assessors? How could he possibly reveal himself as literate? Who could he be in a world made of written words, which is usually more our world—as his teachers—than his.

And yet he wrote.

Educators who study demographics often tell us teachers that in our futures there are many more students like Charles Baldwin: students who will come from worlds unlike our own, students who will not share our stories or the expectations and values, feelings of esteem and power, out of which our worlds are composed.[8] They seldom remind us that those same students who are described as unlike us have much in common with many of our grandparents and great-grandparents, immigrants to this country during the last quarter of the nineteenth century and the first quarter of the present one, individuals whose presence in the country's elementary schools provoked educators then to initiate standardized testing in order that the limited number of seats in the nation's secondary schools and institutions of higher learning would be occupied by those whose words and stories, if not born of hegemonic values, at least appeared to have been formed by them. And then, of course, there were to say nothing of the grandparents and great-grandparents of others of us, potential students in our country for whom purveyors of hegemonic values never troubled themselves to develop exclusionary tests, knowing full well that shades of skin tones would serve quite adequately to effect their exclusion. It is only in more recent years, as some potential students have asserted themselves and earned legal recognition, making their potential more real, that exclusionary tests have been developed for and demanded of them. Hegemonic values inevitably result in culturally biased tests that reflect biases institutionalized in the culture and reproduce—in their effects—existing social structures of inclusion and exclusion.

Although it is apparently ironic that we were guided to develop a pedagogy for teaching critical literacy through work to develop and realize a writing assessment, in the light of this history, it is in fact not so ironic. We played our role as assessors fully mindful of our more comprehensive ones as educators, asking ourselves to become students of our students and of our students' texts, anxious to learn how better to teach all students and especially those students whom we have habitually failed. And, as educators who wished not to fail students, we declined to act like those educators who wish not to fail the existing system and who therefore ask, only, and too easily, which students might learn literacy lessons most readily, which students might be taught most efficiently and hence at least cost to the system.

Charles Baldwin wrote, as did others who sometimes told less melodramatic stories and yet exhibited a similar absence of a making self, a critical self, in the words that constituted their worlds and their places in their worlds. Because they did write, we teachers who concern ourselves with all students' futures had to ask questions about origins and possible openings from them; and we had to ask our questions with an eye toward developing a pedagogy of critical literacy that might enfranchise such students in their futures: How can Charles Baldwin possibly become literate? Given a world in which he lives as marginal, can he become literate? Rather more urgently, given his circumstances, can he be helped toward anything like a critical literacy, one informed by a sense of rights, an awareness of possibility; can he be awakened to a commitment to literacy "as a process of search and creation by which illiterate learners are challenged to perceive the deeper meaning of language and the word"?

Maxine Greene speaks about "the central importance of pedagogy" in times of radical change, of "cataclysmic change" (1978, 96). In our time, which seems characterized by such changes, there is no greater need, if we are to reach toward the possibility of a just social reality in which literacy might overcome illiteracy, than for a pedagogy that meets the needs of Charles Baldwin and other of our students in whose writing we saw selflessness. Greene comments, that for our time "what is most serious and most troubling is the sense that the self as participant, as inquirer, as creator of meanings, has been obliterated?" (12); and she asks the critical question, our question, and suggests its answer:

> What does all this mean for education? One implication has to do with subject matter, with curriculum. Students must be enabled, at whatever stages they find themselves to be, to encounter curriculum as possibility. By that I mean curriculum ought to provide a series of occasions for individuals to articulate the themes of their existence and to reflect on those themes until they know themselves to be in the world and can name what has been up to then obscure (18–19).

In Charles Baldwin's stories—in the fact that he composed them—we are given a point of origin if we are alert enough to recognize it as such in spite of its differences from more familiar ways of forming lives into words. Within a politics of literacy that has promise of overcoming illiteracy, we teachers must be prepared to read different stories, to attend even to the silences of resistance, if we are to find openings into expanding worlds for our students and for ourselves. In Charles Baldwin's texts—in the forms he has given his stories—we are given openings to spaces within which we can meet him and talk with him, not only about the words he has used and the worlds they have made, but about other words as well: the words he implies only—those he seems to understand as calls for reflexive reactions and about words we might propose to him—words that can invite him to reflective actions.

Having read the "First Try" Charles Baldwin composed during the assessment examination, why not invite him to rehearse his cousins' talk on the way to the dance, the taunts of the "boys" who wanted a fight, the words of the girls with whom he danced, the lyrics of the songs to which they danced, the commands of the policeman who put the "boys" out of the school, the "boys" challenges to fight, the emergency room staff's questions, the cousins' answers, the voice of his conscience, the voice of his employer. Having read his "First Free Write," why not ask him to speculate about words as causes of actions? Why not invite him to dramatize one of the times when "this certain person" was called a "square or a nerd," to recollect for himself and us who did the calling? Who looked on? What happened next? Why? Why not ask him to revise the story he composed for his "First Try," by imagining what might have happened if, when he and his cousins were confronted with "bats and chains, knifes," they had turned from the fight, figuring their chances for being hurt were too great?

Moving from the openings he provides us, constructing that space into a place for instruction, we can invite Charles Baldwin to rehearse and inscribe for us the voices that speak words in his world; and we can speak to him and write for him the words that are spoken by the voices that shape our worlds; and then, together, we can reflect upon our words and our worlds, his and ours. It may even come to be that we can use the words we make together—as we tell each other our stories and reflect on them—to make other worlds, worlds demographers have not yet described to us.

The truth of the matter is this: We teachers will play a significant role in shaping the future about which others now tell us. Whether we will do so intentionally or inadvertently, thoughtfully or thoughtlessly, is another matter. The nature of our interactions with our students in our classrooms, the receptiveness of our reactions to our students' texts, the character of the texts we will or will not compose for our students' responsive understanding will constitute a politics of literacy. If it is to be a politics of literacy that has any chance to overcome illiteracy, for any other than the dominant classes, it will require that we make places for instruction of the spaces for negotiating meaning into which our students invite us when they offer us their worlds and their words in texts of their own making.

If Jerome Bruner is right in speculating that "we account for our own actions and for the human events that occur around us principally in terms of narrative," then Charles Baldwin must be encouraged to tell more stories about his life. If he does so and if we enter the space into which his stories invite us, we can create a place for instruction. As readers of his stories, we can make use of our own knowledge and experience as readers of literature by more successful authors to help him toward a use of narrative as a critical account of his actions and of the human events around him. We can invite him, as he writes narratives, to represent others as speaking persons, and to represent himself as speaking with or speaking back, or choosing even at critical moments to remain silent, whether in word or deed.

And as well, if Bruner is right when he asserts that "our sensitivity to narrative provides the major link between our own sense of self and our sense of other," that our commonality as striving humans "may be provided by the forms of narrative that our culture offers us," as teachers we must recognize dual obligations: If it is important for us to be both sensitive listeners and readers, then we must be equally sensitive storytellers. As listeners who would link ourselves to Charles Baldwin in some hope for our common future, we must find place in our literacy, in our own sense of narrative possibility, for the stories he tells us. To do otherwise is to blind ourselves to some of the worlds in which our students' narrative lives are shaped, even as their narratives are; to do otherwise is to drive him into silence even as we speak loudly for the preservation of the society we have inherited, no matter what its values, with no concern for its particular structures of marginalization and exclusion.

And as speakers who care about a future, both for students and for ourselves, we must also tell our own stories, no matter where they came from, and read with students stories of selves as these are inscribed in books, even in books that have become canonical, even in books that are called literary or even Literature. Not to do so, not to tell our own stories and to reread stories inscribed by others who are and are not us, would be to content ourselves to no change in the stories our students' various cultures impose on them: the stories of violence Charles Baldwin has learned; the stories of blandness and class satisfaction electronic media teach us all when we are as apparently without self as Charles Baldwin portrays himself to be in his writing; the stories of consumerism that in commercials frame stories of violence and blandness and class satisfaction.

In a politics of education that allows for a critical politics of literacy, literature has a place, for in spaces where all stories can be told, all heard, and all submitted to responsive understanding, there is some possibility for a cultural literacy in which participation is a matter of informed choice, a matter of making from multiple origins, in common effort, a world worth striving for, a world susceptible of understanding. A critical pedagogy opens out only in a classroom where authorship can flourish, only in a place where students may learn that words have some potential for changing worlds. A critical pedagogy needs a classroom in which starts might be made toward a multivoiced literacy in which all might speak, no matter what language, to reach toward responsive understanding of deeper meanings of language and of the word as they shape worlds we must inhabit.

A Pedagogy for Critical Literacy

CEREMONY

I will tell you something about stories,
[he said]
They aren't just entertainment.
Don't be fooled.
They are all we have, you see,
all we have to fight off
illness and death.

You don't have anything
if you don't have the stories.

Their evil is mighty
but it can't stand up to our stories.
So they try to destroy the stories
let the stories be confused or forgotten.
They would like that
They would be happy
Because we would be defenseless then.

He rubbed his belly.
I keep them here
[he said]
Here, put your hand on it
See, it is moving.
There is life here
for the people.

And in the belly of this story
the rituals and the ceremony
are still growing.

Leslie Marmon Silko

Having read and learned what we could from the texts that Charles Baldwin and other students wrote, those of us who had worked together for two years to assess the writing competencies of high school students in Saginaw turned our attention to developing a pedagogy for critical literacy.[9] Together, in the school year 1987–88, we designed and taught a yearlong twelfth-grade English course that we called *Inquiry and Expression*, a name we borrowed from Theodore Sizer (1984, 132). Persuaded that critical literacy has some space to come into being only in classrooms where all who gather, students and teachers alike, must tell their stories, our plan was to ask our students to join us in researching and inscribing stories from our diverse worlds, stories that defined our selves, and to read with them similar stories written by published writers.

Specifically, we asked students to join us as co-researchers of a set of questions we hoped would be provocative and meaningful to all of us: What has been the nature of your experiences in growing up? What are the stories you tell about it? What has been the nature of others' growing-up experiences? What stories do they tell about them? Are there common themes that capture growing up experiences and characterize growing up stories? In shaping these questions we teachers constructed a purpose for our students' writing and reading that we hoped they would make their own. When in fact they did so, in every way we could imagine we sought to enable them to become a literate discourse community—a community of individuals who use written language to achieve common social purposes, in this case, "to thematize, to problematize, to interpret their own lived worlds" (Greene, 1978, 103). To encourage their sense of authorship in this community, and to make it specifically a literate community, we provided our students such technology and means of distribution for their written words as we could secure in order that they might exercise such literacy as they achieved for a purpose of their own specification. Our aim was for our students to become authors whose works would be published for readerships outside of school.

During the first two months of the course, we provided our students a core of literary selections that we read and discussed aloud together, before one another. We did this for three reasons: to introduce the growing-up theme we would study; to illustrate the variety of ways in which individuals realize that theme in literary language; and to dramatize the multicultural character and worldwide roots of the literature we Americans think of as our own. With our students, we chose to read fiction, poetry, and essays composed by Asian-Americans, African-Americans, Hispanic-Americans, and Native-Americans, among them Ossie Davis, Langston Hughes, Maxine Hong Kingston, Gloria Naylor, Richard Rodriguez, Leslie Silko, Alice Walker. Specifically to illustrate how stories that people tell about themselves and their lives came—in one instance—to be literary texts, we studied Studs Terkel's *Hard Times*, listening to audiotapes of the interviews Terkel conducted with individuals from all walks of life across the United States who lived through the Depression, reading and discussing the written monologues into which these interviews were transcribed by Terkel's secretary as well as the texts into which these monologues were inscribed by Terkel in his book. While we were reading and discussing these works together in class, students were interviewing adults in their families, in their neighborhoods, and in the larger Saginaw community, recording on audiotapes, in their own handwritten accounts, in letters written to them, in whatever forms they chose, the growing-up stories of the adults who have shaped their communities and their cultures.

Acting out the roles we teachers conceived for ourselves within this pedagogy, we joined our students as readers of familiar and unfamiliar texts, and we joined our students as writers. Not only did we read with interest and appreciation our students' and published authors' inscriptions of their stories, but we also wrote our own stories for our students to read, offering them at times lives that were familiar to them; at other times, lives that were strikingly different. In our readings together—in our writings for one another and our readings of these writings—we made spaces, places for instructing one another, so that we might form ourselves into an interpretive community; as we read and wrote together, we asked for clarifications, negotiated toward understanding when others' or our own meanings did not find shapes that were easily comprehended.

When we wrote our own stories for our students to read, our writing for them was as integral a part of our enactment of the critical pedagogy as was theirs for us. It became a fortuitous circumstance that Stock—a co-teacher with colleagues in Saginaw of the *Inquiry and Expression* classes—could not be in the classroom every day. We took advantage of the fact that her schedule enabled her to be in Saginaw only two or three schooldays each week to initiate letter-writing and computer conferencing in the course at its outset. Beginning with a request that they write to her when it was necessary for her to be in Ann Arbor, to keep her informed about classroom activities and the meanings they were making of them, students wrote to Stock, and she answered each letter each student wrote. Because the letter-writing exchanges provided occasions for students to converse with Stock personally, they provided one of the spaces for negotiating meaning that we teachers transformed into places for instruction in the course; and, of course, because they are written, the letters provide us some trace of the kinds of personal interactions that were carefully encouraged in talk in our classrooms.

Examination of a series of these exchanges with one student allows us to illustrate the conduct of the *Inquiry and Expression* course: both the means by which teachers and students realized the theories of literacy learning and use that guided the design of the course and the modalities of social interaction through which teachers and students formed themselves into a productive learning community. The exchanges illuminate our conception of a *politics* of literacy even as they illustrate a pedagogy: how a teacher's beliefs about learning combine with her political and ethical commitments—her sense of self and of other—to influence how a classroom community is constituted and how it functions through interactions that take place in it. As our examination continues, we show the relations of the letter exchanges to other kinds of classroom activities and seek to illustrate, through a display of one student's texts, the movement toward critical literacy—toward reflective authorship—that we hoped our students would make.

The exchange begins this way: When Stock invited students to tell her their thoughts and feelings about writing, Gilberto Sanchez sent her a brief note that he might well have intended, and she might well have understood, as a rejection of her invitation—as a query about her own conception of writing (Is it for school only?), as a question about her role as reader in the class (Do you care about what I write or only about *how* I write?), and as a challenge to her sincerity (Do you really care what I think and feel about writing? What if I say I prefer to talk?).

Gilbert

When I was smaller I use to think I had to learn to right to get an A you know, and as the years went on I started saying to myself I gonna wright how I know how, you know what Im saying, I think about wrighting, letters and stuff, you can express your feelings on paper but sometimes people miss interpret what your trying to say and they get the wrong Idea, now, Today I rather speak out and explain myself rather than put it on paper, You know what Im saying.

With the opening Sanchez provided when he responded frankly, if probingly, to her request that he tell her what he thought about an activity that she—not he—valued, Stock worked to construct a place for teaching and learning. In a letter, she shaped a lesson in literacy especially for him, and in doing so, she meant to assure him that she accepted his words as sincere ones, ones she chose to treat seriously. With her seriousness, she meant to invite his own.

September 30, 1987

Dear Gilbert,

I enjoyed reading your note to me. Your note expresses a concern you share with a famous Greek philosopher, Plato. Plato wrote about it in a piece called a dialogue; the dialogue was entitled *Phaedrus*, after a character in it who had the dialogue with Socrates.

Plato was worried that once words were written down, they might be read by someone who would interpret them differently from the way the author wished them to be understood. Plato was worrying about writing at the time it was becoming a widely used medium in Greece. He also worried that writing would make people forgetful. If people no longer had to commit information to memory, if they could "look it up," Plato believed they would grow mentally lazy.

I thank you for your excellent contributions to our class discussions. You are a very bright young man.

Sincerely,
P. L. Stock

Neither the literacy lesson nor the spirit in which it was composed was lost on Sanchez. In his next letter to her, Sanchez responded to the content of Stock's letter to him, and he did so in a form and a tone she had modeled for him. He accepted a place in the company of Plato, company in which Stock had chosen to think of him; but before he did so, Sanchez worked to establish a relationship with her: he inquired about her well-being ("How are you doing?"); he worried about all the work she was doing (". . . you have to right to so many people besides me"), and he assured her he would not reject her invitations (". . . so you see its not because I didn't feel like or didn't want to right to you its because I was thinking about all the work you have to do").

10/8/87

Dear Dr. Stock,

How are you doing? I didn't want to right to you because I figure Its to much righting for you, cauce you have to right to so many people besides me, so you see its not because I didn't feel like or didn't want to right to you its because I was thinking about all the work you have to do. Its good to know Im not the only one who feels the way I do about writing, meaning Plato. Im sorry this letter is so short, don't work so hard, God Bless You

Sincerely,
Gilbert

Between his letter of 10/8/87 and Stock's next letter to him, Sanchez made an audiotape of a story his mother told him, thereby satisfying a course assignment that asked him to collect a growing-up story from a member of his family. When we invited those students who had made audiotape recordings to share them in class, most were reticent. Although ours was becoming a classroom in which it was clear that every voice was to be heard, attended to, and respected, exposing their parents' and grandparents' voices to their classmates, sharing their family stories in the classroom setting made students understandably nervous. When Gilberto Sanchez offered to be the first to share his taped story, when he offered all of us the following words, spoken in his mother's soft, measured tones, he took a chance. His risk was met with appreciation. As if in church, his classmates listened to his mother's message. They told him they understood what her story meant to him because their parents had versions of that story, too. And they told those versions to one another.

Told in her words, Sanchez's mother's story provided us as Sanchez's teachers an enriched sense of his origins and of the stories that have constructed his self.

We, as a family, the Sanchez, come from a generation of working on the fields. Now, we . . . we learned how to work on the fields by our grandparents. They thought us had to work. And, as we growed up, we learned how to work on the sugar beets, and we used to come from Texas to Michigan, and then we worked for six months, and then went back to Texas. So this kept going on until we were grown up. And then, as we got married, we thought our kids had to work on the . . . on the fields. But, our reason was to show them how to earn their money because working on the field is hard work. And I used to tell my kids, they have to learn how to work, so they can buy their own clothes for school. Which . . . we could afford it, but the main point was for them to learn how to earn their money. And they had to work hard, because I had that experience as I grown up. And this is how our generation, from our parents came, and we passed it to our kids. So, all my three boys, they learned how to work on the fields, and how hard it was to earn their own money.

In a letter she wrote to him shortly after the classroom discussion of his family story, referring both to his letter of 10/8/87 and to his mother's story, Stock offered Sanchez another explicit lesson in literacy by expanding the meaning of his mother's story.

October 19, 1987

Dear Gilbert,

You are so thoughtful. Thank you for thinking about me and the amount of work that I have to do. My schedule is busy, but the truth of the matter is that I really enjoy writing to people so it is kind of nice to have that be a part of my work.

I want to tell you that you have a perfectly beautiful audiotape in the one you submitted to the class. I invite you to work hard as you write about it. The legacy that your mother has given you will also be a gift to your children and their children if you keep it. The story she has told for you is like the stories that are collected in the *Bible*. It has the quality of a parable which is a special kind of story, one that captures truths that outlast a given time, truths to live by, truths to guide us in our efforts to lead good and just lives. As you know, I was quite impressed with your mother's insights and her wisdom. However, I should have guessed that she was very special, for you are gracious and bright.

Sincerely,
P. L. Stock

Stories like the one Sanchez shared, stories that provided occasions for negotiating understanding in our classroom as well as for individualized literacy instruction, did not always originate with students. Enactment of the critical pedagogy we teachers envisioned required us to provide openings too, demanded that we reveal origins, just as we were asking our students to do. A politics of a literacy that hopes to overcome illiteracy realized among teachers and students requires that all tell the stories of their worlds in their words and that all have the opportunity to react to and reflect upon those stories.

In the following letter to all the students in the *Inquiry and Expression* classes, prompted by questions many students were asking her and comments like Sanchez's: "I didn't want to right to you because I figure Its to much righting for you, cause you have to right to so many people beside me . . . ," Stock told a story of her growing up, revealing something of her own origins, providing openings that invited students' reactions:

Dear Students,

I became a serious student in my seventh- and eighth-grades in school. I realize that now. I also realize that I became a *practiced* reader and writer during those two years as well. Furthermore, I believe the two phenomena are related.

At the time I was becoming a serious student and a *practiced* reader and writer, I was a lonely and insecure thirteen- and fourteen-year-old. I was lonely and insecure, in part, because I was a young teenager, but only in part because I was caught between childhood and adulthood. I was lonely also because I was a bit of an outsider in my community. I lived in a Hungarian-American community, and I wasn't Hungarian-American. But my ethnic difference from my schoolmates wasn't the whole reason for my loneliness either. I lived in a small, rural community with few children, and we were separated from one another by distances too great for children to travel alone. Finally, I didn't have many interests in common with my classmates. The boys seemed interested in the cutest girl. And that was not I. The girls seemed interested in the boys and the girl the boys were interested in. The long and the short of it are that I had time on my hands.

I took to books. I checked out all the books I was allowed from the traveling bookmobile that visited my school once a week; I read them in a day or two and then counted the days until the bookmobile would come again.

In the books I read, I found worlds in which I could live and participate. Because my own world was unsatisfactory, I loved the world of books. I read enough to become a *practiced* reader.

The story of how I became a *practiced* writer is related, on the one hand, to my habit of reading and, on the other hand, to how I became a serious student.

When I was in seventh and eighth grades, I attended a first-through-eighth-grade elementary school at the southern tip of Staten Island, one of New York City's five boroughs. Public School #4 was a one-room schoolhouse with rolling walls that slid open and closed on slick tracks. When the rolling walls were opened, all the school's students could be in one room for assemblies or announcements or special programs. When the walls were closed, students in first and second grades studied with a teacher in one room; in third and fourth, with another teacher in another room; fifth and sixth, with another teacher in another room; and seventh and eighth with still another teacher in still another room.

As a result of the fact of the physical arrangement of students in classrooms and the fact that there were usually only fourteen or fifteen students at each grade level each year, teachers at P. S. #4 had a real challenge in helping their students to learn. In my seventh- and eighth-grade classroom, for example, Mr. Romano had twenty-eight pupils, fourteen seventh-graders and fourteen eighth-graders. He taught us English, history, science, mathematics, art, music, whatever he knew.

As I reflect on that time now in an era of departmentalized junior-high-school instruction and speciality teachers, I marvel at what Mr. Romano accomplished. He asked his pupils to help one another, to teach one another. He made each of us believe we were expert at something—at the subject he observed we liked or handled successfully.

Because I liked to read, he asked me to read to others, to help others with reading. I did; and as I did, I learned how to think about reading, how to think about others, how to think about learning. I didn't know it then, but I do realize now that I began to think about learning then.

Mr. Romano made me a writer. He did it kindly when he might have embarrassed me instead. Because I got bored at times in our class of students with varied interests and abilities, sometimes when Mr. Romano was presenting a lesson, I would open a book in my lap, under my desk, and I would read. One day he stopped at my desk when we students were working at some assigned task. He set down a speckled, hard-covered composition book and said, "Those books you read in your lap . . . write about them in here."

I did.

I came to be a good reader because I practiced reading. I came to be a good writer because I practiced writing. Because I read and wrote effectively, I did well in school. Reading and writing have had the most direct impact on my school learning that I can identify.

Sincerely,
Patti Stock

Sanchez chose to react to Stock's story, wondering about the difference between her experience and his, simultaneously expressing concern for her and worrying about himself. Just as Stock had moved into the space he had created in his letters, Sanchez moved into the space she had created in hers. In so doing, he questioned the meanings of her story, its relevance for her, for himself, for others.

Dr. Stock

How have you been? I just finished reading your letter, and I can't help but to wonder why didn't you go out with your friends and do something instead of reading, you must really love to read and write, with my spare time I like to think, I think of mostly my future, I like to be alone when I'm thinking, you know what I mean. Sometimes when every body at home, I take off in the car and drive around anywhere and think, sounds crazy huh? Im at that point were I have to set a goal on what to be, I have to start making plans for my future its hard. Well I'll see you soon Dr. Stock, be careful and God Bless.

Gilbert

In her response to his reflection, once again Stock worked to make a place for instruction of the space for negotiating meaning that he provided. Pressing him to read again, to read even more critically, even more reflectively, to question his assumptions about the meaning of actions and events, she made comments and raised questions that addressed the actions and events in his world even as they challenged him to question the implications of his circumstances and his actions. As she attempted to reinforce the literacy lessons she had been offering him, she revealed the influence on her self of the Protestant ethic of hard work, one so much a part of her world.

December 2, 1987

Dear Gilbert,

Thanks for your nice note. I didn't mean in my letter to suggest that I had no friends. I did. But they were not close friends because we could not be together. We lived too far apart. And, in truth, our interests were not the same. So . . . in my time to myself, I read. That opened up new worlds to me.

I can understand your desire to get off by yourself to think once in a while.
What do you plan for your future? What will you do after high school?

Sincerely,
P. L. Stock

P.S. I've left you notes on my copy of your good essay.
P.P.S. I'm working hard on my stories.

In his reactions to Stock's letters, to the comments his other teachers offered him on his written work, to classroom discussions, Sanchez began to sketch a portrait of himself. To his mother's story, which provided substantial background, he added one narrative after another during the course of the year, stories composed from his world, in his words. This one, which begins where his mother left off, depicts much of Sanchez's world in words quite different from those of his mother. Unlike the parable his mother told in gently moving, softly spoken cadences, Sanchez's words tumbled from his pencil at a frantic pace, in disarray. Taken together, they speak of a world full of sound and, occasionally, of fury.

My mom keeps telling me I need a job, Im gonna go out and some application. So I applied at Little Cersars Pizza. I knew a friend their and he told me he could get me in, he was my girlfriends brother and also my friend, we grew up together playing football in the neighborhood, he was a couple of years older than me, but anyways within a week they called me and told me I started work the following wednesday. I was so excited and happy. My first job. Well not really because my mom would take me to the fields and I would earn my money their. It was kind of traditional for our family to work their, my parents had to work their for a living for a while but now it was different we would go so they could teach us how to work and how hard it was and so we would know how to earn our own money. I called my girlfriend which lived out of town in Holland, Michigan. She use to live down the street from me. I could just run down there and give her a little kiss, now I have to save my money and drive down there and visit for a couple of days. I called her and told her that I got a job, she was happy for me. I started thinking about how it would interfer with my friends because we like to hang out. They told me, the first day of work, if we was going out, I told them I had to work, but they understood. Working their at the pizza place is alright but I don't plan on staying their long. One friday I asked for it off and the manager said ok. So me and my boys went out to a football game, we was all walkin like we was "Bad", just chillin and this guy comes up to me and said are you Rubens brother. I told him "yeah whats it to you" now this guy thought he was bad, he thought he could kick my ass right, excuse my language and he had all his friends with him and I had all my friends with me and me and my boys are real close, its like we all brothers, we blood and blood thicker than water know what Im sayin. so I told the guy "Well I don't like you" and I cocked my fist back and hit him straight in the face, but before that happened while he was talkin I reached in my coat pocket and grabed a lock and then thats when I hit him Im pretty sure I busted his nose he went down for the count and his guys tried to hit me. I kinda moved out of the way and my boy Ken hit him with a right, Pete hit him with his left and Monty "takes" came in and blasted him in the face and he was threw. There was a big fight cause we didn't stop we kicked ass that night. We got a couple of blows from them to. cause I remember going home in pain, my ribs was kinda bruised. I told my girl what happened when I went to see her in next week, she was a little upset, not that I fought, but because I could of gotten hurt, she love me, and I love her. Her parents let me visit her, meaning they let me stay right there, her parents are wonderful people. I still think theirs a lot more adventure to get into cause Im still growing up. When Im alone in my room, sometime I stare at the wall and I say to myself I goes "self, life is hard but it gets harder you know, life is just beginning. Whats gonna happen if your girl goes to a different college out of state, then you go to, whats gonna happen if you don't get a good enough job for you to support your wife, you know what, you have a lot of pressure on your back." just sittin there—chicken. My parent

been gettin on me because I haven't been going to church in a long
time. Part of it is because of work, the other part is I dont want to go.
I have my reasons why, you wouldn't understand or maybe might. I
don't really like having a conversation about the Lord because I feel
like a hypocrite cause here I am talking about him and I don't even go
to church. When you walk with the Lord, it isn't easy cause sometime
you fall down, and the Lord picks you up, and when you fall you have
to try to get up. Know what Im sayin. I fell pretty hard. Its been a
longtime. lately Ive been thinking of my future, its scary sometimes.

While Sanchez's narrative may have been filled with sound and
fury, it is clear that for him, it did not signify nothing. Framing the
dramatic episode he relates, exploring its significance for the world
he is experiencing, indeed, the world he is contributing to make,
Sanchez reflects upon the meanings of events. Informed by his
mother's story, he not only incorporates it in his own, but he also
reflects on it and on the reflections his mother offered in hers. In
part, he demonstrates to us that while his story is not a parable like
his mother's, it is in the tradition of his mother's storytelling, storytelling that explores the significance of events even as it relates
them.

In his words, Sanchez not only describes his effort to get a job,
but he also reflects on his reasons for doing so and demonstrates
how they contrast with the reasons for working that his mother
has described in the story she told him. As he uses words to attach
meaning to his experience, Sanchez means to reveal that his world
is not his mother's world.

My first job. Well not really because my mom would take me to the
fields and I would earn my money their. It was kind of traditional for
our family to work their, my parents had to work their for a living
for a while but now it was different we would go so they could teach
us how to work and how hard it was and so we would know how to
earn our own money. I called my girlfriend which lived out of town in
Holland, Michigan. She use to live down the street from me. I could
just run down there and give her a little kiss, now I have to save my
money and drive down there and visit for a couple of days.

It becomes apparent as his tale unfolds that the center of Sanchez's
story is not so much his finding a job as it is a fight he was in one
Friday night when the manager of "Little Cersars Pizza" gave him
the night off from work. In language that portrays both the perva-
sive violence that characterizes the world in which he lives and his
understanding that he shares with others both a world and words
they may not understand, he writes:

So me and my boys went out to a football game, we was all walkin like
we was "Bad", just chillin and this guy comes up to me and said are
you Rubens brother. I told him "yeah whats it to you" now this guy
thought he was bad, he thought he could kick my ass right, excuse my

language and he had all his friends with him and I had all my friends with me and me and my boys are real close, its like we all brothers, we blood and blood thicker than water know what Im sayin.

And, yes, unfortunately, we did know what Sanchez was saying. In Saginaw, gang fights are too often a way of acting out the tensions that exist between members of different racial and ethnic communities.

Because violence and prejudice are not all Sanchez's story is about, because it is also about his parents' values, his love for Tina and her love for him, because it is also about his fears, it provided us as his teachers many openings. In our efforts to expand those openings into spaces for critical reflection, we asked him questions about the worlds in which he lives, the worlds he describes in more and less detail in his narrative: the world he shares with his family; the world in which he works at a job; the world he shares with his "brothers"; the world he shares with Tina; the world he occupies alone in his room; and as well, one he has not touched in his story—the world of school. We asked him what these worlds had to do with one another, how they did or did not fit together. We asked him if there were differences between the worlds he had inherited and those he was composing with his own actions and his own words.

Sanchez began his next series of writings with a piece about school and what his life is like in school.

> One time me and my friend Pete was in class and the teacher was talkin, teaching class. Pete was talking and the teacher thought that it was me. he said "Gilbert down to the office" I said "for what" in real nice tone of voice and the teacher was being smart he goes "You know for what and quit acting dum" so I got upset I said "Dont talk to me like that Pete my best friend tried to calm me down and Pete told the teacher he said "Gilbert wasn't even talking and he told Pete "shut up or you can go with him Pete told him he said "Man your a ———" the teacher just said "Get out of here" I told him "shut the ———up" the teacher said somethin I can't remember. I said "———you". I lost my temper. I went to the office well we went to the office and the Principle asked us what happened and we told him what happened and we told the truth but then he heard the teacher side of the story and he wasn't telling the truth, he was lyin in front of us. We didn't say anything, Me and Pete just looked at each other and said "man he lyin". So we got suspended I told my Pops everything that happened My Dad told me "you should go apologize for loosing your temper" he was right I shouldin of lost my temper. I waited a couple of weeks before I apologized but my Dad didnt tell me go apologize He just suggest that I do. if he would of told me too I wouldn't have done it. and that what happened.

When he read it with his classmates, many of whom were—like himself—at risk of not graduating from high school, Sanchez's story of school rang a bell. His story inspired others to recite the injustices they had experienced in school. It seems, however, that when teachers join students in remembering the injustices they have experienced in school, the glow of injustice loses some of its warmth. It became a tired topic in our classrooms sooner than we teachers expected it would, perhaps because our students knew and could imagine greater injustices than those usually visited upon them in classrooms.

Alone in his room, when Sanchez was struggling with his fears, it was easy for him to imagine greater difficulties, greater injustices. He composed this story to illustrate the kinds of fears he has for the future when he imagines it.

As I grabe a hold of the iron bars with the cold, dark cell at my back, I look out into the bitter morning, my last day of being locked up in my own world with so little freedom. I cant help but to feel sad when joy should cover the pain I suffered in my heart. the thirty-five years of being seperated from society has come to the end. I have a fresh beginning on life, but I cant ever forget what we once had.

It started from the time when we were all just learning to know what life is about. we were very close friends Brothers is what we use to say we were and we treated each other that way. We were all so similar but yet so different.

Ken came from a rich family, Rich boy, everything came to him so easy. Lazy bumm. Everything came so easy for him, parents handed him everything he needed. wanted, dreamed of. Ken wasn't just another spoled rich kid, he was fun loving and very trusting. He always had this rugged look on him. Ken was the biggest and strongest of the three. He never took anything senior unless it was the business we were all involved in.

Pete came from a broken family and lived with his dad "Pops". Pete was the guy who could talk well with people you know what Im sayin he was the one who could handle people in his own unique way. All the ladies loved him for that and his boyish look in his face. He always held a grug. A grudge against the world.

As for me I carried fear with me everywhere I went. It was just the cold look on my face. I lived on my own in the ghetos staying any where I could mostly with my brothers Pete and Ken accepting their parents as mine. I carried similar trait of both of the guys. I was kinda in the middle of them both. a cross between Pete and Ken I always took everything I did seriously.

We all shared the love we had fore each other, understanding one another. We all shared the love of the same career. Back then we were just Punk low ranksters use to rob banksters.

As every day went buy we grew more mature in our work, our little own maffia. Every day we met new people making new connections all over the States. At our early age we surprisingly ran a whole town. We always new where and what each of us were doin. As you know every business has their competition or apponent.

The Herreras ran their own rob squade. We grew up with them, we were always fighting. with them beating up each other. They had power behind their back. but we had the strongest background from our fathers.

It all went down one day We were all at Kens house just the three of use drinking some quarts of colt 45. The three of us decided to do outside and sit on the porch. Ken walked out first. and I was the last. As Ken stepped out the shooting began. the herraras were there waiting destroy our future. Ken stood alone pulled out his 9mm we all had so many shots against the odds of 10 to 1. Pete jumped behind the railing I jumped behind the wall of the open door. Ken stood their firing his pistol hitting as many as we could. I could here the cry of his voice over the loud thunder of guns. I ran out to watch Ken as he fell to the ground. It was just me and Pete, with no hope. Me and Pete looking at each other stood and shot as many as we could. as I fell the floor all I could think about was that is over. I heard the cars pull away I woke up wounded in several places lying next to my closiest friends my brothers both dead. After being hospitalized for several weeks I was tried for murder among other things and was found guilty sentence to thirty-five years of imprisonment.

Now, here on my last few minute in my cell I think of how the would will accept me my family. I think of how cruel the society could be to an ex-convict. I wonder what my life would have been like after.

As Sanchez imagined the future, in the form of an action-filled fiction, he did so in shapes that are in fact shapes of his present, of the life he lives with the "brothers," of the lives lived by his friends and their families. Violence, murder, are realities in Sanchez's worlds, not just in the world of his imagination, a world that has, no doubt, been exposed to X-rated films as well as hour-long gangster programs that follow half-hour-long sit-coms on weekday night television. At least two of the twenty-seven students in Sanchez's class had known murder in their families. It is perhaps not surprising that, having come close to it, fearing it, Sanchez chose to reflect on it by creating a fictional character who watches his friends being murdered, who murders others, who lives with the consequences of murder, and who wonders what it all means to him and to his family. Even in his fictions, Sanchez had taken up the practice of reflection.

When writing about his girlfriend Tina and members of his family, his reflections were explicit; in fact, in the three brief pieces that follow, written at different times, reflection is the substance of Sanchez's writing.

1

My girlfriend moved out of town not to long ago. I think of her alot. We would tell each other everything solve each others problems. We would talk to each other. She was the only one I could talk to about what I faced everyday. She would make me feel so at ease. Life is much easier to handle with someone to share it with. because you have that someone to rely on. You know what I mean. To help you through those stressful times. but now that she moved I think of how we will live our lives together cause we are both changing into different people shes making her plans and Im making mine. Each of us trying to make our plans fit together. I worry about it sometimes and sometimes I get so frustrated about it, cause it bothers me. And the change of ourselves, the way shes changing and the way Im changing its hard to relate to sometimes and it worries me

2

As you know my girlfriend Tina moved away a while back and it didn't bother me at first but know as we are apart we are thinking of our future trying to put each other in our plans for our lives. We changed so much. Every time I go down to see her shes a different person. Its like we were separated at the time were we change the most and we weren't their with each other to grow in those changes you know. And know I think of whens the next time I'll be with her and what about after we graduate what college will she go to, I'll go to? How far or how much further can we live apart. I love her alot and I would like to marry her one day but the question of me needing a job. I need want a good job to support my wife and maybe family. Life is hard. Sometime I think its not gonna work and I get scared I'm human right. I know their could be worse situations maybe Im worried for nothin but I'll never know til Im old and gray right. It might sould like nothin but theirs more to it than whats mentioned.

3

Ever since my brother moved out the house and went to the army the pressure was on me of being the older brother now, an idol to look at and follow for my little brother and I had to make sure I made the right moves in front of my little brother You know what Im saying. Cause I know everything I did my brother would look at it like it was right cause I never do anything wrong. I had face up to this cause all my life I followed my older brother and did what he told me to do. It was scary being the older brother but now its much easier.

By the middle of the year-long course, writing had become comfortable, perhaps even important to Sanchez. On days when we were writing in class, he came into the room, got busy quickly, and worked purposefully. However, he became a reader more slowly, more grudgingly. In fact, we are not sure if he would have become a reader at all had he not had the opportunity to read stories composed by his teachers and his classmates. Sanchez appeared to mind reading less when the words on the page before him were written by someone he knew, someone to whom he had ready access for conversation. He liked to talk about what he was reading with the author of the piece. In our class, talk and writing were treated as seamless activities; therefore, he had ample opportunities to pursue openings he found in writings with their authors, to push those openings into spaces for negotiating meaning with both the author of a piece of writing and with other members of the interpretative community forming in the classroom. Sanchez became a reader in public, and for him, reading was most meaningful when it was a public activity.

Like other members of his classroom community, he often talked back to an author by writing a story of his own on the subject of a story he had just read. One day, called upon to rehearse a stressful experience from her own teenage years, Stock composed the following narrative about a work experience. She read it at the beginning of a class hour, on a day set aside for writing.

Each summer when I was in high school and college, I worked for a stock brokerage in New York City. Each summer, I worked in a different department. For two of those summers, the work was interesting, even pleasurable; for one of those summers, it was hell.

Hell was having to work with the devil himself—Lloyd Bennett. I shall never forget him. Lloyd Bennett was a big man—about 6 feet 4 inches tall, and he probably weighed 300 pounds. He sat at his desk in his white shirt and dark tie every day when I arrived. He leaned back in one of those sickly-green, pseudo-leather swivel chairs with his feet up on his desk, or he leaned forward over his desk with his barrel chest and arms-like-thighs squished on the papers on his desk. He leaned back in the morning when his work was light, easy. He'd joke and ask questions of his co-workers, and he'd listen to their answers with genuine interest.

"Are you going to college?" he asked me.

"Yes."

"What do you want to study?"

"Literature, I guess. I love to read and write."

"So do I. I read philosophy mostly. I'm a deeply religious Roman Catholic."

In the afternoon, after 3:00 p.m. when the stock market closed and his work load became frantic, Lloyd Bennett turned from Dr. Jekyll to Mr. Hyde. His job required that he borrow the hundreds of thousands or millions of dollars each afternoon that the brokerage needed that day to pay for the securities, bonds, and notes it had purchased that day. From 3:00 p.m. to 5:00 p.m., he was a madman, making one telephone call after another to banks. He'd even make the calls himself because he wasted time yelling at anyone else to make them. On these calls, he'd try to borrow the money he needed at the best rates he could get on overnight loans. He could bargain by checking one bank against another, not by convincing anyone to lower a rate; therefore, he called one bank after another, wrote the loan forms in between calls, screamed to me to run over to his desk to get the form and type it immediately.

The forms were complicated. I wasn't a typist of any merit. I'd sit at my typewriter petrified, clammy-handed. "Please, God, don't let me make a mistake."

"G—, d——, s— o-a b——, get over here. This isn't supposed to be 1¾%; it's supposed to be 1¼%. What the h—are you doing over there?"

"I'm sorry," I half cried, running over to his desk to collect the mistaken form, leaving a half-completed form in my typewriter. I'd pull it out. Replace it with the mistaken one, fix it, and then roll the original back into the machine, trying to find the right line—the one

I had stopped typing when he yelled. From that line back to his illegible notes, I'd try to figure out what he had written. I couldn't ask him; he was on the phone and if I waited for him to finish, we'd get behind and be unable for the runner to get the loan to the bank on time. I was afraid to make mistakes, but I was more afraid of not getting the loan to the bank on time. So I guessed. I typed 1³/₄%. "After all, that had been the rate of the securities he put up as collateral on the last loan. Maybe he's using a lot of them today. He used a lot of bonds at 2¹/₄% yesterday," I reasoned my way to a guess.

I finished the loan form, ran it to his desk, and collected another he had finished. I was in the midst of typing it when the dam burst.

"J——, what the h—— have you done this time? Can't you get anything right? Why the f—— can't you do these things . . . "

It was like that every day of that summer. I cried at night, shook in the morning. I needed the money for school. Jobs were hard to get.

Responding to her story about working, Sanchez wrote one of his own.

It was the moment I walked in the Front door of my work Little Ceasars Pizza. Walked in with my work clothes on brown pants and a tan shirt that said Little Ceasars on it. the momment I walked in I new it was gonna be a hectic night as I looked at the food bar where we make the pizza I could see two of my friend making pizza their was about 6 slips up there to make and that twelve pizzas all together. I could here my manager yelling and working fast like never before. I punched in the clock and put a brown apron on and quickly ran to the oven area where they needed help. So hot as you open the doors. People rushing in the back scrambling to sheet out some doe putting them in pans. It was a real busy day. I put as many pizza I could and 1 shelf in the oven and the oven rotates with four shelves, you can fit eight larges on one shelf and that was it. I started sweating imidiately it being hotter than the hottest day of summer. I remembering opening the oven door checking the pizza melted cheese with the cooked items peperonii, ham etc. I looked in the oven my hair on my arms burnt from reaching in to get the pizza, burning a couple of pizza. The manager just looked at me with this face like you stupid. I got made that day everybody was grouchy and upset cause the phones kept ringing and ringing off the hook. every ones faces all with this mean look on their faces rushing to get the job done, this girl at the til with a fake smile as she serves the customers she just might as well been looking mean. I would pull the pizzas out and put them in boxes and put them up according to their size. we were all so behind hoping and praying that bussiness would slow down. I wanted to go home cause I thought I was gonna faint and fall collapse were I stood.

Sanchez's story offered in response to Stock's was his reading of her story. Rather than commenting on her story in analytic fashion, he offered an analogous account of the pressures of work, one rooted in his own world and expressed in his own words. His story's similarities to Stock's—his presentation of like events and feelings—are clear evidence that he had comprehended her story's meanings.

By February of the academic year, when we teachers presented students with a course pack of essays about the adolescent experience written by psychologists, sociologists, educators, and cultural historians, we invited Sanchez to demonstrate his ability to comprehend in another way: to comment on what he was reading from the perspective of his own authority, authority he and his classmates had earned by collecting, composing, and reflecting on stories of the growing-up experience. Sanchez began reading the writing of published authors with interest. Having studied the experience of growing up with his classmates for six months, having learned to talk and write critically to his classmates and his teachers about the growing-up stories they were composing, Sanchez addressed the authoritative voice he had been practicing in the classroom community to the published authors he was now reading.

After reading "Paths to Adulthood," the first chapter of *Being Adolescent: Conflict and Growth in the Teenage Years*, written by two psychologists from the University of Chicago, Mihaly Csikszentmihalyi and Reed Larson, Sanchez indicated his general agreement with the authors' claims about the importance of adolescence. Reviewing their claims, Sanchez wrote:

> Adolescence is a age between twelve and nineteen, which I think is true. The article says thats when you learn to find out who you are in these years. I agree cause I think between these years you change alot and you make alot of mistakes while your growing up and you learn from those mistakes between these years you learn alot of stuff. The paper says some psychologists claim that early childhood experiences determine the shape of a person's future life. Now all things a child does is going to affect what he does in the future he will now if its right or wrong and learn from it. as a teenager, you have to learn how to become an adult, become more mature.

Sanchez took exception with Csikszentmihalyi and Larson, however, when he thought they drew conclusions based on insufficient evidence.

> The things they predict for the three people mentioned in the article were stupid, I didn't agree cause they make the one sound like a drunk if he took just one beer but he was drunk just having fun that doesn't mean he will become an alcoholic. It was stupid that's the only thing that bothered me.

When Sanchez faulted Csikszentmihalyi and Larson for predicting possible futures for three adolescents based upon one incident from each of their lives, once again he opened a space for negotiating meaning. His critique of "Paths to Adolescence" moved us to ask him questions that invited him to explore the adequacy of his reading of Csikszentmihalyi and Larson's text: Had he interpreted their question, "Would Warren's drinking turn the hopes of a good job and marriage into a nightmare of disappointments?" as a prediction? Was it one? If not, what was it? Was it too soon in his reading of their text for Sanchez to infer from their question the meaning he construed? What would reading the remainder of their book teach him? Would the authors, in fact, reach the conclusions from their argument that Sanchez believed they were implying in the "Introduction" to their book?

When he indicated that he believed the authors of "Paths to Adulthood" were "stupid" to suggest that Warren may become an alcoholic because Warren was just "drunk just having fun," Sanchez was doing what we had encouraged him to do: he was testing the validity of the texts he was reading against his own experience. On the basis of his own experience, he was making a text about a text in order to make both texts subject to critical inquiry, to responsive understanding. As we read together, we elaborated our making of critical texts, making each successive one responsive to questions we formulated for one another. There were our questions for Sanchez: What does it mean to be "drunk just having fun"? Why do you use the word "drunk" to describe the "having fun" you are referring to? There were Sanchez's questions for us: Haven't you ever had something to drink with friends? Just because you were drinking, were you drunk? Are you an alcoholic? And there were the questions all of us asked ourselves together: Are there limits to the understanding we have from our personal experience, limits that might be extended if we entertain the ideas that others compose from their experience?

Increasingly, the openings for instruction that Sanchez provided us in the spring of the 1987–88 academic year originated in the published texts he was reading. Making places for instruction of these openings, at times—as when he wrote about "Paths to Adulthood"—we asked him to reflect on the worlds and the words inscribed by others and on his reading of their worlds and their words; at other times, we asked him to reflect on his own worlds and his words and his composition of them into texts. It became apparent that the interactions of Sanchez's reading and writing experiences were provoking him to think about literature even as his interactions with his teachers and his classmates were provoking him to exercise literacy.

When he began to comment in class discussions not just on the content of the imaginative literature he was reading but also on the ways in which the authors he was reading were shaping their texts, we invited Sanchez to begin to shape something like a theory of literature. For example, when he was reading Stephen King's novella *The Body*, Stock invited him to comment on the following observation made by Gordie Lachance, the narrator/protagonist in the novel, about "Stud City," the first story he had written that "felt like his story":

No, it's not a very good story—its author was too busy listening to other voices to listen as closely as he should have to the one coming from inside. But it was the first time I had ever really used the place I knew and the things I felt in a piece of fiction, and there was a kind of dreadful exhilaration in seeing things that had troubled me for years come out in a new form, *a form over which I had imposed control.* It had been years since that childhood idea of Denny being in the closet of his spookily preserved room had occurred to me; I would have honestly believed I had forgotten it. Yet there it is in "Stud City," only slightly changed . . . but *controlled* (1982, 323).

When she asked Sanchez if he, like the narrator of *The Body*, had given new form to events in his experience and, in so doing, had taken control over them as he was composing them into the piece of writing he was working on at the time, Sanchez responded:

> Now, I feel having control over a story is good. Control, where you can change any part of the story, to make it more interesting or take parts out. Isn't that the only way to make a good story? Take gossip for instance, isn't most gosip a mere exadurated with which makes it a good gossip. Its same case with a story right? Well sometimes the truth can be well good but don't you always add a little here and a little there to make it better. I think having control over a story make it alot better so I agree with gordie on how he wrote his story in having control.

Interestingly, Sanchez's analogy of gossip with story is one Patricia Meyer Spacks explores in a book-length analysis of "the analogy between gossip and literature" (1985, 262). For Sanchez, the likeness lies in the notion of control: If a gossiper exaggerates to make gossip "good," a storyteller "can change any part of the story, to make it more interesting or take parts out." For Spacks,

> the analogy between gossip and literature serves a double hermeneutic function: it both emphasizes the importance of gossip's procedures and insights and illustrates some of literature's roots in ordinary experience. Writing and speech (whatever the laws of priority) generate sister arts. If gossip empowers the subordinated into liberated discourse, imaginative literature frees its practitioners for speculation and invention (262–63).

Both the professional literary critic, Spacks, and the unpracticed one, Sanchez, observe that the writing of imaginative literature empowers authors to remake the worlds of their ordinary experience into worlds they can imagine—worlds in which speculation and invention find some space to figure actions that transcend the constraints of ordinary experience, to expand limits imposed by the merely past. Freed by control into "liberated discourse," freed by imagination into the powers of "speculation and invention," perhaps Gilberto Sanchez could be freed as well into "a critical presence in the real world" so that life might imitate art and authorship lead to deliberate agency.

Having been invited by us to use desktop publishing equipment to produce a collection of their literature for actual distribution, at the conclusion of their course of study in *Inquiry and Expression,* Sanchez and his classmates chose to become authors. They selected and reworked favorite growing-up stories which they gathered into an anthology they entitled *The Bridge.* [10] For his contribution to the collection, Sanchez composed "It's a Cold World," a literary tapestry woven of the worlds and words of his prior texts. Constructing a textual warf from strands of the stories he had told about his work experiences, he wrote in the "liberated discourse" Spacks has named, the "liberated discourse" he himself had defined. Freeing himself of the reality of his previous experiences and of the constraints of his previously told stories about those experiences, he composed imaginative literature. As we read "It's a Cold World," we saw visions and heard sounds from the worlds about which Sanchez had written during the time we studied together, and we saw the visions and heard the sounds of the world of our classroom—the world in which he composed his text. It appears that as he "speculated and invented"—as he reconstructed events, revised sequences, replaced connections—Sanchez used the processes of speculation and invention to reflect on both the world of experiences that informed his composition and his act of composition itself. The visions we saw and the sounds we heard in his composition reminded us of Mikhail Bakhtin's observation that the writer of imaginative literature

> does not strip away the intentions of others from the heteroglot language of his works, he does not violate those socio-ideological cultural horizons (big and little worlds) that open up behind heteroglot languages—rather, he welcomes them into his work. The prose writer makes use of words that are already populated with the social intentions of others and compels them to serve his own new intentions, to serve a second master (1981, 300).

"IT'S A COLD WORLD"

Gilberto Sanchez

Parents are always telling you to do this and that and they say, "You better start thinking of your future." My mom would take me and my older brother to work in the fields, cutting weeds and separating cabbages, and we would earn our money there. Working there made me realize I needed to think of my future, to think of my goals in life. My mom was right. Working there made me realize I was becoming an adult even though I was still young. Maybe you could call it maturing.

It seems like problems started coming up the summer I was fourteen years old, when I started thinking of my future. When the season ended for working in the fields, I told my mom and dad I wasn't ever going back. That job wasn't for me. It was hard working there with the sun beating down upon your back and all those mosquitos and bugs.

I wasn't going back for sure. It was kind of traditional for our family to work there. My parents had to work there for a living for a while. When they were small, they would work in the fields to help my grandparents' finances. But now it was different, we would go so that our parents could teach us how to work hard for our money.

After a while my parents got on my case about my being lazy. They complained that I should be working, telling me I needed a job. I decided to go and fill out some applications. I applied at Little Caesar's Pizza. I knew a friend there, and he told me he could get me in. He was my girlfriend's brother and also my friend. We all grew up together, playing football in the neighborhood—me, my brother, and all our friends. Within a week Little Caesar's called me and told me that I could start working the following Wednesday. I was so excited and happy. My mom thought I'd never get out of the crib. Everything was going great, so I thought.

But it wasn't. My brother Robert had moved out of the house and gone into the army. He had been gone for just one week, and I already missed him. Ever since he left, the pressure has been on me. I have had to be the older brother. I have had to be a model for my little brother, Ruben. I have had to make sure I make all the right moves in front of my little brother. You know what I'm saying? Because I know that everything I do, Ruben will look at it as right. Because I never do anything wrong, is what he thinks. I have had to face up to the fact that I am the older brother and that I have to make my own decisions. All my life, I followed my older brother and did what he did and did what he told me to do. It's scary at times being the older brother.

Things got worse. My girlfriend moved out of town. My girlfriend Tina's pop got a better job offer. He's an electrician. His getting a better job offer was good. Nothing was wrong with that, but the job was out of town. Their family ended up moving to Holland, Michigan. I remember when Tina used to live down the street from me. I could just run down there and give her a little kiss. Now I have to save my hard-earned money and drive three hours to go to see her for the weekend. Her parents let me visit her, meaning they don't mind me visiting for the weekend and staying the night.

I think of Tina a lot. We can tell each other everything, solve each other's problems. We can talk to each other. She is the only one I can talk to about what I face everyday. She can make me feel so at ease, so secure. Life is much easier to handle with someone to share it with. You have that someone to rely on, you know what I mean?

Now that she moved, I think of how we will live our lives together. We are both changing into different people. She's making her plans, and I'm making mine. Each of us is trying to make our plans fit together. The change in ourselves—the way she's changing, and the way I'm changing—makes it hard to relate sometimes, and it worries me. We keep in touch. I call her, and she calls me, and we run up the phone bill. I'm in love.

When I started work, I did pretty good. Working there was all right. I didn't plan on staying there long. I find when I go to work, I'm not thinking of work, but of all the problems I face. Working can be a problem in itself. There are times we get so busy that everyone working is behind in their work, and everyone just has a mean look on their face. I sometimes have to work this huge oven cooking pizzas. The managers yell, people scream that they need help. No one can help because they need help themselves. It's hectic sometimes working there, especially when you are not thinking of work.

I started thinking about how work interfered with my friends because we would like to hang out sometimes. One of my friends, Pete, had asked me the first day of work if we were going out. I told him I had to work, but he understood. One Friday I asked for time off and the manager said, "Okay." So me and my boys went out to a football game. We were all walking like we were "bad," just chillin', and this guy came up to me and he started to front me. He had been wanting to fight me since the eighth grade and three years had passed since then. He started talking his shit. Now this guy thought he was bad. He thought he could kick my ass. I was a little scared, but then again who isn't when they are getting ready to fight.

While he was talking, I reached into my coat pocket and felt a lock so I grabbed it like a weapon. He had all his friends with him and I had all my boys with me and me and my boys are real close. It's like we are all brothers. We are blood, and blood's thicker than water, know what I'm saying? I told the guy, "Look, you want to fight, let's go then," and I cocked my fist back with the lock in my hand and hit him with the hood part of the lock, holding it like brass knuckles. Aiming for the face, I hit him. I'm pretty sure I busted his nose. He went down for the count, and this guy tried to hit me. I kinda moved out of the way and my boy, Ken, hit him with a right. Pete came in and hit him with a left hook, and Monty came through the crowd and blasted him in the face and that dude was through. This all happened in a split second. There was a big fight because we didn't stop. We kicked ass that night. We got a couple of blows from them, too. Well, at least I know I did, cause I remember going home in pain. My ribs were kinda bruised. That was a rough night that night.

The next week I went to see Tina, and I told her what happened. She was a little upset, not that I fought, well, that too, but mainly because I could have gotten hurt. She loves me, and I love her.

Life is hard when you're growing up, being a teenager. When I'm alone in my room, sometimes I stare at the wall and try to figure out my problems. Sometimes it seems there is no solution. Life is just beginning for me, but sometimes it seems to get harder and harder as I get older. The stress is always gonna be there, the problems, the trouble. I guess it's just something you have to live with. Growing up is hard to do; it's hectic sometimes. When it comes right down to it, you might want to say, "It's a Cold World" (Sanchez, 89–92).

Reflecting on "It's a Cold World," we have been reminded of Bakhtin's characterization of prose art:

If the art of poetry, as a utopian philosophy of genres, gives rise to the conception of a purely poetic, extrahistorical language, a language far removed from the petty rounds of everyday life, a language of the gods—then it must be said that the art of prose is close to a conception of languages as historically concrete and living things. The prose art presumes a deliberate feeling for the historical and social concreteness of living discourse, as well as its relativity, a feeling for its participation in historical becoming and in social struggle; it deals with discourse that is still warm from that struggle and hostility, as yet unresolved and still fraught with hostile intentions and accents; prose art finds discourse in this state and subjects it to the dynamic unity of its own style (1981, 331).

Informed by Bakhtin's insights, we may conclude that Sanchez is well on his way toward becoming a prose artist. Mindful of the worlds in which he lives, however, as well as the worlds in which we as his teachers live, we are less able to conclude that Sanchez is well on his way toward becoming literate, if by calling him literate we mean to imply that no one will label him a "marginal man," that no one will deny him ready access to the sets of "social and intellectual practices" that shape public discourse and determine who gets to speak to whom about what and when. But, we would argue, Sanchez's artistry, his growing control of his words, gives him the right to ask for a hearing and perhaps, too, sufficient sense of self to claim that right.

How Will They Be Received, This Politics, This Pedagogy, This Young Man?

What is most serious and most troubling is the sense that the self as participant, as inquirer, as creator of meanings, has been obliterated (Greene, 1978, 12).

The people of the United States need to know that individuals in our society who do not possess the levels of skill, literacy, and training essential to this new era will be effectively disenfranchised, not simply from the material rewards that accompany competent performance, but also from the chance to participate fully in our national life (A Nation at Risk, 1983, 7).

Business and military leaders complain that they are required to spend millions of dollars on costly remedial education and training programs in such basic skills as reading, writing, spelling, and computation. The Department of the Navy, for example, reported to the Commission that one-quarter of its recent recruits cannot read at the ninth grade level, the minimum needed simply to understand written safety instructions. Without remedial work they cannot even begin, much less complete, the sophisticated training essential in much of the modern military (A Nation at Risk, 1983, 9).

While it is important that teachers be invested with the authority and responsibility to exercise their professional judgment over a wide range of matters over which they currently have little control, that judgment . . . must be subject to certain constraints. Governing authorities will have to develop means to assure themselves that students are making satisfactory progress toward agreed upon goals. They will also have to be prepared to take action to either reduce teacher discretion or change the makeup of the school leadership team if student learning falls substantially below expectations (Carnegie Forum on Education and the Economy, 1986).

The topic of a speaking person takes on quite another significance in the ordinary ideological workings of our consciousness, in the process of assimilating our consciousness to the ideological world. The ideological becoming of a human being, in this view, is the process of selectively assimilating the words of others (Bakhtin 1981, 341).

In our time again, there are many persons speaking about education: some speak to teachers and students and about them to the public, others speak for teachers and students (as we are doing here) as if they could not, or had no right to, speak for themselves. When teachers raise their voices in the heteroglossia that constitutes the current discourse of education, and especially the discourse of public education, theirs are likely to be anxious ones. Teachers of language use particularly—those who teach things that are named by others "basic skills," "reading, writing, spelling," skills identified as fundamental to making it in the world—find it difficult to use a language that is anything other than a language of anxiety. In the language of teachers of reading and writing—in our language—a listener hears words of concern for Charles Baldwin's and Gilberto Sanchez's future as speaking persons: a concern for a self "as participant, as inquirer, as creator of meanings"; a hope for a self who might say new things, things that might redefine the relations of self to others. But in our language, one hears words of other concerns as well: the assimilated words of others who express their concerns for students' futures in terms of economic well-being and social stability, terms that speak to the needs of the marketplace and the state. Perhaps as his teachers we can persuade and enable Charles Baldwin to find a voice for himself, to become a speaking person as Gilberto Sanchez has, to some extent, done; but will his speech or Sanchez's, especially in their written versions, ever land them jobs? Will Baldwin's even enable him to get through high school?

The minds of teachers, their dialogic imaginations, provide space enough—even if others were not speaking loudly—for contending voices expressing apparently conflicting values: a genuine concern for Baldwin's and Sanchez's selves must of course include concern for their economic well-being—even if many of us conclude, as teachers merely, that our efforts and actions will not be the real forces that will determine it. And if such a concern is not of our own making, of our own authorship, there are powerful means to assure that we will nonetheless assimilate it through listening to the words and heeding the actions of authoritative others. There are always assessments, and they are always rooted in hegemonic values, in the values of authoritative others. Assessments speak to students, ordering them into ranked groups; and of course they speak, perhaps more loudly, to us, those students' teachers, telling us where we have failed and pointing out the consequences of failure, not simply for us but also for our students. And there are also, of course, always agencies to give expression to hegemonic values, agencies that have the power to enforce them: Teachers are to "be vested with the authority and responsibility to exercise their professional judgment," but only if that authority is made subject to clear restraints:

> Governing authorities will have to develop means to assure themselves that students are making satisfactory progress toward agreed upon goals. They will also have to be prepared to take action to either reduce teacher discretion or change the makeup of the school leadership team if student learning falls substantially below expectation (Carnegie Forum, 1986).

In this way of looking at the world, in this conception of a politics of education, the means of assurance are most likely to be the methods of assessors; and the "agreed upon goals" with their resultant expectations are most likely to reflect the ideologies of those who in fact govern. Assessments, as we found out ourselves, are not very good devices for measuring the growth of a self "as participant, as inquirer, as creator of meanings."

Of our work in Saginaw, it might be said—in fact, it has been said—that we are making in our classrooms unreal worlds, worlds that do not mirror the competitive ones outside the walls of the schoolhouse, worlds that do not prepare students for success in the competition for jobs and goods. In fact, there is truth in these charges. In fact, we are trying to make our classrooms safe havens from the violent worlds some of our students, Charles Baldwin and Gilberto Sanchez among them, have to live in, because they are there. And in the midst of a world that works to drown individual voices in seas of commercial and political messages, messages that seem to be made by no one or to invite any other response than acquiescence, we are trying to make little worlds in which single speaking persons may say what they are able to say in the full expectation of responsive understanding from others.

In a way, our own assessment, or rather our assessment of our assessment as teachers, did lead us toward our attempts to build the kinds of worlds we have imagined in our classrooms. In studying the efforts of students whose texts we had judged illiterate, we did find evidence (why should we have been surprised?) of lack of sense of agency, of the ability to choose, of the opportunity for choice. In trying to find new ways to teach students who find themselves at risk both in the classroom and in the worlds that surround it, we are trying to find ways to encourage agency, to find sources for its exercise, to give latitude for its development. We are encouraging students to tell stories and write them about the worlds they live in and to become critical about their presences in those worlds; we are encouraging students to read stories in which others have found critical presence in other worlds. We are, quite deliberately, trying to fashion in the classroom an inhabitable world for students, one in which they might safely raise such voices as they have to make meanings for themselves and others, voices that will be valued for such agency as they can manage.

In asking ourselves why we build such classrooms, we do not mean to avoid the inevitable questions of authoritative others; quite otherwise, we have assimilated them in our own imaginations. We do ask their questions because they are ours as well. What are our obligations to the worlds constituted through public discourse, through sanctioned discourse, through the literacy of "the dominant classes"? What are our real-world obligations to Charles Baldwin, Gilberto Sanchez, and others? Can we care for their futures as selves, as human beings, as critical presences in a world that needs remaking, and still prepare them to meet the expectations of assessors, in school and after school?

But if in building our classrooms, we have left them open to the questions from authoritative others, we have also used them as openings to ask something of authoritative others. We ask others not to avoid our questions, and these questions in particular: Because they have labored for literacy, fought for the right to tell their stories, struggled to compose selves for themselves in literate discourse, will you read our students' texts and read them with responsive understanding? Because they have recognized the power of hegemonic values and have labored to compose and publish their literature in something like conventional modes, will you distribute our students' texts? Will you ask your students to read our students' texts as Sylvia Robins does at Delta College in her course in *Introductory Composition*; as Marian Mohr and Marion MacLean do at George Mason University in their course, *The Teacher as Researcher*; as Loren Barritt does at the University of Michigan in his course, *The Psychology of Education*; as Marni Schwartz does in her classes in Niskayuna Middle School in Schenectady, New York?

As Freire reminds us, *illiterate* is a label by means of which those near centers of power push others to peripheries, to function as "marginal men" and women. When those on the margins can be enabled to write texts, reading those texts can become a powerful political act. For authoritative others who teach reading and writing, it is one within their full competency and power.

Those of us who are teachers and researchers in the nation's institutions of higher learning have the opportunity—and we would argue the responsibility—to act in the spirit in which we speak. While we all appear to agree that our students have a right to literacy, too many of us are content to allow such literacy as our students do achieve to go unrecognized, too many of us are content to blame others for making our students into "marginal men" and women. We would argue that our students' right to literacy asks something of us. It obliges us to read their words about their worlds, to study those words, to circulate them, and to respond to them; it obliges us, too, to read through those words toward human and humane interpretations of the selves *in situ* who have composed them, to read in texts from the margins attempts to recompose a sense of self, to reconstitute the meanings of self in relation to others.

In the world we inhabit with our students, one is not made literate or taught to become so; one chooses to become literate, in circumstances where choice is made available; one learns how to become literate by using words in situated actions that are rendered personally meaningful by social and intellectual practices that are socially meaningful. No one becomes literate who does not see some opening, however small, toward active participation in a literate world that is part of the reality in which he or she lives. No one becomes literate who does not glimpse, and then come to feel, some possibility, no matter how tightly constrained, to shape the meanings that inevitably control one's life. Even as assessors, we see little hope for Charles Baldwin, or for Gilberto Sanchez either, unless we can join with them in a polity of literacy in which all are speaking persons and all alike listeners who offer responsive understanding. And, of course, there is little hope for such a polity unless we can constitute a politics of education that makes for openings, nourishes beginnings, no matter when they happen, and honors difference—even resistance—when it is uttered or inscribed or expressed in meaningful silences. Charles Baldwin did write, and in spite of our judgments, we honor him for that: for opening his world to us to enrich ours. Given his example, may we all write as separate selves to compose a better one in forms of public discourse open to participation by all who choose to become speaking persons. If we would be literate, and help others to become so, it is a time for thoughtful listening to those voices that come from the margins; it is time for reflective reading of texts that inscribe those voices as centrally human ones.

Notes

1The work is being done under the auspices of the School District of the City of Saginaw and the Center for Educational Improvement through

Collaboration (CEIC) of The University of Michigan. Work has been funded by both agencies, and by the W. K. Kellogg Foundation and the State Department of Education in Michigan. Patricia L. Stock has served as Coordinator of the project; other University of Michigan workers have included Colleen Fairbanks, Cathy Fleischer, Richard Harmston, and David Schaafsma.

[2]The following English teachers from Saginaw deserve special mention for their imaginative and committed work: Linda Bush, Jean Cole, Alena Dancy, Jane Denton, Sharon Floyd, Louise Harrison, Robert Hoard, James Jones, Mary Lane, Gail Oliver, Kathie Smith, Sheila Smith, Bea Ugartechea, Rosa Winchester, and Carol Woolfolk.

[3]We particularly wish to thank and commend Foster B. Gibbs, Superintendent; Burris Smith, Director, K-12 Education; Gene Nuckolls, Assistant Superintendent, Secondary Education; Lochie Overbey, Coordinator, Staff Development; James Jones, former Language Arts Coordinator; Jane Denton, Language Arts Coordinator; Thomas Sharp, Principal, Arthur Hill High School; Wilson Smith, Principal, Saginaw High School.

[4]For an account of an assessment with similar aims, see Stock and Robinson, 1987.

[5]It is amazing that reports of test results rarely take account of the fact that students may either not care about performing well or refuse what seems to them a meaningless task, even though any teacher will tell any tester that not all students care much about playing a game that is rarely one in which they have much investment. And yet one reads every day, as reportable news, that 54 percent of American eleventh graders can't do something or other.

[6]Similar issues about the implications of reading assessment essays are treated in Barritt, Stock, and Clark, 1986.

[7]The assessment was entirely designed and conducted by teachers, some from the Saginaw schools and some from the University of Michigan. On the first of the four days given to it, teachers in their own classrooms prompted students to write an account of some incident in which they or someone they knew had experienced stress; the stories were then shared. On the second day, students were asked to compose an account of another incident, something brought to mind by accounts told the previous day by other students, and "language lists" were collected on chalk boards in the classrooms: lists of words and phrases that seemed best to capture the notion of stress.

On the third day, the students were given the following prompt and asked to take about half an hour to write a response to it:

TEENAGE STRESS

"Get off my case!"

"Get outta my face!"

"Just forget it!"

At some time or other, most teenagers have observed or experienced stress. Have you ever felt life was coming down on you pretty hard and you didn't know how much more you could take? Think about a time when you or someone you know felt stressed, frustrated, or uptight.

Write an essay based in your own experience that tells Saginaw English teachers what stresses teenagers feel and why teenage stress is a problem.

You may begin your essay however you choose, but if you need suggestions for how to begin, here are several:

Sometimes, I lose my cool.

There are days when I just can't stand it anymore.

The adults I know seem to think that a teenager's life is free of pressures.

After students had been writing for about half an hour, teachers asked them to set their essays aside and turn their attention to a letter that was distributed to each student, explaining that the letter would tell them how to help a partner whose essay they would read to earn the best evaluation possible for his or her essay. The letter read:

Dear Student Writers:

As you and your partner read the first drafts of each other's essays for the purposes of helping each other write even better final essays, it may help you to know that your final essays will be evaluated by two English teachers, who will each award your essay a numerical score from 1 to 4.

4 equals Excellent
3 equals Proficient
2 equals Interesting but Flawed
1 equals Unsuccessful

As you underline the parts of your partner's essay you like and ask your partner questions about aspects of his/her essay, keep in mind these questions that teachers will be asking themselves as they evaluate your essays:

1. Has this writer made clear to me his/her *own* understanding of what stress is?

2. Has this writer illustrated his/her *own* understanding with specific, appropriate examples?

3. Does this writer illustrate his/her ideas and illustrations in a way that allows me to understand them as he/she does? That is, are the ideas and illustrations organized so that I can follow them and understand the connections between them? Are they written in language that is clear and interesting? Are there so many usage and mechanical errors in this essay that I cannot understand what the writer wants me to understand?

With these questions in mind that teachers will be asking themselves, offer your partner the best help you can as you underline and question what he/she has written.

GOOD LUCK TO YOU AND YOUR PARTNER.

Students then exchanged papers with a classmate, who underlined sections he or she particularly liked in the partner's essay and wrote questions to the author asking about what was unclear or understated.

On the fourth day, students were asked to revise or write another version of the essay written as a response to the prompt. Because teachers gave the assessment in their own classrooms, and were invited to use techniques for eliciting writing that were familiar to their students, there was much variation in how the assessment was conducted, which would not please most kinds of assessors.

The aims behind the assessment were these: to give students every opportunity to perform as ably as they could; to invite variety in student responses; to encourage students to use recollection, in the form of personal or close experience, as a basis for reflection and assertion.

Below are the descriptive labels teachers attached to the rankings they assigned and criteria teachers devised as a guide to their readings and ratings:

CRITERIA FOR EVALUATION

(4) EXCELLENT

The essay *fully* engages the reader because of its originality of thought and its accuracy, appropriateness, and freshness of expression. Overall unity and coherence are evident. The writer assumes a clear and definable stance toward his or her materials, makes a claim, and develops the claim through appropriate illustrations or particular demonstration. There is shape and clarity in the organization; functional units (introductions, illustrations, elaborations, and so on) are marked or obvious. There is appropriate variety both in sentence structure and in the vocabulary employed in sentences. Technical errors either do not occur or are so rare that they do not interfere with the writer's message or the reader's engagement.

(3.5) EXCELLENT TO PROFICIENT

(3) PROFICIENT

Although the essay engages the reader, it may lack originality of thought or it may demonstrate weaknesses in expression, development, coherence, clarity, or correctness. Clarity of claims, soundness of thought and development, clear organization, and general correctness of expression are all required for an essay to be ranked 3.

(2.5) PROFICIENT TO INTERESTING BUT FLAWED

(2) INTERESTING BUT FLAWED

The essay engages the reader, although not fully, because of failures in imagination, inconsistencies, inaccuracies or inadequacies in development, imprecision or staleness of expression, and/or serious problems with the requirements of correctness. Illustrative problems might be:

Thought and Development: Superficiality of thought; reliance on facile generalizations; incorrect statements of fact from which inferences are drawn; irrelevant statements or evidence; needless repetition; inaccurate use of expressions and words.

Organization and Style: Lack of discernible organization; lack of coherence; absence of transitional sentences, phrases, or words. Inappropriate and uncontrolled sentence structure; inappropriate level of usage and diction; vague reference; dangling elements.

Technical Errors: Sentence run-ons, misspellings, agreement errors, missing or inaccurate paragraphing. *Errors like these must leap out at the reader and cause the writer's message to be lost for an essay to be rated 2.*

(1.5) INTERESTING BUT FLAWED TO UNSUCCESSFUL

(1) UNSUCCESSFUL

The essay interests the reader in spite of the fact that the reader has to work throughout the essay to make meaning or perceive form or does not interest the reader because of a combination of problems: superficiality or staleness of thought; lack of clarity in the claims; lack of development; incoherence in organization; inaccuracy and/or uncertainty in expression; serious lack of control of the mechanics of written English.

[8]For a useful summary of the demographic data, see the special edition of *Education Week,* May 14, 1986.

[9]The two Saginaw teachers engaged with us in this effort were Jane Denton (Arthur Hill High School) and Sharon Floyd (Saginaw High School). Without their commitment and imagination the effort would not have produced the results it did, for they were there, every day, to turn into real activities the ideas we were forming together. We hope this essay will stand as a tribute to their generous capacity to add still other tasks to those that customarily require of public-school teachers more energy than most humans have. In the academic year 1989–90, Sheila Smith joined Jane Denton, and Kathie Smith joined Sharon Floyd, to work as co-teachers of new Inquiry and Expression courses offered to tenth-graders. The two teams will teach the same students for three years in an attempt to see how deeply student literacy can develop in the classroom we are trying to construct. But that is and will be another story.

[10]In June 1988, two classes of twelfth-grade students in the two high schools in Saginaw published a book entitled *The Bridge,* a collection of their own accounts, their own stories, of what it means to grow up in communities like Saginaw's various ones. The book has now sold over 3,000 copies. It is available for $5.00 a copy from The Center for Educational Improvement Through Collaboration, 2018 School of Education Building, University of Michigan, Ann Arbor, MI 48109.

Afterword

Since I wrote "Literacy in the Department of English" and "Constitutive Literacy: The Department of English Revisited," the world has changed in some ways and in some places but remained impermeable in others. There seems to be, in some academic regions, a warming of the climate for studies that conceive of literacy as something like conversation; and in some academies (still too few, and fewer still in those academies that think of themselves as "major research universities") strong rhetoric and composition programs have found homes in good English departments or have found means to operate in peaceful coexistence with English departments if their home is elsewhere. Yet one must still raise questions and tinge them with a sincere if not militant skepticism.

We talk often nowadays about our profession as if it were one, and we often ask ourselves where it and we are going. But maybe we should still talk about our several professions—as college teachers or school teachers; teachers, critics, theorists of literature, or teachers, researchers, theorists of composition; as experts in British or American or African-American literature; and after doing so, probably we should then ask ourselves whether we are marching toward some commonly perceived future or walking in separate directions toward places that will leave us far apart. I think about the inertial forces that impel our steps, and especially about the ways those forces find embodiment in the institutions within which we live our lives and shape our minds. Some of our theories and methods do now seem convergent—those in some forms of rhetoric and those in some forms of critical theory, for example. But yet our everyday preoccupations and concerns and the ways these find value in our institutionalized lives seem still as divergent as ever.

Ours as an institutionalized profession still finds divisions established and variously valued among teaching, research, and service. Ours is a profession whose work is variously separated into that which is internally or externally funded, federally funded, or foundation funded, or in some cases client funded (in some universities in recent years students have been required to pay extra for so-called remedial instruction they have been required to take). And then, of course, there are the various and separate cultures signified, and with their separateness enforced, by the presses and journals that do or do not publish our work. We know as a result of our professional upbringing where to send the various inscriptions of our thoughts; and we have learned how to speak in different social dialects in *PMLA*, in *College English*, in *College Composition and Communication*, in *Language*, in *Research in the Teaching of English*, in *English Education*, and in the growing variety of still more specialized journals. And, of course, in promotion and salary decisions various hierarchies of value enforce socially constitutive rules for who may say what to whom in which language and in what place. In theory we may be coming together, but in our published discourse, in the conversations we have or almost have with one another at conferences, both in our discourse and in the discursive practices that shape and regulate it, we remain separated.

Yet in spite of this, we should still make attempts at conversation: each of us should speak out in forums where some opportunity is open to talk our separate ways toward means for making our theories convergent; each of us should try to converse our way toward Geertz's useful miracle ("that rarest of phenomena"), finding means as specialists and members of different cultures to "find something circumstantial to say to one another," to "give a credible account of [ourselves] to each other." And how much more useful (and rarer still) that miracle would be if we should find in the ways we talk with one another in the academy means to talk with and give a credible account of ourselves to others outside it: Fred Albright, for example, or Charles Baldwin and Gilberto Sanchez.

In the essays offered in this collection, my colleagues and I have played with various metaphors that capture for us both something of the complexity of language use and our hopes for it: "literacy as conversation," "talk as text," "conforming and informing literacy," "literacy as a common language" or as a search for one. I will end my Afterword with another metaphor: If we look toward a future in which our various ways of talking may converge, in which we may converse with one another, I think we need to put aside "efficient" languages for "inefficient" ones—well-ordered languages that serve like newly cleaned-up desks in neatly ordered studies for messy languages that serve like cluttered desks in rooms that are more like public browsing rooms than studies.

Efficient languages, neat ones, with their special vocabularies and with their institutionalized systems of invisible discourse, have led us—as members of cultures of specialization—to some real benefits, to some valuable understandings about human beings and the worlds they inhabit. But efficient languages work as well as they do because they are exclusive languages—languages that exclude those who have not learned the specialized vocabularies; worse, they exclude those who have not found or been granted opportunity to learn, through birth, participation, or experience, those moves of preferring and valuing that remain invisible to those who live lives on the margins of efficiently functioning communities. Charles Baldwin hears invisible discourse in the brutally efficient languages that control his life; but in hearing that discourse, in having to act out its imperatives, he is rendered always marginal to worlds that are more subject to personal control, and hence more open to willed opportunity. All efficient languages work because the presuppositions and assumptions embedded in them remain invisible, never brought into open daylight, never made explicit for reflection and critique; when they are favored languages, languages assumptive of the power that makes imperatives work, they are never open to questions Charles Baldwin might want to ask. He could never find the words.

Messy languages might work better to include a range of others in a common aim to "find something circumstantial," something substantive, "to say to one another." Messy languages, like conversations, can't leave much invisible: presuppositions and assumptions, when talk is messy, can always be inquired after if conversation breaks down, can always be called up for explicit statement to be made subject to understanding, to critical reflection and challenge.

Maybe we should go beyond a conception of literacy as conversation to think of it as Mikhail Bakhtin thinks of the novel—as heteroglossic, as inevitably a dialogic or multilogic form of coming together or refusing to in worlds made of words. Maybe we need, as writers, teachers, readers who would talk to students—all students—novelization of the languages we use. In novelized languages, no one speaks with a single voice because any utterance contains within it traces of past conversations; in novelized languages, all claims and all propositions contain within them their own adversatives, their own contradictions, their own contingent modifiers. It is that kind of language that may open itself to possibilities for convergence in its openness to past and future human concerns, those that concern us all.

There may be one other advantage to the messy language of novelization. The novel grew up, Bakhtin tells us, to treat as subject not what is past but "contemporaneity" itself. And contemporaneity, he tells us,

> ... was a subject of representation only in the low genres. Most importantly, it was the basic subject matter in that broadest and richest of realms, the common people's creative culture of laughter.... Precisely here, in popular laughter, the authentic folkloric roots of the novel are to be sought. The present, contemporary life as such, "I myself" and "my contemporaries," "my time"—all these concepts were originally the objects of ambivalent laughter, at the same time cheerful and annihilating (1981, 20–21).

Could it be that in laughter, "ambivalent laughter," "self-annihilating" but "cheerful" laughter, real convergence, real conversation, real community might be rendered possible? Laughter that opens itself to another's opens, too, to conversation among equals, for to be able to take one's self unseriously annihilates any possibility to talk merely as an authority, to talk ever as an authoritarian. Laughter that leads to that kind of self-annihilation may offer some possibility for a self to come to a deep and deeply understood sense of common humanity—to a recognition of common participation in a struggle to say, a struggle that is rendered humane in messy languages that allow for a sense of humor, for human laughter. Since nothing final can ever be said about topics that endure in human conversations, play and laughter may be all we have to make ourselves humanely serious in our attempts to control and change our worlds.

It all has to do with how we see worlds and with how we would make them, if we could. It all has to do with how we talk about our worlds with others and how many we invite into the conversations we seek to have.

References

Aarons, A. C., Barbara Y. Gordon, and William A. Stewart, eds. *Linguistic-Cultural Differences in American Education. The Florida FL Reporter* 7.1 (1969).

Abrahams, Roger D. "Black Talk and Black Education." *Linguistic-Cultural Differences in American Education. The Florida FL Reporter* 7.1 (1969): 10–12.

Achebe, Chinua. *Things Fall Apart*. Portsmouth, NH: Heinemann, 1962.

Allen, Harold B. *A Survey of the Teaching of English to Non-English Speakers in the United States*. Champaign, IL: NCTE, 1966.

Aronowitz, Stanley, and Henry A. Giroux. *Education Under Siege*. South Hadley, MA: Bergin & Garvey, 1985.

Austin, J. L. *How to Do Things with Words*. Ed. J. O. Urmsson and Marina Sbisa. 2nd ed. Cambridge: Harvard UP, 1977.

Bach, Kent, and Robert M. Harnish. *Linguistic Communication and Speech Acts*. Cambridge, MA: MIT P, 1979.

Bailey, Richard W., and Robin M. Fosheim, eds. *Literacy for Life*. New York: MLA, 1983.

Bailey, Richard W., and Jay L. Robinson, eds. *Varieties of Present-Day English*. New York: Macmillan, 1973.

Baker, Sheridan. "The Literate Imagination." *Michigan Quarterly Review* 9.1 (1970): 12–18.

———. *The Practical Stylist*. 2nd ed. New York: Thomas Y. Crowell, 1969.

323

Bakhtin, Mikhail. *The Dialogic Imagination.* Ed. Michael Holquist. Trans. Caryl Emerson and Michael Holquist. Austin: U of Texas P, 1981.

——. *Speech Genres and Other Late Essays.* Ed. Caryl Emerson and Michael Holquist. Trans. Vern W. McGee. Austin: U of Texas P, 1986.

Baldick, Chris. *The Social Mission of English Criticism, 1848–1932.* Oxford: Clarendon, 1983.

Baratz, Joan C. "Educational Considerations for Teaching Standard English to Negro Children." *Teaching Standard English.* Ed. Ralph W. Fasold and Roger W. Shuy. Washington, DC: Center for Applied Linguistics, 1970. 20–40.

——. "Teaching Reading in an Urban Negro School System." *Language and Poverty.* Ed. Frederick Williams. Chicago: Markham, 1970. 11–24.

Baratz, Joan C., and E. Povich. "Grammatical Constructions in the Language of the Negro Preschool Child." Paper presented at American Speech and Hearing Association, 1967.

Baratz, Joan C., and Roger W. Shuy, eds. *Teaching Black Children to Read.* Washington, DC: Center for Applied Linguistics, 1969.

Baratz, Stephen S., and Joan C. Baratz. "Negro Ghetto Children and Urban Education: A Cultural Solution." *Linguistic-Cultural Differences in Education. The Florida FL Reporter* 7.1 (1969): 13–14, 151.

Barnes, Douglas. *From Communication to Curriculum.* Harmondsworth, Eng: Penguin, 1975.

——, et al. *Language, the Learner and the School.* 3rd ed. Portsmouth, NH: Boynton/Cook, 1986.

Barritt, Loren, Patricia L. Stock, and Francelia Clark. "Researching Practice: Evaluating Assessment Essays." *College Composition and Communication* 37:3 (1986): 315–27.

Bartholomae, David, and Anthony Petrosky. "Facts, Artifacts and Counterfacts: A Basic Reading and Writing Course for the College Curriculum." *Facts, Artifacts and Counterfacts: Theory and Method for a Reading and Writing Course.* Ed. David Bartholomae and Anthony Petrosky. Portsmouth, NH: Boynton/Cook, 1986. 3–43.

Bazerman, Charles. "Scientific Writing as a Social Act: A Review of the Literature of the Sociology of Science." *New Essays in Technical and Scientific Communication: Research, Theory, Practice.* Ed. Paul Anderson, R. John Brockmann, and Carolyn R. Miller. Farmingdale, NY: Baywood, 1983.

Becker, Alton L. *Correspondences: An Essay on Iconicity and Philosophy.* (in press.)

——. "The Poetics and Noetics of a Javanese Poem." *Spoken and Written Language: Exploring Orality and Literacy.* Ed. Deborah Tannen. Norwood, NJ: Ablex, 1982. 217–38.

Bellack, Arno A., Herbert M. Kliebard, Ronald T. Hyman, and Frank L. Smith. *The Language of the Classroom.* New York: Teachers College P, 1966.

Bereiter, Carl, Siegfried Engelmann, et al. "An Academically Oriented Pre-School for Culturally Deprived Children." *Pre-School Education Today.* Ed. Fred M. Hechinger. Garden City, NY: Doubleday, 1966. 105–35.

Berger, Peter L., and Thomas Luckmann. *The Social Construction of Reality: A Treatise in the Sociology of Knowledge*. Garden City, NY: Doubleday, 1967.

Berthoff, Ann E. *Forming/Thinking/Writing: The Composing Imagination*. Portsmouth, NH: Boynton/Cook, 1981.

———. *The Making of Meaning*. Portsmouth, NH: Boynton/Cook, 1981.

Birnbaum, June C. "The Reading and Composing Behaviors of Selected Fourth- and Seventh-Grade Students." *Research in the Teaching of English* 14 (1982): 197–222.

Bleich, David. *Subjective Criticism*. Baltimore: Johns Hopkins UP, 1978.

Bloome, David, ed. *Literacy and Schooling*. Norwood, NJ: Ablex, 1987.

———. *Classrooms and Literacy*. Norwood, NJ: Ablex, 1989.

———. "Reading as a Social Process." *Advances in Reading/Language Research*. Vol. 2. Ed. Barbara A. Hutson. Greenwich, CT: JAI, 1983. 123–49.

Britton, James. *Language and Learning*. Harmondsworth, Eng: Penguin, 1970.

———. "Talking to Learn." *Language, the Learner and the School*. Ed. Douglas Barnes, James Britton, and Mike Torbe. Portsmouth, NH: Boynton/Cook, 1986.

Britton, James, Tony Burgess, Nancy Martin, Alex McLeod, and Harold Rosen. *The Development of Writing Abilities* (11–18). Houndmills: Macmillan, 1975.

Brown, Gillian, and George Yule. *Discourse Analysis*. London: Cambridge UP, 1983.

Brown, Goold. "Of the Science of Grammar." *English Linguistics: An Introductory Reader*. Ed. Harold Hungerford, Jay Robinson, and James Sledd. Glenview, IL: Scott, Foresman, 1970. 41–54.

Bruner, Jerome. *Actual Minds, Possible Worlds*. Cambridge: Harvard UP, 1986.

———. "Vygotsky: A Historical and Conceptual Perspective." *Vygotsky and the Social Formation of the Mind*. Ed. J. Wertch. Cambridge: Harvard UP, 1985. 21–35.

Bussis, Anne M., Edward Chittenden, Marianne Amarel, and Edith Klausner. *Inquiry into Meaning: An Investigation of Learning to Read*. Hillsdale, NJ: Erlbaum, 1985.

Calhoun, Daniel H. *The Intelligence of a People*. Princeton, NJ: Princeton UP, 1973.

Carnegie Forum on Education and the Economy. *A Nation Prepared: Teachers for the 21st Century*. New York: Carnegie Forum, 1986.

Carothers, J. C. "Culture, Psychiatry, and the Written Word." *Psychiatry* 22.4 (1959): 307–20.

Cazden, Courtney B. "Can Ethnographic Research Go Beyond the Status Quo?" *Anthropology & Education Quarterly* 14.1 (1983): 33–41.

The 1980 Census of Population. Vol. 1. Chapter C. Washington, DC: U.S. Government Printing Office, 1983.

The 1980 Census of Population. Vol. 1. Chapter D. Washington, DC: U.S. Government Printing Office, 1984.

Chase, Geoffrey. "Accommodation, Resistance, and the Politics of Student Writing." *College Composition and Communication* 39.1 (1988): 13–22.

Clark, Katerina, and Michael Holquist. *Mikhail Bakhtin.* Cambridge: Harvard UP, 1984.

Clark, Michael. "Evaluating Writing in an Academic Setting." *fforum: Essays on Theory and Practice in the Teaching of Writing.* Ed. Patricia L. Stock. Portsmouth, NH: Boynton/Cook, 1983. 59–79.

Clifford, Geraldine Goncich. "Buch und Lesen: Historical Perspectives on Literacy and Schooling." *Review of Educational Research* 54.4 (1984): 472–500.

Cohen, Arthur M., and Florence B. Brawer. "Functional Literacy for Community College Students." *Literacy for Life.* Ed. Richard W. Bailey and Robin M. Fosheim. New York: MLA, 1983. 207–22.

Coles, Peter, and J. L. Morgan. *Syntax and Semantics III: Speech Acts.* New York: Academic P, 1975.

Commission on the Humanities. *The Humanities in American Life: Report of the Commission on the Humanities.* Berkeley: U of California P, 1980.

Cook-Gumperz, Jenny. *The Social Construction of Literacy.* Cambridge: Cambridge UP, 1986.

Corbett, Edward P. J. "The Status of Writing in Our Society." *Writing: The Nature, Development and Teaching of Written Communication.* Vol. 1 of *Variation in Writing: Functional and Linguistic Differences.* Ed. Marcia Farr Whiteman. Hillsdale, NJ: Erlbaum, 1981. 47–52.

Csikszentmihalyi, Mihaly, and Reed Larson. *Being Adolescent: Conflict and Growth in the Teenage Years.* New York: Basic. 1984.

Culler, Jonathan. *The Pursuit of Signs: Semiotics, Literature, Deconstruction.* Ithaca, NY: Cornell UP, 1981.

D'Angelo, Frank J. "Literacy and Cognition: A Developmental Perspective." *Literacy for Life.* Ed. Richard W. Bailey and Robin M. Fosheim. New York: MLA, 1983. 97–114.

Dewey, John. *Democracy and Education.* New York: Macmillan, 1916.

Disch, Robert, ed. *The Future of Literacy.* Englewood Cliffs, NJ: Prentice-Hall, 1973.

Donaldson, Margaret. "Speech and Writing and Modes of Learning." *Awakening to Literacy.* Ed. Hillel Goelman, Antoinette Oberg, and Frank Smith. Portsmouth, NH: Heinemann, 1984. 122–30.

Eco, Umberto. *The Role of the Reader: Explorations in the Semiotics of Texts.* Bloomington: Indiana UP, 1979.

Education Week. 14 May 1986: 14–39.

Elbow, Peter. *Writing Without Teachers*. New York: Oxford UP, 1973.

Emig, Janet. *The Web of Meaning*. Portsmouth, NH: Boynton/Cook, 1983.

———. "Writing as a Mode of Learning." *College Composition and Communication* 28 (1977): 122–28.

Engelmann, Siegfried. "How to Construct Effective Language Programs for the Poverty Child." *Language and Poverty*. Ed. Frederick Williams. Chicago: Markham, 1970. 102–22.

Entwisle, Doris R. "Semantic Differences of Children: Some Assessments of Social Class and Ethnic Differences." *Language and Poverty*. Ed. Frederick Williams. Chicago: Markham, 1970. 123–39.

Erickson, Fred. "Classroom Discourse as Improvisation: Relationships Between Academic Task Structure and Social Participation Structure in Lessons." *Communicating in the Classroom*. Ed. Louise Cherry Wilkinson. New York: Academic, 1982. 153–81.

———. "Tasks in Times: Objects of Study in a Natural History of Teaching." *Improving Teaching*. Ed. K. K. Zumwalt. Alexandria, VA: Association for Supervision and Curriculum Development, 1986. 131-47.

Everhart, Robert B. *Reading, Writing, and Resistance*. Boston: Routledge & Kegan Paul, 1983.

Evertson, Carolyn, and Judith Green. "Observation as Inquiry and Method." *Handbook of Research on Teaching*. 3rd ed. Ed. Merlin C. Whittrock. New York: Macmillan, 1986. 162–213.

Fader, Daniel. "Literacy and Family." *Literacy for Life*. Ed. Richard W. Bailey and Robin M. Fosheim. New York: MLA, 1983. 236–47.

———. *The New Hooked on Books*. New York: Berkeley, 1976.

Farrell, Edmund J. *Deciding the Future: A Forecast of Responsibilities of Secondary Teachers of English, 1970–2000 A. D.* Urbana, IL: NCTE, Research Report No. 12, 1971.

Fasold, Ralph W. "Orthography in Reading Materials for Black English-Speaking Children." *Teaching Black Children to Read*. Ed. Joan C. Baratz and Roger W. Shuy. Washington, DC: Center for Applied Linguistics, 1969. 68–91.

Fasold, Ralph W., and Roger W. Shuy, eds. *Teaching Standard English in the Inner City*. Washington, DC: Center for Applied Linguistics, 1970.

Fasold, Ralph W., and Walt Wolfram. "Some Linguistics Features of Negro Dialect." *Teaching Standard English in the Inner City*. Ed. Ralph W. Fasold and Roger W. Shuy. Washington, DC: Center for Applied Linguistics, 1970. 41–86.

Ferreiro, Emilia, and Ana Teberosky. Trans. Karen Goodman Castro. *Literacy Before Schooling*. Portsmouth, NH: Heinemann, 1982.

Fetterman, David M., ed. *Ethnography in Education*. Beverly Hills, CA: Sage, 1984.

Fish, Stanley. *Is There a Text in This Class?* Cambridge: Harvard UP, 1980.

Fishman, Joshua A. "The Breadth and Depth of English in the United States." *Linguistic-Cultural Differences in American Education. The Florida FL Reporter* 7.1 (1969): 41–42.

Flanders, Ned A. *Analyzing Teacher Behavior*. Reading, MA: Addison, 1970.

Fleming, Robben W. "Literacy: Who Cares?" *Literacy for Life*. Ed. Richard W. Bailey and Robin M. Fosheim. New York: MLA, 1983. 63–6.

Foucault, Michel. "What Is an Author?" *Textual Strategies: Perspectives on Post-Structural Criticism*. Ed. Josue V. Harris. Ithaca, NY: Cornell UP, 1979. 141–60.

Freire, Paulo. *Pedagogy of the Oppressed*. New York: Continuum, 1970.

———. *The Politics of Education: Culture, Power, and Liberation*. South Hadley, MA: Bergin & Garvey, 1985.

Fries, Charles C. *American English Grammar*. New York: D. Appleton Century, 1948.

Fulwiler, Toby. *Teaching with Writing*. Portsmouth, NH: Boynton/Cook, 1987.

Gadamer, Hans-Georg. *Philosophical Hermeneutics*. Ed. and Trans. David E. Linge. Berkeley: U of California P, 1976.

———. *Truth and Method*. New York: Crossroad, 1975.

Gee, James Paul. "Orality and Literacy: From *The Savage Mind* to *Ways with Words*." *TESOL Quarterly* 20.4 (1986): 719–46.

Geertz, Clifford. "Blurred Genres: The Refiguration of Social Thought." *Local Knowledge: Further Essays in Interpretive Anthropology*. New York: Basic, 1983. 19–35.

———. "Deep Play: Notes on the Balinese Cock Fight." *Daedalus* 101.1 (1972): 1–37.

———. *Local Knowledge: Further Essays in Interpretive Anthropology*. New York: Basic, 1983.

———. "The Way We Think Now: Toward an Ethnography of Modern Thought." *Local Knowledge: Further Essays in Interpretive Anthropology*. New York: Basic, 1983. 147–63.

Gere, Anne Ruggles. *Writing Groups: History, Theory, and Implications*. Carbondale: Southern Illinois UP, 1987.

Gere, Anne Ruggles, and Ralph S. Stevens. "The Language of Writing Groups: How Oral Response Shapes Revision." *The Acquisition of Written Language*. Ed. Sarah Warshauer Freedman. Norwood, NJ: Ablex, 1985. 85–105.

Gilmore, Perry, and Allan A. Glatthorn, eds. *Children In and Out of School: Ethnography and Education*. Washington, DC: Center for Applied Linguistics, 1982.

Giroux, Henry A. *Ideology, Culture, and the Process of Schooling*. Philadelphia: Temple UP, 1981.

———. *Theory and Resistance in Education*. South Hadley, MA: Bergin & Garvey, 1983.

Glazer, Nathan, and Daniel Patrick Moynihan. *Beyond the Melting Pot*. Cambridge: MIT P, 1963.

Goelman, Hillel, Antoinette Oberg, and Frank Smith, eds. *Awakening to Literacy*. Portsmouth, NH: Heinemann, 1984.

Goffman, Erving. *Forms of Talk*. Philadelphia, PA: U of Pennsylvania P, 1981.

———. *Interaction Ritual*. New York: Pantheon, 1967.

Good, Thomas L., and Jere Brophy. *Looking into Classrooms*. New York: Harper & Row, 1978.

Goodlad, John I. *A Place Called School: Promise for the Future*. New York: McGraw-Hill, 1984.

Goodman, Kenneth S., "Reading: A Psycholinguistic Guessing Game." *Language and Reading*. Ed. Doris V. Gunderson, Washington, DC: Center for Applied Linguistics, 1970. 107–19.

Graff, Harvey J. *The Literacy Myth: Literacy and Social Structure in the Nineteenth-Century City*. New York: Academic, 1979.

———., ed. *Literacy and Social Development in the West: A Reader*. New York: Academic, 1981.

Gramsci, Antonio. *Selections from the Prison Notebooks*. Ed. and Trans. Quinten Hoare and Geoffrey Smith. New York: International, 1971.

Graves, Donald. *Writing: Teachers and Children at Work*. Portsmouth, NH: Heinemann, 1983.

Graves, Donald, and Virginia Stuart. *Write from the Start: Tapping Your Child's Natural Writing Ability*. New York: Dutton, 1985.

Greene, Maxine. *Landscapes of Learning*. New York: Teachers College P, 1978.

———. "Literacy for What?" *Phi Delta Kappan* 63.5 (1982): 326–29.

———. "Toward Possibility: Expanding the Range of Literacy." *English Education* 18.4 (1986): 231–43.

Grice, H. P. "Logic and Conversation." *Syntax and Semantics Vol. 3: Speech Acts*. Ed. Peter Cole. NY: Academic, 1978. 41–58.

Gunderson, Doris V., ed. *Language and Reading*. Washington, DC: Center for Applied Linguistics, 1970.

Halliday, M. A. K. *An Introduction to Functional Grammar*. London: Arnold, 1985.

Halliday, M. A. K., and Roqaiya Hasan. *Cohesion in English*. London: Longman, 1976.

Hansen, Jane. "First Grade Writers Who Pursue Reading." *fforum: Essays on Theory and Practice in the Teaching of Writing*. Ed. Patricia L. Stock. Portsmouth, NH: Boynton/Cook, 1983. 155–62.

Heath, Shirley Brice. *Ways with Words: Language, Life and Work in Communities and Classrooms*. New York: Cambridge UP, 1983.

Heath, Shirley Brice, and Amanda Branscombe. "'Intelligent Writing' in an Academic Community: Teacher, Students, and Researcher." *The Acquisition of Written Language: Revision and Response*. Ed. Sarah Warshauer Freedman. Norwood, NJ: Ablex, 1985. 3–32.

Heath, Shirley Brice, and Charlene Thomas. "The Achievement of Preschool Literacy for Mother and Child." *Awakening to Literacy*. Ed. Hillel Goelman, Antoinette Oberg, and Frank Smith. Portsmouth, NH: Heinemann, 1984. 51–72.

Hendrix, Richard. "The Status and Politics of Writing Instruction." *Writing: The Nature, Development, and Teaching of Written Communication.* Vol.1 of *Variation in Writing: Functional and Linguistic Differences.* Ed. Marcia Farr Whiteman. Hillsdale, NJ: Erlbaum, 1981. 53–70.

Hirsch, E. D. *Cultural Literacy.* Boston: Houghton Mifflin, 1987.

Horner, Winifred Bryan, ed. *Composition and Literature: Bridging the Gap.* Chicago: U of Chicago P, 1983.

Hungerford, Harold, Jay L. Robinson, and James Sledd, eds. *English Linguistics: An Introductory Reader.* Glenview, IL: Scott, Foresman, 1970.

Hunter, Carman St. John, and David Harman. *Adult Illiteracy in the United States: A Report to the Ford Foundation.* New York: McGraw-Hill, 1979.

Hymes Dell. *Foundations in Sociolinguisitics: An Ethnographic Approach.* Philadelphia: U of Pennsylvania P, 1974.

Iser, Wolfgang. *The Act of Reading.* Baltimore: Johns Hopkins UP, 1978.

Jagger, Angela. "Observing the Language Learner." *Observing the Language Learner.* Ed. Angela Jagger and M. Trika Smith-Burke. Urbana: NCTE, 1985. 1–18.

Kelly, George. *The Psychology of Personal Constructs.* New York: Norton, 1955.

King, Stephen. "The Body." *Different Seasons.* New York: Signet, 1982.

Knoblauch, C. H., and Lil Brannon. *Rhetorical Traditions and the Teaching of Writing.* Portsmouth, NH: Boynton/Cook, 1984.

Kozol, Jonathan. *Illiterate America.* Garden City, NY: Doubleday, 1985.

Labov, William. "The Logic of Nonstandard English." *Language in the Inner City: Studies in the Black English Vernacular.* Philadelphia: U of Pennsylvania P, 1972a.

———. "Some Features of the English of Black Americans." *Varieties of Present-Day English.* Ed. Richard W. Bailey and Jay L Robinson. New York: Macmillan, 1973. 236–55.

———. "The Study of Language in Its Social Context." *Sociolinguistic Patterns.* Philadelphia: U of Pennsylvania P, 1972b: 183–259.

———. *The Study of Nonstandard English.* Champaign, IL: NCTE, 1970.

Labov, William, and Clarence Robins. "A Note on the Relation of Reading Failure to Peer-Group Status in Urban Ghettos." *Language and Reading.* Ed. Doris V. Gunderson. Washington, DC: Center for Applied Linguistics, 1970. 208–18.

Lamont, Corliss. *Dialogues on John Dewey.* New York: Horizon, 1959.

Langer, Susanne. *Philosophy in a New Key.* Cambridge: Harvard UP, 1942.

Lanham, Richard A. "One, Two, Three." *Composition and Literature: Bridging the Gap.* Ed. Winifred Horner. Chicago: U of Chicago P, 1983. 14–29.

Lather, Patti. "Research as Praxis." *Harvard Educational Review* 56 (1986): 257–77.

Leech, Geoffrey. *Explorations in Semantics and Pragmatics.* Amsterdam: Benjamins B. V., 1980.

———. *Principles of Pragmatics.* New York: Longman, 1983.

Lockridge, Kenneth A. *Literacy in Colonial New England.* New York: Norton, 1974.

Lopez, Barry H. *Of Wolves and Men.* New York: Charles Scribner's Sons, 1978.

Lunsford, Andrea. "The Pedagogy of Collaboration." Paper presented at the Conference on College Composition and Communication. Atlanta, GA, 1987.

Macrorie, Ken. *Searching Writing.* Portsmouth, NH: Boynton/Cook, 1980.

———. *Telling Writing.* 4th ed. Portsmouth, NH: Boynton/Cook, 1985.

"Martin Luther King Junior Elementary School Children v. Ann Arbor School District Board, Defendant." *Federal Supplement*, vol. 473. St. Paul, MN.: West, 1979. 1371–91.

Martin, Nancy, Pat D'Arcy, Bryan Newton, and Robert Parker. *Writing and Learning Across the Curriculum*, 11–16. London: Ward Lock, 1976.

McDavid, Raven I. "The Dialects of American English." *The Structure of American English.* Ed. Nelson W. Francis. New York: Ronald, 1958. 480–543.

Mehan, Hugh. *Learning Lessons.* Cambridge: Harvard UP, 1979.

Meiland, Jack W. *College Thinking: How to Get the Best out of College.* New York: New American Library, 1981.

Milz, Vera. "First Graders Can Write: Focus on Communication." *Theory into Practice* 19 (1980): 179–85.

Mishler, E. "Meaning in Context—Is There Any Other Kind?" *Harvard Educational Review* 49:1 (1979): 1–19.

Modern Language Association, Ohio State University, and the Federation of State Humanities Councils. "Call for Papers." *The Right to Literacy.* Conference in Columbus, OH. September 1988.

Moffett, James. *Teaching the Universe of Discourse.* Boston: Houghton Mifflin, 1968.

Moll, Luis. "Writing as Communication: Creating Strategic Learning Environments." *Theory into Practice* 25.2 (1986): 102–8.

Moll, Luis, and Rosa Diaz. "Teaching Writing as Communication: The Use of Ethnographic Findings in Classroom Practice." *Literacy and Schooling.* Ed. David Bloome. Norwood, NJ: Ablex, 1987. 193–221.

Murray, Donald M. *Learning by Teaching: Selected Articles on Writing and Teaching.* Portsmouth, NH: Boynton/Cook, 1982.

National Commission on Excellence in Education. *A Nation at Risk: The Imperative for Educational Reform.* Washington, DC: U.S. Department of Education, 1983.

Ohmann, Richard. "Call for Articles: Literacy and 'Basics.'" *College English* 37.8 (1976): 819.

———. "Literacy, Technology, and Monopoly Capital." *College English* 47.7 (1985): 675–89.

Ohmann, Richard, and W. B. Coley, eds. Editorial. *College English* 38.5 (1977): 441–2.

Ong, Walter J. "The Writer's Audience Is Always a Fiction." *Interfaces of the Word.* Ithaca, NY: Cornell UP, 1977. 53–81.

Oxenham, John. *Literacy: Writing, Reading, and Social Organization.* London: Routledge & Kegan Paul, 1980.

Paley, Vivian G. *Wally's Stories: Conversations in the Kindergarten.* Cambridge: Harvard UP, 1981.

Polanyi, Michael. *Personal Knowledge.* Chicago: U of Chicago P, 1962.

Radway, Janice. "Interpretive Communities and Variable Literacies: The Functions of Romance Reading." *Daedalus* 113.3 (1984): 49–73.

———. *Reading the Romance: Women, Patriarchy and Popular Literature.* Chapel Hill: U of North Carolina P, 1984.

Resnick, Daniel P., and Lauren B. Resnick. "The Nature of Literacy: An Historical Exploration." *Harvard Educational Review* 47.3 (1977): 370–85.

Robinson, Jay L. "Literacy in the Department of English." *College English* 47.5 (1985): 482–98.

———. "Literacy in Society: Readers and Writers in the Worlds of Discourse." *Literacy and Schooling.* Ed. David Bloome. Norwood, NJ: Ablex, 1987. 327–53.

———. "The Social Construction of Readers and the Social Uses of Texts." *Works and Days* 4.1 (1986): 17–41.

———. "The Social Context of Literacy." *fforum: Essays on Theory and Practice in the Teaching of Writing.* Ed. Patricia L. Stock. Portsmouth, NH: Boynton/Cook, 1983. 2–12.

———. "The Users and Uses of Literacy." *Literacy for Life.* Ed. Richard W. Bailey and Robin M. Fosheim. New York: MLA, 1983. 3–18.

Rosenblatt, Louise M. *The Reader, the Text, the Poem: The Transactional Theory of the Literary Work.* Carbondale: Southern Illinois UP, 1978.

———. "Viewpoints: Transaction Versus Interaction—A Terminological Rescue Operation." *Research in the Teaching of English.* (1985): 96–107.

Rosenthal, Robert, and Lenore Jacobson. *Pygmalion in the Classroom.* New York: Holt, Rinehart and Winston, 1968.

Ruddock, Jean, and David Hopkins. *Research as a Basis for Teaching: Readings from the Work of Lawrence Stenhouse.* Portsmouth, NH: Heinemann, 1985.

Sanchez, Gilberto. "It's a Cold World," *The Bridge.* Saginaw, MI: The Public Schools of the City of Saginaw, 1988.

Scardamalia, Marlene, and Carl Bereiter. "Development of Dialectical Processes in Composition." *Literacy, Language, and Learning: The Nature and Consequences of Reading and Writing.* Ed. D. Olson, N. Torrance, and A. Hildyard. New York: Cambridge UP, 1985.

Scholes, Robert. *Textual Power: Literary Theory and the Teaching of English.* New Haven: Yale UP, 1985.

Schön, Donald A. *The Reflective Practitioner: How Professionals Think in Action.* New York: Basic, 1983.

Scribner, Sylvia, and Michael Cole. *The Psychology of Literacy.* Cambridge, MA: Harvard UP, 1981.

Searle, John R. *Expression and Meaning: Studies in the Theory of Speech Acts.* New York: Cambridge UP, 1979.

———. *Intentionality, An Essay in the Philosophy of Mind.* New York: Cambridge UP, 1983.

———. *Speech Acts.* New York: Cambridge UP, 1969.

Shapiro, Michael J. *Language and Political Understanding.* New Haven: Yale UP, 1981.

Shaughnessy, Mina. *Errors and Expectations: A Guide for the Teacher of Basic Writing.* New York: Oxford UP, 1977.

Sherman, Katharine. *Spring on an Arctic Island.* Boston: Little, Brown, 1956.

Shor, Ira. *Critical Teaching and Everyday Life.* Boston: South End, 1980.

———. *Freire for the Classroom: A Sourcebook for Liberatory Teaching.* Portsmouth, NH: Boynton/Cook, 1987.

Shuy, Roger W. "A Linguistic Background for Developing Beginning Materials for Black Children." *Teaching Black Children to Read.* Ed. Joan C. Baratz and Roger W. Shuy. Washington, DC: Center for Applied Linguistics, 1969. 117-37.

Silko, Leslie Marmon. *Ceremony.* New York: Signet, 1977.

Sinclair, John McHardy, and R. M. Coulthard. *Towards an Analysis of Discourse.* London: Oxford UP, 1975.

Sizer, Theodore R. *Horace's Compromise: The Dilemma of the American High School.* Boston: Houghton Mifflin, 1984.

Sledd, James. "Doublespeak: Dialectology in the Service of Big Brother." *College English* 33.4 (1972): 439–56.

Smith, Frank. Introduction. *Awakening to Literacy.* Ed. Hillel Goelman, Antoinette Oberg, and Frank Smith. Portsmouth, NH: Heinemann, 1983.

Spacks, Patricia Meyer. *Gossip.* Chicago: U of Chicago P, 1985.

Stock, Patricia L., ed. *fforum: Essays on Theory and Practice in the Teaching of Writing.* Portsmouth, NH: Boynton/Cook, 1983.

———. "Writing Across the Curriculum." *Theory into Practice* 25 (1986): 97–101.

Stock, Patricia L., and Jay L. Robinson. "Taking on Testing: Teachers as Tester-Researchers." *English Education* 19.2 (1987): 93–121.

Stock, Patricia L., and Karen Wixson. "Reading and Writing—Together." *fforum: Essays on Theory and Practice in the Teaching of Writing.* Ed. Patricia L. Stock. Portsmouth, NH: Boynton/Cook, 1983. 201–19.

Strassmann, Paul A. "Information Systems and Literacy." *Literacy for Life.* Ed. Richard W. Bailey and Robin M. Fosheim. New York: MLA, 1983. 115–21.

Taba, Hilda. *Teacher's Handbook for Elementary Social Studies.* Reading, MA: Addison-Wesley, 1967.

Tannen, Deborah, ed. *Coherence in Spoken and Written Discourse.* Norwood, NJ: Ablex, 1984.

———, ed. *Spoken and Written Language: Exploring Orality and Literacy.* Norwood, NJ: Ablex, 1982.

Tax, Sol. "Group Identity and Educating the Disadvantaged." In *Language Programs for the Disadvantaged: The Report of the NCTE Task Force on Teaching English to the Disadvantaged.* Eds. Richard Corbin and Muriel Crosby. Champaign, IL: NCTE, 1965. 204–15.

Tax, Sol, and Robert K. Thomas. "Education 'for' American Indians: Threat or Promise." *Linguistic-Cultural Differences and American Education. The Florida FL Reporter* 7.1 (1969): 15–19.

Thomas, Lewis. *The Medusa and the Snail: More Notes of a Biology Watcher.* New York: Viking, 1979.

Thorndike, Robert L. "Pygmalion in the Classroom by Robert Rosenthal and Lenore Jacobson." *American Educational Research Journal* 5.4 (1968): 709–11.

Threadgold, Terry. E. A. Grosz, Gunther Kress, and M. A. K. Halliday, eds. *Semiotics Ideology Language.* Sydney: Pathfinder, 1986.

Tompkins, Jane P. *Reader-Response Criticism: From Formalism to Post-Structuralism.* Baltimore: Johns Hopkins UP, 1980.

Toulmin, Steven, Richard Rieke, and Allan Janik, eds. *An Introduction to Reasoning,* 2nd ed. New York: Macmillan, 1984.

Tyler, Ralph W. "Testing Writing: Procedures Vary with Purposes." *Literacy for Life.* Ed. Richard W. Bailey and Robin M. Fosheim. New York: MLA, 1983. 197–206.

Volosinov, V. V. *Marxism and the Philosophy of Language.* New York: Seminar, 1973.

Vygotsky, Lev Semenovich. *Thought and Language.* Cambridge: MIT P, 1962.

Wagner, Daniel A., ed. "Literacy and Ethnicity." Special Issue of *International Journal of the Sociology of Language* 42. New York: Mouton, 1983.

Weisz, Paul B. "English and Science in Symbiosis for Survival." *Literacy for Life.* Ed. Richard W. Bailey and Robin M. Fosheim. New York: MLA, 1983. 125-36.

Wertsch, James V. *Vygotsky and the Social Formation of Mind.* Cambridge: Harvard UP, 1985.

White, James Boyd. *Heracles' Bow: Essays on the Rhetoric and Poetics of the Law.* Madison: U of Wisconsin P, 1985.

———. "The Invisible Discourse of the Law: Reflections on Legal Literacy and General Education." *fforum: Essays on Theory and Practice in the Teaching of Writing.* Ed. Patricia L. Stock. Portsmouth, NH: Boynton/ Cook, 1983. 46–59.

———. *The Legal Imagination.* Boston: Little, Brown, 1973.

———. *When Words Lose Their Meaning: Constitutions and Reconstitutions of Language, Character, and Community.* Chicago: U of Chicago P, 1984.

Whiteman, Marcia Farr, ed. *Writing: The Nature, Development, and Teaching of Written Communication.* Vol. 1. of *Variation in Writing: Functional and Linguistic-Cultural Differences.* Hillsdale, NJ: Erlbaum, 1981.

Wilkinson, Louise Cherry. *Communicating in the Classroom.* New York: Academic, 1982.

Williams, Frederick, ed. *Language and Poverty.* Chicago: Markham, 1970.

Williams, Raymond. *Marxism and Literature.* Oxford: Oxford UP, 1977.

———. *The Sociology of Culture.* New York: Schocken, 1981.

———. *Writing in Society.* London: Verso, 1980.

Winterowd, W. Ross, ed. *Contemporary Rhetoric: A Conceptual Background with Readings.* New York: Harcourt Brace Jovanovich, 1975.